Getting str[illegible] doesn't have to be a mystery...

these practical, concise, and affordable study guides will tell you how!

The Harbrace Guides to

STUDENT SUCCESS

from Harcourt Brace Canada

Fit to Print: The Canadian Student's Guide to Essay Writing 3/e
Joanne Buckley

Learning for Success: Skills and Strategies for Canadian Students 2/e
Joan Fleet, Fiona Goodchild, Richard Zajchowski

Power over Time: Student Success with Time Management
Joan Fleet, Denise Reaume

Success in the Social Sciences: Writing and Research for Canadian Students
Richard Floyd

Getting into Law School: The Canadian Guide
Trevor Johnson

Speaking for Success: The Canadian Guide
Anthony Lieb

Transitions: Succeeding in College and University
Greta Hofmann Nemiroff

Graduate Student Success: The Canadian Guide
Manfred Szabo

Making your Mark: Learning to do Well on Exams
Catherine Taylor, Heather Avery, Lucille Strath

Career Success: The Canadian Guide
Shannon Whelan

Print Out: Using the Computer to Write
Wendy Wilson

Look for copies of these best-selling books in your college or university bookstore.

SEEING OURSELVES

MEDIA POWER AND POLICY IN CANADA

Second Edition

Helen Holmes
University of Calgary

David Taras
University of Calgary

HARCOURT BRACE CANADA

Harcourt Brace & Company, Canada

Toronto Montreal Fort Worth New York Orlando
Philadelphia San Diego London Sydney Tokyo

Canadian Cataloguing in Publication Data

Main entry under title:

Seeing ourselves

2nd ed.
ISBN 0-7747-3378-0

1. Mass media - Canada. I. Holmes, Helen, 1944-
II. Taras, David, 1950-

P92.C3S44 1996 302.23'0971 C95-931393-1

Publisher: Heather McWhinney
Senior Acquisitions Editor: Christopher Carson
Projects Manager: Liz Radojkovic
Developmental Editor: Laura Paterson Pratt
Editorial Assistant: Martina van de Velde
Director of Publishing Services: Jean Davies
Editorial Manager: Marcel Chiera
Supervising Editor: Semareh Al-Hillal
Production Editor: Laurel Parsons
Production Manager: Sue-Ann Becker
Production Co-ordinator: Sheila Barry
Copy Editor: Linda Collins
Cover Design: Steve Eby Production & Design
Interior Design: Dave Peters
Typesetting and Assembly: Sharon Moroney
Printing and Binding: Edwards Brothers Incorporated

Cover Art: Joanne Tod, *Two Perspectives*, 1986, oil on canvas, 152.4 × 312.4 cm. Courtesy of S.L. Simpson Gallery. Photo by Peter MacCallum. Reprinted with permission of the artist.

This book was printed in the United States of America.

1 2 3 4 5 00 99 98 97 96

This book is dedicated to Joel and Matthew Taras, and to Lindsey and Paula Holmes with great thanks for their continued love and support.

ACKNOWLEDGEMENTS

To say that many hands make light work and that two (or more) heads are better than one are, of course, clichés. But as in many clichés, there is a good deal of truth, particularly when it applies to an edited volume such at this. We would like to thank the literally dozens of people who have helped bring it about. Our thanks go to the Faculty of General Studies at the University of Calgary for providing the environment which makes such efforts possible, and to Laura Paterson Pratt and all the others at Harcourt Brace for their help and enthusiasm. Our thanks also go to the reviewers of the first edition of *Seeing Ourselves* who provided detailed and helpful feedback which we happily embraced in preparing this second edition, and to the nameless reviewers supplied by Harcourt Brace who offered useful comments and insights on early drafts of many of the articles in the present edition. Thanks also to Janet Alford, Ellen Eastwood, and Marie Rajic for pulling together the statistical information in Appendix A. And many, many thanks to the contributors whose enthusiasms and expertise enabled us to bring together such a wealth of provocative material.

We wish to thank those who gave permission to use previously published material in this volume:

Communications Canada. *The Broadcasting Act of 1991*. Reprinted with permission of the Minister of Supply and Services Canada, 1995.

Colin Hoskins and Stuart McFadyen. Adapted from "The Mandate, Structure, and Financing of the CBC." *Canadian Public Policy* 18 (1992), pp. 275–89. The 'Postscript' and some of the other revisions draw heavily on "Cost Saving through Restructuring the CBC," March 1995, proposal entered in the 1995 Fraser Institute Economy in Government Competition.

Gertrude J. Robinson and Armande Saint-Jean. Adapted from "Women Politicians and Their Media Coverage: A Generational Analysis." In *Women in Canadian Politics: Toward Equity in Representation*. Research Studies, Royal Commission on Electoral Reform and Party Financing and Canadian Communications Group. Publishing, Supply and Services Canada, 1991.

A NOTE FROM THE PUBLISHER

Thank you for selecting *Seeing Ourselves: Media Power and Policy in Canada*, Second Edition, by Helen Holmes and David Taras. The authors and publisher have devoted considerable time to the careful development of this book. We appreciate your recognition of this effort and accomplishment.

We want to hear what you think about *Seeing Ourselves: Media Power and Policy in Canada*. Please take a few minutes to fill in the stamped reader reply card at the back of the book. Your comments and suggestions will be valuable to us as we prepare new editions and other books.

CONTENTS

INTRODUCTION: SEEING POWER AND CHANGE IN THE CANADIAN MEDIA

In this second edition of *Seeing Ourselves,* we tried to offer students a rich collection of articles spanning a wide spectrum of issues and concerns. There are omissions, and not all aspects of this broad and expansive field of study could be covered. The goal was to give students not only strong descriptions of the concepts or history that pertain to particular topics but also a sense of the consequences of actions taken, where battles have been fought and where they are looming, the choices that the country and its citizens face. The collection will give students much to debate about the Canadian mass media—a world that has enveloped them almost since birth.

Authors were given the freedom to spread their wings and deal with their topics in the manner that they thought appropriate. They were not asked to fix their gaze on a single, unifying theme or adhere to a particular point of view. Nonetheless, a number of strong currents run through the collection and bring unity to the book.

A number of authors dealt with the problem of Canadian cultural identity in the face of the overpowering influence and shadow of the United States. Others carried the argument further, suggesting that there was now an international marketplace—an international cultural shopping centre—where consumer identities are being shaped and national identities blurred. People wear the same clothes, consume the same products, watch the same television shows, go to or rent the same movies, and listen to the same music almost everywhere in the Western world and far beyond. It can even be argued that global economic forces and pressures threaten to undermine genuine American culture—the local and vibrant cultures of New York, the Deep South or New England—as much as genuine Canadian culture appears to be under attack.

John Meisel, one of Canada's pre-eminent thinkers, believes that Canadian culture can survive the onslaught, that it is growing and prospering. Beverly Rasporich, Mark Starowicz, and Seth Feldman see the country as being capable of remarkable innovation, triumph, and accomplishment even in the face of relentless cultural assaults. Martin Laba is worried about the commercial power that underlies the commodification of youth culture.

A central thread that links all of these articles is the question of what role, if any, should be played by the Canadian state. In a time of shrinking budgets and a shrinking state, many citizens are questioning whether monies spent on the Canadian Broadcasting Corporation (CBC) or on supporting a Canadian music industry are "frills" that can no longer be justified when so many Canadians depend on food banks and have to wait many months for medical procedures. The role of governments and that of private media industries is vigorously debated in this collection.

At the centre of the debate is the future of the CBC. Some observers believe that the CBC plays an increasingly important role at a time when a small clutch of corporate behemoths so dominate the presses and the airwaves. The CBC is not only an alternative voice but one that sometimes probes deeply into public issues, even at the risk of making the country's political leaders and large numbers of listeners and viewers acutely uncomfortable. This is something that private outlets are often reluctant to do. "Feel good" news or "news you can use" is far too lucrative. The argument is that the CBC keeps others honest and that without its influence, standards of journalism would drop like a stone. The CBC remains, to some, a national town hall, an electronic spinal cord, that has been and continues to be central to Canadian nation-building. The private networks and services have simply not delivered in quite the same way.

Others believe that the CBC is not only expensive but antiquated. Subsidies from Telefilm Canada, protections and incentives given to private broadcasters, initiatives by a new generation of independent producers, and the Canadian-content provisions of the Broadcasting Act are enough to ensure that fine Canadian programs continue to be made. Desbarats contends that private broadcasters are no longer the "villains of the piece." Opponents of the status quo also argue that the CBC can be melted down to its core, leaving for instance, CBC "Newsworld," national radio, and regional television to survive. The rest can be sold off and millions of dollars saved.

Another theme that runs through the collection is the challenges that have been brought by new media technologies; the articles by Starowicz, and Ray Straatsma and Catherine Murray tackle the issue head on. There have been a cornucopia of new developments since the publication of the first edition of *Seeing Ourselves* in 1992. Vincent Mosco of Carleton University, one of Canada's foremost experts on information technologies and policies, has compared the advent of the much discussed information superhighway with the changes that occurred with the arrival of electricity in the late nineteenth century. "White magic" and "the great white way" fundamentally altered the structure of society.[1] In the same way, changes are now occurring along a number of key intersections. The following list is no more than a rough guide to this changing horizon.

The Explosion of Channels through Cable

The arrival of new digital-compression technology has allowed more signals to be compressed into the same electronic space, hence the capacity to launch a 500- or 1000-channel universe. In the United States, there are already cable systems that broadcast over 125 channels. Television production has become a new experience as the audience seems to be dividing into narrower and narrower subgroups. A myriad of news, sports, shopping, and religious channels, as well as boutique channels devoted to such topics as pets, music videos, books, gardening, court cases, political parties, war, old movies, and video games, all compete against the major networks. Some systems even have a video "red light" district where salacious movies can be seen. Each year the audience share of the American networks is chipped away little by little. The mass audience that once came together in the tens of millions to watch the same networks, the same shows, to witness the same events—thus creating a common culture of viewing and experience—will, it can be argued, be splintered into many disparate pieces. While it may be too early to predict the demassification of the mass media, there are certainly trends in this direction.

In 1995, ten new services were added to cable offerings in Canada. Others are being lined up for the next rounds of decisions. Some of the services now in place, TSN, YTV, and the Discovery channel, for instance, seem to have found their niche. Others may gradually fall by the wayside. All of these services, however, may eventually cut sharply into the CBC's audience and those of the main private networks and stations. Advertisers have already discovered some of the benefits of "narrowcasting"—being able to reach the most desirable demographic groups for their products by advertising on specialty channels to specialty audiences. A sports equipment manufacturer can reach the sports audience by advertising on TSN, a young singles audience can be reached by advertising on MuchMusic. While the new services remain a sideshow in terms of audience size, we are only at the early stages of the cable explosion.

Direct Broadcast Satellites (DBS)

The arrival of DBS, or "Death Stars" as they have been called, opens another, if similar, horizon. There are signs that some Canadians, increasingly frustrated by the rates and offerings of cable monopolies, will turn to satellite services that will deliver well over 100 channels. While the Canadian Radio-television and Telecommunications Commission (CRTC) is attempting to impose regulations that will ensure Canadian content, some observers see the potential for a great deal of unregulated traffic with the government unable to regulate the signals that reach Canadian living rooms. The term "Death Star," with its sinister Darth Vader connotation, refers to the death of Canadian culture as the ability to protect and regulate the airwaves in Canada might be lost amid a thunderstorm of new channels that originate from outside the country.

The Coming World of Convergence and Interactive Television

Convergence is the term used to describe the merging of television, telephone, and computer systems. Although extensive research and investments are being made in these areas, the dream of being able to do one's banking at home, or to call up movies on demand, is not likely to be widespread until well into the twenty-first century. But convergence is occurring at a number of levels. Clearly the merging of technologies is the main focus of business investment. At least one new product combines a computer, a colour TV, a CD-Rom player, a speaker phone, and an answering machine. Even the shape of the television screen is changing. Xerox has just developed a television monitor using liquid crystal technology that has the thickness of a pad of paper. The high costs of research and development, and the need for major corporations to hurdle protectionist walls, has spurred a new generation of corporate alliances or corporate convergence.

Huge corporate empires such as Time-Warner or Sony dominate production and distribution. While citizens may feel that they are being exposed to a dizzying array of channels, programs, and options, control over what people are exposed to now rests in fewer and fewer corporate hands.

In addition to technical and corporate convergence, there is also concern about what some scholars believe is a convergence in media content. Media production seems to have become increasingly homogenized. The same shows, the same advertising, the same sounds pulsate across the globe. Martin Laba illustrates the problem in his analysis of the manufacturing of a global youth culture, a culture based on common themes, rhythms, and products. The question of whether Canadian culture is being smothered by this new international convergence is addressed by a number of authors in this collection.

There is also the new interactive capability of modern cable systems. While still at a relatively rudimentary stage in development, viewers who subscribe to some cable services in Canada can control the camera angles at hockey games, choose the commercials that they want to watch, and have a choice of video games. Many parents are looking forward to the V-chip and its potential to block out programs with sex or violence.

The Internet and the Information Highway

Much has been written about the new webs of communication that allow people to connect instantly across the world and the communities of conversation and exchange that have mushroomed in increasing numbers. While it still lacks the resonance and power of conventional mass media, many of those who "surf the net" have found that it can be a vital forum for exchanging views and information. The great advantage, and great disadvantage perhaps, is that it is unregulated. Repressive regimes are unable to stop the ceaseless tide of connection, information, and conversation. Moreover, as one observer recently explained, "Electronic conversations, to our benefit, allow people to circumvent the managed dialogue that politicians and PR-types try to shape to serve their own ends."[2]

But unwanted intruders—commercial exploitation, pornographic fantasies, vicious hate, and a great deal of mischief—are also part of this new world. It is as if the anonymity of cyberspace allows for the unleashing of raw emotions and aggressive activities that are suppressed in normal everyday encounters. Some have argued that as the Internet comes to attract a larger and larger number of flamers and cranks and people who "have little of interest to say but a lot of room in which to say it," the more educated and refined users will migrate to more exclusive preserves.[3]

Not everyone will be able to afford these new media and information services. There may be new stratifications and disparities based on people's ability to access the information highway. Pay-per-view TV, pay TV, the many new services offered by cable and satellite, CD-Roms, and interactive television are all costly, and while some Canadians will be able to buy into this new world, others will not. Those who can pay will be able to dine from a virtually unlimited menu of options, and that menu will be customized to suit individual tastes to an almost astonishing degree. The elite groups that John Meisel believes are keeping Canadian culture alive are also those who can most easily afford, and may be the most attracted to, the new international menus of culture.

The articles in this book focus on three central concepts: power, regulation, and the rights of citizens. In Part I of the book, entitled "Canadian Media in the Looking Glass," we present readers with a series of articles that are meant to delve beneath the surface and ask difficult and probing questions about the impact that the mass media has had and continues to have on Canadian society. Political reporting, the role and coverage of women, the problems of children and television, the politics of "Hockey Night in Canada," the commercialization of the youth and music culture, and the centrality of Canadian humour are tackled in articles that we believe readers will find insightful but also filled with questions that will generate discussion, challenge conventional wisdom, and stir thinking and ideas.

Part II on Media, Law, and Regulation describes the many difficulties of managing and bringing fairness to a media system that must balance a variety of competing claims. Marc Raboy describes the anguished and aching question of Quebec, language, and nationality. He argues that communication reflects and is central to resolving the Canadian constitutional dilemma. Lorna Roth deals with broadcasting north of 60 and the problems encountered by First Peoples in their struggle to use the modern media to connect with one another and to have their voices heard by other Canadians.

Stephen Kline and William Leiss provide a systematic overview of the dilemmas faced in advertising regulation. The problems are complex and messy as a balance must be struck between commercial free speech and the need to protect the rights of citizens. Ray Straatsma and Catherine Murray warn readers about the perils of electronic databases and about how these are used by corporations to monitor and target consumers. Consumer records have become a product that is gathered, traded, and sold as a commodity. What may be lost in the transaction, however, is the right of citizens to maintain their privacy.

The other two articles in this section are on the legal aspects of the mass media. Mary Gerace Gold has written about defamation law, and Janice Dickin has analyzed pornography legislation. Both authors provide students with refreshing and provocative insights and critical perspectives about the nature of and legal reasoning behind these laws.

In Part III, Power and Change in the Canadian Media, Robert Hackett, Richard Pinet, and Myles Ruggles describe the power of media conglomerates and ask whether citizens are being exposed to a full bouquet of ideas and stories or whether commercial imperatives curtail and narrow the information and perspectives that citizens are exposed to. Gillian Steward, the former managing editor of the *Calgary Herald*, has similar concerns and links the decline of newspapers with their inability to reflect their changing communities.

The book will also provide readers with what is likely to be new intellectual equipment. Concepts such as hegemony, framing, moral panic, and commodification are explained in ways that readers will easily understand. The sometimes dense and impenetrable tangle of law and regulation is presented by scholars who have much experience teaching these subjects and untangling their complexities.

During the lifetime of this second edition of *Seeing Ourselves*, there will undoubtedly be significant changes in the Canadian media landscape. The question of the role of the state during a period in which there is likely to be severe budget-cutting and moves toward decentralization and privatization, decisions about the future of the CBC, the continued expansion of channels and services (even as some of those that have already been launched fall by the wayside), the advent of new technologies, pressures toward convergence and globalization and the drive toward larger and larger media empires are likely to be a volatile mix. We will see the reflection of these changes in virtually all aspects of the mass media and their relationship to society. We will see it in the nature and quality of news reporting, in children's television, in how gender is depicted in the media, in music and sports programming, and in how Canadians see their own reflection in the ever changing tempests of the mass media.

NOTES

1. Vincent Mosco, "Information Policy: The Superhighway Meets the Great White Way." Paper presented at the meeting of the Canadian Library Association, Vancouver, June 1994.
2. Gary Chapman, "Flamers," *The New Republic* 10 (April 1995): 14.
3. Ibid.

PART I

CANADIAN MEDIA IN THE LOOKING GLASS

TELEVISION NEWS FRAMES IN THE 1993 CANADIAN ELECTION

***Matthew Mendelsohn*[1]**

Election coverage, like all communications processes, exists within certain constraints. The news media cannot discuss everything it considers important. It must assume certain things to be true and certain objectives to be worthy if any political discussion is to take place. This discussion depends on which aspects of reality are reported and how they are bounded, or framed; it depends on how the infinite and discursive world of the "real" is reconfigured and transformed into "news stories." Newsworkers must constantly make decisions about 1) what is real, 2) what is important, and 3) what is the overriding objective of their reporting. These decisions are only sometimes conscious, while oftentimes they are the product of the socialization of newsworkers and the obligations of news reporting (like time, availability of visuals, and ratings). This essay deals with the assumptions that shape campaign reporting, particularly the frames of interpretation television news applied to the 1993 Canadian election campaign. By understanding how campaign reports are framed, we are able to understand what information is available to voters when they make decisions, and how this political communication may affect eventual election outcomes and policy debates.

WHAT IS A "FRAME"?

Frames can be understood as those persistent patterns of interpretation, presentation, emphasis, and exclusion by which symbol-handlers routinely organize discourse (Gitlin, 1980, 7). Frames are thus the assumptions used to structure discourse and "define situations" (Goffman, 1974, 9-13). The selection of a news "angle" or "storyline" which transforms an occurrence into a news report is a frame. For example, newsworkers can view an election campaign as a contest between competing parties, interests, or values; as a partisan game played for personal advantage and power; as a battle of leaders; or as a discussion among citizens about their collective future. Each of these descriptions is in some way "true," but if the media presume that only one is an accurate representation of "reality," the media will seek out different aspects of the campaign and structure their reports accordingly. These media frames become an implicit part of discourse and help determine what viewers eventually understand about the campaign.

Frames are, of course, an inevitable part of discourse. All language is inherently bounded and news reports are no exception to this rule. Assumptions are necessary, and choices must be made about what to report and how. In this way, there is no such thing as "objectivity." Journalists can try to treat major parties equally and be fair on the issues, but their own values, the values of news reporting, and the dominant values of society determine the answers to a thousand questions, including the definition of which parties are "major" and which issues warrant scrutiny. The media are not entirely "transparent" in that they cannot simply present a window on the world. News frames put things in context; they communicate assumptions; and they assume certain causal relationships for why things happen as they do.

Where Do Frames Come From?

During a political campaign, the frames are set by an interplay between political parties and the media. For the most part, the media rely on parties and their strategists for the political information that eventually gets reported. Parties thus set the bounds for debate, and present the frames of discussion. However, the media have certain demands, and parties tailor their strategies with an understanding of these media expectations. News conventions constrain which frames get selected. The media therefore are dependent on the approaches of the parties, but the latter are designed with a knowledge of news conventions. Individual journalists usually have little control over what is reported, but the news media as a whole define what their conventions will be, and, by so doing, reinterpret the messages that parties can communicate. Those parties that better understand news conventions will be more successful in the communication of their messages to voters, as there will be less need for mediation.

However, this interplay between parties and the media exists within certain constraints. Some suggest that the selection of frames is related to organizational needs (Epstein, 1973). What becomes "news" is not dictated by daily choices made by newsworkers. Rather, stories are the result of the specific ways newswork is organized. Reports that deal with the manifest actions of well-known people are reported because newsworkers know where to find these stories. Breaking events are reported because they ensure the creation of an audience who will come back the next day to find out more (Entman, 1989). Altheide (1976) describes "the news perspective" (73), by which stories must have a beginning, a middle, and an end. While the news perspective began as a practical way to separate one event from another and make plausible statements about them within a given amount of time, it has now come to set the criteria for importance and coverage. Events become news when they are discrete (i.e., they occur in a particular time and place and then finish), can be told simply through an easily developed angle, when colourful visuals are available, when conflict is present, and when interesting characters are involved, not because of their inherent importance. There are thus a number of organizational and sociological constraints placed on the media.

Tuchman (1978) adds, however, that it is not only organizational needs that define newsworthiness; those events that conform to the expectations of legitimized institutions and dominant ideology are also more likely to be deemed newsworthy. News conventions are based on collective myths and reside within mainstream beliefs and ideology; they are built on this ideology and depend on it. The interactive relationship between the news media and politicians, whereby they both conform to media conventions and expectations, is thus bounded by the ideological consensus of elites at the moment. Parenti (1986) makes the point more emphatically. That the media favour personality over issues, events over content, official positions over popular grievances, the atypical and sensational over the structural and systemic, is a conscious choice made by the news media to withhold from citizens the information that they need to question elite consensus. The very bounds of the expressible are limited by elites, and these limits are accepted by newsworkers because they are dependent on this elite consensus. They are dependent on it for their jobs, for advertising dollars, and for continued privileged access to those in positions of authority who "make news" (Chomsky, 1989).

What Have Others Said about Campaign Reporting?

A certain consensus has developed about how media conventions structure election coverage. There must always be a clear narrative in news stories. Winning and losing are the frames which glue stories together (Robinson and Sheehan, 1983) and campaigns are seen as horseraces, as standing and polls structure news reports about polls and standings (Brady and Johnston, 1987; Patterson, 1980; Wagenberg et al., 1988). Campaigns are interpreted as a game played for personal advantage. The language and culture of television encourages campaigns to be portrayed as war, as a game, as drama, but rarely as a competition between alternate visions (Fiske, 1987). News reports focus on campaign events and campaign strategy, and neglect substantive differences between the parties (Fletcher and Everett, 1991); campaign reporting focuses on the political process, rather than political content. News reporting is always more concerned with events and happenings—the "episodic"—rather than more structural, systemic, and permanent aspects of political reality—the "thematic" (Iyengar, 1991). Elections are framed as choices of leadership (Wattenberg, 1991). When differences are reported, they are presented in symbolic terms (Jamieson, 1992).

Methodology

This essay provides examples of typical news coverage from the CBC National Prime Time News. To analyze frames, one cannot simply extract unrepresentative passages from news coverage. To ensure that this did not happen, four guidelines were followed.

First, examples that were the opening or closing passages of the reports were selected—the words that "framed" reports. Second, identification was made of the causal relationships that were assumed: what subjective explanations do newsworkers offer for why things happen? Third, I identified the questions that newsworkers were trying to answer in their reports. And fourth, I restricted the analysis to one network (the CBC) and a very narrow time period (the first week of the campaign, September 8–15). This restriction reduces the choice open to the researcher: it is almost impossible to choose unrepresentative passages to prove a point because frames are taken from almost every campaign report over the time period.[2]

TELEVISION NEWS FRAMES IN 1993

The frame of strategy is used as an interpretive device in most reports:

Anchor: "To news from home now, starting with the federal election campaign and Jean Chrétien on the attack. Keith Boag begins our coverage on board the Liberal campaign plane." *Reporter*: "Six days into the campaign, Liberal leader Jean Chrétien has travelled across most of the country and given more than a dozen speeches. A clear strategy has emerged, it has two parts: the first, to hammer home that a Liberal government would play a more active role than the Tories have and that creating jobs would be their priority. The second part is to attack Kim Campbell" (Sept. 13).

The news report assumes the strategy of the leader is important, as are his activities, and ties it together with the metaphor of war.

This theme repeats itself throughout reports.

Anchor: "In the campaign today, Kim Campbell did a little fine-tuning to some of her own statements about jobs. The prime minister was in the Montreal area, making her first visit to the province of Quebec since the campaign began. Denise Harrington is covering the Campbell tour.... *Reporter*: " 'Chrétien will run up the deficit to pay for fairytales,' Campbell said. Still, Chrétien's promise that the Liberals will create jobs now has pushed Campbell into tempering her message. Tories are worried that Campbell's coming across as a leader who cares more about the deficit than about the unemployed." *Campbell*: "There is hope for Canadians. There is real hope. Real hope in real solutions to real problems, not the empty hope of short-term solutions." *Reporter*: "Polls show Campbell is popular in Quebec, and here in a suburban shopping centre, for example, the party is eager to show that a prime minister from outside the province can connect with French-speaking voters....Campbell said she knows people are suffering. All week, Campbell has been arguing she's only being honest when she says Canadians will have to wait a while for improvement on the job front. Conservatives insist that's still the right message, but say Campbell has to deliver it in a more sensitive way" (Sept. 11).

Candidates fine-tune their messages, they do so in response to the tactics of opposing camps, and they worry about the manner in which messages are delivered. The dispute itself—how to deal with the questions of unemployment and the deficit—is assumed to be unimportant. It is only discussed by the media as a tableau on which strategies and counterattacks are played out. How well the leader can "deal with the issue" as a strategic obstacle to overcome, rather than as a national political problem to solve, is assumed to be most important. "The press magnifies certain aspects of politics and downplays others, which are often more central to issues of governing" (Patterson, 1993, 29).

TV news sets out to answer the questions: What are leaders trying to convince voters to believe? What are their strategies? and Are these strategies working? We see this in a particularly striking way when the Liberals' platform is released.

Anchor: "The document is 112 pages long, and the Liberals believe it is their passport to power. The party released its entire election campaign platform today. It is an attempt to weigh cuts against spending while trying to boost the economy. It's the dilemma faced by all politicians, but the Liberals say their solution is unique. The CBC's Keith Boag reports on Jean Chrétien's game plan." *Reporter*: "The platform is called 'Creating Opportunity' and the Liberals took the unusual risk of releasing it all at once rather than bit by bit through the course of the campaign. Reporters got to look at it early and were encouraged to question Liberal staff members on the details. That was partly an attempt to ensure reporters understood the platform, partly to demonstrate the party is confident it can withstand the scrutiny" (Sept 15).

According to the journalist, the party took risks by releasing their game plan, their passport to power. These acts were consistent with their strategy of demonstrating they were confident they could withstood scrutiny. It is assumed that if the platform withstood the scrutiny of reporters—presumably meaning that it has no glaring errors of fact or obvious contradictions—it has passed a test and fulfilled its strategic goal. Its programmatic and ideological content—its very political ideas—are considered less important. Because the relationship between strategists and reporters remains close, both groups come to see election campaigns through the same lens: strategy, tactics,. and process, rather than ideas.

The tactical motivations of party leaders were used as interpretive devices. Providing viewers with more background on politicians' motivations can be grouped into two broad categories: tactical or ideological. Political leaders have tactical as well as ideological motivations. Parties do hope to do well, but they also have some vision of "The Good Community" and some idea about the mechanisms to arrive there (the NDP was not interested in creating the same country as were the Liberals, who were not interested in creating the same country as the Reform Party). During the 1993 election, the parties had very different attitudes toward fundamental questions like the role of the state and the role of the market. The media is thus presented with a choice: the focus can be on the partisan, tactical, and vote-oriented motivations, or the programmatic, theoretical, and goal-oriented motivations. Television's choice in the 1993 election was the former, as motivations always equalled strategy. Policy positions were treated as mere campaign devices to attract votes.

As we have seen, the media assume a very particular reason for these various strategies: standings in the polls.

Anchor: "And Jean Chrétien was also making stops in Montreal today. The Tory years have reduced the Liberal strength in Quebec to just nine seats. Now Chrétien is trying to fight back. Keith Boag is with the Liberal leader's tour." *Reporter*: "There was a time when Jean Chrétien was one of the most loved politicians in Quebec. Not any more. A Quebec poll published in *La Presse* today showed him trailing both Kim Campbell and Lucien Bouchard in public opinion polls. Because of their leader's unpopularity, the Liberals are facing as tough a fight here as anywhere else in the country. It's also a crucial fight. The party's best case scenario still shows it would have a tough time forming a majority government without at least doubling the number of seats it now holds in Quebec" (Sept. 11).

Anchor: "To the election campaign now. The NDP had the biggest policy splash today. Audrey McLaughlin came out with charts and graphs to illustrate her economic programme. The CBC's Paul Adams is covering the NDP." *Reporter*: "Winnipeg is one of the few places the NDP has realistic hopes of gaining seats in this election. So it was a natural first stop on the Audrey McLaughlin tour.... Tomorrow, Audrey McLaughlin will fix her guns on free trade during a meeting with Ontario's NDP premier Bob Rae. The party is hoping its opposition to NAFTA can help revive its fortunes, which have been sagging in Ontario with the unpopularity of the provincial government" (Sept. 9).

It should be noted that this report did include some detail on policy proposals, as did a minority of other reports. What is more important though is that the small amount of detail on policies is put in a strategic context, is seen as a response to polls, remains unconnected to a general ideology or principles, disappears the next night, and only emerges if the leader talks about it. McLaughlin talking about NAFTA is framed as an isolated episode and a tactic, rather than framed as an example of the economic vision of the NDP.

We have begun to see how reports are framed in an "episodic" manner, meaning that they focus on isolated events as episodes and happenings: poverty is not a story, a child dying of malnutrition in Toronto would be; the level of crime is not news, a murder is. Through events, speeches, photo ops, and press conferences parties try to create news by manufacturing "episodes."

Anchor: "Kim Campbell officially opened her Quebec campaign today. She and dozens of other Conservative candidates held a rally in Montreal. Quebec is crucial for the Tories. And polls there put them behind the Bloc Québécois. So today Campbell tried to undercut Bloc support. Our campaign coverage begins tonight with Denise Harrington in Montreal." *Reporter*: "It's the kind of show Quebec Conservatives love to put on: 800 cheering, flag-waving supporters, and 70 MPs and candidates, all led by Kim Campbell with a helping hand from Jean Charest" (Sept. 12).

Reporter: "Bloc Québécois leader Lucien Bouchard walked with his wife through his home town today, heading to his riding office, getting ready for what he hopes will be the last federal election ever in Quebec" (Sept. 12).

Campaign events and the actions of leaders are deemed important aspects of the electoral process. Whether campaign events go well acts as a frame because it provides a simple, though questionable, metaphor: how well a leader can run the campaign indicates how well he or she will be able to run the government. The question of efficient management is deemed important; which ideas a leader actually intends to manage are not. When discussing the strategic frame, we saw how policies were interpreted through these assumptions. It is, however, important to examine in more detail the framing surrounding policy differences.

Reporter: "Jean Chrétien interprets the criticism that he's yesterday's man as an attack not on his policies, but on his age and fitness. So when the camera is on, he goes out of his way to look robust and energetic. But Chrétien freely admits he is the same kind of Liberal he was 30 years ago. He believes some government economic policies that were used in the past are just as useful now. He took reporters on a little walk through Halifax's historic properties renovation, a government-sponsored building project that once created jobs where they were needed and now is a thriving tourist site" (Sept. 9).

Policies exist on the news. Here there is talk of government intervention in the economy. But they exist in the background, away from the central action of campaign events, photo ops, and leaders trying to create images.

Reporter: "This is Denise Harrington in Utica, Ontario. This scene might look familiar. Kim Campbell has taken a page out of Bill Clinton's book, a town hall meeting." *Campbell*: "I would like to lead the process." *Reporter*: "Questions for the prime minister on farming, railways, the economy." *Citizen*: "Why did they phase that out?" *Reporter*: "There was a mix of people: farmers, businesspeople, not all Tories." *Campbell*: "And I've been hearing from people across the country, their very great concern, that we get the deficit eliminated, because they understand that only when we do that can we ease up on the tax burden of Canadians." *Reporter*: "The style is supposed to smooth the way for the tough message. Campbell's still insisting there's no quick fix for the unemployed." *Campbell*: "There is a direct link between the growth in jobs and the reduction in the deficit. It is not possible to increase the deficit and increase overall employment in Canada." *Reporter*: "This is the image Conservatives want voters to see over and over again: Kim Campbell out listening to people" (Sept. 9).

Policies are used as ammunition, named by the media but not discussed. The image of dialogue is more important than the dialogue itself. When the real question of how we go about creating employment and reducing the deficit comes up, the debate is not joined; it is used to create images and construct political personalities.

The news media have their own priorities, and sometimes the political communication of parties is heavily reformulated to conform to the media's own agenda.

Anchor: "Liberal leader Jean Chrétien talked about job training today. He repeated an earlier promise to create more apprenticeships for young Canadians. Chrétien said the Liberals would put an additional 60 000 people in apprenticeship programs. The cost: 576 million dollars. Reporters following Chrétien's campaign are enjoying unusually good working conditions. Liberal party organizers have gone out of their way to make the media feel comfortable. The CBC's Keith Boag explains how, and why." *Reporter*: "Courting the media has always been part of the game, but in this campaign the Liberals are taking that game to a higher level. Take their media bus: it has seduced reporters. They're in love with it. Not only is it roomy and comfortable, with televisions, and so on, but each reporter also has a work space with a table, a lamp, and a telephone. And there's a fax machine in the back. For print and radio reporters, that means deadlines are suddenly easier to meet. They can file stories straight off the bus. On the Tory bus, organizers are aware that reporters covering them feel they're not treated as well as reporters covering the Liberals. The party is trying harder: last night the Tories offered reporters and technical crews with tickets to the Montreal Expos game. The Liberals insist their service to the media is not an attempt to jolly reporters into sympathetic coverage" (Sept. 12).

We can see how television does in fact see policies and promises as mere tactical devices.

Anchor: "And when we come back, our political panel looks at the start of the election campaign. Tonight's focus, the jobs issue, and did Kim Campbell make a costly strategic error?" (Sept. 12).

There is no desire to engage in debate over Keynesian economics, economic policy, or any of the other real differences that divided parties during the 1993 election that come to mind based on Campbell's comments concerning unemployment. Rather, the news sets out to answer the question: Was it a strategic error? By doing so, citizens are marginalized. They are not provided with information that could help them pass judgement on economic policy. Instead, they are given pundits' assessments of elite strategies to get (presumably) gullible and easily manipulated citizens to change their votes.

Though I have distinguished between the frames of strategy, tactical motivation, polls, and assessments of events, they usually come together in the same report in an attempt to answer the question: How will what happened today affect who will win? Standing is thus used as an interpretive device for the events. The central goal of television news during the election is predicting the election outcome. It is this frame that could be defined as the "metaframe," since it holds together all election reports. A focus on strategy, tactical motivations, and polls are the frames which enable this to take place. This metaframe may suffice in the coverage of foreign campaigns because viewers have no possible influence on the eventual outcome. "Who is going to be President of the United States?" may be an acceptable question for Canadian news, but "Who is going to be prime minister?" is somewhat limiting. It assumes that elections are ends in themselves, to be observed, rather than means by which citizens participate in making important decisions. Viewers are provided with information about who is winning, not with information to help determine who *will* win. Citizens are treated as mere spectators, framed outside the story, not participants integral to the election. Who will win? is one possible frame. What do parties stand for? What would they do? How would life be different, and for whom? could be others.

This frame was used to structure the campaign because the news media have determined that politics is a game played for power:

Reporter: "At the end of this, their first week on the road, the Liberals are feeling very pleased with themselves. They believe they've taken control of the election agenda and pushed the Tories onto the defensive. On Wednesday though, they've set themselves the difficult task of explaining exactly how they'll finance their entire election platform without adding a nickel to the deficit" (Sept. 13).

Leaders themselves succumb to participation in the game.

Reporter: "Kim Campbell and other political leaders hastened to pay tribute to Robert Bourassa" [following his retirement announcement]. *Campbell*: "His devotion to federalism...is something that's important for all Canadians." *Reporter*: "But there was also puzzlement about the timing, and above all, the effect of Bourassa's departure on the federal election." *Campbell*: "It's very difficult to say what impact it will have, but perhaps it will focus attention on the importance of Quebec's role in Canada." *Reporter*: "Jean Chrétien insisted Bourassa quit for personal, not political, reasons. As for suggestions in Quebec that the premier did it to harm the Bloc Québécois"—*Chrétien*: "For me, you know, anything that hurts the Bloc will be welcomed by me." *Reporter*: "But will it?" *Chrétien*: "I don't know. I hope so, but I don't know." *Reporter*: "But, he added, Bourassa's departure will not change his campaign" (Sept. 14).

The frame is how the departure of Bourassa will affect the dynamics of the campaign and the outcome of the election, and leaders are asked to play the role of pundit and pollster as they enter into the fray of predicting effects. All along though, citizens—the ones who will determine these outcomes—are provided with little information on which they can base their democratic decisions. The effect of campaign strategies on citizens is discussed as if they had no ability to exercise independent judgement. Citizens are permitted to participate in town halls of various kinds, or shout at a campaign leader, but the effect of politics and policy-making on the lives of individual members of our democratic community is considered inconsequential.

The frames that recurred were strategy, tactical motivations, polls, episodic events, the leaders' activities, and the illusions they were trying to communicate. Campaign journalists understand their role as one of narrating activities, and explaining the strategic political process. Kathleen Hall Jamieson (1992) concluded that they act as campaign consultants and theatre critics, as they give personal suggestions about what strategies should be followed in the days to come and evaluate the theatrical performance of leaders and their show (173). I would add the roles of sportscaster and war correspondent to the list, as they provide play-by-play action from the frontline trenches. They construct the political spectacle consistent with the vision that "politics is a phony show played for political advantage" (which it is). However, after having identified the artificial aspects of the political spectacle, there is no attempt to identify and explain the important and genuine aspects of politics (which also exist).

The Effect of Television Frames

Identifying frames is not simply an amusing intellectual exercise. Because most citizens get most of their political news from TV, and because we can only make judgements based on the information available to us, the recurring presentation of reality in a particular way will likely change the way we think and will have political effects. Iyengar (1991) demonstrated in controlled experiments that when episodic framing is used—that is, a focus on isolated events and incidents—viewers were more likely to attribute responsibility to the character of individuals rather than to social or political forces. When thematic framing was used—that is, a focus on structural and systemic forces, causes, and consequences—viewers avoided personalizing complex problems. Marlier (1989) has also demonstrated how the framing of a political issue affects public opinion. When the Iran-Contra hearings began to frame the issue through the motivations and character of Oliver North, support for his actions rose. Though individuals were still responding to the same set of facts, their responses changed because of the media's framing of these facts in a personalized way. During the 1988 Canadian election, it was demonstrated that as individuals' exposure to the media went up, they became more likely to base their votes on their opinions of leaders rather than on their judgements of parties or issues (Mendelsohn, 1994) because the media framed the election as a matter of "which leader is to be trusted on the question of free trade" (Mendelsohn, 1993). Others have also argued that the effect of television news has encouraged candidate-centred politics, whereby our collective judgements are reduced to choices of personality (Wattenberg, 1991; Keeter, 1990). Avoiding discussion of the fundamental differences separating parties and the stakes of the election may communicate to voters that *nothing* is at stake: no party would be any different than any other. In this manner, elections become ways to choose likeable and honest leaders and reject unpopular governments, but nothing more. With the use of an episodic frame to cover the campaign, voters may be unable to make links between disparate issues and to develop coherent philosophies which could help them pass judgement on a whole range of issues (Iyengar, 1991). The episodic frame thus encourages citizens to treat each issue as an isolated discrete event, rather than encouraging a recognition of the organizing first principles inherent in most political disagreements.

These trends may have serious consequences for policy-making: because parties cannot count on loyal supporters who are committed to their broad agenda, governments must constantly seek to buttress support by engaging in popular short-term policy-making. In the process, vision and long-term planning decline because there is no payoff for parties in pursuing such strategies.

The indeterminate view of political issues, whereby nothing can really be resolved, is offered by television news. Television news does not pretend to be able to resolve issues, but in so doing, television demeans the possibility for philosophical or political argument. Television news communicates the message that it is *impossible* to determine certain things. Though the conventions of objective reporting prevent journalists from resolving issues, these conventions do not preclude the possibility for journalists to frame issues so that viewers are provided with the tools and cues to resolve the issues for themselves. Instead, viewers are offered two conflicting soundbites on complicated questions, often leaving confused and frustrated citizens to say: "Well, if the economists can't agree, how can I make a decision?" The news media frame the issue of deficit reduction as impossible to resolve as parties use the issue in tactical terms, rather than assuming that different approaches to deficit reduction are grounded in different views of the market and government intervention.

The frames used encourage a trivialization of politics, and contribute to a general decline in political discourse and the quality of political life. The frame of the horse race coupled with a lack of ideological, philosophical, group, or social frames that would help viewers interpret events and understand issues guarantee that viewers and parties will turn to that which is easier and more apparent, namely, symbolic and visceral issues. Politics is of course always in some way about symbols, and voters often reason in a symbolic way (Sniderman, Brody, and Tetlock, 1991). However, what is new is that for many voters, the differences between the parties are not clear. And, unfortunately, whenever politics degenerates to a battle uniquely of symbols, we usually witness a growth in political intolerance and nastiness. Intolerance in a political community grows when political leaders encourage citizens' worst instincts. Because the media respond to simple, easily explained and easily depicted symbols, politicians have an interest in using a discourse that is simple and symbolic—one that relies on the polarization of complex issues and the assignment of blame. Media conventions and the electoral interests of politicians coincide to encourage a discourse which makes no room for nuance, whether it be on the question of Quebec sovereignty, crime, or immigration. The decline of political discourse is thus complemented by the incline of symbolic battles and scapegoating.

Moreover, because parties know that the complexity and reality of their proposals will be simplified as symbolic battles between "the party of jobs versus the party of deficit reduction," they become hesitant to make daring or complicated suggestions; they become reluctant to engage in more sophisticated political argument. In the process, citizens lose democratic control of their governments because they do not know how the parties would behave if elected and cannot hold them accountable for their actions. The Liberals may have a mandate to increase employment (and, of course, to not be Brian Mulroney), but it was not clear during the campaign how they would go about this; nor was it clear how they intended to deal with issues like NAFTA or the GST. Citizens' ability to impose democratic control declines as parties' reluctance to discuss their positions inclines.

Presuming constant tactical motivations on the part of parties may have contributed to a decline in the confidence citizens have in their elites. This in itself is neither good nor bad as some elites are worthy of confidence while others are not. But the journalist's assumption that "all politicians are liars" makes it difficult for any political leader to mobilize citizens for a particular project. Robinson and Sheehan (1983) concluded that the media "do seem to want to make the public aware of the frailties and inadequacies of their elected leadership" (381). A political system in which there is generalized alienation and disillusionment on the part of citizens prevents the possibility of rectifying the situation because anyone who suggests mechanisms of improvement is greeted with the same scepticism (and tactical frames) as anyone else. A general cynicism, alienation, and depoliticization can be the result, preventing citizens from coming together and clearly expressing a political direction. A decline in linkages between the governed and the governors (not a particular set of governors but *any conceivable* group of governors) can only be unhealthy.

A failure to frame events in terms of competing interests may leave many voters confused. The last three Canadian election campaigns produced huge swings in vote intentions. This volatility was partly due to the fact that voters did not know who represented them and who spoke for their interests, and I suggest that this lack of understanding was related to news frames that ignored competing interests, making it difficult (though not impossible) for viewers to make sense of the election in a meaningful way, as democratic citizens.

Conclusions and Suggestions

The specific ways newsworkers went about organizing the campaign, to make it comprehensible to themselves as well as to viewers, focused on what leaders did, what their tactical motivations were for doing it, how they looked while doing it, and on understanding their actions and statements as a reaction to their standings in the polls. They framed their reports to answer the question: Who will win? and set out to answer this question by reference to campaign events, campaign strategy, and leader performance. Newsworkers did not organize the campaign in ideological terms, with reference to competing values, interests, groups, or visions. When the media did ask questions about the consequences of policies (rather than the strategic questions), they posited a world free from class or ideological divisions. Newsworkers asked the question: Is the Liberal platform good for Canada? rather than asking the question: For whom is it good? The first question ignores class, group, and ideological conflict, while the second recognizes this conflict as an integral part of politics. Though there is a great deal of partisan squabbling and bickering on television news, there is no real substantive conflict over values and direction. In this way, politics on TV is not Political.

While political parties attempt to have their frames accepted by the news media, ultimately the news media hold power by accepting or rejecting these attempts at information management. Even within accepted news conventions, changes can be made to help viewers become more active participants and more informed citizens. The media could assume that all motivations are not tactical, and they could try to explain the underlying differences between parties. They could explain these differences and connect them to the different beliefs of parties. They could try to explain why politics matters to citizens' lives. They could decrease their focus on leaders, polls, and episodic campaign events. They could also assume that fundamental differences exist within Canadian society, and try to identify these. In sum, when newsworkers approach an election campaign, they could take a "problem-promise-performance (on that problem)" approach (Jamieson, 1992, 191).[3] If the media were prepared to more radically change their criteria for news selection and construction, they could even eliminate the bogeyman of "objectivity," hire journalists with a wide range of political leanings, and permit them to explain the news in more detail through reference to specific values and beliefs (what is sometimes called "advocacy journalism").

These suggestions, however, are unlikely to be adopted. Rather, we have witnessed a move in the opposite direction: Action News (with its increased focus on disaster and isolated episodes), Tabloid News (with its increased focus on scandal and personality), and newspapers that increasingly mimic the trends and epistemology of television. The new news is still personality and events, but it is also bits of gore, scandal, outrageousness, and tragedy. Moreover, as journalists spend more of their time covering this kind of news, they become increasingly likely to apply these same frames and foci to the decreasing number of political stories that do make it to the screen.

Media reliant on advertising must always do two things: they must deliver audiences for advertisers, and, to do this, they must be as entertaining as possible. Media, to which we invariably turn for entertainment, may be ill-suited for the political responsibility of informing voters during democratic exercises.

The media recognize that election campaigns involve spectacle and illusion: creating false appearances and images. But while the media point this out—indicating, by definition, that what we are watching is unimportant—they continue to report it, thus, by definition, suggesting that it is important. This is because there is an unresolvable dilemma inherent in the coverage of election campaigns: the things that are important to television—events, personalities, dynamics (polls), colourful visuals, emotional outbursts, the drama of crisis and emergency (even if such urgency must be artificially created by pseudo-events)—are precisely those things that are unimportant to citizens engaged in democratic decision-making. Unless decision-makers within media organizations make a conscious choice to change current news criteria—which they are unlikely to do because this then implies that current news is not an "objective" mirror-like representation of "reality"—there is little room for individual journalists to make a healthier contribution to the democratic exercise. I ask the questions: If it is only appearance, why cover it at all? and If there are real differences between the parties, why not cover them? In 1993, we saw how TV news was reconceptualizing its role in the direction of action and tabloid news.

Anchor: "Later on Prime Time, we'll be introducing a special segment that we'll be featuring until election day, "Campaign Update." We'll include late-developing news and stories that take us beyond the day's events. Tonight, a look at how candidates pursue the farm vote at a time when farmers are too busy for politics, and a look ahead to tomorrow" (Sept. 14).

Going "beyond the day's events" is thus conceived as three things: stories that are even more recent than the day's activities, an increased focus on the tactical pursuit of votes, and a focus on the next day's activities in order to create a mood and a market of anticipation for episodic reports.

This essay has been concerned with textual rather than semiotic analysis, but, of course, TV news is visuals and imagery, not simply words. However, it should be underlined that the imagery of campaign reporting is consistent with the frames identified here. Reporters follow the leaders' tours to communicate that this spectacle is where the important action is. They couple this with the visual depictions of leaders' actions and performances, campaign events, and campaign rallies.

In sum, let us answer the questions posed at the beginning: What is assumed to be real? What is seen as important? What is understood as the objective of reporting? TV news media understand their objective as one of predicting who will win. They believe it is most important to explain strategy and standing to voters, and they believe that politicians rather than citizens are the actors of importance. They assume that process rather than content, and events and activities rather than ideas, are real. These are the things of importance to TV news; they have become the things of importance to parties; it remains uncertain whether they are the things of importance to the large numbers of citizens trying to make up their minds about how to vote.

NOTES

1. I am very grateful to my colleague Jonathan Rose who provided insightful and penetrating comments on an earlier version of this paper. Transcripts of news coverage were made available by the National Media Archives.
2. For a complete analysis of news frames over an entire campaign, see Jamieson, 1992. It should be noted, though, that news frames remain fairly consistent throughout campaigns.
3. This has all been suggested before. As a matter of fact, in response to criticism from various quarters following the 1988 election, the Canadian news media and political parties stated that they might deemphasize the leaders' tour in the next election (see "The Voters Reflect," p. 19). This clearly did not happen.

References

Altheide, David L. (1976). *Creating Reality: How TV News Distorts Events.* Beverly Hills: Sage.

Brady, Henry E., and Richard Johnston. (1987). "What's the Primary Message: Horse Race or Issue Journalism?" In *Media and Momentum: The New Hampshire Primary and Nomination Politics*, edited by Gary R. Orren and Nelson W. Polsby. Chatham, NJ: Chatham House.

Chomsky, Noam. (1989). *Necessary Illusions: Thought Control in Democratic Societies.* Toronto: CBC Enterprises.

Entman, Robert. (1989). *Democracy Without Citizens: Media and the Decay of American Politics.* New York: Oxford University Press.

Epstein, Edward Jay. (1973). *News from Nowhere.* New York: Random House.

Fiske, John. (1987). *Television Culture.* New York: Methuen.

Fletcher, Frederick, and Robert Everett. (1991). "Mass Media and Elections in Canada." In *Media, Elections and Democracy*, edited by Frederick Fletcher, 179–222. Toronto: Dundurn Press.

Gitlin, Todd. (1980). *The Whole World is Watching: Mass Media in the Making and Unmaking of the New Left.* Berkeley: University of California Press.

Goffman, Erving. (1974). *Frame Analysis.* New York: Harper & Row.

Iyengar, Shanto. (1991). *Is Anyone Responsible? How Television Frames Political Issues.* Chicago: Chicago University Press.

Jamieson, Kathleen Hall. (1992). *Dirty Politics: Deception, Distraction, and Democracy.* New York: Oxford University Press.

Johnston, Richard, André Blais, Henry Brady, and Jean Crête. (1992). *Letting the People Decide: Dynamics of a Canadian Election.* Montreal: McGill-Queen's University Press.

Joslyn, Richard. (1984). *Mass Media and Elections.* Reading, Mass: Addison-Wesley.

Keeter, Scott. (1987). "The Illusion of Intimacy: Television and the Role of Candidate Personal Qualities in Voter Choice." *Public Opinion Quarterly* 51:344–58.

Krosnick, Jon, and Donald R. Kinder. (1990). "Altering the Foundations of Support for the President Through Priming." *American Political Science Review* 84:497–512.

Maclean's. (1988). "The Voters Reflect." *Maclean's*, December 5, p. 19.

Marlier, John. (1989). "Fifteen Minutes of Glory: A Burkean Analysis of Press Coverage of Oliver North's Testimony." *Political Communication and Persuasion* 6:269–88.

Mendelsohn, Matthew. (1993). "Television's Frames in the 1988 Canadian Election." *Canadian Journal of Communication* 18:149–71.

————. (1994). "The Media's Persuasive Effects: The Priming of Leadership in the 1988 Canadian Election." *Canadian Journal of Political Science* 27:81–97.

Parenti, Michael. (1986). *Inventing Reality: The Politics of the Mass Media.* New York: St. Martin's.

Patterson, Thomas E. (1980). *The Mass Media Election: How Americans Choose Their President.* New York: Praeger.

————. (1993). *Out of Order.* New York: Vintage.

Robinson, Michael J., and Margaret Sheehan. (1983). *Over the Wire and on TV.* New York: Russell Sage Foundation.

Sniderman, Paul, Richard Brody, and Philip Tetlock. (1991). *Reasoning and Choice: Explorations in Political Psychology.* New York: Cambridge University Press.

Tuchman, Gaye. (1978). *Making News: A Study in the Construction of Reality.* New York: Free Press.

Wagenberg, R.H., W.C. Soderlund, W.I. Romanow, and E.D. Briggs. (1988). "Campaigns, Images, and Polls: Mass Media Coverage of the 1984 Canadian Election." *Canadian Journal of Political Science* 21:117–28.

Wattenberg, Martin. (1991). *The Rise of Candidate-centered Politics: Presidential Elections of the 1980's.* Cambridge: Harvard University Press.

FROM FLORA TO KIM: THIRTY YEARS OF REPRESENTATION OF CANADIAN WOMEN POLITICIANS[1]

Gertrude J. Robinson and Armande Saint-Jean

A recent article in *The Globe and Mail* entitled "Life after Ottawa" investigated the question "Whatever happened to Kim?" Kim, of course, is Kim Campbell, Canada's first female prime minister, who governed for a short three months in 1993 before the Progressive Conservative party all but disappeared from the Canadian electoral map. Women politicians, the article implies, are still a novelty in the male domain of politics, and the fact that Campbell was defeated must have had something to do with her gender. Even today, after 30 years of public service, it seems that many party stalwarts and the public still view women as intruders, as a bit out of place in the halls of Parliament. What is at the heart of this assessment, and why has it persisted to this day?

Part of this puzzle must be sought in traditional social values, which continue to assign women to the "homemaker" and men to the "breadwinner" roles. Yet, these values have begun to erode both as a result of the activities of the North American women's movement and because of economic change. In the 1990s, women need to work outside the home to assure an adequate living standard for their families. It appears that other forces must be at work to reinforce the marginalized view of women in politics. Among these, media institutions play an important role because they create and reinforce our understandings of the political world. While it is well known that the media cannot tell the public *what* to think, agenda-setting research has demonstrated that they have a strong influence on what we think *about*.

To investigate the symbolic reinforcement role of the media in the representation of Canadian women politicians, we sought answers to three distinct questions:

1. Are there organizational barriers to recruiting women candidates to party posts, and how do these impact on media coverage?
2. Are there differences in the narrative descriptions of female and male politicians since the 1960s?
3. What are the implications of these different narrative styles for a female politician's ability to achieve political legitimacy and to play an active role?

Graham Fraser, writing in *The Globe and Mail*, notes that the Royal Commission on Electoral Reform and Party Financing addressed these questions by listing some of the barriers facing women who want to enter federal politics. Among them are "sexual stereotyping; the difficulty of juggling career, family, and political responsibilities; problems of child care; jobs that are less flexible for entering politics than those held by men; negative attitudes within parties; the fact that men tend to have better networks to help them in politics; and the question of how female politicians are portrayed in the media" (Fraser, 1993). In the following sections, we will demonstrate that sexual stereotyping, outmoded social attitudes, party barriers, and skewed media portrayals are all interrelated and create a social "sense-making" framework that continues to marginalize the contributions of women politicians in Canada's governmental setup.

The Media Implications of Women's Minority Status in Canadian Parties

At both the provincial and federal levels, the election of female representatives was insignificant until 1970. During the last two decades, however, women have made substantial gains, so that in 1988 there were 39 women in Parliament, representing 13.4 percent of all federal MPs. On the provincial level, the number of female politicians varies from an insignificant 2 percent in Newfoundland to 22 percent in Ontario, with Quebec registering a close 19 percent representation (Brodie and Chandler, 1992). Even though these figures show progress for women politicians, they indicate that Canada has only about half the female political representation that is found in some Scandinavian parliaments, such as Sweden, where 38 percent of MPs are women. Sociologists suggest that it takes at least 30 percent for a minority to succeed in improving its access to a guarded profession such as politics. Sweden has achieved this threshold, but even there, the iron rule of power prevails: the greater the power, the scarcer the women. In both countries, gender still appears to be a factor in the appointment of ministers and committee chairpersons. Canadian and Swedish women have also not yet penetrated the top and most powerful Finance and Economics domains, though Defence was assigned to Barbara McDougall in the last Mulroney cabinet, Health to Diane Marleau in the Chrétien government, and Audrey McLaughlin became leader of the New Democratic Party (NDP).

The media implications of female politicians' minority status are twofold: women politicians have virtually no visibility in three of the country's ten provinces; thus successful female politicians constitute a very small subgroup of candidates available for media attention. Even in Ontario, Sylvia Bashevkin notes that only a total of 85 women participated in the 1990 Ontario provincial election, although there were 99 contested seats (1992, 70). That constitutes only about 21 percent of all of the candidates who ran. Added to these gender-related obstacles in the political system (Burt, Code, and Corney, 1988), there is a further media-specific barrier: the virtual annihilation of women from major network television programming, including the news. Not only are there very few women's *representations* in television programming generally, but women's *perspectives* are also always left undiscussed. In 1986, Tannis MacBeth-Williams and her colleagues found that nearly two-thirds of all program characters were male and only one-third female. This discrepancy is further reinforced in news and public-affairs coverage, where 77 percent of news readers, 91 percent of experts, and 70 percent of voice-overs are male (Jeffery, 1989). Women are also denigrated with respect to their *capacities*: they are less likely to be featured as being in leadership positions, as taking risks, or as powerful, authoritative, and knowledgeable personalities.

All of these journalistic selection norms tend to make the appearance of women on the television screen rare and to feature women in their traditional supporting and homemaker roles. Only 38 percent of programs show women doing nontraditional work of *any* kind, thus reinforcing the notion that women's public place is in the "pink ghettos" of nursing and teaching or in low-paying service jobs. Such norms work against the accurate description of women politicians who are engaged in a nontraditional social role. Because these norms have remained constant since the 1950s, one must conclude that the media themselves contribute to an interpretive framework that carries the implicit message that women have only a small, secondary role to play in Canadian public life (MacBeth-Williams et al., 1986).

Television's gendered framework for political reporting is reinforced by the ways in which Canada's parties function. Robert Mason Lee (1989) argues that television as a medium has drastically changed the strategy, the conduct, and the functioning of electoral campaigns. Television magnifies the leader and views politics as a strategic game. This has eroded the central role once played by political parties because the media focus on leaders rather than on other party personnel.

Because women are rarely selected for strategic and visible party positions, they also receive less media exposure *prior* to their candidacy. This disproportion is the outcome of two sets of gender-related party practices: women candidates have had unequal access to the parties' available seats and were also disproportionately assigned to run in "lost cause" ridings (Brodie, 1985, 113–17). In the 1988 federal election, female candidates contested only 45 percent of all open seats.

Cumulatively, these gender-related constraints have serious consequences for the media coverage of female contenders. The electronic media, with their overwhelmingly male personnel and a "games" approach to election coverage, associate "winning" with male politicians, while women politicians, whose campaigns are often linked to lost-cause ridings, are associated with the "Flora syndrome." Sheila Copps had to contend with this negative association in her 1982 bid for Ontario's premiership. Though she garnered many votes, she was neither credited with having done well in the campaign nor with having leadership potential. This same negative assessment continues to dog her today as Minister of the Environment in the Chrétien government. Together, these gender-linked party barriers translate into negative media selection and biased descriptions.

Narrative Differences in the Descriptions of Female and Male Politicians

To explore the differences in narrative styles, we undertook a narrative analysis which probed both the *context* of media descriptions and the *patterns* these descriptions formed in the 30-year period between the 1960s and the 1990s. It highlights that while "maleness" is a fact of nature, "masculinity" is also a culturally constructed notion. The notion of masculinity affects social sense-making by being subtly touted as the "norm" and thus becomes the standard in relation to which "femininity" is constructed. It furthermore demonstrates that though the descriptions of women's political activities have changed in 30 years, the differential nature of women's and men's representations continues to exist. Even today, a "nongendered" reporting style is rarely achieved. The 30-year comparison permits us to link the changing media portrayals of women politicians to the three historical periods in which they occurred, and to particular generations of political women who were implicated. We also discover that journalism, like politics, continues to be a largely male-dominated activity whose professional values reinforce and amplify traditional notions about women's place in society. In summary, our historical comparison permits us to relate advances made by the women's movement to journalistic reporting *styles* with regard to women politicians.

The Traditional Period (before 1970): Focus on Biology

In the period up to 1970, before the second wave of the North American women's movement changed attitudes, women's role in society was circumscribed. Social life was divided into the private sphere of home and family, for which women had the main responsibility, and the public sphere of politics, business, and labour, which were dominated by men. Although the Second World War had drawn more women into the paid labour force, the ideology of the 1950s once again relegated women to their "proper" place in the home (Friedan, 1963). This traditional role assignment provided a formidable barrier to the recruitment of women into the male domain of Canadian politics. Only 17 female politicians were elected to Parliament in the 50 years between 1920 and 1970. Clearly, these conservative social attitudes also affected the ways in which the first generation of women politicians and their activities were narrated. Among this group were Quebec's Claire Kirkland-Casgrain, the first woman appointed to the Senate, Ellen Fairclough, Diefenbaker's immigration minister, and Pearson's Minister of Health, Judy LaMarsh. It also included Flora MacDonald, who later became the first woman to be appointed external affairs minister in the short-lived Conservative Clark cabinet of 1979–80.

The "traditional" narrative style of the period assumed that women and men operate in different, mutually exclusive social spheres. Assignment to these spheres was by biological criteria. "Biological difference" was therefore the means for talking about the first generation of women politicians. Being viewed as the biological "other" made it very difficult to discern, let alone talk about, these early female politicians' competence and capabilities. Yet, their biographies show that they had more in common with male politicians in terms of training and experience than with the typical housewife/mother of the time. Reporters of the fifties and sixties, including female reporters, were preoccupied with women politicians' "private" (biological) affairs; their sex lives if they were single; their cooking and child-rearing capabilities if they were married; their clothes; and their "ladylike" behaviour. Today we would call this the "human interest" approach to a female politician's public role. Through the "traditional" narrative lens, *visible biological difference* became the primary point of narrative reference.

We discovered that four sets of biologically related descriptions were used for the activities of women politicians, all of which belittle their social and political contributions. We have called these stereotypical foci *wife of, spinster, femme facile,* and *club woman*. The *wife of* label was used in the coverage of women MPs Martha Black (1935–40) and Cora Casselman (1941–45), whose elections were explained away on familial grounds. They were portrayed as wife/widow "inheritors" of their powerful husbands' seats in Parliament rather than as qualified in their own right. The *spinster* label, in contrast, was usually applied to unmarried women of a certain age who resembled nurses or teachers (Gray, 1989, 19). It may have curtailed the professional esteem accorded to older politicians like Flora MacDonald, Pat Carney, and Pauline Jewett, who served in the Trudeau, Clark, and Mulroney cabinets respectively. In politics, the label *spinster* was used to describe someone who had independent ideas and was free of obligations usually expected of a wife, while at the same time subtly suggesting their sexual lacunae, their inability to attract a husband. Women politicians viewed through this lens were portrayed as serious, preachy, competent, hard working, and celibate. Not only were these early woman politicians belittled by the *spinster* label, the women we interviewed acknowledged that journalists frequently showed more interest in their sex lives than in their contributions to the solution of political issues such as the Iranian hostage crisis, in which American diplomats were spirited out of the country by Canadian embassy personnel. Flora MacDonald as external affairs minister was initimately involved in this situation but never received any recognition for her role.

The *femme facile* and *club woman* labels were attached to a different group of women politicians, those who rejected the conventional demarcations between private and public activities, or who espoused opinions which were in opposition to those of the male establishment. Both of the labels imply that it is "proper" for women to engage in social and civic activities such as garden clubs, reading groups, and educational associations but that the tough world of commerce and politics is best left to men. Claire Kirkland-Casgrain's decade long fight for Bill 16, which gave full legal status to married women in Quebec (1964) was not narrated as a revolutionary achievement but as going beyond what a *club woman* was supposed to be doing. A condescending headline and an irrelevant comment about her looks substituted for a detailed description of the content of the revolutionary bill. In an article in the *Financial Post* (May 23, 1964), which bore the headline "A striking political heroine plans to save Quebec women from their medieval bondage," Amy Booth observes that "This charming champion of women's rights, herself the first woman elected to the Quebec legislature, has brought two years of campaigning to a climax with a bill she describes as the first step toward first class citizenship for Quebec women...The lady from Jacques-Cartier is a lot easier on the eyes than any of the current inhabitants of Quebec's Red Chamber." The publisher of *Le Bien public* of Trois-Rivières (1964) was even more acerbic about Mme. Kirkland-Casgrain's political accomplishment and admonished her to return home where she belonged and "cook, sew, embroider, read, card wool, play bridge—anything rather than persist in her dangerous role of issuer of directives [in the public domain]."

The coverage of women politicians up to the 1970s demonstrates that the exceptional status of women politicians was reinforced in press representations on the ground that their "gender" would normally make them ineligible for political work. Marie Allard (1987, 106) catches the negativism implied in this label: "If she is a widow, she is suspected of having killed her husband. If she is divorced, she is unstable. If married, she neglects her husband and if single, she is abnormal." Such media descriptions use the fixed characteristics of biology to erase the fact that gender characteristics are *socially constructed* and therefore changeable. In addition, the biological focus sets up special expectations with respect to the looks, figure, hair colour, "proper" clothing, and "speech patterns" that were considered appropriate for women. Many of these expectations are considerably less stringent for the male politician who, because he is part of the "majority," is never queried about the legitimacy of his public role. Women were in a "double bind" situation, illustrated in an article once written about Immigration Minister Ellen Fairclough entitled "A minister well 'hatted,'" which tells us much about her hats and little about her ministerial accomplishments. It notes: "Our immigration minister Mrs. Ellen Fairclough travels, meets people and wears a hat much more often than do the majority of Canadians. Since becoming a federal cabinet minister in 1957, she has travelled some 240,000 miles... and has worn more than three dozen hats... even some that are not specifically feminine. While flying she wore a helmet used by pilots for protection in case of accidents" (translation).

The "Transitional" Narrative (1970-1980s): Focus on Power

In the fifteen years between 1970 and 1985, the public view of women's social role changed dramatically. Three occurrences contributed to this change in social outlook: The Royal Commission Report on the Status of Women in Canada (1970); the changing market requirements of our postindustrial society; and the growth and radicalization of the women's movement beginning in the late seventies. The report explicitly called on parties to recruit more women into politics (Kieran, 1968, 42). The postindustrial economy, with its multiplication of service jobs, propelled married women (68 percent) and mothers (54 percent) into the labour market and coined the concept of the "working mother" (Bashevkin, 1983, 147–48). Women's experiences outside the home led to calls for pay equity in the workplace and initiatives for full legal equality in the 1980s (Burt, Code, and Corney, 1988, 140–41). Furthermore, the 1979–82 debate over the Charter of Rights and Freedoms sensitized women's groups to the need to mobilize and convinced grass-roots organizers that extensive lobbying would be required to bring women's issues before Parliament (Hosek, 1989, 507).

These experiences led to a qualified public acceptance of an enlarged role for women in the political sphere. Although there were few initiatives to recruit women candidates in the Liberal and Conservative parties, the NDP introduced gender-related criteria into its party recruitment activities in the 1970s (Brown, 1989, 144). This greater consciousness began to have an effect. Women now account for about 20 percent of the membership in the legislatures of Canada's three largest provinces, and women hold close to 30 percent of the seats in Canada's largest city governments (Lavigne, 1990, 5).

Two additional social developments have drawn attention to the changing role of women in Canadian and American politics. The first was a change in women's electoral participation, the second an emergent differentiation in women's and men's voting patterns. Together these became known as the "gender gap." In the United States, the advantage in voter participation that men held over women during the 1950s (10 percent) has been reversed. By 1984, women had a 7 percent lead over men in voter participation (Mueller, 1988b, 22). In Canada, Janine Brodie (1985,126) noted a similar numerical shift in favour of women and also discovered that, by 1983, women preferred the Liberal party by a margin of ten points. Flora MacDonald confirmed that all parties in the 1984 election campaign took this gender gap extremely seriously, because it seemed to suggest that women were going to vote as a block. Yet, subsequent research has shown that such block voting is likely to appear only on a few selected issues: child care, abortion, and health and social services. Yet, these votes may have given the Liberals their landslide majority in the 1993 federal election because the gendered electorate perceived them as more socially responsible.

The narrative approaches used during this "transitional" period were profoundly influenced by the ideology of feminism. Feminism clarified and documented the difficulties and injustices that women encountered in the male worlds of business, the top professions, and the media. Even though the women's movement has changed the perception of most Canadians, both women and men, it remains difficult to integrate a female perspective into media descriptions, because the profession remains overwhelmingly male-dominated, even in the 1990s. Only 27 percent of daily print journalists, our most recent survey indicates, are women (Robinson and Saint-Jean, forthcoming).

Three new stereotypes captured these ambivalences, though they frame female politicians in a "power" network that is superficially more complimentary. They are the *superwoman*, *champion*, and the *member of the gang* designations. The *superwoman* description is applied to the young, intelligent, active, and ambitious female politician who succeeds on "all levels" and who "has it all." She combines family with her career, and she is as well-groomed as she is competent in her political responsibilities. The *superwoman* is a hybrid; she embodies both traditional characteristics (family and children) with the modern traits of the successful businesswoman (superior IQ, enormous capacity for work, an iron constitution, as well as charm and generosity). Canadian politicians described in this manner were Sharon Carstairs, the Liberal leader in Manitoba; Chaviva Hosek, an Ontario Liberal cabinet minister; and Iona Campagnolo, an MP from British Columbia and later President of the Liberal party. As Hubert Bauch once described Iona Campagnolo: "Campagnolo has been an instinctive climber all her life...from the time she blew into Ottawa eight years ago (she) has been tagged as a contender for the whole bag of marbles....As if to prove them right, she made it into the Cabinet in less than two years....She was Iona "la Camp" who had clawed her way from Cannery row to Parliament Hill (1982).

The second stereotype in descriptions of female politicians in the 1980s is that of the *champion*. This descriptive approach is close to that of the *superwoman* but tends to be applied to women politicians "of a certain age" who have led a more traditional life. Often a woman described in this way has come to politics after she has proved herself in another domain, perhaps business, sports, or various charitable organizations. Her children are usually older, and her family obligations more compatible with her public duties. She pays attention to her grooming, is open to the media, and is aware of her previous accomplishments. Among the politicians who have been described as being "tough" like men and therefore "ready" to hold political power are British Columbia's Pat Carney and Quebec's Lucie Pepin, as well as Great Britain's Margaret Thatcher. Under the headline "Tough Woman Tory has skill to be party leader: next MP" *The Gazette* (1975) comments, "The right honourable Margaret Thatcher, 49, is no ordinary woman: that she is being even seriously considered as the next leader of the Conservative Party, a body with more than its fair share of male chauvinists, is in itself a remarkable achievement. Those who have worked with her have no doubt that she has the ability to be leader... She has stamina and talent. Her appetite for work is prodigious. She enjoys making decisions. Thatcher is tough, not ruthless." Kim Campbell also acquired this male honorific when *Actualité* compared her with Trudeau and said "she presents herself as alternately arrogant, funny, spirited, not particularly beautiful, but certainly sexy" (Vestel, 1993).

The third label we encountered in our analyses is one we have called *member of the gang* or being *one of the boys.* This narrative scheme is applied to women politicians who have been accepted into the ranks by the male political establishment, as part of the "gang." This type of female politician adopts a "masculine" stance in politics, which means either that she does not resort to what are called "feminine wiles" to achieve her goals (charm, coquetry) or that she accepts and operates by the conventional rules of the game. A female who is "one of the boys" benefits from this kind of acceptance but is, at the same time, continually reminded that she is an anomaly and may be placed in the unenviable position of being used as an excuse for not forwarding women's interests. Examples are legion, among them the situation where the first female justice minister, Mary Collins, was appointed just as anti-abortion legislation (Bill C-43) was being reintroduced by the Mulroney government. Politicians who qualified for the "one of the gang" label are Barbara McDougall, Mary Collins, Kim Campbell, and Sheila Copps. A *Maclean's* article described Copps's run for the leadership of the Ontario Liberal party this way: "Copps earned a reputation among her Tory opponents as a shrill firebrand...and the most vocal member of the Liberal 'Rat Pack'—a small group of MPs known for their aggressive Question Period attacks during the Conservative government's first term."

In contrast to the first set of stereotypes—*spinster, wife of*, etc.—which have to do with the traditional roles of women, the stereotype of female politicians during the 1970s and early 1980s was that they were "sisters" mobilized to accomplish particular ends—a special interest group. Their legitimacy as players in the political realm can therefore no longer be ignored. Yet, this participation must be that of "help-mate," not that of an autonomous equal. Women politicians' power and behaviour are still described and evaluated in relation to the political performance of their male colleagues. The political *superwoman* performs like a woman in the home and like a man in the political realm. The *champion* uses her contacts with men in other organizations. The *members of the gang* play the political game like men.

Public narrations recreate and incorporate social changes not as passive mirrors but as active prisms through which public understandings are subtly fashioned and influenced. Although recent stereotypes describe female politicians in a power-game context, they still fail to evaluate women's political competence in the terms that are *routinely* applied to men. Instead, women are judged on their personal abilities to be "tough" like men and play by the masculine rules of the game. These include personal aggressiveness, adversarial performance in Question Period, hard-headedness, and coolness under fire. Evaluations of Sheila Copps and Sharon Carstairs as more aggressive than their male counterparts continue to imply that men are the norm, thus leaving the gendered misconceptions intact.

In the early 1980s, the American media discovered a "gender gap" in attitudes toward the Reagan administration, and by the 1984 elections, the Tories thought that this gap might affect Canadian women voters as well. Consciousness-raising activities were consequently undertaken in party caucuses, and these activities were picked up by the media. In 1987, a Decima poll confirmed that there was a male/female difference in voting preference and that the Tories were particularly disliked by working women (only 28 percent would vote Conservative) (Gray, 1989, 18). In 1987, the Tories overcame this resistance by sending customized letters to various undecided women voters, promising child-care tax credits and day-care places. The "gender gap" failed to materialize, and by 1993 these broken promises had turned working women even more strongly against the Progressive Conservative party.

By the late 1980s, journalists had learned a lesson and began to report feminist groups as having the power to change the political rules. This stance became a prominent aspect of the coverage of Audrey McLaughlin's December 1989 win over Dave Barrett for the NDP leadership in Winnipeg. The two reasons that were immediately offered for McLaughlin's NDP convention success were her gender and her feminist support, *not* her varied professional credentials such as her social work background, her experience with community organizations in the Yukon, or her Third World engagement. *The Globe and Mail*'s Jeffrey Simpson (1984) argued that it was McLaughlin's sex that got her elected: "From the moment Ms. McLaughlin declared her candidacy, she became the New Democrat to beat for one simple, compelling and ultimately decisive reason—her sex.... For seven consecutive elections, the NDP has been mired in the rut of 15 to 20 percent of the national vote. Maybe a woman leader, wondered many New Democrats, would produce a larger number of voters."

Hugh Winsor (1989) another *Globe and Mail* columnist, added the second theme: a "feminist" network had (illegitimately?) helped her to win over Dave Barrett. The real factors behind the McLaughlin win, however, seem to have been other: her new platform ideas and her campaign organization. McLaughlin's varied background enabled her to reconceptualize the party's social policy and she additionally had by far the largest number of riding workers. Many were indeed borrowed from the feminist movement, but headquarters had been set up in each province and territory, a computerized delegate tracking system had been developed, which gave her floor captains great advantages in targeting delegates during the convention. The negative connotation of the "feminist" connection was used even more aggressively by Dalton Camp (1989) in *The Toronto Star*: "I thought the NDP convention suffered from an excess of feminist militancy at the barricades. Against the militants stood the rest of the delegates, as though barefoot on a floor of ground glass, weighing each word, idiom, and simile on the gender scale." The charges and countercharges traded among print reporters indicate that the media establishment continues to be as unprepared as the political establishment to admit female players *on their merits* into the game of high-stakes politics. Whether Audrey McLaughlin was a great leader of Canada's NDP in the 1990s remains an open question. What is not open, however, is her right to be taken seriously by the press as the leader of what was Canada's third largest party.

Toward a More Egalitarian Discourse in the 1990s

In spite of attempts to redress women's social inequality in the male preserve of politics, only slow progress has been made in the corporate and media worlds. Women are now integrated into provincial and local political bodies, but continue to be underrepresented in the federal domain. The "glass ceiling" also remains in place in the media professions (Robinson and Sixt, 1975; Crean 1987), where women have gained access to middle management but not to the top level. Today women make up only 9 percent of the editors-in-chief and 6 percent of managing editors in the Canadian Daily Newspaper Publishers Association. The picture is no better in television and film production where, according to a U.S. study by the National Commission on Working Women, women made up 15 percent of producers, 25 percent of writers, and 9 percent of directors. In prime-time TV shows, furthermore, women held 43 percent of the roles but were rarely depicted after age 40 (*The Gazette*, 1990). This "glass ceiling," which is less pronounced in broadcasting than in print, is being kept in place by a complex web of social and professional factors. Among these are traditional career-access barriers for women, organizational practices determined by male chief editors (many of whom are in their late fifties), and a dearth of women at the top, who because of small numbers lack the power to change the rules (Robinson and Saint-Jean, forthcoming).

Though there have been changes in the representation of female politicians and older stereotypes have been replaced by new ones, this constitutes only small progress for the third generation of Canadian women politicians. In the 1990s, there has been a backlash against feminist demands for women's social equality. Powerful elites, among them journalists, continue to belittle women's contributions to politics by falsely proclaiming the "postfeminist era" or the "death of the women's movement." Even today the narrative focuses for female politicians are much narrower than those for males and continue to stress women's personal characteristics: dress, looks, and hair style, rather than the substance of their speeches. Graham Fraser (1989), writing in *The Globe and Mail*, picked up this different coverage when he noted in his "View from the Hill": "As the first woman to lead a Canadian federal party, Ms. McLaughlin still seemed to be subject to a different kind of scrutiny on Wednesday. One reporter inquired about the mark on her cheek...a national columnist noted that she had worn a green silk dress on her first day as NDP leader.... One of the women reporters within earshot did a double-take when the NDP leader was asked if her knees had been shaking (after her first address to the House of Commons as Leader). 'Give me a break,' she muttered. 'Do you think that will be his first question to Paul Martin if he becomes Liberal leader?'"

Another way of undermining women politicians is to distinguish between "female" and "male" types of governance, with the latter acknowledged as the "norm." Susan Delacourt's *Globe and Mail* article (April 6, 1993), explicitly makes this distinction and thus sets up a comparison which does not work the other way around. She notes: "As women have moved farther into the influential reaches of politics and business, their (feminine) style of leadership has started to become more evident." This "feminine" way of governing is described as including the capacity to listen, to prefer cooperation rather than competition, and in the realm of power, to being good managers of people and keeping their feet on the ground. Evenhanded reporting practices would require that the same criteria be applied to all politicians, female and male. Nathalie Collard, in *Elle Quebec* (October 1993), uses such an approach when she reports Mulroney cabinet minister Monique Landry's consternation "at having the cleaner or the grocer be surprised to see me in person. Yet, this surprise is not grounded in my being the Minister, but rather in my doing these errands personally."

While these more positive media descriptions of female politicians may reflect a general disenchantment with traditional modes of governing, they indicate that male and female office holders continue to be evaluated differently. They also show that women have to live up to higher standards of excellence and looks than do men. Only the outstanding and photogenic woman politician will make it into the political arena. Remember the famous photograph of Kim Campbell, showing her bare shoulders, which prompted so much media comment about her "image"? Michel Vestel (1993) of *Le Soleil* commented on the media preoccupation with "image," observing that "the only question which interested the English media was whether she was in the nude behind the robe...nobody asks what she has in her head." Gavin Scott (1993) in *Time* agreed that "In the eyes of some Canadians, her legislative skills took second place to a celebrated 1992 photograph that showed her bare shouldered and coyly holding a judge's black robe in front of her."

Kim Campbell as justice minister commented to the Women in Journalism conference held in Ottawa November 12, 1992: "I was raised on Charlotte Whitten's wonderful comment that a woman has to be twice as good as a man in order to be considered half as good" (*The Gazette*, November 20, 1992). In addition, as we have seen, women politicians also continue to have to live up to a higher code of sexual abstention, never imposed on men. Again, Kim Campbell illustrates the burden of this code, commenting to Warren Carragata (1993) of *Maclean's*, "I don't know why there is this prurient interest in my private life. When I spoke last year about the unspeakable loneliness of life in Ottawa, which is very true, I wasn't just talking about myself. I was talking about the life of politicians and I was talking about men as well. Yes, I have a social life (she has been reported to be involved with Montreal inventor Gregory Lekhtman) and one of the compensations of not being prime minister is to have both the time and privacy to pursue it. It's just such an invasion of my privacy to be talking about that." A final differential criterion is that women politicians can be branded "feminist," as Audrey McLaughlin was, and thus have their political contributions denigrated, while "masculinist" men face no such charges.

The Implications of Media Descriptions for Female Politicians

Such differential narrative focusses and evaluative criteria raise a series of questions. To what extent do the media adequately perceive the difference in attitudes, goals, and understandings that motivate female and male politicians? Why are women drawn in greater numbers to local, municipal, and regional political activity than to provincial and national politics? How adequate is the picture the media construct of the political arenas in which women prefer to operate? And, even more fundamentally, is there any difference in the motivations that propel women and men into political life? Since the media provide society with the words and concepts for naming and constructing social and political reality, how adequately are they performing this task for women and women's concerns? The veracity with which the media represent female politicians and their views are inextricably linked to the effectiveness with which political women can shape their society. Conversely, inaccurate and biased media descriptions deprive women of the right to be heard in and to influence the public domain.

There is evidence today that women readers and viewers are profoundly troubled by the restrictive media reporting of their social concerns and by the irrelevance of many media reports to their common life experiences. Recent analyses confirm that newspapers, which supply their readers with an overwhelmingly white, male, middle-class view of the world, have lost 25 percent of the female readership in the past decade (Cornacchia, 1990; Walker 1990). These kinds of evidence indicate that women have different notions about the nature of political activity, and that they are becoming alienated from Canada's governing bodies such as Parliament and the Senate.

The question for the future is how to translate these differing outlooks into viable programs for more women-friendly legislation and institutional change. Political scientist Carol Mueller, exploring the historical development of women's political agendas, points out that two different strategies have been proposed (1988a,291). One argues that equal rights are the best foundation for women's needs; the other contends that women have special needs grounded in their reproductive capacities, and that "human difference" must therefore inform social legislation. This leads us to conclude that women are *needed* in government. The women ministers we talked to or whose biographies we consulted have all made contributions to furthering women's social equality through legislative initiatives. Claire Kirkland-Casgrain legally established married women's property rights in Quebec; Monique Begin introduced universal health insurance; Pat Carney provided for greater job equality in the federal bureaucracy; and Flora MacDonald inserted a women's equality clause into the latest Broadcasting Act.

Second- and third-generation politicians continued this agenda. Though Campbell had a short tenure as minister of justice and then prime minister, she introduced the "no means no" rape law, and is widely credited with taking a progressive stance on such social issues as homosexual rights, abortion, and gun control.

Extra commitment will be needed in the 1990s as North American economic restructuring submerges women's political agendas under the weight of staff and budget cuts. It is at these times that the growing number of feminist politicians among third-generation incumbents in municipal and provincial councils will make the greatest difference, for they will have the fresh ideas to set a new course for the future.

Notes

1. This paper is based on a more extensive study by Gertrude Robinson and Armande Saint-Jean (1991) and on additional analyses performed between 1992-1994 by Martine Gingras.

References

Adelson, Andrea. (1990). "TV Downplays Women On, Off Screen: Study." *Montreal Gazette*, Nov. 21, p. B7.

Allard, Carole Marie. (1987). "Ottawa: les femmes emménagent." *Commerce* (October):102–6.

Bashevkin, Sylvia. (1983). "Social Change and Political Partisanship: The Development of Women's Attitudes in Quebec, 1965–79." *Comparative Political Studies* 16 (July):147–72.

———. (1992). "Women's Participation in Political Parties." In *Women in Canadian Politics: Toward Equity in Representation*, edited by Kathy Megyery, 61–80. Toronto: Dundurn Press.

Bauch, Hubert. (1982). "Campagnolo: Can She Climb to PM's Job?" *The Gazette* (Montreal), November 13, p. B5.

Booth, Amy. (1964). "A Striking Political Heroine Plans to Save Quebec Women from their Medieval Bondage." *The Financial Post*, May 23, p. 23.

Brodie, M. Janine. (1985). *Women and Politics in Canada.* Toronto: McGraw-Hill Ryerson.

Brodie, M. Janine, and Celia Chandler. (1992). "Women and the Electoral Process in Canada." In *Women in Canadian Politics: Toward Equity in Representation*, edited Kathy Megyery, 3–60. Toronto: Dundurn Press. 3–60.

Brown, Rosemary. (1989). *Being Brown: A Very Public Life.* Toronto: Random House.

Burt, Sandra, Lorraine Code, and Lindsay Corney, eds. (1988). *Changing Patterns: Women in Canada.* Toronto: McClelland & Stewart.

Camp, Dalton. (1989). "Let's Treat Audrey Like One of the Boys." *The Toronto Star*. December 6, p. A23.

Canada, Royal Commission on Electoral Reform and Party Financing. (1990). Symposium on Women's Participation in Political Parties, Montreal, October 31–November 2.

Carragata, Warren. (1993). "A Very Strong Person." *Maclean's*, December 6, p. 19.

Collard, Nathalie. (1993). "Femmes politiques: la Revolution de l'intérieur." *Elle Quebec*, October, p. 70, 72.

Cornacchia, Cheryl. (1990). "Pressing on: Women's Perspective Important to the News." *The Gazette* (Montreal), November 19, p. D1.

Crean, Susan. (1987). "Piecing the Picture Together: Women and the Media in Canada." *Canadian Woman Studies* 8 (Spring):15–21.

Delacourt, Susan. (1993). "These Women Not Two of a Kind." *The Globe and Mail*, April 6, p. A1, A6.

Fraser, Graham. (1989). "Bye, Mr. Broadbent: Hello There, Audrey." *The Globe and Mail*, December 9, p. A5.

————. (1993). "Why So Few Women Run for Office." *The Globe and Mail*, January 26, p. A15.

Friedan, Betty. (1963). *The Feminine Mystique*. New York: Dell.

Fruman, Leslie. (1984). "Lucie Pépin Is a Proven Feminist." *The Toronto Star*, December 7, p. D1, D2.

Gazette (Montreal). (1975). "Tough Woman Tory Has Skill to be Party Leader, Next PM," February 5.

————. (1990). "TV Downplays Women On, Off Screen: Study," November 21.

Gray, Charlotte. (1989). "The New F-Word." *Saturday Night*, April:17–20.

Hosek, Chaviva. (1989). "How Women Fought for Equality." In *Women and Men: Interdisciplinary Readings on Gender*, edited by Greta Hoffmann Nemiroff, 493–511. Toronto: Fitzhenry and Whiteside.

Jeffery, Liss. (1989). "Waiting for the Results." *Scan*, March/April:7–10.

Kieran, Sheila H. (1968). "Who's Downgrading Women? Women." *Maclean's*, August 18–19, 40–42.

Lavigne, Marie. (1990). "Femmes et Pouvoir Politique: Une Intégration à Réussir." In *Women and Power: Canadian and German Experiences*, edited by Gertrude J. Robinson and Dieta Sixt. Montreal: McGill Studies in Communication & Goethe Institut.

Lee, Robert Mason. (1989). *One Hundred Monkeys: The Triumph of Popular Wisdom in Canadian Politics*. Toronto: MacFarlane Walter and Ross.

MacBeth-Williams, Tannis, D. Baron, S. Phillips, L. Travis, and D. Jackson. (1986). "The Portrayal of Sex Roles on Canadian and U.S. Television." Paper presented at a conference of the International Association for Mass Communication Research, New Delhi.

Mueller, Carol M. (1988a). "Continuity and Change in Women's Political Agenda." In *The Politics of the Gender Gap*, edited by Carol Mueller, 284–99. Beverly Hills: Sage Publications.

————. (1988b). "The Empowerment of Women: Polling and the Women's Voting Bloc." In *The Politics of Gender Gap*, edited by Carol Mueller, 16–36. Beverly Hills: Sage Publications.

Robinson, Gertrude J., and Dieta Sixt. (1975). "Women Journalists in Canadian Dailies: A Social and Professional Profile." *McGill Working Papers in Communications*. Montreal: McGill University.

————. (1990). *Women and Power: Canadian and German Experiences*. Montreal: McGill Studies in Communications & Goethe Institut.

Robinson, Gertrude and Armande Saint-Jean. (1991). "Women Politicians and Their Media Coverage: A Generational Analysis." In *Women in Canadian Politics: Toward Equity in Representation*. Vol. 6, Research Studies, Royal Commission on Electoral Reform and Party Financing and Canadian Communications Group—Publishing, Supply and Services Canada. Toronto and Oxford: Dundurn Press.

————. (Forthcoming). "Women in the Canadian Media: Twenty Years of Progress.".

Scott, Gavin. (1993). "In Kim We Trust." *Time*, June 28, pp. 20–21.

Simpson, Jeffrey. (1989). "From the Crucible, a Determined Pro." *The Globe and Mail*, December 4, p. A7.

Vestel, Michel. (1993). "L'effet Campbell." *L'Actualité*, May 1, pp. 20–26.

Walker, Robert. (1990). "In Byline Game Men Win 67–30: National Study Suggests Gazette Ratio Is Typical." *The Gazette* (Montreal), September 24, B3.

Winsor, Hugh. (1989). "Keen Organization and Networking Compensated for Lacklustre Speech." *The Globe and Mail*, December 4, A 10.

CHILDREN AND TELEVISION: A CONTEMPORARY LOOK

Jeffrey L. Derevensky and Carolyn Klein

"Mighty Morphin Power Rangers," "Roseanne," "Teenage Mutant Ninja Turtles," "Barney," "The Simpsons," and "Sesame Street." These program titles clearly demonstrate how dramatically children's television has changed since the early days of "Captain Kangaroo," "The Mickey Mouse Club," and "Howdy Doody." While television, beginning in the 1940s, is a relatively recent phenomenon, few if any other innovations have had such an extreme impact upon children and society. Initially created for the affluent few, television sets are now found in over 98 percent of all Canadian and American households.

In addition to commercial and public television programming, the proliferation of cable and pay-per-view channels has significantly altered television viewing habits since the late 1970s, and has exploded in the 1990s. These cable networks have provided a more diversified, centralized, and focussed approach, intended to address specific markets, of which children are one. Programs on the Disney Channel, Nickelodeon, YTV, and the Family Network are directly aimed toward children. Reports by the A.C. Nielsen Company (1988) indicate that within the United States, more than half of all homes subscribe to at least one cable channel, with the numbers growing at a rapid rate. Within Canada, 75 percent of all households have cable, and the proportion of homes having at least one specialty channel approaches 40 percent (Lavallée-Farah, 1992). In Canada, access to many American commercial television channels may only be achieved through cable and/or satellite dishes, a basic necessity in many homes. More recently, videocassette recorders (VCRs), introduced in 1975, have become increasingly used by the general population. As of 1993, as many as 75 percent of Canadian homes had at least one videocassette recorder, as many as have microwave ovens (Statistics Canada, 1994). The growth and widespread use of videocassette recorders has been even more dramatic in European (Hellman and Soramäki, 1985) and Third World countries (Boyd and Straubhaar, 1985). Rentals of prerecorded instructional programs and movies on cassette have similarly experienced a dramatic increase in popularity. Virtually overnight, the video rental store has created a new industry, which reported over $800 million in sales during 1991 in Canada alone (Lavallée-Farah, 1992). Video stores in many communities remain open 24 hours per day, seven days a week. Classic adult and children's films have experienced a resurgence in popularity. Further, both children and adults now have the ability to record specific programs while simultaneously viewing others. The purchasing price of home movies, previously only available at the theatre, have dropped dramatically. For example, the video-release versions of *Jurassic Park, Snow White and the Seven Dwarfs*, and others have sold millions of copies. A recent marketing report found that since its recent release, *Snow White* has already sold more than 27 million copies. Large personal home-video libraries are being developed, likely resulting in increased viewing time.

The age at which children become video-sophisticated is becoming younger with each generation. We are reminded of a cartoon depicting a young child and his mother seated in front of a television set. The 3-year-old child proudly professes to his mother that "I'm not in school yet, but I already know my numbers:...zero, one, two, three, four, five, six, seven, eight, nine, pause, fast forward, rewind, play and record" (Glasbergen, date and origin unknown). Children not yet old enough to tie their shoelaces can often operate remote-control devices for VCRs and television sets. Teachers report that many children unable to recite their multiplication tables are "walking TV Guides," able to accurately recite the daily sequence of programs on many channels.

The increased frequency and impact with which television has entered our daily lives has heightened the importance of examining its effects upon children and the family. According to a recent report (Statistics Canada, 1994), the average Canadian watches 23 hours of television weekly, with residents of Newfoundland surpassing other Canadians with an average of 25.4 hours of television viewing per week. The average North American spends more time watching television than on any other activity, save sleep and work (Huston et al., 1990). That 98 percent of all North American households have at least one television set is indicative of the status television holds in contemporary family life (Statistics Canada, 1994). The magnitude of television's role in our daily lives is punctuated by Sohn (1982), who states that the average American watches approximately 1200 hours of television per year yet spends only five hours per year reading books.

Since 1960, when television became widely accessible, television viewing time has significantly increased. Reports indicate that the average American television set is on approximately seven hours per day (Steinberg, 1985). However, this figure may not be truly reflective of individual viewing time, since many households report that the television set is frequently on when no one is watching. Regardless, there is substantial evidence indicating considerable viewing time.

Children are certainly not immune to the lure of television. On the contrary, children can be found sitting mesmerized in front of a television set for hours, if not watching public or commercial channels, then watching a prerecorded movie or television show, or playing a video game. Children whose parents report them as having poor attention spans often have little difficulty sustaining attention while watching their favourite television programs. A typical 6–9-month old is reported to be seated in front of a television approximately one-and-a-half hours per day (Hollenbeck and Slaby, 1979). By the time the child reaches three years of age, he or she will spend as many as three to four hours per day in front of the TV (Pearl, Bouthilet, and Lazar, 1982; Singer and Singer, 1981). Canadian children between the ages of 2 and 11 watch an average of 18.5 hours of television per week (Statistics Canada, 1994).

During the preschool years, the average child will watch two-and-a-half hours of television per day. However, viewing time has been shown to be as individual as the child, with weekly exposure ranging between 0 and 75 hours (Huston et al., 1990). As children's bedtime increases, so does the amount of television they watch. Overall, by the time the average American youth has graduated from high school, he or she will have spent approximately 15 000 hours watching television (National Institute of Mental Health, 1982).

It is interesting to note that Saturday morning cartoons, which are explicitly aimed at children, account for a relatively small percentage of children's viewing time (13 percent for 2–5 year olds, 15 percent for 6–11 year olds) (Nielsen Report, 1988). The vast majority of viewing time is centred during the week, in early morning, late afternoon, and early evening hours (Comstock et al., 1978; Kunkel and Watkins, 1987). As well, evidence exists that children in elementary school exhibit viewing preferences for dramatic and adult-oriented programs, a phenomenon which likely increases their total viewing time (Comstock et al., 1978; Statistics Canada, 1994), and has significantly altered their viewing content. It has been shown that 2–11 year olds devote one-third of their television viewing time to dramatic programs, and another 17 percent to comedies (Statistics Canada, 1994).

Considerable research evidence has contributed to our understanding of significant variables that influence viewing patterns and behaviours. Specific individual characteristics have been shown to be related to television viewing habits. Ethnic minorities, women, individuals in low socioeconomic strata, and those with low education levels are all reported to watch considerably more television than others (Greenberg, 1986; National Institute for Mental Health, 1982; Statistics Canada, 1994; Williams, 1986).

Television viewing can be a passive or active experience. While remaining in their seats, children can be stimulated, entertained, educated, horrified, or intrigued (Van Evra, 1990). It appears that boys watch more violent action cartoons than girls (Lyle and Hoffman, 1976); however, there is some evidence that this pattern is changing as more aggressive female role models have been incorporated into cartoons (e.g., "Wild C.A.T.S.") (Eron et al., 1983). Still further, children with emotional disorders watch more television overall, and more aggressive programs in particular, than typical children (Sprafkin, 1988). In their study of children's leisure activities, Meldrich, Roizen, Ruben, and Buckley (1982) found that children from the least advantaged homes were roughly three times as likely to have heavy television viewing diets as compared with children from higher socioeconomic groups.

Television viewing undoubtedly consumes a great deal of children's time and attention. Its role in society, its effects upon children, and its limitations are only beginning to be understood. Its potential has yet to be fully realized. Successive generations of children will continue to view television. While the programs will change, its societal effects can no longer be considered casual. A large-scale report of the National Institute of Mental Health (1982) concluded that:

> Almost all evidence testifies to television's role as a formidable educator whose effects are both pervasive and cumulative. Television can no longer be considered...an electronic toy. Research findings have long since destroyed the illusion that television is merely innocuous entertainment. While the learning it provides is mainly incidental rather than direct and formal, it is a significant part of the total acculturation process. (p. 87)

The relationship between television viewing and children is complex. It has been studied from multiple perspectives by researchers from varying disciplines. Researchers have studied the effects of television on children's aggression, socialization, development of sex roles, and cognitive development. Television's impact upon children's academic performance, reading proficiency, and information-processing skills have all been empirically studied. Most recently, researchers have been examining the complexity of the television experience, and how a number of features and the interaction among them affect the outcome of exposure to television. Van Evra (1990) provides a graphic representation of this complex interaction, which is presented in Figure 1. She argues that what is needed is a careful examination of the interactions among the child, program, technical, familial, experimental, motivational, and contextual variables in order to gain a meaningful understanding of children's viewing behaviour and its subsequent impact.

While all these factors remain crucial, and many questions remain unanswered, this essay examines how television influences children in four distinct ways: through social learning, education, entertainment, and advertising.

Social Learning

Television's ability to affect children's behaviour has grown stronger as social factors continue to change the structure of the family. For many years, researchers and theorists have recognized the family as the crucial socializing agent for the child. However, since the 1970s, the structure of the family has been significantly altered, and other sources of socialization have taken on added importance. The demise of the extended family, and of the nuclear family (as a result of the high incidence of divorce), have significantly altered the socialization process. No longer are grandparents in the home; frequently they do not even live within the same community. No longer do mothers have as their sole occupation the raising of their children. All too frequently, children return to empty homes in which television serves as both a friend and companion. Television viewing behaviour has, to a large extent, become uncontrolled, as parents are unavailable or unable to monitor its use and/or to set limits. Certainly, television plays a crucial role in the child's socializing process, understanding of the world, knowledge of current events, and development of values, attitudes, and social skills.

As a medium, television has radically changed family behaviour. Johnson (1967) reports that 60 percent of families have changed their sleeping patterns because of television programming, 55 percent have altered meal times, and 78 percent have

FIGURE 1

Summary Chart of Variables Involved in Children's Television Viewing Experience

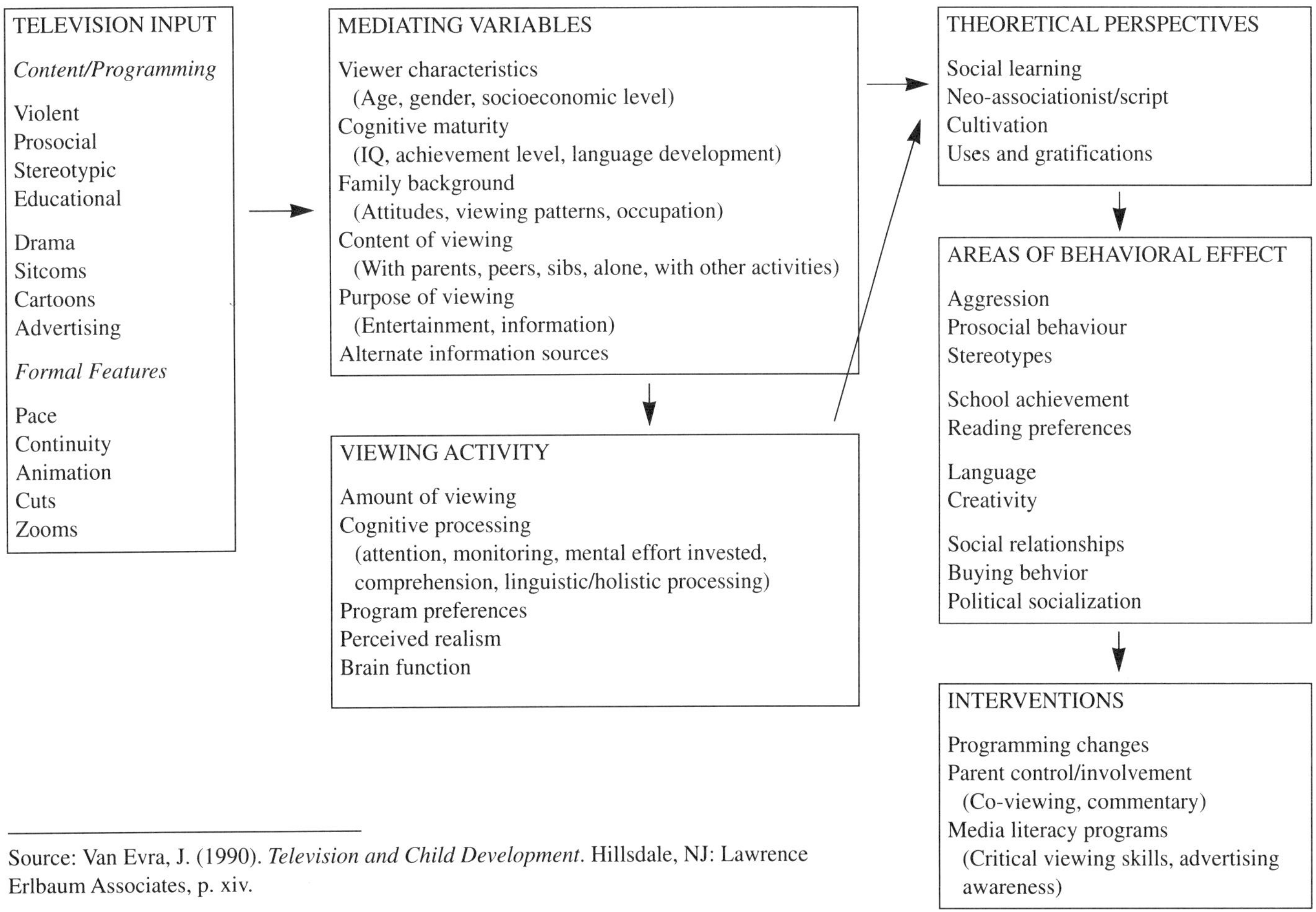

Source: Van Evra, J. (1990). *Television and Child Development*. Hillsdale, NJ: Lawrence Erlbaum Associates, p. xiv.

incorporated television as the ultimate electronic babysitter. Leisure time activities are often scheduled around television viewing patterns. In a study in Western Canada, in which a small community had only recently received television broadcasts, Williams and Hanford (1986) found that while television did not determine the number of community activities available, it clearly had a negative effect upon participation in those activities. Involvement in community activities fell dramatically after television was introduced. The effect was particularly strong for sports-related activities by adolescents, however, it also affected their attendance at community dances, suppers, and parties; and the adult attendance at meetings of clubs and other organizations. The authors also suggested that television may lead to greater age segregation and may qualitatively influence community life by reducing contact between individuals of different generations (Williams and Handford, 1986).

While most adults tend to believe that television is merely a form of entertainment that has relatively few negative consequences and limited social influence (Steiner, 1963), there remain serious questions as to its effects upon children's cognitive, social, affective, and personality development, and, subsequently, upon their behaviour. Certainly, questions concerning the role of television in shaping children's stereotypes, attitudes, perceptions, acquisition of aggressive behaviour, and its educational utility, remain to be answered.

In order to explain the influence television has had upon children, a number of theoretical positions have been proposed. One of the most cogent and widely accepted perspectives remains that of Social Learning Theory, as proposed by Albert Bandura (1977). Central to this theory is the view that learning can occur through vicarious and symbolic modelling. Proponents of this theory recognize that an individual's cognitive perceptions, feelings, and actions, which are indisputably influenced by direct experience, can also be distinctly shaped through modelling and imitation.

According to social learning theory, an individual's psychological functioning is defined through continuous shared interaction between personal and environmental determinants. Figurative, vicarious, and self-regulatory mechanisms assume dominant roles. Whereas other theories, such as behaviorism, propose that learning can only occur through direct experience of behaviour and its consequences, social learning theory assumes that learning can occur vicariously by observing the consequences of others' actions (Bandura, 1977). The ability to learn through observation permits behaviour patterns to be acquired without a lengthy trial-and-error process required for learning through performance. Observational learning facilitates the acquisition process, and ensures that specific behaviour will be reproduced with greater accuracy. Such learning need neither be direct nor formal. Instead, incidental learning can occur without the child even being aware.

In order to more fully understand social learning's impact upon children, knowledge of the factors that affect the modelling process is essential. If television, more specifically television characters, can influence children's behaviour, it is necessary to delineate among three sets of conditions which have been shown to influence the modelling process. These conditions include (1) specific characteristics of the child; (2) characteristics of the observed behaviour; and (3) characteristics and attributes of the model (Bronfenbrenner, 1970).

Certainly, the complexity of a behavioural act is critical for children's acquisition of knowledge. While letter sequences from "Sesame Street" as an example, are readily acquired, more complex phenomena such as reading are not as easily acquired (e.g., "Electric Company"). More importantly, certain qualities of the model will determine the extent to which they influence children. These factors include the model's competency and status, the degree of support and control that the model exhibits over the environment, the similarities between the model and the child, aspirations of the child to be a member of a group to which the model belongs, and, lastly, the consequences of the behaviour itself (Bronfenbrenner, 1970). Accordingly, these conditions and attributes interact to influence the probability that a model's behaviour will be imitated. Bandura's (1965) research contends that individuals are more likely to imitate a model who has been rewarded for his or her behaviour. Similarly, observers are less likely to pattern their behaviour after models who have been punished for their actions (Bandura, 1973; Bandura, Ross, and Ross, 1963). In instances of violent depictions by television characters, it follows, therefore, that the modelled aggression should have an inhibitory effect when the protagonist is punished for this behaviour. Conversely, an instigative effect should arise when the "good guy" is rewarded for his or her actions (Turner, Hesse, and Peterson-Lewis, 1986). Persistence of the viewed behaviour appears to be unrelated to the role model but instead remains a function of the way in which the child's behaviour is rewarded (Bandura, 1965).

Observational learning has also been shown to vary as a function of age, with two-year-old children being able to imitate quite accurately what they view on television (Collins, Berndt, and Hess, 1974; Eron et al., 1972), clearly a phenomenon that educational television and advertisers have attempted to capitalize upon. However, since young children do not fully understand the relationship between aggression and its underlying motives, they become most vulnerable to the effects of aggressive depiction on television.

Social learning theorists predict that viewing televised models (whether in cartoon or human form) behaving violently facilitates children's aggressivity. There has been considerable support from laboratory studies that children do indeed imitate aggressive behaviour depicted on television immediately following its presentation (e.g., Hicks, 1968). Additional research has demonstrated that such learning occurs in real-life situations as well (e.g., Parke et al., 1977).

In 1972, the Surgeon General of the United States published the results of a series of examinations into the relationship between television violence and aggression. The results of these studies led the Surgeon General to conclude that a causal relationship between watching television violence and aggressive behaviour does indeed exist. Ten years later, the National Institute of Mental Health (1982) published results of a compendium of follow-up studies that cemented the conclusion of the original report. Rubinstein (1983), in a summary of the NIMH report, states:

> Granted that the data are complex and that no single study unequivocally documents the connection between televised violence and later aggressive behaviour, the convergence of evidence from many studies is overwhelming and was so interpreted in the NIMH report (p. 821).

Cartoons, representing the vast majority of programs directed solely toward young children, have repeatedly been shown to have the highest occurrence of violent incidents per episode (Williams, Zabrack, and Joy, 1982). Researchers and clinical investigators have placed great emphasis upon examining cartoons' violent content. Numerous studies have documented increased aggression in children following exposure to cartoon violence (e.g., Ellis and Sekyra, 1972; Ross, 1972), with no studies reporting a decrease in aggression following exposure to cartoon violence (Stein and Friedrich, 1975). This increase in acquired aggression has been noted for both boys and girls, across various socioeconomic strata, and for children of different ages (e.g., Lovaas, 1961).

The incidence of violence on commercial television remains consistently high (Signorielli, Gross, and Morgan, 1982). One cannot deny the plethora of evidence which suggests that in the short and long term, television violence influences childhood behaviour. Results gathered in the laboratory, in the field, and from studies spanning several decades, despite methodological shortcomings, have all shown that violent television elicits aggressive behaviour in children.

A critical period during which exposure to violent television has the most deleterious effects has been postulated. It appears that the greatest effects of television violence occur when viewed in the late preschool and early elementary-school years (Eron et al., 1983; Huesmann et al., 1984). Still further, many of these studies report that these harmful effects are long lasting and increase proportionately with the amount of violent television viewed (e.g., Eron et al., 1983).

A variety of research studies have concluded that children's imitation of aggressive models occurs through incidental and vicarious learning. This finding is particularly important for the young child who attends intermittently to television (Anderson and Lorch, 1983), who may be unaware of and/or may fail to comprehend the links between aggressive actions and perceived punishment (Collins, 1983). Continued exposure and concomitant aggressive behaviour have repeatedly been observed across a variety of populations, in studies incorporating various methodological approaches. The physiological arousal, stimulated in large part by the fast-paced action of television programs aimed at children, and cognitive arousal, associated with children's attentiveness, may also facilitate this learning (Williams, 1986). Moreover, Williams (1986) reports that frequent observations of aggression as a successful method of conflict resolution may reduce inhibitions against aggressive behaviour. Coupled with an increased desensitization, propensity for increased tolerance for aggressive behaviour and violence may result in children's increased aggression and tolerance for verbal abuse. Still further, a number of studies have concluded that aggressive behaviour, while acquired, may not necessarily be immediately exhibited but may occur much later. On a more positive note, research has also shown that aggressive behaviour may be inhibited and modified through viewing appropriate models (Huesmann et al., 1984; Williams, 1986).

Singer and Singer (1983), reporting on their longitudinal study of preschool children, have suggested that television's effect upon children may not be so straightforward. Rather, they have attempted to examine a combination of television and family variables which place a child at risk for problematic behaviour by early elementary-school age. They conclude that the high-risk child comes from a home in which a) television viewing is uncontrolled; b) there exists heavy viewing of television during the preschool years; c) there has been recent heavy viewing of violent programs; d) parents tend to emphasize physical punishment as the primary form of discipline; and e) parents fail to stress curiosity, creativity, and imagination, traits which tend to mediate the influences of television. Thus, while there appears to be overwhelming evidence that television viewing behaviour can lead to increased aggressivity and violence in children, it is not a pure, unidirectional consequence; rather it may be a mediating variable. Television alone cannot negate the impact of parents.

Since the 1970s, parents and educators have been interested in how television could be used to reinforce desirable or prosocial behaviours, such as sharing, helping, cooperation, problem-solving, and imaginative play (Lovelace and Huston, 1983). In general, studies examining television's effects on prosocial behaviour have been conducted with young children, and, characteristically, only short-term effects have been reported (Eron, 1986). Over the past two decades, empirical evidence has emerged in support of the potential of prosocial learning through television (Gunter, 1984). Through observational learning, children have been shown to acquire prosocial behaviours and appropriate conduct from watching television characters behave in a prosocial manner (Gunter, 1984). Similar results have been reported in laboratory and field studies (e.g., Zuckerman, Singer, and Singer, 1980). Lesser (1974), in writings concerning "Sesame Street," has noted that observational learning of prosocial behaviours need not necessarily require direct instruction. He suggests that displaying activities that convey an implicit prosocial attitude can result in effective modelling. "Altruism, kindness, courage and tolerance can be communicated indirectly through the actions of the televised characters without explicit labelling" (p. 86).

A study conducted by Paulson (1974) during the first season of "Sesame Street" examined the effects of special inserts of scenes involving the modelling of prosocial and antisocial behaviour as a method for teaching cooperation. During a six-month field study, children who viewed these segments demonstrated significantly more cooperative behaviour when placed in similar situations. Unfortunately, these behaviours were found to be situation specific and did not transfer or generalize to other situations (Paulson, 1974).

Other researchers have demonstrated that television can encourage generosity. Bryan and Walbeck (1979) showed 6–9-year-old children a television program depicting a child successfully playing a bowling game and winning gift certificates. In different versions, the boy either donated his winnings to charity stating that it was the right thing to do, or kept the winnings for himself. Children who viewed the "giving" version were more likely to subsequently donate their own winnings. A replication of this study was carried out in England and found similar short-term effects (Rushton and Owen, 1975).

In what situation will prosocial behaviour have the greatest likelihood of being transmitted? Prosocial content appears on television in three forms: (1) model(s) displaying prosocial behaviour without introducing any antisocial behaviour; (2) model(s) are depicted in conflict, and then prosocial means are used for conflict resolution; and

(3) model(s) are presented exhibiting prosocial behaviour, with the same or similar models being presented in conflict (Lovelace and Huston, 1983).

While prosocial behaviour can be acquired by watching unambiguous portrayals on television, programs of this type are rare. More common are programs that depict the "good guys" winning over the "bad guys," or good overcoming evil. Frequently, Western, police, and detective programs fit into this mould, although their moral purity has come into question (e.g., "NYPD Blue.") Other shows, such as "Mister Rogers' Neighborhood" and "Sesame Street" continue to attempt to reinforce positive prosocial behaviour. Content analyses of "Mister Rogers' Neighborhood" programs revealed in a sample of 20 episodes (10 hours), 1223 (95 percent) examples of positive reinforcement, and 67 (5 percent) instances of punishment (verbal criticism, ignoring) (Coates and Pusser, 1975). Studies by Friedrich and Stein (1973) and Friedrich-Cofer and colleagues (1979) have shown that under certain conditions, children's viewing of "Mister Rogers' Neighborhood" promotes an increase in prosocial behaviours, albeit for a relatively short term. Similarly, for "Sesame Street," 78 percent instances of positive reinforcement and 22 percent instances of punishment occurred. While these programs differ in terms of their pace, overall design, and degree of prosocial and antisocial content, they both employ conflict resolution as a means of modelling prosocial behaviour (Lovelace and Huston, 1983). Prosocial interactions such as altruism and sympathy are portrayed in many programs (Harvey, Sprafkin, and Rubinstein, 1979). A number of films have also been used to reduce fear and anxiety in children (Lovelace and Huston, 1983), and to present appropriate social skills (O'Connor, 1969; 1972). Empirical support indicates this prosocial content can provide an effective model for children to acquire appropriate prosocial behaviour (Harvey, Sprafkin, and Rubinstein, 1979). However, while short-term effects may be present, the long-term consequences have not been well established (Van Evra, 1990).

Television as Teacher of Educational Material

When television first appeared in 1940, children's programs were an important part of the broadcast schedule. Most shows were in the form of puppet shows and other short programs. By 1953, the first educational television station began operation, and by the end of the decade, 44 stations existed (O'Bryan, 1981). Many of these stations operated with restricted budgets and had low visibility. Frequently, these stations were operated by local community groups, school systems, and universities. The majority of the educational programs were adult-oriented, with relatively few aimed at children (Liebert and Sprafkin, 1988). Early educational television, limited by a lack of technology, colour, and sophistication, was often found to be boring and repetitive.

Historically, educational television had two distinct faces from its inception. The first to be emphasized was the master teacher model, in which teachers, appearing as "talking faces," were broadcast into the classroom via closed-circuit television. These programs were intended to combat both overcrowding in the classroom and the effects of poor teaching. The other type of educational television, now by far the stronger of the two, maintains that educational programming should be as interesting and as well-produced as commercial television, and should be considered as an aid to, and not a replacement for, the classroom teacher. By 1980, closed-circuit master-teacher television had virtually disappeared (O'Bryan, 1981), and Educational Television (ETV) had become stronger than ever.

The growth of ETV was slow due to scheduling and technical difficulties and lack of financial resources. In the 1960s, however, the industry realized its potential, and a report from the Carnegie Commission (1967) encouraged the establishment of a Corporation for Public Television and recommended support from local and national sources. One year later, Children's Television Workshop (CTW) was founded. CTW's philosophy was that children's television should meet the standards and withstand the competition of commercial programming, and a complete revamping of children's television ensued.

"In 1969 two significant events took place: Neil Armstrong set foot on the moon, and 'Sesame Street' went to air" (O'Bryan, 1981, 5). During the late 1960s, planned programs designed to educate the young child became widely noticed. Along with "Sesame Street," early child-oriented programs such as "Mister Rogers' Neighborhood" and "Mr. Dress-Up" began to appear. "Sesame Street" is by far the most popular and successful educational television program ever broadcast (Palmer, 1984; Rice et al., 1990). Its estimated audience of 10.4 million American households, and its target audience of 3–5-year-olds, make "Sesame Street" an ideal vehicle for teaching preschoolers a variety of basic concepts and skills. From its inception, Joan Ganz Cooney and Lloyd Morrisett, the planners and architects of Children's Television Workshop, were concerned about the paucity of highly entertaining, quality educational programs for young children. Cooney and Morrisett had a strong belief that "the wasteland of children's programming was too vast for a major effort not to attract at least some audience" (Cooney, 1974, XV). They were concerned about the plight of the preschoolers, the lack of progress in educating young children, and the predicament of underprivileged children for whom "experimental" preschool programs were then unavailable. As such, CTW became the agent through which television would begin to teach young children, regardless of socioeconomic status, some basic cognitive skills, such as letter recognition and basic arithmetic, and prosocial behaviours like sharing and cooperation.

Today, "Sesame Street" is broadcast in nine languages to over 50 countries. "Sesame Street" has been viewed by an entire generation of children, successfully broadcasting for 25 years, making it the longest running television series of all time. Liebert and Sprafkin (1988) contend that "Sesame Street" remains the world's most famous and popular television show and is viewed by almost half of all American preschoolers on a weekly basis (5.8 million children between the ages of 2 and 5), watching an average of three episodes per week. In many cities, "Sesame Street" is broadcast several times each day. The Canadian version of "Sesame Street," "Sesame Street North," has met with considerable success, and its content has been distributed worldwide.

Considerable research has been presented suggesting that "Sesame Street" has successfully achieved many of its initial goals, that is, teaching a number of school-readiness skills (e.g., Ball and Bogatz, 1970). Instead of attempting to heighten general cognitive ability, "Sesame Street" attempts to teach specific content such as letters, numbers, and relational concepts. Summative evaluations performed after the first two seasons of "Sesame Street" revealed that children who watched the program regularly gained more new knowledge than children who did not (Ball and Bogatz, 1970; 1972). Further, benefits were found across all socioeconomic groups, in that disadvantaged frequent viewers often learned as much as advantaged frequent viewers, and more than advantaged infrequent viewers. Today, the Muppet characters, Big Bird, Ernie, Bert, Kermit, Oscar, Cookie Monster, and Miss Piggy created by Jim Henson are household names for preschoolers throughout the world. Along with the Disney characters, "Sesame Street" characters remain the most desired licensed products by parents of preschool children. However, with all the praise has come criticism, and some researchers have questioned the magnitude and longevity of the show's effects (Cook and Connor, 1976).

According to Gerald Lesser, the main lesson of "Sesame Street" was that television can directly teach children without hiding its educational intentions, and yet attract a large and devoted audience while being broadcast over noncommercial, public broadcasting stations. As well, it provided new evidence of "the remarkable rate at which young children can learn from television" (1974, 234).

While studies suggest that television can be used to promote vocabulary development (Rice et al., 1990) and social skills (Van Evra, 1990), positive benefits of viewing television have been noted for few programs. Older children's general exposure to television has been found to negatively affect academic achievement in general (Gadberry, 1980), and reading skills in particular (for a review of this literature, see Hornik, 1978).

Many researchers and educators have argued that television viewing severely impedes reading development (e.g., Gunter, 1982; Morgan and Gross, 1982). There is much support for the contention that television, by occupying a significant amount of time per day (Pearl, Bouthilet, and Lazar, 1982; Singer and Singer, 1981), limits the time children spend reading. Television often replaces reading as a leisure time activity, which in turn has limited children's ability to use language (Gunter, 1982). These generally negative results are related to the amount of time children view television, often to the exclusion of reading, doing homework, and performing other academic type tasks.

An 18-month longitudinal investigation of 6–11-year-old children in New York reported by Gunter (1982) revealed that a negative correlation existed between television viewing and effort placed on school achievement. From her research findings, Williams (1986) concludes that comparisons among the communities in Canada prior to and two years after the arrival of television broadcasting indicated that "T.V. probably slows down the acquisition of fluent reading skills" amongst young prereaders. However, she quickly noted that once reading skills were acquired, these skills failed to deteriorate. Children who had a greater number of television viewing hours tended to be poorer readers than those who watched fewer hours, even after the effects of intellectual ability were removed. Better readers were found to use, and to have a greater reliance upon, print media (books, newspapers, and magazines) than less efficient and poorer readers. Gunter (1982) found that academic effort and persistence were negatively correlated to a propensity for adult-oriented and action-adventure programming.

Further, for young children, a positive relation between a preference for children's educational programs and academic ability was found. Taken together, these results suggest that television may be used to promote academic achievement and provide valuable information, but the types of programs watched must be carefully monitored. Nevertheless, when television viewing time reaches an unreasonable level, the amount of academic tasks a child performs will likely decrease, resulting in poorer performance on achievement tests.

Zuckerman, Singer, and Singer (1980) examined the relationship between television viewing and a number of variables related to school performance (reading ability, reading habits, and attitude toward school in general) among 10- and 11-year-old children. It was found that when compared to children who spent little time reading, children who spent more time reading scored higher on standardized tests of intelligence, had more educated fathers, and watched fewer hours of action-adventure type television programs. Children rated by their teachers as being highly imaginative also tended to be those who watched fewer of these programs (Zuckerman, Singer, and Singer, 1980). The authors conclude that it is not the violent television programs that appear to have replaced reading; instead, it seems that programs aimed at facilitating fantasy, involving superhuman characters and fast-moving action, fulfil children's fantasy needs (1980).

It is important to note that within the educational realm, television provides a daily course on current events. There remains little doubt that many children, as well as adolescents, turn to television for their basic current events; this may represent a means of escaping from frustrating experiences with print (Van Evra, 1990) Both for children and adults, large amounts of information are acquired through television viewing. Science programs, recreations of significant historical events, instructional programs designed to teach viewers how to use computer programs, courses in cooking, psychology, fine arts, and man's exploration of space are but a few examples of how the television medium can successfully be used as an educational tool.

Anecdotally, parents frequently report that their children will "rush through" their homework so they can watch television. Certainly, there is considerable "time on task" research demonstrating that the amount of time a child is working on a particular academic task is highly correlated to achievement in that domain (Rosenshine, 1976). A series of studies done in California showed a negative relationship between heavy television viewing and achievement (California Assessment Program, 1980). If television viewing time is precluding the performance of school-related tasks, albeit voluntarily, performance and achievement are likely to suffer. While television can help to fulfil the "fantasy" role in a child's development, excessive viewing behaviour can limit the school-age child's acquisition of important basic skills and concepts.

Television as Entertainment

Certainly, television's primary purpose is as a source of entertainment for children and adults. There is considerable evidence that children, like their parents, are committed to watching each and every episode of their favourite programs. Children can sit motionless, viewing program after program. With the widespread use of VCRs, favourite shows along with popular movies can be taped, saved, and replayed at a later date.

The use of television as a primary source of entertainment and escapism is widespread. Schramm, Lyle, and Parker (1961) have suggested that the young child's process of maturation, with its concomitant difficult experiences, limitations, and frustrations, leads the child to seek escape from conflicts, to seek aid for problems, and to use television as a form of pure entertainment and escapism. Through animation, the child's favourite cartoon characters come to life, and perform feats which can only be realized in the child's imagination. Schramm, Lyle, and Parker (1961) differentiate between two types of content: reality-based and fantasy. Reality-based material has the function of providing children with information. Although Huston et al. (1990) report that children's information-type programs are relatively rare on commercial television, programs such as "Pee Wee's Playhouse," "Fat Albert and the Cosby Kids," and "Pryor's Place" should be commended for their creative efforts. They have successfully provided children with some educational and prosocial content, while entertaining them. It is interesting to note that these programs are no longer being produced. While other programs such as "Street Cents," and "Bill Nye the Science Guy" are available, there still remains a lack of quality educational programs. In contrast, fantasy material is often used to vicariously solve the child's problem. According to this theoretical argument, fantasy becomes a primary function of television, both for children and adults.

Still, today, many television programs and cartoons depict child characters in heroic and central roles. These characters have the ability to perform tasks, feats, and solve problems in ways the child cannot. Generally, these characters are able to exert significant control over their environment, an attribute upon which the child fantasizes and desires to possess. As a result, a strong attachment, albeit an unconscious one, occurs with the character. From a psychoanalytic perspective, children's identification with cartoon and real-life models supports this perspective. Several research reports have noted that children have a propensity for fantasy-type programs as opposed to reality-type programs. Still further, empirical results support the contention that for some children television viewing is a temporary means of escapism (Bailyn, 1959; Maccoby, 1954; Riley and Riley, 1951). While this perspective is speculative, observations of childhood television-viewing patterns certainly lend some credence to this perspective. Undoubtedly, children and adults will continue to enjoy vicariously the adventures of their favourite television characters.

ADVERTISING

Children under the age of 13 constitute more than one-quarter of the North American population of more than 70 million people. They spend considerable time watching television, with as much as 40 percent of their viewing time taken up by commercials directed specifically toward them. Children have been reported to watch between 1500 and 1800 hours of commercial television annually (Cheney, 1983). Given that most television commercials are 30 seconds long, children may view as many as 130 commercials daily,

900 per week, or 45 000 per year (Himmelstein, 1984). The enormity of this can be overwhelming. Coincidentally, the Greek parliament has acknowledged the power that commercials hold over children and has passed a law to limit their potential influence. This law, passed in October 1994, banishes toy commercials from television between 7 a.m. and 10 p.m. It will be interesting to see if other free market countries follow this trend-setting legislation.

Children have become a prime target for advertisers trying to promote toys, cereals, candy, and other childhood products (Barcus, 1977). Television remains the prime vehicle through which advertisers reach large numbers of children. Whether this advertising is aimed at a select group of children, based on characteristics of age, sex, race, etc., or children in general, the message is powerful. While children have very little purchasing power, the commercials remain child-driven, encouraging them to request that their parents purchase specific products or brands. To illustrate television's advertising impact, Jennings (1970) reported that in 1955, Mattel Toy Company increased its annual sales from $500 000 to $12 million after launching a television-based advertising campaign. Today, toy manufacturers often spend in excess of $1 million to promote a given product. The strength of store purchases is often contingent upon the amount of money manufacturers have committed for television advertising.

Huston, Watkins, and Kunkel (1989) report that a convincing body of research accumulated during the 1970s demonstrating that children under eight years of age have difficulty distinguishing program material from advertising. Likewise, children often do not comprehend the "selling intent" of television commercials, and misleading impressions are prevalent and created by commercials despite any accompanying disclaimers (Liebert and Sprafkin, 1988). In testimony before the Federal Trade Commission in the United States, representatives of the Action for Children's Television group alleged that advertising techniques are frequently used to deceive, cajole, and exploit the youngest and least knowledgeable members of society. Naturally, marketers deny such allegations and cite evidence indicating that advertising serves mainly to reinforce existing attitudes and opinions, and that parents ultimately remain the key influence in their child's cognitive development and determine which products are purchased. However, extensive research suggests that advertisers are capitalizing upon the child's ability to understand and act upon persuasive messages. Still further, they rely upon their knowledge of developmental stages to provide the most persuasive message possible. For certain, marketing researchers are aware that early consumer patterns are relatively durable and are resistant to change over time (Bever et al., 1975). Therefore, it is to the advantage of advertisers to attend to this potential market at a time when children are most susceptible to developing their consumer behaviours and brand loyalty.

Research performed in this area suggests that children's attitudes toward television commercials and their ability to evaluate them are influenced by the child's cognitive ability. The capacity to evaluate television commercials and recognize the advertiser's intent increases with age such that children aged 9–12 indicate some understanding of the meaning of the message (Ward and Wackman, 1973). Moreover, as children mature, their attitudes become more materialistic; they become more cynical and considerably more sceptical about the truth underlying television advertising. However, for the young child, seeing is believing. Children not only believe the claims presented in advertisements but they frequently perceive some underlying message. Commercials for board games generally include the entire family playing a particular game. Children subconsciously believe that if their parents purchase this game, then the entire family will play together. Unfortunately, games and toys are frequently purchased in order for the child to be engaged in solitary play. Other products may be even more deceiving. What looks so very interesting in a 30-second commercial may maintain the child's interest for a similar period of time.

Young children often fail to differentiate between the program and the product. Liebert and Sprafkin (1988) refer to these television shows as "program length commercials." These television shows (e.g., "Mighty Morphin Power Rangers," "Teenage Mutant Ninja Turtles") feature characters that are available in toy stores. Gone are the days when toys were developed following the success of television shows. Today, toys may precede, or be introduced simultaneously to, the television program or movie. Toy manufacturers have now become the developers and producers of children's television programs. Kindergarten children watching the television cartoons "The Transformers" and "She-Ra" found the Transformer and She-Ra toys to be much more appealing than children not exposed to these shows (Bryant, 1985).

Regardless of conflicting results, and age and gender differences, it remains clear that television advertising influences both children's social behaviour and patterns of consumption, at least in the short term. However, it has yet to be determined what effects the same advertising message has on their behaviours over longer periods of time. Advertising's potential ability to persuade children seems especially plausible when the child is unsophisticated or relies on television for his or her view of reality. The preschooler, lacking in knowledge and cognitive defences, becomes the most vulnerable to television advertising.

Given the influence that powerful models have upon children, the concept of product endorsement by an individual or cartoon character fits well within the advertiser's domain. Current examples can be seen with the proliferation of products bearing the name Bart Simpson, Mighty Morphin Power Rangers, Barbie, and Barney. Manufacturers capitalize upon the popularity of these shows by producing everything from Halloween costumes to toys, clothes, and even cereals. This technique, aimed at children, remains effective in increasing consumer purchases (e.g., Iskoe, 1976; Ross et al., 1984).

The question of what effects television advertising has upon children's attitudes and behaviours is a problem in which correlation and causal relations often are confounded. The advent of television was accompanied by dozens of other important social changes, one of them being the proliferation of television advertising. Which ones are causes of children's behaviours and which are not is still unknown.

Certainly, many mediating variables are important to consider. Parental responsiveness to children's requests is critical. It is interesting to note that when parents refuse to purchase a requested product, large-scale, heated arguments frequently ensue. In fact, Atkin (1978) reports that 65 percent of parental refusals of children's requests prompted by television advertisements were accompanied by parent-child conflicts and arguments. Still further, mothers often blame advertisers for their children's negative behaviours, since their perceptions are strong that television significantly influences their children's requests (Ward, 1976).

It is generally agreed that older children become jaded to commercials, pay less attention to them, and are less likely to be persuaded by their messages. Younger children, however, appear to be potentially more persuadable. They remain more passive viewers than older children and show less resistance to commercial interruptions.

Given these findings, stronger governmental legislation has been proposed. To some, television should be totally unregulated, with the onus of children's viewing behaviour and habits placed upon parents. Others would prefer to see a total ban on all aggressive programs and advertising on programs aimed at children (Linz, Penrod, and Donnerstein, 1986).

Conclusions

Technological innovations, the demise of the extended family, the incidence of divorce, and other societal reorganizations have forever altered childhood. Today's children develop and live in a world where crime is rampant, drugs are plentiful, and working mothers are the reality. Today's child is more mature and sophisticated than children in previous generations and requires more entertainment. Parents, busier than their parents were, have come to rely upon television, video games, video machines, computers, and other fast-paced innovations to entertain their children. Children have become more sophisticated consumers, and no longer merely entertain themselves, but instead turn to television to satisfy a multitude of their needs.

It has been shown that television can teach children skills, such as letter and number recognition, can help develop their vocabulary, and can foster prosocial behaviour. Many have urged the introduction of a television-viewing curriculum into the schools as a means to encourage and develop more appropriate critical viewing skills (Van Evra, 1990). Considerable research has emphasized the deleterious effects of heavy exposure to television, that is, increased aggression following repeated exposure to violent television and decreased academic performance. It has been shown that the effects of television violence are cumulative and last well into adulthood.

We have attempted to examine several aspects of television's influence upon children. Neither governmental legislation nor more responsible programming alone will suffice. While television can help to educate and to socialize children, it cannot replace effective and responsible parenting. According to Gerald Lesser:

> Television does not hover over children with demands and expectations. They can watch without being tested, graded, reprimanded or even observed by others. They are safe from the threat of humiliation or ridicule for not living up to what is expected of them. There is little doubt that we all need retreats, some sanctuary from forces that correct and direct us. But, we have not made up our collective mind about whether they should exist. We fear that they may engulf us in escape and illusion, and that the indulgence may become addictive. Yet periodic

> escape from surveillance and exacting expectations need not be equivalent to escape from reality. For those children who need it, television used in moderation can provide a temporary refuge (1974, 246).

Broadcasters, more cognizant of the impact of television upon children, have established more laudable goals. In what will likely become a landmark decision in Canada, the Canadian Broadcast Standards Council, a self-regulatory body established by Canadian private broadcasters, in a controversial decision in 1995, withdrew "The Mighty Morphin Power Rangers" from the air, due to its excessive violence and lack of alternative prosocial means for conflict resolution. It is the first time that this voluntary television-industry violence code has been imposed. YTV, a cable channel geared toward children, though not obliged to adhere to the council's decision, has decided to keep the program off the air until it conducts an in-house "program review."

Research evidence continues to suggest that under proper parental supervision, and in moderation, television can serve to provide children with valuable information, knowledge, new perspectives, entertainment, and an escape from daily pressures. However, like any addictive substance, when used to excess, and under specific circumstances, negative effects are bound to ensue.

References

Anderson, D.R., and Lorch, E.P. (1983). "Looking at Television: Action or Reaction?" In *Children's Understanding of Television: Research on Attention and Comprehension* edited by J. Bryant and D.R. Anderson, pp. 1–33. New York: Academic Press.

Atkin, C. (1978). "Observation of Parent-Child Interaction in Supermarket Decision Making." *Journal of Marketing* 42:41–45.

Bailyn, L. (1959). "Mass Media and Children: A Study of Exposure Habits and Cognitive Effects." *Psychological Monographs* 73, 1:1–48.

Ball, S., and G.A. Bogatz. (1970). *The First Year of Sesame Street: An Evaluation*. Princeton, NJ: Educational Testing Service.

————. (1972). "Summative Research of *Sesame Street*: Implications for the Study of Preschool Children." In *Minnesota Symposia on Child Psychology*, Vol. 6, edited by A.D. Pick. Minneapolis: University of Minnesota.

Bandura, A. (1965). "Influences of Model's Reinforcement Contingencies on the Acquisition of Imitative Responses." *Journal of Personality and Social Psychology* 1:589–95.

————. (1973). *Aggression: A Social Learning Analysis*. Englewood Cliffs, NJ: Prentice-Hall.

————. (1977). *Social Learning Theory*. Englewood Cliffs, NJ: Prentice Hall.

Bandura, A., D. Ross, and S.A. Ross. (1963). "Imitation of Film-Depicted Aggressive Models." *Journal of Abnormal and Social Psychology* 66:3–11.

Barcus, F.E. (1977). *Children's Television: An Analysis of Programming and Advertising*. New York: Praeger Publishing.

Bever, T., M. Smith, B. Bengen, and T. Johnson. (1975). "Young Viewers' Troubling Responses to TV Ads." *Harvard Business Review* 53(6):109–20.

Boyd, D.A., and J.D. Straubhaar. (1985). "Developmental Impact of the Home Video Cassette Recorder on Third World Countries." *Journal of Broadcasting and Electronic Media* 29(1):5–21.

Bronfenbrenner, U. (1970). *Two Worlds of Childhood: U.S. and U.S.S.R.* New York: Simon & Schuster.

Bryan, J. H., and N.H. Walbeck. (1979). "The Impact of Words and Deeds Concerning Children." *Child Development* 41:747–57.

Bryant, J. (1985). Testimony at hearings before the U.S. House of Representatives' Subcommittee on Telecommunications, Consumer Protection, and Finance, October 28.

Californa Assessment Program. (1980). *Television and Student Achievement.* Sacramento, CA: California State Department of Education.

Carnegie Commission. (1967). *Public Television: A Program for Action.* New York: Harper and Row.

Cheney, G.A. (1983). *Television in American Society.* New York: F. Watts.

Coates, B., and H.E. Pusser. (1975). "Positive Reinforcement and Punishment in 'Sesame Street' and 'Mister Rogers' Neighborhood.'" *Journal of Broadcasting* 19:143–51.

Collins, W.A. (1983). "Interpretation and Inference in Children's Television Viewing. In *Children's Understanding of Television: Research on Attention and Comprehension*, edited by J. Bryant and D.R. Anderson, 125–50. New York: Academic Press.

Collins, W.A., T.J. Berndt, and V.L. Hess. (1974). "Observational Learning of Motives and Consequences for Television Aggression: A Developmental Study." *Child Development* 45:799–802.

Comstock, G., S. Chaffee, N. Katzman, M. McCombs, and D. Roberts. (1978). *Television and Human Behavior.* New York: Columbia University Press.

Cook, T. D., and R.F. Connor. (1976). "The Educational Impact." *Journal of Communication* 26:155–64.

Cooney, J. (1974). Foreword. *Children and Television: Lessons from Sesame Street*, edited by G. Lesser, xv–xix. New York: Random House.

Ellis, G.T., and F. Sekyra. (1972). "The Effect of Aggressive Cartoons on the Behavior of First Grade Children." *Journal of Psychology* 81:37–43.

Eron, L.D., L.R. Huesmann, P. Brice, P. Fischer, and R. Mermelstein. (1983). "Age Trends in the Development of Aggression, Sex Tying, and Related Television Habits." *Developmental Psychology* 19:71–77.

Eron, L.D., L.R. Huesmann, M.M. Lefkowitz, and L.O. Walder. (1972). "Does Television Violence Cause Aggression?" *American Psychologist* 27:253–63.

Friedrich, L., and A. Stein. (1973). "Aggressive and Prosocial Television Programs and the Natural Behavior of Preschool Children." *Monographs of the Society for Research in Child Development* 38 (4, Serial No. 51).

Friedrich-Cofer, L.K., A. Huston-Stein, D.M. Kipnis, E.J. Susman, and A.S. Clewett. (1979). "Environmental Enhancement of Prosocial Television Content: Effects on Interpersonal Behavior, Imaginative Play, and Self-Regulation in a Natural Setting." *Developmental Psychology* 15:637–46.

Gadberry, S. (1980). "Effects of Restricting First Graders' TV-viewing on Leisure Time Use, IQ Change, and Cognitive Style." *Journal of Applied Developmental Psychology* 1:45–57.

Greenberg, B.S. (1986). "Minorities and the Mass Media." In *Perspectives on Media Effects*, edited by J. Bryant and D. Zillmann, 165–88. Hillsdale, NJ: Lawrence Erlbaum Associates.

Gunter, B. (1982). "Does Television Interfere with Reading Development?" *Bulletin of the British Psychological Society* 35:232–35.

————. (1984). "Television as a Facilitator of Good Behaviour Amongst Children." *Journal of Moral Education* 13(3):152–59.

Harvey, S.E., J.N. Sprafkin, and E. Rubinstein. (1979). "Prime Time Television: A Profile of Aggressive and Prosocial Behaviors." *Journal of Broadcasting* 23(2):179–89.

Hellman, H., and M. Soramäki. (1985). "Economic Concentration in the Videocassette Industry: A Cultural Comparison." *Journal of Communication* 35(3):122–34.

Hollenbeck, A.R., and R.G. Slaby. (1979). "Infant Visual and Vocal Responses to Television." *Child Development* 50:41–45.

Hornik, R. (1978). "Television Access and the Slowing of Cognitive Growth." *American Educational Research Journal* 15:1–15.

Huesmann, L.R., L.D. Eron, M.M. Lefkowitz, and L.O. Walder. (1984a). "Stability of Aggression Over Time and Generations." *Developmental Psychology* 20:1120–34.

Huston, A.C., B.A. Watkins, and D. Kunkel. (1989). "Public Policy and Children's Television." *American Psychologist* 44:424–33.

Huston, A.C., J.C. Wright, M.L. Rice, D. Kerkman, and M. St. Peters. (1990). "Development of Television Viewing Patterns in Early Childhood: A Longitudinal Investigation." *Developmental Psychology* 26:409–20.

Iskoe, A. (1976). "Advertising Via Famous Personalities and the Effects on Children." Unpublished manuscript. The Wharton School, University of Pennsylvania, Philadelphia.

Jennings, R. (1970). *Programming and Advertising Practices in Television Directed to Children.* Boston: Action for Children's Television.

Johnson, N. (1967). *How to Talk Back to Your Television Set.* Boston: Little, Brown, & Co.

Kunkel, D., and B. Watkins. (1987). "Evolution of Children's Television Regulatory Policy." *Journal of Broadcasting and Electronic Media* 31:367–89.

Lavallée-Farah, M. (1992). "Beyond the Big Screen: Competitiveness of Film Markets." *Focus on Culture* 4(4):1–3.

Lesser, G. (1974). *Children and Television: Lessons from "Sesame Street."* New York: Vintage Books.

Liebert, R., and J. Sprafkin. eds. (1988). *The Early Window: Effects of Television on Children*, 3rd ed. New York: Pergamon Press.

Linz, D., S. Penrod, and E. Donnerstein. (1986). "Issues Bearing on the Legal Regulation of Violent and Sexually Violent Media." *Journal of Social Issues* 42(3):171–93.

Lovaas, O. (1961). "Effect of Exposure to Symbolic Aggression on Aggressive Behavior." *Child Development* 32:37–44.

Lovelace, V.O., and A.C. Huston. (1983). "Can Television Teach Prosocial Behavior?" *Prevention in Human Services* 2(1/2):93–106.

Lyle, J. and H. Hoffman. (1976). "Television Viewing by Preschool Age Children. In *Children and Television*, edited by R. Brown, 45–61. Beverly Hills, CA: Sage Publications.

Maccoby, E. (1954). "Why Do Children Watch Television?" *Public Opinion Quarterly* 18, 3 (Fall):239–44.

Meldrich, E., J. Roizen, V. Rubin, and S. Buckley. (1982). *The Serious Business of Growing Up: A Study of Children's Lives Outside School.* Berkeley: University of California Press.

Morgan, M., and L. Gross. (1982). "Television and Educational Achievement and Aspiration." In *Television and Behavior: Ten Years of Scientific Progress and Implications for the Eighties*, Vol. 2, edited by D. Pearl, L. Bouthilet, and J. Lazar, 78–90. Washington, DC: U.S. Government Printing Office.

National Institute of Mental Health. (1982). *Television and Behavior: Ten Years of Scientific Progress and Implications for the Eighties.* Rockville, MD: NIMH.

Nielsen Report. (1988). *Television: 1988 Neilsen Report.* Northbrook, IL: A.C. Nielsen.

O'Bryan, K.G. (1981). "The Teaching Face: A Historical Perspective." In *Children and the Faces of Television: Teaching, Violence, Selling*, edited by E.L. Palmer and A. Dorr, 5–18. New York: Academic Press.

O'Connor, R.D. (1972). "Relative Efficacy of Modeling, Shaping, and the Combined Procedures for Modification of Social Withdrawal." *Journal of Abnormal Psychology* 70:327–34.

Palmer, E.L. (1984). "Providing Quality Television for America's Children." In *The Future of Children's Television*, edited by J.P. Murray and G. Salomon, 103–24. Boys Town, NE: Boys Town Center.

Parke, R., L. Berkowitz, J. Leyens, S. West, and R. Sebastian. (1977). "Some Effects of Violent and Nonviolent Movies on the Behavior of Juvenile Delinquents." *Advances in Experimental Social Psychology* 10:135–72.

Paulson, F.L. (1974). "Teaching Cooperation on Television: An Evaluation of Sesame Street Social Goals Programs." *Audio-Visual Communication Review* 22:229–46.

Pearl, D., L. Bouthilet, and J. Lazar, eds. (1982). *Television and Behavior: Ten Years of Scientific Progress and Implications for the Eighties*, Vol 2. Washington, DC: U.S. Government Printing Office.

Rice, M.L., A.C. Huston, R. Truglio, and J. Wright. (1990). "Words from 'Sesame Street': Learning Vocabulary While Viewing." *Developmental Psychology* 26:421–28.

Riley, M.W., and J.W. Riley. (1951). "A Sociological Approach to Communication Research." *Public Opinion Quarterly* 15:445–60.

Rosenshine, B. (1976). "Recent Research on Teaching Behaviors and Student Achievement." *Journal of Teacher Education* 27:61–64.

Ross, R.P., T. Campbell, J.C. Wright, A.C. Huston, M.L. Rice, and P. Turk. (1984). "When Celebrities Talk, Children Listen: An Experimental Analysis of Children's Responses to TV Ads With Celebrity Endorsement." *Journal of Applied Developmental Psychology* 5:185–202.

Rubinstein, E.A. (1983). "Television and Behavior: Research Conclusions of the 1982 NIMH Report and Their Policy Implications." *American Psychologist* 38:820–25.

Rushton, J.P., and D. Owen. (1975). "Immediate and Delayed Effects of TV Modelling and Preaching on Children's Generosity." *British Journal of Social Clinical Psychology* 14:309–10.

Schramm, W., J. Lyle, and E.B. Parker. (1961). *Television in the Lives of Our Children.* Stanford, CA: Stanford University Press.

Signorielli, N., L. Gross, and M. Morgan. (1982). "Violence in Television Programs: Ten Years Later. In *Television and Behavior: Ten years of Scientific Progress and Implications for the Eighties*, Vol. 2: Technical Reports, edited by D. Pearl, L. Bouthilet, and J. Lazar, 158–73. Washington, DC: U.S. Government Printing Office.

Singer, J.L., and D.G. Singer. (1981). *Television, Imagination and Aggression: A Study of Preschoolers.* Hillsdale, NJ: Erlbaum Associates.

———. (1983). "Psychologists Look at Television: Cognitive, Developmental, Personality, and Social Policy Implications." *American Psychologist*, 38:826–34.

Sohn, D. (1982). "David Sohn Interviews Jerzy Kosinski. A Nation of Videots." In *Television: The Critical View*, 3rd ed., edited by H. Newcomb, 351–66. New York: Oxford University Press.

Sprafkin, J. (1988). "Television and the Emotionally Disturbed Child." In *The Early Window: Effects of Television on Children*, edited by R. Liebert and J. Sprafkin, 260–66. New York: Pergamon Press.

Statistics Canada. (1994). *Annual Television Viewing in Canada: 1992 Culture Statistics.* Ottawa: Minister of Supply and Services Canada.

Stein, A.H., and L.K. Friedrich. (1975). "Impact of Television on Children and Youth." In *Review of Child Development Research*, Vol. 5, edited by E.M. Hetherington, 183–256. Chicago: University of Chicago Press.

Turner, C.W., B.W. Hesse, and S. Peterson-Lewis. (1986). "Naturalistic Studies of the Long-Term Effects of Television Violence." *Journal of Social Issues* 42(3):51–73.

Van Evra, J. (1990). *Television and Child Development.* Hillsdale, NJ: Lawrence Erlbaum Associates.

Ward, S. (1976). "Effects of Television Advertising on Children and Adolescents." In *Children and Television*, edited by R. Brown, 279–319. CA: Sage Publications.

Ward, S., and D.B. Wackman. (1973). "Children's Information Processing of Television Advertising." In *New Models for Mass Communication Research*, edited by P. Clarke, 119–46. Beverly Hills, CA: Sage.

Williams, T.B., ed. (1986). *The Impact of Television: A Natural Experiment in Three Communities.* New York: Academic Press.

Williams, T.H., and A.G. Handford. (1986). "Television and Other Leisure Activities. In *The Impact of Television: A Natural Experiment in Three Communities*, edited by T.H. Williams, 143–213. Orlando, FL: Academic Press, Inc.

Williams, T.B., M.L. Zabrack, and L.A. Joy. (1982). "The Portrayal of Aggression on North American Television." *Journal of Applied Social Psychology* 12:360–80.

Zuckerman, D., D. Singer, and J. Singer. (1980). "Television Viewing, Children's Reading, and Related Classroom Behavior." *Journal of Communication* 30:166–74.

THE PRIME MINISTER OF SATURDAY NIGHT[1]: DON CHERRY, THE CBC, AND THE CULTURAL PRODUCTION OF INTOLERANCE

James Gillet, Philip White, and Kevin Young

INTRODUCTION

Among the many manifestations of popular culture in Canada, professional hockey is unique. As one of our national sports, hockey plays a central role in the material, cultural, and life processes of our society. The many hours that television devotes to hockey, the packed arenas of National Hockey League (NHL) teams, and the popularity of team-inspired paraphernalia and memorabilia testify to the game's powerful grip on the emotions of many Canadians. Far from peripheral, hockey has a significant effect on the everyday lives of thousands of Canadians—witness the front-page newspaper coverage enjoyed by Canada's Junior Hockey team following their gold medal performance in the 1995 World Junior Championships. Remarking on how their childhoods were steeped in hockey and its lore, authors Gruneau and Whitson (1993) recall:

> pleading with our parents to allow us to stay up to watch "Hockey Night in Canada,"...flipping hockey cards in the schoolyard, and...arguing about which was the better team, the Leafs or the Canadiens. These memories of sights, sounds, and feelings are the stuff of nostalgia. But they are also the stuff of identity—part of the attachments both of us have to the places, times and social influences that shaped our developing conceptions of self" (p. 1).

As these authors imply, much of what we know and understand about hockey is shaped through the media. In Canada, a cherished ritual of hockey spectating involves "Hockey Night In Canada," a weekly television show broadcast by the Canadian Broadcasting Corporation (CBC), which has consistently enjoyed one of the largest viewing audiences of any Canadian television program. For instance, Gruneau and Whitson (1993) report that in the early 1960s, "Hockey Night in Canada" drew audiences as large as 3.5 million English Canadians and 2 million

French Canadians. Though not quite as large, audiences for the 1993-94 season were still sizeable, averaging 1.4 million viewers per broadcast.[2] Such is the popularity of this show that during the 1995 disruption of the NHL, because of a lockout of the players by the owners, the CBC's Saturday night audiences fell by an average of 20 percent and on some Saturday nights the audience fell by as much as 50 percent (Strauss, 1995).

In recent years a highly popular component of "Hockey Night in Canada" has been an intermission segment called Coach's Corner. The segment's principal character is Don Cherry, a former NHL coach turned hockey commentator. Addressing controversial issues with theatrical and confrontational style, Cherry has become one of Canada's most recognized personalities (S. Young, 1990). Alan Fotheringham has argued that "Cherry, with his 'Hockey Night in Canada' act, is better known than Jean Chrétien's finance minister and undoubtedly has more influence on the body politic" (1994).

This essay takes stock of Cherry's place in Canadian popular culture with an eye toward the complicity of the CBC in Cherry's success, although it should be noted that we are not addressing the *effects* on viewers or listeners of watching Don Cherry. Although the latter remains a separate and so far unresearched issue, what is clear is that the viewing audience is not one great homogeneous mass. Rather, a phenomenon like Don Cherry may be decoded or "read" in many different ways—which explains why some people love him, why some hate him, why some have never heard of him, and why it is also possible for the same person to both like him and be offended by him either simultaneously or at different times.

We focus here on two central issues. First, we examine why Cherry has been cultivated by the media and advertising industries. Beginning with a description of his idiosyncratic style, we consider the broader forces that are involved in the construction of Don Cherry as a media personality and commodity. This is followed by a description of how he is marketed, how he markets himself, and the power structures within which he is located. This is of interest for determining how some groups have had more power than others in exercising influence over the ensconcement of Don Cherry on "Hockey Night in Canada" and the communication of intolerant political attitudes. This is particularly significant because the CBC is a publicly owned national network. Second, we scrutinize the messages that are produced for the audience by Don Cherry, and which are implicitly endorsed by the organizations for which he works. We analyze these messages and what they reveal about culturally dominant assumptions in Canadian society.

On Schtick Work: The Man and His Style

'If we (Hamilton) got an NHL franchise here, Toronto would want one too' (Don Cherry quoted in the Hamilton Spectator, October 16, 1987).

Don Cherry is a native of Kingston, Ontario. Now in his early sixties, Cherry progressed as far as Grade 9 in school, played hockey professionally for eighteen years (all but one game—with the Boston Bruins in the NHL—were as a journeyman with various teams in the minor leagues), coached various teams including the Colorado Rockies and the Boston Bruins, and finally turned his hand to hockey commentary. In his private life, he is a family man who lives in Mississauga and who, paradoxically, given his public persona, is said to love gardening, animals, and constructing model boats, and who gives of himself generously to charities.

As a public persona—"When I'm on there, (i.e., television, radio, advertisements), I'm doin' my job" (quoted in Scrivener, 1993)—Cherry sometimes seems omnipresent. He appears to audiences in various media formats—television, radio, print, and commercial videotapes—although the style and content of his appearances are predictably similar and are based on his high profile as a hockey analyst. That Cherry is quite a different person in his private life, and that there seem to be contradictory versions of the man, tends to inflate interest in him. It is as if he is so outrageous in public that it is difficult to conceive of him behaving that way all the time, or at least when he is out of the limelight. Harry Neale, a popular colour commentator on many "Hockey Night in Canada" broadcasts, who has worked alongside Cherry extensively, has suggested that: "If he's sitting there having a beer and there's just two or three of us, you'd think the guy is a little out in left field, just a good guy, but if he saw a mike over there somewhere, into his act he goes" (quoted in S. Young, 1990, 22). Cherry's professional "style" has visual and oral components which are sufficiently vivid that he is instantly recognizable as an original character. Hockey writer Roy MacGregor, for instance, refers to him as "the most outrageous act on Canadian television" (1992). Both to look at and to listen to, Cherry's performance is so compelling that his appeal extends from television to print advertisements to radio performances. On television, Cherry, or "Grapes" (short for "Sour Grapes") as he is also known because of his caustic style, is a visual concoction with several trademark characteristics. Perhaps most striking is his penchant for custom-tailored shirts with three-and-a-half inch collars and monogrammed cuffs, and his equally outrageous ties. This attention-grabbing combination is invariably complemented by a suit or suit jacket with an equally outlandish cut and fabric component. His seeming willingness to flout conventional sartorial taste, which led him to be named "Canada's Worst-Dressed Man," (*The Globe and Mail,* 1994) is, needless to say, part of his theatricality. Cherry seems to consciously caricature the role of the dandy by referring to himself boldly, but also one suspects with tongue in cheek, as a "sharp-dressed guy."

Once described as a "human hand grenade" (Brioux, 1994, 16), Cherry matches his garish costume with a public persona that is belligerently opinionated, hyper-flamboyant, and self-promotingly controversial, which probably helps explain why he remains a fixture on one of Canada's most watched television programs. Because of his style, Cherry tends to elicit extreme responses. It is difficult to be neutral, to ignore him, or to be indifferent. Throughout the long Canadian winter, Cherry assaults the senses with a voice that is both beloved and despised.[3]

In constructing this media persona, Cherry claims to speak on behalf of the "average worker." As he suggests: "There's nobody speaking for the people who are paying the freight, the average worker, the guys in construction and the mechanics and people like that, but me." (MacGregor, 1992), and: "I'm talkin' to the guy that goes in the beverage hall" (quoted in Brunt, 1987). Thus, part of Cherry's appeal may lie in his adoption, quite intentionally, of a working-class voice that is pointedly different from the predominantly middle-class journalistic discourse of television. As Knowles (forthcoming) has argued:

> Cherry's aggressively bad grammar (consciously class-coded), his championing of old-fashioned and unfashionable causes such as the tolerance of fighting and violence in sport, and above all his xenophobia and anti-feminism, have made for much of the show's popularity as well as its controversial quality, particularly on the CBC, which is noted for its broadcaster's "neutral"... accents and respectably liberal-humanist opinions.

Ex Says It All: Coach's Corner and Corporate Interpendencies

> *He is everywhere, doing everything. Talking, hawking, conglomerating*
> *(Maki, 1992)*

During the economic downturn of the late 1980s, the Conservative government reduced spending on numerous public services including the CBC, which experienced an extensive reduction of resources and services. Coincidental with these cutbacks and reflecting a broad trend toward greater corporate sponsorship for public enterprises, the CBC moved toward what S. Young (1990, 208) has called a "Molson-ization" process, a closer connection between the brewery giant and the CBC's NHL broadcasts, which led to the name of the program being changed to "Molson Hockey Night in Canada." As part of this arrangement, revenues are guaranteed in exchange for the association of the corporation with the title of the broadcast.

A second, and related, change involved an increased emphasis on Cherry's segment of the program. The conservative populism that has become the trademark of Cherry's patois and style fits perfectly with the corporate interests of both Molson Breweries and the CBC. As Gillmor (1992) has noted:

> Cherry has the mannerisms of the tavern fan, voicing outrage, jabbing his finger, making his opinions heard above the din and against the objections of twits. He is a five minute subliminal beer ad, the embodiment of the Molson Export tag line—*There's nothing half-way about it, Ex says it all* (p. 61).

Thus, on the one hand, Cherry generates controversy with his extravagant personality and strident views about hockey, violence, and the place of Canadians in the NHL. On the other hand, love him or hate him, Cherry's financial impact is considerable. He creates interest in "Hockey Night in Canada" which is beneficial not just to

Molson Breweries but also to other sponsors and advertisers, particularly when the grass roots support of hockey in Canada may be waning.[4]

But for all its ratings success, and probably a major cause of it, Coach's Corner always appears to be surrounded by uncertainty and tension. The viewer gets the impression, which is frequently reinforced by Cherry's many references to the tenuousness of his job, that his shoot-from-the-hip delivery might finally self-destruct. As Gillmor (1992, 61) observes, the appeal of Coach's Corner, for a large part of its audience, lies precisely in the unpredictability created by placing a loose cannon in an unrehearsed, live broadcast: "Like racing car fans, the audience waits for flames and destruction. A call to invade Sweden perhaps, or a slur, an expletive, an uppercut to Ron's chin." Despite sometimes being uncomfortable with Cherry's views which are hardly consistent with the philosophy of a network that aspires to be politically correct, the CBC is keenly aware of the commercial value of Coach's Corner. As Alan Clarke, head of CBC's sports programming has suggested, "television is entertainment, and Don is entertaining" (Gillmor, 1992, 61). For Molson Breweries, meanwhile, Cherry not only sells beer and helps to legitimate beer consumption as a Canadian pastime, he also helps to consolidate Molson's powerful position in the Canadian alcohol industry.

But the commercial ramifications of Coach's Corner extend beyond the mutually beneficial relationship between Molsons and the CBC. Cherry has astutely parlayed his popularity into his own entrepreneurial ventures. By the late 1980s, Cherry's brash but evidently likeable persona had become an endorsement leviathan penetrating numerous, and surprisingly diverse, markets. The television show, "Don Cherry's Grapevine" currently appears on The Sports Network (TSN).[5] The current series is presented as a compilation of "classics" from the past. He has a short, but regular, radio segment called "The Grapeline" which is heard on FAN radio, a 24-hour sport-programming station located in Toronto (in which he appears with Brian Williams, who acts as Cherry's foil). This syndicated radio slot is heard in over 100 markets across Canada. Then there is *Don Cherry's Rock 'Em, Sock 'Em Hockey* videotape series. Currently in its sixth edition, these 60-minute compilations of vicious and often injurious body checks and fistfights have sold over 750 000 copies, and routinely top the best-seller list for Canadian videos (the current edition has Cherry referring to one of the authors of this article as a "left-wing pinko"!). Cherry also appears in an assortment of television advertisements in which he acts as the pitchman for products such as after-shave lotion, automobiles, home insulation, pizza, and provincial sport lotteries. He also lends his name to over a dozen "Don Cherry's Grapevine" sports bars across the country. And finally, he is also involved in endorsements for organizations such as the Ontario Federation of Anglers and Hunters. Indeed, the potential marketability of Cherry's image and opinions is so strong that he promotes himself by acquiescing to literally hundreds of interviews each year, and maintains a hectic schedule of charity work, talk shows, banquets, and other appearances.

Many, if not most, of Cherry's products are hawked using the same intimidating rhetoric, the same controversial point of view. When author Stephen Cole remarks that

"Watching 'Don Cherry's Grapevine' feels like being trapped on a long bus ride with the guy from high school who beat you up for your homework" (Houston, 1994b), he hints not only at the tedious predictability with which Cherry pitches his products but also at the paradox Cherry's immense popularity represents. And Cole is exactly right; Cherry is indeed "superb" for huge numbers of Canadians. For example, while his hockey videos and the violence contained in them carry cultural meaning in and of themselves, their success must be understood in terms of the broader appeal of Cherry's values for working-class philosophy and lifestyle. As writer Allan Maki (1992) points out, "the 'Rock 'Em, Sock 'Em' image sells—it sells shirts, drinks, burgers *and* (emphasis added) logic for the common man."

Other than acknowledging the importance of appeasing Molsons ("when the beer guys like me, that means I'm doin' my job," (quoted in *TV Guide,* April 16, 1994, p. 18), Cherry remains coy on the broader economic implications of his Coach's Corner slot. He has routinely denied, for example, any strategy to what many critics have observed appears to be a straightforward entrepreneurial codependency between the pro-violence views he sells from the broadcast booth and the huge success of his videotapes which show bone-crushing hits. The apparently not-so-self-evident possibility of an exploitive relationship between Cherry and the CBC has, remarkably, seldom been raised, though it has not escaped Roy MacGregor's (1993) notice:

> There is also the matter of how Cherry profits from hockey violence. For several years now, Cherry has conducted a lucrative side-business marketing video compilations of hockey hits and fights. His first, *Don Cherry's Rock 'Em Sock 'Em Hockey* sold more than 150 000 copies, making it the top-selling video in Canada. Two successful sequels have followed. If no new products were available, the series would come to an end, which means that Don Cherry has a direct vested interest in having fighting continue in the NHL. Fisticuffs is money in his pocket (p. 141).

Moreover, even more serious questions might be raised regarding the complicity of the CBC in the sale for profit of clearly pro-violence and otherwise dubious values. Again, MacGregor is right on the mark here:

> Why have Cherry's business activities never become an issue with the CBC, which does not produce the "Hockey Night In Canada" broadcasts but does carry them? Cherry himself has said, "It's a modern miracle that I'm still on CBC." And the CBC, as the past has shown, is highly sensitive to conflict of interest or even the appearance of it. In 1988 Dale Goldhawk was removed as host of "Cross-Country Checkup" because he was also head of a broadcasters' union that had spoken out against free trade. It was deemed that Goldhawk was unable to be unbiased on that issue. Cherry is clearly unable to be unbiased on the issue of hockey violence. Goldhawk received no money for his work on the free trade issue. Yet Cherry makes money out of hockey violence (p. 142).

That the CBC, a public network, has taken no action against Cherry may well be tied to the fact that it can no longer afford to control the broadcasts it carries. In the same years that Cherry's star has been soaring, the CBC has become strapped for cash. For the network, the Stanley Cup playoffs represent about $60 million a year in advertising. The impact of that much money is enormous: a cutback in federal funding of $108 million in 1990 led to the closure or gutting of eleven television stations across the country. Money from playoff hockey is obviously of critical importance to the CBC. The Stanley Cup involves between 80 and 150 hours of viewing time each year, with an average audience on the English network, where Cherry appears, of 1.8 million viewers. "Coach's Corner" is generally conceded to be more popular with many viewers than the games themselves. Nonhockey programming in similar time slots would bring in perhaps one-quarter of the revenues. On this issue, the CBC seems to be driven by the same force that drives the game's owners: money. As MacGregor writes, "Don Cherry's potential conflicts of interest go unnoticed by the CBC because the CBC cannot afford to notice them" (1993, 142-43).

Finally, in light of this apparently symbiotic relationship, it must be said that it is also difficult *not* to notice the complicity of the CBC in setting up Cherry as the "comic" against Ron Maclean's "straight man" (Brioux, 1994). Despite the efforts of the CBC in many of the Coach's Corner segments to distance the corporation from Cherry's controversial views (witness Maclean's frequent raised eyebrows, disapproving glances, reprimands, and corrections), are we really expected to believe that this is not a quite deliberate attempt to cash in on a proven television routine? As with other television personalities like David Letterman, outrageous views lure audiences and the advertising revenues that are attracted by them. This successful formula has paid in the case of Coach's Corner for the CBC, for Molsons, and for a host of spin-off business interests for Cherry. Although there has been some public pressure to curb the views of Cherry on CBC, as long as ratings remain stable Coach's Corner will most likely continue—with the same content and format.

Man of the People: Canadiana, Xenophobia, and Intolerance

> *This is my home town, Kingston, Ontario. We have the Hockey Hall of Fame. We put 75 percent of players in the National Hockey League and the Yankee Doodie Dandles [sic] are telling us we can't have a franchise?*[6]

To a great extent, Cherry is controversial because of his self-acknowledged intolerance. As he has said of himself, "I'm the Anglo redneck of all time" (MacGregor, 1993, 141). Although purportedly a commentator on hockey, and one who is widely regarded as a source of considerable insight following his long association with hockey in various roles, it is his views on social and political issues that most often lead to controversy. His more famous transgressions have become well known. They include:

> ...pleading for someone to break the arm of Pittsburgh Penguin defenceman Ulf Samuelson; waving an eight-foot long Canadian flag during a Gulf War tirade against "wimps and creeps"; making fun of Finnish-born coach Alpo Suhonen's name ("Alpo—That's a dog food, isn't it?"); publicly backing Washington Capitol Dale Hunter following a vicious playoff mugging ("Hang tough, Dale"); a jaw-dropping snipe at CBC News, which had the gall to cut into his "Corner" last spring with reports about, in Cherry's words, "lower Slobovia attacking Slimea" (Brioux, 1994, 16).

Cherry is famous for making such intolerant statements, often having nothing to do with hockey, often directed toward various groups including immigrants to Canada, "foreigners" of different types, women, and gays. It is not unusual, particularly on his radio spots, for him to discuss political issues such as capital punishment, immigration policy, and corporal punishment without mention of hockey.

While many viewers find Cherry's intolerance repugnant, his fierce sense of nationalism tends to elicit more ambiguous and even supportive responses. His staunchly pro-Canadian rhetoric implicitly assumes that there is such a thing as a "typical" Canadian and a homogenous Canadian culture. Thus, his rhetoric goes beyond promoting his definition of what it is to be Canadian to lamenting Canada's undeniable cultural heterogeneity—a feature of Canada's make-up that has been established as long as Canada has been a country. In Cherry's view, Canadian culture has a definable quality that is being threatened by what he mistakenly and ironically refers to as Canada's policy of "multi-racialism":

> We're too liberal of people coming over here telling us we can't have Jesus Christ in our prayers, and we can't do this and we can't do that. I'd like to go over there...to some of those foreign lands and...tell them that they've got to change their prayers and their customs. Trouble is, there's no Canadian heritage anymore, absolutely none (quoted in Brioux, 1994, 19).

Cherry's views, then, could be seen by some as xenophobic; their vitriol often being aimed mostly at European countries and cultures. Thus, Finns, Swedes, and Russians are denigrated, not only for taking the jobs of "good Canadian boys" in the NHL but also because they lack, seemingly without much variation within those groups, qualities Cherry deems desirable—notably gritty, masculine toughness: "Wait in the weeds, then stick 'em. Fucking guy. There's a Swede trick" (quoted in Gillmor, 1992, 110). Interestingly, selecting these targets does not appear to elicit as much of an outcry as would be the case if he attacked other cultural groups. As Fotheringham has suggested:

> If he said the same thing about blacks and Jews that he does about Swedes and Russians he would be hauled before some human rights

> commission, but he gets away with it because all he's talking about is violence and Canadian men love it (1994).

Locating examples of Cherry's hockey-related xenophobia is not difficult. For instance, Cherry called former Calgary Flame Pekka Rautakallio "as yellow as duck's feet" and Pavel Bure of the Vancouver Canucks and Sergei Fedorov of the Detroit Redwings "sissy foreigners." On these matters he has made his views quite plain:

> Yes, I think there are foreign hockey players who are overpaid and don't deserve to be in the NHL. Check the playoffs last year. There was one in the TOP 20 scoring. They're like magicians. They disappear in the playoffs. Yeah, I'll take Canadian and American boys any day (quoted in Brioux, 1994, 19-20).

If there is an underlying theme to Don Cherry's banter, it is a nostalgic defence of the changing nature of hockey. For Cherry, hockey is increasingly moving away from its essentially "Canadian" character. There appear to be two central features of this defence. First, Cherry takes issue with the trend toward a less violent version of the game. In fact, using traditional but widely criticized explanations, Cherry is outspoken in his endorsement of fistfighting, arguing that it is inherent to the game. Second, Cherry focusses on the growing involvement of non-Canadians in professional hockey, both on the ice and off. Germane here is the noticeably greater presence in the NHL of American interests, and the increasing involvement of European players. This aspect of Cherry's defence typifies his conservative populism; jobs, as he sees it, are being taken away from young working-class Canadians—jobs that "real" Canadians have a more natural right to because, after all, Canadians invented the game, and produce the best players.

To be fair, Cherry's spirited promotion of hockey and Canadians is in some ways honourable. At a time when participation and interest in hockey is declining, it is important that Canadians are encouraged and given the opportunity to play the game. In these respects, changes in hockey, for Cherry, serve as a metaphor for broader changes in Canada's social make-up: "I'm trying to keep this country together, I'm the fucking *glue* that holds it together" (quoted in Gillmor, 1992, 58). However, in his defence of hockey, Cherry paints a portrait of the relationship between hockey and Canadian identity that is based on exclusion and dominance. Advocacy of toughness and violence in hockey is not only gendered, but reflects and reproduces a definition of masculinity that requires the dominance of others, and discourages many men and women from participating.

By making the claim that there is something intrinsically *Canadian* about hockey, Cherry is able to limit participation on the basis of race and nationality. It is clear that for Cherry the people who have a right to play hockey are white Anglo-Saxon (and to lesser degree francophone) working-class and/or rural men. At a time of economic retrenchment and occupational instability in Canada, this sounds very similar to the conservative view that immigrants are stripping Canadians of jobs. Cherry's intentions may be pro-Canadian, but his version of Canada and hockey is both limited and limiting.

On Turtlists and Left-wing Pinkos: Don Cherry and the Defence of Aggressive Masculinity

> *Once upon a time we had a rough and tumble game when everyone took care of themselves. Then came along Wayne Gretzky, who had a credit card to set all kinds of records because he had a guy like Dave Semenko looking out for him. But then Wayne went out there to La La Land and became friends with Arsenio Hall and Chevy Chase and all those Hollywood types, and they didn't like fighting. So we said, "Let's get fighting out of the game"*
>
> *(quoted in Sports Illustrated, 1993).*

When he referred to one of us as a "left-wing pinko" on "Coach's Corner" during the final game of the 1994 Stanley Cup playoffs, Don Cherry not only called into question alternative ("left-wing") readings of hockey and alternative versions of masculinity ("pinkos"), he also unwittingly revealed the seriously limiting potential of dominant versions of both. Of course, Cherry has not been slow to comment on such issues before. On the contrary, his explicit and openly acknowledged conservatism and class bias, coupled with his more implicit sexism and homophobia, have become cornerstone elements of his image and his schtick.

Whether it is his insistence that a fistfight is the best way to settle an argument, or wearing an earring on camera and speaking with an exaggerated lisp and a contrived camp style to mock the "candyass" "Hollywood-ization" of a tough Canadian game, Don Cherry's views are constant reminders of the inhospitability of hyper-macho sports culture to certain social groups and alternative ways of playing. As he has routinely noted himself: "There's a lot of mothers and women who don't like it ... There's a lot of college profs that don't like it. But I'm talkin' to the guy that goes in the beverage hall" (Brunt, 1987). Or again: "I speak for the average guy. Truck drivers give me the thumbs up. The professors and the guys who drink Perrier water and white wine don't like me. I don't care about them" (Maki, 1992). Nowhere does Cherry's commitment to "masculinism"—a term Brake (1985) uses to refer to the championing of a particular brand of maleness based on physicality and excess—show itself more clearly than in his position on fighting in the NHL. It is evident that like many other hockey people, Cherry has "bought into" what former hockey great and respected student of the game Ken Dryden (1983, 189) calls the "NHL theory of violence." What is ironic here is that the theory that fighting is inevitable in hockey because players need an outlet for their pent-up frustrations has been comprehensively discredited. Sociological research has shown that hockey violence is essentially a learned phenomenon and that continued reference to catharsis theory is part of the process of rationalizing the retention of fighting as "part of the game." Cherry, and to be fair, many other hockey commentators, routinely adopts additional arguments to embellish crude catharsis theory (K. Young, 1991). We hear, for example, that the elimination of fighting would lead to more stick work; that no one actually gets hurt in a fistfight; that there is an art to fighting; that fighting is instinctive among males and that nothing can be done about it; and so on.

But for Cherry, fistfighting is not only a way of purging aggressive tendencies in a fast-paced contact sport, it is also a means of establishing honour and respect. Indeed, this is a view which has been confirmed many times by research into the subculture of male sport (Faulkner, 1972; K. Young, 1993). The result for audiences is that Cherry's *Rock 'Em Sock 'Em Hockey* videotapes and his numerous television and radio spots are punctuated by laudatory commentaries on hockey's tough guys, goons, and pugilists. For example: "Cox and Probert. Folks, you're never gonna see a better one than this. We counted the punches—71 in 50 seconds. Back and forth.... Probert is something else. But Cox doesn't back down I'll tell ya. Nobody backs down on this one. This was the talk of hockey for a long time. See how everybody stands back. Two tough guys goin' at it. They want to go, let 'em go. They're not hurtin' anybody but themselves."[7] Conversely, Cherry is scathingly critical of players who avoid physical confrontation and refuse to fight when challenged. "Foreign" players, with their supposed preference for skill over force, are especially vulnerable to Cherry's wrath but so, for that matter, are North American players who adopt equally nonviolent orientations to the game. For example, when Pittsburgh Penguin Larry Murphy covered his head in a 1992 game to protect himself from an attack by Chris Chelios of the Chicago Blackhawks, Cherry saw fit to question Murphy both as a player *and as a man*: "This is what we've come to? Turtlism?... That's not manly. I remember Bobby Hull, broken jaw, still playing. The Rocket... *little Guy Lafleur*, a hundred and seventy-five pounds, best right wing who ever played, he *never* whined, never took a dive" (quoted in Gillmor, 1992, 59). For Cherry, Murphy's retreat into his shoulder pads symbolizes the passing not only of a violent hockey era but also the transformation of what it means to be a man in our culture: "The image of hockey as the one place where a man stood up for himself, where there was honour, that's almost gone" (quoted in Gillmor, 1992, 59). And just as Cherry laments less aggressive player styles, efforts by officials to eliminate fistfighting in hockey leave him enraged. Such was the case in 1987 when the government's Fair Play Commission, fronted then by Federal Sport Minister Otto Jelinek, issued two advertisements depicting hockey as a dangerous sport. One contained a photograph of an empty rink with the headline "The Scene of the Crime" superimposed on it. Predictably enough, and following his well-established pattern of invoking bigotry and intolerance when anyone challenges *his* version of hockey, Cherry's response to the advertisements took aim at "left-wingers" and "pinkos" everywhere: "To me, when I saw those ads, I was incensed. That's detrimental to hockey. It's socialist thinking.... We've got a figure skater telling us what's wrong with hockey" (quoted in the Hamilton *Spectator,* October 16, 1987).

Though we suspect Cherry intentionally embellishes his pro-violence views for effect (knowing full well that being provocative enhances the *spectacle* of "Coach's Corner"), it is equally clear that for him, like many others in the still male-dominated world of sport, the brutality of hockey contains a certain appeal and connotes a particular brand of masculine integrity. His daunting physical presence, his I-can-yell-louder-than-you schtick; his bull terrier dog; his video series; his aversion to safety equipment (particularly visors) and the intervention of officials during fights; his transparent rationalizations for violence on the ice ("you don't have to maim 'em, but hit them to hurt"); his lending his name to traditional male preserves such as the Ontario Federation of Anglers and Hunters; his poking fun at alternative notions of what it means to be a man ("I'm a 90s guy") and at opponents of hockey fighting ("so if you don't like the odd tussle, go out in the kitchen and make a pot of tea"): everything about Cherry's public image represents a defence of a traditional, but decreasingly socially acceptable, aggressive masculine style.

Conclusions

Beneath Cherry's bluster is a sense of powerlessness, an inability to stem the tide of inexorable change. Whether change is perceived as shifts in the control of hockey, particularly in the form of current processes of de-Canadianization that mirror new economies of free trade and the globalization process (Cantelon and Murray, 1993; Jackson, 1994), or trends toward the aestheticization of the game and making it a safer place to play, Cherry represents an attempt to reclaim traditional ways of thinking about hockey and an attempt to reassert *his* way of playing as *the* way of playing.

A similar dynamic has been identified in studies of the "lovable" bigot Archie Bunker, a famous television character from the 1970s, whose derisive, but popular, racist humour was grounded in his feelings of economic impotence (see, for example, Raney, 1981). Interestingly, Bunker's patent racism was cosmeticized for television by his being made to appear ignorant because of his working-class status—a destructive stereotype connecting bigotry with class membership (Berk, 1977). But clearly, there are parallels between Bunker and Cherry's overt association with "beer guys," and his constant stream of malapropisms. In both cases, comedy is used as a technique of neutralization to make intolerance seem more palatable. The message seems to be that intolerance, like ignorance, is indigenous to the lower classes and is consequently a legitimate source of humour. Future research might investigate how Cherry's intolerance is "read" by viewers, whether his views are recognized for their comedic appeal (as a comic nature, as a put-on, as an exaggerated spectacle), or whether for some people the humour is not recognized and his views serve to legitimate their own.

There are those, of course, who might argue that making Don Cherry the subject of academic research is unwarranted because sports issues are trivial or that they are removed from "real," pressing issues of everyday life. As sociologists of sport, we are concerned, as Cantelon and Gruneau (1988) have put it, about "the degree to which the apparent innocence of sport provides a significant site for the construction of myth and ideology (184). In this essay, we have also attempted to illuminate a complicity between sport, the media, and corporate interests in the active production of ideologies.

As a huge critical literature on the mass communication process has indicated (see, for example, Gans, 1979; S. Hall et al., 1978; Said, 1981; Tuchman, 1978), conceiving of television production as neutral or objective is naive in the extreme. By examining Coach's Corner and Don Cherry's contribution to it as "texts," it quickly becomes obvious that the production of hockey for Canadian television involves the promotion of identifiable political messages. Cherry's well-known, and self-acknowledged, intolerance is only barely rationalized by its being framed as reflecting his opinions alone. In appearing to be a guy who is willing to face the music and "say it like it is," unlike others who are silenced by the forces of "political correctness," his views seem less malicious because he claims to speak for a large (but not verified) proportion of Canadians. The overt conservatism of this stance is, at least in part, disguised because it is placed in a sport context that has been shown to be both macho (Gruneau and Whitson, 1993; K. Young, 1993) and ethnocentric (A. Hall et al., 1991). On this basis, there is some reason to question the appropriateness of broadcasting Cherry's views on Canada's publicly funded television network, particularly when it is clear that he profits personally from the promotion of sport violence.

Notes

1. Although we are uncertain as to its exact origins, we have borrowed the appellation "The Prime Minister of Saturday Night" from one of Roy MacGregor's many thoughtful commentaries on Don Cherry (1993, p. 139).
2. Information provided by Debbi Crossen, publicist for CBC Sports, January 27, 1995.
3. Although many of Cherry's opponents come from outside of the hockey world, many players, administrators, and observers of the game have also had critical things to say about him. For example, Calgary Flame Frank Musil has remarked, "He's a total idiot. He's a goof. I ignore him" (quoted in *The Toronto Star*, May 23, 1993, p. D1), and Mordecai Richler has referred to Cherry as a "role model for cretins" (quoted in MacGregor, 1993, p. 139).
4. Many amateur hockey jurisdictions across the country reported diminished rates of participation throughout the 1980s. Meanwhile, alternative styles of hockey, notably the noncontact version, continue to call into question risk and injury factors associated with the way the game has traditionally been organized for youngsters.
5. As further evidence of the complicity of the beer industry in Don Cherry's success, it is interesting to note that TSN is one of the most profitable companies owned by the John Labatt Ltd. empire (Houston, 1994a).
6. Don Cherry made this comment on Coach's Corner during the 1993–94 NHL playoffs.
7. Don Cherry made this comment on Coach's Corner during the 1993–94 NHL playoffs.

References

Berk, L. (1977). "The Great Middle American Dream Machine." *Journal of Communication* 27:27–31.

Brake, M. (1985). *Comparative Youth Culture*. New York: Routledge.

Brioux, B. (1994). "True Blue: Hockey Night in Canada's Don Cherry." *TV Guide*, April 16, pp. 15–21.

Brunt, S. (1987). "A Hoser in Paradise." *The Globe and Mail*, January 17, p. C1.

Cantelon, H., and R. Gruneau. (1988). "The Production of Sport for Television." In *Not Just a Game: Essays in Canadian Sport Sociology*, edited by J. Harvey and H. Cantelon, 177–95. Ottawa: University of Ottawa Press.

Cantelon, H. and S. Murray. (1993). "Globalization and Sport, Structure and Agency: The Need for Greater Clarity." *Loisir et Société* 16:275–91.

Dryden, K. (1983). *The Game.* Toronto: Macmillan.

Faulkner, R. (1973). "On Respect and Retribution: Toward an Ethnography of Violence." *Sociological Symposium* 9:17–36.

Fotheringham, A. (1994). "Pointy-heads Take a Run at Don Cherry." *Financial Post*, June 14, p. 11.

Gans, H. (1979). *Deciding What's News*. New York: Pantheon.

Gillmor, D. (1992). "Don Cherry Unleashed." *Saturday Night,* October 6, pp. 56–110.

The Globe and Mail (1994, December 29). "Best and Worst Dressed," p. D4.

Gruneau, R. and D. Whitson. (1993). *Hockey Night in Canada: Sport Identities and Cultural Politics.* Toronto: Garamond Press.

Hall, A., T. Slack, G. Smith, and D. Whitson. (1991). *Sport in Canadian Society.* Toronto: McClelland and Stewart.

Hall, S., C. Critcher, T. Jefferson, J. Clarke, and B. Roberts. (1978). *Policing the Crisis: Mugging, the State, and Law and Order.* London: Macmillan.

Houston, W. (1994a). "Real TV Means Real Profits." *The Globe and Mail*, August 27, p. A16.

Houston, W. (1994b). "The 'Superb' Don Cherry." *The Globe and Mail*, January 14, p. C11.

Jackson, S. (1994). "Gretzky, Crisis, and Canadian Identity in 1988: Rearticulating the Americanization of Culture Debate." *Sociology of Sport Journal* 11:423–46.

Knowles, R. (forthcoming). "Post-, 'Grapes,' Nuts and Flakes: Coach's Corner as Post-Colonial Performance." *Modern Drama* 38.

MacGregor, R. (1992). "Grapes of Wrath (or Grapes of Gaffe.)" *Calgary Herald*, March 29, p. F6.

————. (1993). *Road Games: A Year in the Life of the NHL.* Toronto: Macfarlane, Walter & Ross.

Maki, A. (1992). "No Sour Grapes." *Calgary Herald*, November 11, p. F1.

Raney, M. (1981). "The Normalization of the Bigot: The Case of Archie Bunker." *Free Inquiry in Creative Sociology* 9:149–52.

Sports Illustrated. (1993, November 29). "Bad Influences," p. 11.

Said, E. (1981). *Covering Islam: How the Media and Experts Determine How We See the Rest of the World.* New York: Pantheon.

Scrivener, L. (1993). "Cherry on Top." *The Toronto Star*, May 23, p. D1.

Strauss, M. (1995). "NHL Faces Loyalty Test." *The Globe and Mail*, January 12, p. B1.

Tuchman, G. (1978). *Making News*. London: Free Press.

Young, K. (1991). "Writers, Rimmers, and Slotters: Privileging Violence in the Construction of the Sports Page." Paper presented at the annual meetings of the North American Society for the Sociology of Sport, Milwaukee, Wisconsin, November 1992.

————. (1993). "Violence, Risk, and Liability in Male Sports Culture." *Sociology of Sport Journal* 10:373–97.

Young, S. (1990). *The Boys of Saturday Night: Inside Hockey Night in Canada.* Toronto: McClelland and Stewart.

NO BORDERS, NO PROBLEMS: MIXED MEDIA, CULTURES OF YOUTH, AND MUSIC IN THE MARKETPLACE

Martin Laba

MARKETING THE GLOBE

"Planet Teen," an article that appeared in a Canadian business publication a few years ago, offered "a look at the promise and perils of selling to a young generation that knows no borders."[1] The article provided a strategic profile of youth and consumerism around the world, and served up a map for marketers and advertisers as they make their way through the nuances and complexities of selling to kids in the apparently endless economic horizons of the global marketplace.

Music, fashion, and fast food were identified as the key commodities, and as powerful purveyors of the culture of youth—goods that are consumed voraciously and that carry in their advertising images the conditions and capacities for deep identity investments. Global media marketing and promotional strategies of transnational corporations and transnational advertising agencies have been substantial and effective. The cola giants have done battle worldwide for the tastes and cash of "global youth" by regarding culture as a "minefield" to be explored cautiously and exploited smartly for local and national-specific appeals. The provocative print ad campaigns of Benetton have decisively blurred the distinctions between commercial and social advertising—clothes and social/global awareness are encapsulated and communicated simultaneously. Benetton has created a compelling myth of youthful unity, well-being, and multiracial harmony in bold and pristine representations of the young. The company has also distilled and packaged in riveting images for its ads (actually news photos), as well as for its promotional magazines, tragedies around the globe (AIDS, poverty, hunger, violence, environmental degradation). Young consumers buy social awareness along with their sweaters and pants. The Levi-Strauss corporation has created stylized, romantic images of American western ruggedness, images clad in denim and offered to fire the fantasies of young audiences already steeped in manufactured American mythologies. Sports shoes, fast food, rock and rap—the list of products and strategies of transnational youth marketing is considerable and ever-expanding.

Strategies of transnational manufacturers and their advertising and marketing divisions have worked to develop a global youth market since the mid-1980s, and this market has demonstrated a singular vitality and expansion and profit potentials. The assumption behind these strategies is that transnational conquests in the marketplace are in large measure the consequence of addressing the youth market as a globally united culture in tastes and sensibilities, give or take a few necessary adaptations to local, regional, or cultural differences. "Global messages," whether corporate logos for fashion or sports equipment, or sponsored social-awareness messages emblazoned on T-shirts, represent both the foundation and direction of a promotional culture of youth.

As "Planet Teen" documents, transnational advertising and market research companies engaged in global surveys of consumerism and consumer attitudes among youth, First to Third Worlds, have suggested that numerous young consumer groups transcend national borders and cultural differences in terms of market orientation and attitudes. These are groups of teens "almost alarming in their precocious levels of consumer sophistication and self-interested demands," whether they have the economic capacity to buy, or not.[2] Analyses of globalization, media, and consumerism that have moved beyond traditional "cultural imperialism" theses, have argued that transnational advertising agencies are not merely trying to sell goods around the globe (though they are doing precisely that). Rather, they are involved, as all marketers, in developing and promoting—"engineering"—social and cultural change conducive to the reception, expansion, and maintenance of a global consumer culture and of a relatively standardized global retailing technique—this is the professional practice of marketing and advertising.[3] Without a doubt, the scope and the intensity of the media presence globally have endowed the media with an unprecedented socializing efficiency—transnational media corporations have successfully tapped into, and promoted, consumerism and consumer preferences in the Third World, and elsewhere. As Armand Mattelart has noted, the enterprise of contemporary industries of cultural production is to develop and transform global audiences into consumers of transnational commodities.[4] And youth are regarded as the key and lucrative market for these transnational products. Train the young in consumerism, make those messages frequent, accessible, riveting, sexy, even socially conscious, and develop, expand, and sustain markets.

This profile of global youth is crucial for an understanding of popular music, clearly the eye of the global youth marketing hurricane, and to engage with the current theoretical debates around popular music, culture, and society. Further, this profile is important for approaches that seek to identify and elaborate the "national" character, strength, and direction of popular music (as in "Canadian music") in the prevailing communication and cultural contexts in which borders are eroding, and which involve the development of a transnational, nationless form of culture. This study examines the changing meanings of popular music in the transnationalization of music markets, musical styles, and youthful fans and consumers.

Mixed Media

In his discussion of the promotional dimensions of music television, Andrew Goodwin details the multidimensional nature of media in the business and the meaning of popular music:

> It is important to establish at the outset that pop music is, and always has been, a multidiscursive cultural form, in which no one media site is privileged. The implication of this for music video analysis is that it becomes impossible to understand the meaning of any individual clip without considering its relation to the wider world of pop culture....The commodity forms of the music industry are records, cassettes, and compact discs. These are products that have to be shifted in order to make profits. And yet these products do not sustain pop meaning, which has always had to draw on other forms—including posters, teen magazines, live performances, film, radio, and TV.[5]

As with music video, all forms of commercial musical expression are understood only in the wider, complex media environment. Music cannot be analyzed apart from the interconnected interests, orders, forms, and technologies of commercial media that structure, promote, and disseminate the widest range of commodities and messages. These commodities and messages—advertising images, television programs, popular film, fashion, and others—inform the meaning and significance of music for fans. In other words, an encounter with the media and market environments of popular music is revealing in terms of the ways in which popular music becomes meaningful within those environments.

The mixed media realities of popular music are basic to what Andrew Ross has called the "bone-crunching contradictions that have become a daily item in postmodern youth culture."[6] Recent contemporary popular musical styles and expressions, particularly rap and other hip hop forms, the diversity of club and dance music, and the wide range of rock forms still vital, have developed and thrived within the sheer and blatant materialism of the commercial media, its products and messages. Stylistic diversity in musical tastes, from hip hop to grunge, work to expand profit margins while they also serve the creative identity investments of youthful devotees and subcultural members. Rap, for example, has been celebrated for its political and oppositional significance and condemned for its complicity with consumer capitalism.[7]

In fact, rock music has served promotional interests for some time, and has served those interests well. Through the late 1980s, the rank and file of performers of mainstream rock and pop (Whitney Houston, Michael Jackson, David Bowie, Paula Abdul, Robert Palmer, Elton John, Madonna, and others) rented their faces and performances to soft drink companies. While Pepsi ads were particularly prominent in the televisual landscape, corporate rockers were to be found strategically punctuating the promotional messages for all manner of goods—junk food, automobiles, jeans, beer, and more. Rock music, both old and recent, was (and continues to be) hijacked, incorporated, willingly delivered, imitated, and bought out to serve as the soundtrack for promotion and consumption.

Today, in the constant shifting and repositioning of popular musical products in global marketplaces, the relationship between music and marketing is more intensely interdependent than ever. The technological capacities that provide for, and elaborate, this interdependence are decisive in the ways in which media are mixed and tied for profitability in the music business. The industries of cable and satellite-TV rock video, electronics, video rental, television and movie production and distribution, publishing, merchandising, and others, are fundamental to the media tie-ins by which popular music is produced and promoted, bought and sold. Major multinationals are engaged in the production, promotion, merchandising, distribution, and sales of entertainment goods around the globe. The bleeding of content, design, and production values between music, music video, fashion, advertising, television programming, magazines, and films is, in large measure, rooted in the multinational marketplace's "facts of life"—profitability and mixed media strategies.

In Canada, consumers spend over $1 billion a year for recorded music; globally, the figure approaches $20 billion. These figures do not include the additional billions in revenues generated and investments in the ancillary industries driven by popular music—the concert production and promotion industry, the video production industry, the radio industry, the cable music and satellite video industry, the home audio-equipment industry, musical instruments and sound equipment sales and rentals, manufacturing and merchandising, and royalty revenues. While this litany of dollar potentials offers a compelling economic statement on the well-being of the music/media marketplace, the meaning of popular music is found nowhere in these figures.

Throughout its history, popular music has always been a particularly contradictory cultural form. Musical goods and audiences are manufactured and assessed for market viability and profit potential; and at the same time, pleasures are taken within the confines of a market culture that at once limits imaginings and is the rich and vital ground on which imaginings are moulded and asserted. Youth is both a market, and a complex and highly differentiated range of cultural practices. It turns profits and it constructs urgencies and identities. Youthful fans, clearly the pivot of the business and culture of popular music, must be accounted for in terms of their relations to global entertainment conglomerates, and their continual, mostly unselfconscious negotiation of space and identity within those relations.

Taking Aim: Selling the Youth Markets

The confinement of youth, and the ongoing dismantling and remanufacturing of youth, is not a new phenomenon. The question to contemplate is to what extent the terms and degrees of this manufacturing of youth have changed in the contemporary conditions of transnational markets and mixed media. And further, how have cultures of youth continued to work out their places in the ongoing redefinition and shifting of musical goods in the marketplace?

The mechanics, strategies, and imperatives of that marketplace are central to these questions. There is a distinct pattern that runs throughout the media and marketing trade journals of the last 40 years—*Printer's Ink, Advertising Age, Sponsor, Billboard*, and others. From the concentration on "the teen" as a market segment in the post-war period (an invention which proved to be an almost immediate boon to emerging consumer-based economies, particularly in North America), to the prevailing realities of "planet teen," the marketplace has been the decisive ground for popular music production, use, and meaning. Since the earliest product tie-ins of the 1950s (music and film, music and soft drinks, for examples of the period), the ebb and flow of the music business, and the movement of audiences through the commercial and cultural processes of popular music, have been structured and tracked in a market landscape.

While "youth" was defined as a market category as early as the 1920s, it was in the postwar period that marketers trained their sights in a focused manner on this expanding segment—the "teenage market." The baby boom of the postwar era eventually "turned the idea of youth into mass market reality"—youth acquired both cultural and economic significance and power.[8]

The October 4, 1947, issue of *Business Week* ran a feature entitled, "Selling the Youth Market," a call to arms for marketers to get in on the enterprise of commercially exploiting youth. The article detailed the numerous and varied ways and contexts within which promotional campaigns could be carried out on behalf of manufacturers of youth-oriented commodities, and urged that such campaigns be tied to the preferred media and leisure activities of teens. Citing the findings of Eugene Gilbert's Gil-Bert Teen Age Services and the specific research data from Gilbert Youth Surveys, the article made the observation that for teenagers, "social acceptability depends largely on material possessions."

By the early 1950s, the marketing of youth was already in a frenzied state of activity. Betty Betz, writing for *Nation's Business* in January 1953, provided American business with some very seductive figures. She argued that retailers and advertisers who were neglecting the high-school or teen market were missing out on a massive profit potential. Betz created a marketing vision of a vast, virtually untapped, and enormously affluent segment. For graphic reinforcement, the article was accompanied by photographs of teenage girls standing at the magazine rack of the local drug store/soda fountain, bedecked in rolled up blue jeans, bobby socks, saddle shoes and penny loafers, plaid pleated skirts and blue jean jackets, engrossed in the pictorial fantasies of teen fashion magazines.

The demographic bulge of youth inspired marketers to wage a full-scale commercial assault on the burgeoning teen market. Product tie-ins and media buys soon became standard and effective strategies in the development and expansion of youth markets. In 1959, for example, Sales Communications Incorporated, a branch of McCann-Erickson Advertising Agency, devised "The Hi-Fi Club" for Coca-Cola, a massive media buy described in *Sponsor* as "the most exciting thing to hit radio in a long time":

> Cause of the excitement: the Hi-Fi Club, sponsored on some 325 radio stations by local bottlers of Coca-Cola and custom-tailored to fit the rather discriminating entertainment tastes of that mammoth—though shudderingly young (under 20)—population segment which plays a major role in helping Coca-Cola sell 23,243,819,904 bottles of Coke a year.[9]

Program packages of commercial scripts, playlists, merchandising and other promotional tie-ins were conceived and produced at a New York production house and distributed to designated Hi-Fi Club DJs at local radio stations across the continent.

Coca-Cola targeted and designed its youth market with precision, served up a formula of bland pop stylings and covers (Pat Boone, Julius LaRosa, Andy Williams, for example) with product tie-ins, and sold millions of bottles of their product.

Media marketing frenzies have moved in waves since the 1950s. In the contemporary context, the concentration of marketing energies devoted to the youth segments is substantial. Referring to 1992-93, Andrew Ross notes, "Not since the late fifties had American youth been scrutinized in such a frankly exploitative way."[10] "Generation X," "20-Somethings," "Baby Busters," or in the designation in the premier issue (November 1994) of *Swing* magazine, "The Paradox Generation"—the upper reaches of the "youth" demographic has been positioned as a particularly privileged market force. In his "Letter From the Editor," *Swing* publisher and editor-in-chief David Lauren rejects the notion of Gen X as an aimless and disconnected culture of "slackers," and provides an impressive clutter of glossy advertising (eight ads introduce *Swing* before the "Contents") to make his point. His editorial declaration specifies, above all, the economic power and influence of his generation:

> *Swing* is a vehicle for twentysomething dreamers and doers, once perceived as apathetic slackers, to recognize their potential influence.... We are a generation of 46 million strong with hundreds of billions of dollars in spending power. We have the influence to "swing" public policy and political decisions one way or the other. We influence the way major corporations act and the way advertisers market their products. We influence the songs chosen to be played on the radio and the films Hollywood decides to greenlight.[11]

This influence has been decisive. In music, "alternative" became a powerful and dominant form, particularly with the emergence of Seattle grunge, and its self-conscious (and thoroughly exploited) dressed-down style. While numerous "noize" musics have maintained their sonic assaults (industrial, speed metal, thrash, hardcore postpunk, and others) and inspire subcultural devotees to remain firmly outside the mainstream, numerous grunge and hip hop forms have been powerful modifiers of radio programming. Stations switching to "alternative formats" have experienced massive listening audience increases, along with queues of advertisers.

Music is situated as one of numerous, co-determinate commodities/identity vehicles available for purchase by the appropriate target segment. As Generation Next emerges as a dominant cultural and market force, music will continue to constitute a critical component in the mix of media aimed at youthful hearts, minds, and cash. As always, music maintains its substantial signifying power for youth cultures, along with, of course, its enormous profitability.

Art as Commerce

Criticism and commentary on popular music, both academic and popular, have asserted and supported an enduring set of dichotomies—art versus commerce, authentic versus commercial, original versus plagiarized. Michael Jarrett argues against such dichotomies and suggests that the "model of conventionalization" used to describe and analyze the progress of popular music mythicizes a purity and authenticity of "real" music in the context of popularization: "[P]opularization: the process whereby 'authentic' music (a narrowcast code) is translated into 'commercial' music (a broadcast code) for the purpose of selling music to wide audience."[12] This model has produced a "common sense" among audiences of popular music that see rock as a history of deterioration and degradation of authentic music (most often black musical forms) into commercialized, formulistic musical commodities.

Martha Bayles, for example, asserts that the "decline" of popular music is rooted in the ways in which the blues was "bludgeoned into 'rock,' 'hard rock,' 'heavy metal,' and beyond—developments that you need not be a philistine, prude, or old fogey to deplore."[13] Bayles maintains that current speed metal, grunge, and rap, among other forms, are evidence of the unsettling nature of contemporary popular music and its effects on youth. The anxieties and frustrations of youth are evoked with no balancing emotional influences ("tenderness, grace, and wit"), a balance which, in her view, has been a fundamental characteristic of the finest popular music.

Jarrett's metaphor for conventionalization is "compost"—as decay turns organic materials into compost, which itself transforms into new materials, so conventionalization creates the conditions within which innovation and musical renewal take place. Others assault the theoretical dichotomies around popular music by emphasizing the continual interplay between innovation, opposition, and the market. In his analysis of youthful popular expression (especially hip hop music, dance, locale-specific vernacular, images, and identities) in the context of "racialized social crisis" (unemployment, poverty, alienation, and crime among youth, and the rise of neoconservative political power in the United States), George Lipsitz offers a compelling case against culture-commerce dichotomies.[14] In particular, he warns that "market considerations" are never by themselves determining factors of cultural practices and, further, that commodities are invested in by youth because of the power of commodities to shape "the contours of personal and collective identity."[15] Media representations and consumer goods become for youth subcultures in crisis crucial identity vehicles to be appropriated, used, contested. In this way, consumerism is neither opiating nor passive, but a cultural practice of important symbolic dimensions, and a cultural space for the pleasures and struggles of identity formations of youth.

Tricia Rose's analysis of identity politics and style, rap, and the urban context offers a similar conclusion concerning the vital role of commodities in the communicative and symbolic dimensions of hip hop cultural practices.[16] She notes that hip hop has always been a dynamic and contested expressive culture, "articulated via commodities and engaged in the revision of meanings attached to them."[17] Above all, hip hop has relied on technologies and commodity systems (from DJs to rappers to consumers) to plunder, revise, invent, and create its sounds and images. This reliance and creativity, together with the reality that rap is the music of choice among youth in North America, that it cuts across national, regional, and local borders in its popularity, and that it is produced, promoted, and consumed in an intense media market environment, attest to the unviable nature of dichotomization concepts of popular music.[18]

Originality and authenticity in music have become increasingly problematic and unworkable notions in the realities of new musical technologies and techniques which routinely revise, version, and sample. Artistic creation, invention, and re-invention, and the everyday appropriations and uses of musical goods and symbols, are practices that are vitally connected to commodities and media technologies in the marketplace.

Dichotomization has also encouraged "active" versus "passive" concepts of audiences and consumption. The theorization of "active" audiences has often concluded a kind of "cultural populism," to employ John Clarke's term.[19] The power and decisiveness of marketing strategies and media technologies are somewhat obscured in accounts of almost "heroic" cultural practices in everyday life. As Clarke has suggested, "Cultural populism has been right to argue against the notion of the people as cultural dupes, but the alternative is not necessarily a population of cultural activists conducting cultural guerilla war."[20] The "use" of music does not automatically make for counter-hegemonic practices, and "resistance" is a term that overstates the uneven and contradictory character of social consumption practices by multitudes of fans in, and outside of, the mainstream of popular music. Still, the concept of "use" is key in the analysis of youth cultures and music. "Symbolic work" and "symbolic creativity" are notions that address the active, and often deep involvement, that youthful fans have in their music, and attendant dress and fashions, language, images, and styles.[21] In the everyday and commonplace use of musical and related goods in the marketplace, youth cultures engage in the "meaning-making" process of appropriating, recontextualizing, and transforming commercial sounds into personal and collective identities and pleasures. Musical and other popular commercial commodities are neither benign nor static, and as with the concept of "youth," "the music industry" is not monolithic. Meanings in music are never determined in the manufacture of commodities and images; but those commodities and images are "used"—reworked, redefined, made meaningful—in the social lives and cultural spaces of the young.

No Borders: Canadian Music, World Music

The contradictions of music and its images in the world market are considerable. This market both conventionalizes and revitalizes. In the mixes, shifts, and recompositions of cultural forms in transnational media networks and through borderless technologies of communication, this market both constrains, and is a rich and vital ground for musical expression and invention. Mixes, genre fusions, and crossovers of music of specific local cultures around the world have produced musical styles (bangra meets reggae meets rap meets dub meets techno meets rai meets acid house/jazz meets zulu meets rave meets indie rock meets soca, and the list goes on and on) that defy market categorization for an industry that works entirely by its capacity to categorize.

The recognition of a world culture has necessarily engaged persistent theories of cultural imperialism, and, specifically, notions of political and economic engineering of weak societies by First World capitalist societies. Dependency models are also inflected with the cultural imperialism thesis, as in the analyses of the negative impacts of an overwhelming U.S. media and promotional culture on other First World countries (Canada, Australia, and others). Leslie Sklair defines four main types of criticisms of cultural and media imperialism theories:

> First, what is often identified as "U.S. cultural and media imperialism" is really just advanced professional practice. Second, there are quite different processes at work in different countries and national variations can be more important than global patterns. Third, all countries develop internal cultural and media forces which counteract the external influences of U.S. cultural products. Fourth, U.S. media flows may work for as well as against national autonomy."[22]

These criticisms focus on the possibilities that national, regional, and local variations of cultural, social, political, and economic dimensions can be more significant than global patterns. As well, these criticisms point out that in an emergent world culture, no "total homogenization of systems of meaning and expression has occurred," despite the constant global flow of people, meanings, and commodities.[23]

Studies of popular music and world markets have demonstrated that the prominence, sweep, and penetration of U.S. commercial culture does not entail a corresponding degradation or subversion of established or traditional cultural values of a society, and that those societies possess and develop cultural and media forces which counteract or torque the influences of U.S. cultural products.[24] In numerous cases, indigenous musical forms of various local and national cultures around the world have modified significantly the directions, styles, and sensibilities of the most mainstream, commercial popular music (Jamaican ska, reggae, and dub, for examples).

The strategies behind "Planet Teen" are obvious. Transnational advertising and marketing contribute to, and are structured by, the conditions of globalization, and have tapped into the economic and technological potentials of world cultures and world markets. While the marketing of youth culture has pursued a global strategy of producing a uniform and borderless market for a myriad of image/style products—and to a large degree this strategy has been successful—a homogeneity of cultural meanings is not the consequence. The significances of cultural expression cannot be read through sales strategies and sales successes, and the volatility and complexities of cultural practices are always problematic, often uncontainable for the homogenizing intentions of global marketing.

Popular music in Canada demonstrates the same tendencies and contradictions as music around the globe, both within the country and in the relations between Canadian popular music and world music and markets. Notwithstanding Canadian-content regulations guiding production and airplay, the amount of music of Canadian origin cannot be regarded simply as a feature that sustains cultural identity. And the amount of foreign music available and sold in Canada is not automatically a demonstration of a subversion or erosion of cultural identity and values. The sheer density of transnational encounters and exchanges (through trade, finance, telecommunications, mass media, and other means) has meant the emergence of global musical, and other cultural forms, that defy notions of culture as an integrated or integrating system of common histories, values, sensibilities, experiences, and knowledge.

In the market strategies of homogenization and the realities of cultural diaspora and heterogeneity through globalization, Canadian music is not unique in its economies and cultural struggles. The ongoing significance and contributions of Canadian artists and music worldwide is unquestioned. At issue here, however, is the fact that Canadian popular music is one musical force in a global melange of forms and influences that cannot be denied or avoided. Attempts to limit conceptions of culture to national boundaries against the processes of globalization are questionable, and as analysts have argued, culture can be understood today only in continental or global terms.[25] The frequency, quality, and significance of cultural exchanges and influences in globalization, and the technological capacities and applications for stylistic invention and intervention in musical creation, unfold and are realized in a world context.

Whether produced in the severely formulaic demands of mainstream "corporate pop," or created in the mix and meld of musical traditions and expressions that have no borders, the popular music in Canada consumed by youth circulates in cultural spaces in which the "nation of origin" is increasingly difficult to isolate, and not a compelling feature in the use of and pleasures taken in music.

NOTES

1. Jim Cormier, "Planet Teen," *Vista* (October 1989):68–77.
2. For example, Cormier cites the Global Scan survey of consumer attitudes on five continents, carried out by the U.S ad agency Backer Speilvogel Bates Worldwide in 1988. Youth were revealed as highly materialistic, heavily involved in brands, driven to acquire, and consistent in consumerist aspirations.
3. See Leslie Sklair, *Sociology and the Global System*, particularly Chapter 5, "The Culture-Ideology of Consumerism in the Third World" (London: Wheatsheaf, 1991).
4. Armand Mattelart, *Transnationals and the Third World: the Struggle for Culture* (South Hadley, Mass.: Bergin & Garvey, 1983).
5. Andrew Goodwin, *Dancing in the Distraction Factory: Music Television and Popular Culture* (Minneapolis: University of Minnesota Press, 1992), pp. 25–26.
6. Andrew Ross, "Introduction," in Andrew Ross and Tricia Rose, eds., *Microphone Fiends: Youth Music & Youth Culture*. (New York: Routledge, 1994), p. 1.
7. Greg Tate, writing on commercialism of hip hop in the 1992 premier issue of the hip hop magazine *Vibe*, argued that the rage of rap has "boosted the profits of the record, radio, junk food, fashion, and electronic industries," and has the demonstrated but unrealized potential to push for action "towards bona fide social change." Quoted in Ross and Rose, *Microphone Fiends*, p. 1.
8. See Jon Savage's account of the postwar emergence of youth, "The Enemy Within: Sex, Rock, and Identity," in Simon Frith, ed., *Facing the Music* (New York: Pantheon, 1988), pp. 171–82.
9. *Sponsor* (1959, 30 May):29.
10. Ross, in Ross and Rose, *Microphone Fiends*, p. 4.
11. *Swing* (November 1994), p. 20.
12. Michael Jarrett, "Concerning the Progress of Rock & Roll," in Anthony DeCurtis, ed., *Present Tense: Rock & Roll and Culture* (Durham: Duke University Press, 1992), p. 169.

13. Martha Bayles, "Rock 'n' Roll Has Lost Its Soul," *Utne Reader* (November/December 1993):102.
14. George Lipsitz, "We Know What Time It Is: Race, Class and Youth Culture in the Nineties," in Ross and Rose, *Microphone Fiends*, pp. 17–28.
15. Ibid., p. 26.
16. Tricia Rose, "A Style Nobody Can Deal With: Politics, Style and the Postindustrial City in Hip Hop," in Ross and Rose, *Microphone Fiends*, pp. 71–88.
17. Ibid., p. 83.
18. SoundScan, the computerized scanning system of CDs, tapes, and records at the point of purchase that profiles not only sales for charting, but also demographics, offers an accurate read of who, and how many, are buying what.
19. John Clarke, "Pessimism Versus Populism: The Problematic Politics of Popular Culture," in Richard Butsch, ed., *For Fun and Profit: The Transformation of Leisure into Consumption* (Philadelphia: Temple University Press, 1990), pp. 28–44.
20. Ibid., p. 42.
21. See Peter Jackson, "Towards a Cultural Politics of Consumption," in Jon Bird, Barry Curtis, Time Putnam, George Robertson, and Lisa Tichner, eds., *Mapping the Futures: Local Cultures, Global Change* (London: Routledge, 1993), pp. 207–28; and Paul Willis, *Common Culture* (Milton Keynes: Open University Press, 1990).
22. Sklair, *Sociology and the Global System*, p. 133.
23. Ulf Hannerz, "Cosmopolitans and Locals in a World Culture," in Mike Featherstone, ed., *Global Culture: Nationalism, Globalization and Modernity* (London: Sage, 1990), p. 235.
24. See David Laing, "The Music Industry and the 'Cultural Imperialism' Thesis," *Media, Culture and Society* 8 (1986):331–41.
25. See Anthony D. Smith, "Towards a Global Culture?" in Featherstone, *Global Culture*, pp. 171–91.

CANADIAN HUMOUR IN THE MEDIA: EXPORTING JOHN CANDY AND IMPORTING HOMER SIMPSON

Beverly Rasporich

A long line of thinkers through the ages have argued that humour is not as funny as it seems. Sigmund Freud, for example, found jokes to be akin to dreams, and joke-telling, like dreaming, a means of releasing unconscious wishes, feelings, anxieties—even aggression. Since Freud's time, theorists of humour in a variety of disciplines have elaborated on the complexities of humour in its many forms. Pared down to its essence, humour is a sociocultural and group phenomenon, and the humorist a spokesperson for a group that shares common language, experience, attitudes, and value systems. The successful joker is in complicity with the audience, reflecting the group back to itself, affirming its identity. Consequently, the humour of a group can tell us much about its collective conscious and unconscious life (Sypher, 1956, 242).

Clearly, as the French philosopher Henri Bergson claimed in *Le Rire*, a person must first belong to the parish in order to appreciate parish laughter (Bergson, 1956, 64). In the first instance, however, we need to recognize that humorous parishes can be many and diverse and that we, as individuals, can belong to a number of them simultaneously. A humorous parish can be local, regional, or national; it can be rural or urban; it can be recorded via books and the media; or it can be unrecorded, transmitted orally between like-minded people and groups. It can be limited by gender, ethnicity, or religion, or any combination of these. One would not expect, for example, a group of football players in the locker room to be telling the same jokes as a group of female lawyers at a legal convention, unless, of course, they all belonged to an inclusive common parish. In Canada, we have had a broadly encompassing national parish of humour that has happily touched many Canadians, most obviously through a rich tradition of political caricature, comedy, and satire.

Beginning with J.W. Bengough's relentless political cartoons of Sir John A. Macdonald, and his drinker's nose, in the comic periodical *Grip* in the 1870s, comic assaults on Canadian politicians have contributed to a superior tradition of political cartooning. In the 1990s, in other media such as CBC radio and television, popular political comedy, like "The Royal Canadian Air Farce" and "Double Exposure," demonstrates that Canadians enjoy mocking and ridiculing their national leaders and pundits. Unlike the Americans who are less comfortable than Canadians satirizing their heroes and heads of state, Canadians have shown continually that they don't need to take their leaders so seriously. Given the legacy of a colonial past where the reins of power and privilege were held from afar in England, and held in respect by the colony, it seems that Canadians need to feel free to strike out at authority—to comically correct, dress down, or "send up" their less-than-sacrosanct leaders. In the words of the Canadian poet, Dennis Lee, about our ninth prime minister:

> William Lyon Mackenzie King
> Sat in the middle & played with string
> And loved his mother like *any*thing—
> William Lyon Mackenzie King (1981, 23).

Although Canadians enjoy this national sport of gleefully shredding their elected officials, humour in the national vein also acts like a community glue; it brings the country together in the country's interest.

Since historically the Americans have always presented a potential threat to Canadian national sovereignty, it is not surprising that they have also been a constant comic butt in the humour of the nation. Traditionally, by identifying and ridiculing the American threat, the Canadian parish has been kept on alert, and relieved of anxiety through laughter. This process was begun by Thomas Haliburton, the Nova Scotian judge who wrote *The Clockmaker* in 1835 and created the character of Sam Slick, the archetypal, enterprising, fast-talking American Yankee, for whom time and money is all, and who recognizes the wealth of the natural resources in Nova Scotia. The "sayings and doings" of Sam was developed partly as a cautionary tale to Haliburton's fellow Nova Scotians, and was published outside the colony, reaching international audiences in Europe and the United States in the 1840s and 1850s. As our first humorous export, Sam Slick ironically caused Haliburton to become known as "the father of American humour" (McDougall, 1958).

During the 1870s, the cartoonist Bengough also vilified the American national persona of Uncle Sam by presenting him as a would-be seducer of a young Miss Canada. From Bengough on, a permanent popular theme in Canadian cartooning has been American–Canadian relations, with many cartoons in newspapers across the country offering comic resistance to the possible threat of American domination. As well, a long suffering object of Canadian ridicule has been the American woman, who as a society figure was characterized as vulgar and indecorous from our British-derived perspective in nineteenth-century comic periodicals (Allen, 1967, 15). More recently, a visiting American female relative in the Canadian film *My American Cousin* is lampooned in the same spirit. Popular books of humour published within the country have also often appealed to the national parish by affirming the country and its differences from the United States. Eric Nicol's *The U.S. or US—What's the Difference, Eh?* comically trades on the distinctions, providing the serious message that Canadians want to maintain their cultural identity. In his anxiety about free trade, Nicol pens his final chapter, "Do We Conclude with 'God Bless Americanada'"? Similarly, "This Hour Has Twenty-Two Minutes," a current CBC program of political and social satire, points to the 1994 Grey Cup game won by British Columbia against Baltimore as a lucky thing, concluding, with some tongue-in-cheek, that we need, as in the Canadian national anthem, to be always on guard (against the Americans).

Although a fear of the Americans is projected through humour at their expense, we know that our attitude toward our neighbouring country is complex. In humour, it has been double-sided: our anxious disrespect has been counterbalanced in effect by an undeniable attraction. Haliburton's Sam Slick, for example, exuded a wildly appealing comic energy and applaudable enterprise; he was to be emulated even as he was presented as a threat. In contemporary light-hearted made-in-Canada films, cultural differences between Americans and Canadians are respected, but the continuous appeal of the United States persists. In *My American Cousin* and *Highway 61*, for example, contact with the American way of life is presented as humorous adventure. In *Highway 61*, a trip into the United States is entry into the land of the comically and culturally bizarre, but it is nonetheless fascinating.

Perhaps more important than our humour of disrespect and attraction for Americans is that, beginning with Haliburton, Canadian humorists soon learned that careful study of America and American behaviours could be beneficial to humour. Stephen Leacock, the Canadian literary humorist and political economist who became a national icon and our unofficial "official" humorist, certainly cast his humorously astute eye southward. Leacock, a prolific writer of humour in the first half of the twentieth century, did not believe that Canada had a tradition of humour and turned to the Americans for inspiration. He critically applauded the American tradition and its great humorists in his serious book *American Humour*. Paradoxically, in the process of writing his 33–odd books of humour and a number of serious books touching on Canadian nationhood, he himself set the standards for a national humour.

Leacock's Canadian humour included an ambivalent ironic stance, born of the imperial squeezes of Mother England and the United States, and presented in such humorous pieces as "Oxford As I See It." Here Leacock simultaneously pokes fun at both British and American systems of education. He also had a penchant for comic imitation through literary burlesque and parody—a talent which is perhaps a colonial legacy in that mimicry is one way of reducing the distance between one's self and the authorities. As well, Leacock held fast to a nonaggressive Victorian sentimental ideal of humour, which in its highest form is "where we mingle smiles and tears as we look down upon the vanity of life" (1939, 253). The proof that Canadians take humour seriously is that Leacock, both through his person and his humour, became a national symbol and helped shape the Canadian identity. In his person, mythologized in a famous Karsh photograph that shows him as a smiling, genteel, fatherly figure playing at being a farmer on his country estate in Orillia, Ontario, Leacock implicitly contributed to the national ideal of the amicable and somewhat rural Canadian. As a nostalgic humorist in the Canadian classic, *Sunshine Sketches of a Little Town*, considered by some as the most Canadian book ever written, and adapted for both CBC radio and television in the 1950s (Legate, 1970, 256), he tempered humour with humanity and helped to advance the ideal of a caring Canada.

Like Haliburton, Leacock also set a precedent for future comic artists in Canada by inventing humour that was North American in scope and appealed to a continental parish. In 1896, he wrote a national humorous classic "My Financial Career," more than half a century later (1962) made into an animated film by the National Film Board (Legate, 1970, 32). Leacock's creation of a man who feels little as he goes into a bank, only to be overwhelmed by the institution, signalled the beginning of an American comic parade of naive and neurotic bumblers. At the turn of the century, Americans and Canadians shared a fear and anxiety about technological change and the growing complexities of modernity. Leacock's "little man," who humorously offered resistance to banking practice, initiated a modern comic prototype that would include Charlie Chaplin's little tramp in Hollywood films, Dagwood Bumstead, the oppressed husband, employee and father in the comic strip "Blondie" (Yates, 1964, 223-25), and even Woody Allen's more recent existential persona in Hollywood film. At least one American humorist, Robert Benchley, acknowledged his debt to Leacock (Curry, 1957, 14).

Even as Leacock's little man was recognized by American critics as a typical North American figure, Canadian critics read in him nuances of cultural difference. For R.E. Watters, Leacock's little man archetype is firmly rooted in the ironic posture that is reflective of the inner strength of a small nation that has survived the imperialism of larger powers. Watters suggests that as powerless and subordinate as Leacock's little men may seem to be, they are in control of themselves. Although they wear masks of "calculated diffidence," their comprehension of self is full and ironic. The comic archetype is therefore "radically different in outlook from such a character as Benchley's befuddled little man in an incomprehensible world or Thurber's Walter Mitty, who can live only by escaping into a fantasy of his own making" (Watters, 1960, 31). If one accepts Watters's argument, Leacock's little man cannot be singularly described as a continental comic figure; rather, he is a tricky character who holds dual citizenship, passing easily as a North American, but remaining a Canadian.

Leacock, who understood himself and his humour to belong to print culture, was rightfully concerned with new technologies of communication and their impact on humour. In 1937 he acknowledged the developing technologies of radio, film, and television and anticipated the worst:

> Here is a new world of mechanical voices and illusive visions, of inconceivable rapidity, things made, executed, and forgotten in a fraction of a second. Here appreciation turns into a spasm, ecstasy to a twinge and humour to a bark. From the "bark" of a moving-picture audience one can perhaps forecast the outline of the "humour" that is to come—short and snappy, sarcastic—a bark, a snarl...."(Leacock, 1937, 231).

Leacock himself failed as a radio humorist in 1934 when he was commissioned to read sections from his books on a weekly broadcast. A highly successful humorist as a public speaker, he discovered that his successful live-lecture technique of chuckling as he developed a joke displeased radio audiences. He sounded self-satisfied. The humorist was forced to abandon his radio contract prematurely (Legate, 1970, 195). He need not have worried, however, about humour rapidly turning into jolts per seconds, at least in the Canadian media. The relaxed, thoughtful, pastoral—and Canadian—way of life that Leacock and his humour symbolized was maintained in subsequent Canadian radio humour. Rawhide was born on a Saturday in 1946 and grew into the national conscience of Canada with his satirical comments on Canadian institutions and personalities. This rustic radio character, a cowboy philosopher with a husky drawl, was created by the urbane radio announcer Max Ferguson, who, himself a CBC radio personality, kept Rawhide on the air for over seventeen years. Rawhide even went to Parliament when a humorless Toronto MP rose to denounce him for his "meaningless ravings" and "illiterate English" (Ferguson, 1983, 54). In the 1950s, another successful humorous radio program also projected a rural Canada, and the sentimental humour that Leacock favoured. W.O. Mitchell's *Jake and the Kid* series was set in Crocus, Saskatchewan, where Jake, the hired man, dispensed homely wisdom to the kid, and penetrated hypocrisy and social conventions in the interest of the human heart. In the 1950s, too, Wayne and Shuster as the country's national comedians, on radio and later on television, also remained much like Leacock in that they were fond of parodying European and American literature. Burlesque and parody were for Wayne and Shuster a mainstay. Wayne and Shuster parodies, such as that of the infamous *Julius Caesar* routine, burlesqued in an American vernacular ("I told him Julie, don't go!" became the often quoted line of Caesar's wife) also went over well in the United States. Their skits, too, sometimes smacked of American vaudeville, and echoed, with an Anglo-Canadian overlay, a familiar Jewish comic voice in American humour. No doubt American audiences responded favourably to this nuance. Like Leacock, then, Wayne and Shuster found their humour to be exportable to the United States. Paul Rutherford suggests that as "superb clowns," Johnny Wayne and Frank Shuster showed that "it was not impossible" to export "Canadian Pop-Cult"; "they appeared sixty-seven times on the Ed Sullivan show, far more than any other comedians" and their humour "pleased American audiences as least as much as Canadians" (Rutherford, 1993, 276).

In the 1970s, Canada's most successful funny men (and some women) not only proved that in the great Canadian tradition, they were brilliant comic imitators, but that they were now "plugged in" to media culture. "SCTV," the enormously popular television program that was produced in Toronto, delivered in Canada, and successfully exported to the United States, was a parody of television itself. With "SCTV," media humour about the media flowed easily across national boundaries, completely satisfying the comic tastes of Americans and Canadians alike—or so it seemed.

Rick Salutin has written about the Bob and Doug Mckenzie popular-culture phenomenon of "SCTV," explaining that when the CBC asked for an extra two minutes of Canadian content per show to fill in where the Americans ran commercials, the actors Dave Thomas and Rick Moranis created a talk show called "The Great White North." As the Mckenzie brothers with toques and bush boots, they were unlike any American talk show: they had no guests, no subjects, only "topics" that were Canadian in nature, like beer, snow chains, and back bacon. The result was a national craze, with Canadians across the country imitating the style of the Mckenzie brothers and a Hosers Parade held in Toronto. Salutin explains this mass appeal as that of Canadians discovering their own "voice" (Salutin, 1984, 269). "SCTV" proved, despite itself, that Canadians have an ongoing need to see themselves specifically reflected back, as Canadians, in humour. These "little men," like Leacock's little man in the bank, were nonconforming in the face of conventions. They struck a sympathetic response in the Canadian psyche.

In the 1990s, there is free trade in humour across the 49th parallel, with some attention still consciously being paid to national differences. In September, 1994, "Due South," a campy police series produced by Alliance, about a steady Canadian mountie with a husky named Diefenbaker who doesn't listen, and an excitable Chicago policeman, created CBS history, by being the first non-American production to be shown on prime time in the United States. The CBC continues, too, to present programs that are explicitly Canadian in their political and social satire. The homogeneity of daily urban life in North America and the ubiquity of American media culture, however, has solidified a North American humorous parish. Canada's talented comics have taken advantage of this broad parish in a way that is amazing (although not unpredictable, given our history of exporting humour). Canadians are not only creating humour from the margins in Canada and exporting it to the United States, they are, and have been for quite some time, producing it for North American audiences from within America itself.

Canada's Hollywood

Canadian comics have invaded the mass media in the United States; as the paranoid television spoof "The Canadian Conspiracy" revealed a few years ago, the Canadians, enemy agents, have secretly infiltrated the American entertainment industry. The Americans themselves have discovered that "Thanks to their nearly undetectable accent and their proximity to the United States, Canadians have insinuated themselves into the pop culture of the United States...."(Marin, 1993). Writing from the New York Times Service, reporter Marin continues,

> They are indeed among us but it's in the realm of comedy—on both sides of the camera—that their presence seems so weirdly disproportionate. Scratch the surface of television comedy over the last three decades and you'll find Canadian writers and producers behind such shows as "The Smothers Brothers Comedy Hour," "Rowan and Martin's Laugh-In," "The Sonny and Cher Comedy Hour," "Hee-Haw," "Taxi," "Fernwood 2-Night," "SCTV," "Major Dad," "Home Improvement," "Seinfeld," "The Simpsons," and "The Ren and Stimpy Show."
>
> Those familiar Canadian faces on stage and in front of the camera include Dan Aykroyd, John Candy, Martin Short, Catherine O'Hara, Mike Myers, Michael J. Fox, Rich Little, Phil Hartman, Rick Moranis, Dave Thomas, Jim Carrey, Howie Mandel, Mort Sahl, David Steinberg, Alan Thicke, the Kids in the Hall. *(Marin, 1993).*

The Canadian tradition of studying the Americans and their humour has paid off. As cultural outsiders, the Canadians have the advantage. As Martin Short is reputed to have suggested to Mike Myers, "When Americans watch TV, they're watching TV, but when Canadians watch TV, they're watching American TV. That distinction," Myers says, "makes you notice things" (quoted in Marin and Hustak, 1993). Canadians are also better educated in humour. They have a broader, more sophisticated experience of humour because of their experience with two traditions, British and American. Matthew Cope, comedy research archivist for the short-lived Museum of Humour in Montreal, points to the Canadian middleman position as allowing for a great range in the Canadian repertoire of humour. He explains that Canadian humour was born in part out of the more literate theatrical tradition of humour in England and the racy, physical comedy of the commedia dell'arte tradition, thus the ready appreciation of the "cross-dressing, pants-down humor of Monty Python's Flying Circus" (Marin and Hustak, 1993). On the other hand, the Americans, suggests Andrew Malcolm, former correspondent for the *New York Times*, "don't always get it" (quoted in Marin, 1993).

Canadian comedians and humorists have done well in the United States for practical reasons as well. Many of them had the chance for professional experimentation before they emigrated. Norman Jewison acknowledges that "By the end of the 1960's, American variety television was controlled by Canadians," and "Many...cut their teeth on CBC television" (quoted in Marin and Hustak, 1993). Second City, a theatre troupe based in Toronto, has also been enormously popular as a training ground. The patriarch of popular comedy in Canada, Frank Shuster, however, has a simpler explanation for why Canadians left in droves in the 1960s and took over in the United States. There simply was no alternative. "All those people who left in the '60's and did so well, the endless number of Canadians who left, went because they couldn't get their own shows here. At that time there was only one television network in Canada, and there were three in the United States. They went where the work was" (quoted in Marin and Hustak, 1993). The force of the cultural impact of Canadians creating the humour of North America is almost impossible to measure. Lorne Michaels, the Canadian who created "Saturday Night Live," underscores the need to compromise with American cultural norms. He recalls that when he first went to NBC, there was curiosity about his wish to do political comedy, one of the strongest traditions in Canada, "because it was a sure ratings killer." Michaels goes on to say, "America was founded on the distrust of authority. In Canada, you don't feel secure in that right, so you exercise it. Defying authority in a small way is a big Canadian thing" (quoted in Marin and Hustak, 1993).

The Canadian penchant for defying politicians through humour, while it is not wholly explicable, is probably a legacy of colonialism in Canada, possibly serving as a substitute for direct criticism or action. In any event, not suprisingly, like Canadians, Americans wish to see themselves, their culture and cultural myths, in their humour. One can only assume that the cultural history of America and its own myth-making must necessarily continue to dominate the made-in-the-USA media—and that Canadians abroad need to accommodate this reality. While Michael J. Fox felt that as a Canadian he brought a parodic distance to the arch-conservative Republican teenager he played so successfully on the long-running sitcom "Family Ties" (quoted in Marin, 1993), he nonetheless was playing a Republican. Similarly Norman Jewison, viewed suspiciously as a Canadian with suspect political tendencies when he wanted to make the satirical film *The Russians are Coming! The Russians are Coming!*, ultimately persuaded Hollywood to produce the film (Gzowski, September 9, 1994). Yet the victory was not as radical as it might first seem. The obsession with the Russians fit nicely into the Americans' cold war mythology, even if the satire seemed a daring Canadian venture.

The clearest contemporary example of the impact of Canadian culture from within the United States resides with the late John Candy. Candy died unexpectedly in March 1994 a Canadian hero, with news of his untimely death a front page item. Canadians felt that they had lost a personal friend in Candy who, before his passing, had become "a Canadian comic king" (Johnson and Gregor, 1994), and whose comedy was light years away from the jolts and snarls and jokes-per-minute demanded by modern media comedy. Candy was in the tradition of Leacock, a sentimental humorist, and like the old humorist, a national symbol. In his person, Candy was a gentle and kindly man, a "nice" Canadian who, even like Leacock, lived in pastoral retreat in the Canadian countryside when not working. His comic genius resided in his person—"of all the comic actors who have led the Canadian invasion of Hollywood.... John Candy had a singular quality. He could be as funny as anyone. But what set him apart was tenderness, a gentle emotional candour that made him instantly credible and lovable" (Johnson and Gregor, 1994).

Candy was clearly not in Hollywood's tradition of comic fat men whose personas had hostile edges. The legend of W.C. Fields included a hatred of children; Oliver Hardy often played an angry, frustrated recipient of Stan Laurel's innocent errors in their comic films, and Jackie Gleason in one of America's favourite television comedies, "The Honeymooners," played a raging comic bull. John Candy as Steve Martin's sidekick in the comic film classic *Planes, Trains and Automobiles* is a superb example of Stephen Leacock's faith that the most sublime form of humour is humour with pathos and humanity. While Martin plays a successful, rational suburbanite, Candy plays a not-so-successful salesman of shower-curtain rings who measures his life not by technology and the frustrations of the uncontrollable schedules of planes, trains, and automobiles, but by human interactions. Candy plays a version of a good wife in his caring after Martin, and his insistence on the importance of heart over head. As a Canadian, he takes up this role of playing a thoughtful feminine alter ego to an American protagonist with traditional ease. The mythology of Canada's feminine role-playing to her masculine, aggressive, continental partner is a well-worn cultural observation, but one that is often imagized to Canada's disadvantage: "The metaphor of a masculine America's penetration of a feminine Canada has been frequently evoked by those seeking a vivid imagery for the Canadian experience on a continent shared with an incontinent partner" (Manning, 1993, 4). John Candy's popularity as a comic and Hollywood hero with a heart of gold suggests that a different, more positive reading of Canada's metaphorical position in the Canadian-U.S. marriage is possible. John Candy proved the impossible, that a happy, overweight Canadian could go to Hollywood and become a comic legend, and even challenge the sexual stereotypes of mass culture by playing the romantic hero, as he did in the light romantic comedic film *Only The Lonely*. It seems that Candy and other members of the "SCTV" troupe such as Dave Thomas, Martin Short, Rick Moranis, and Catherine O'Hara have been contemporary trailblazers. They have led the way for other, younger Canadians like The Kids in the Hall, who are continuing the tradition of humorous export to the larger North American parish, but with somewhat more radical challenges to American humour and culture.

The Kids in the Hall—Pushing the Limits from the Margins

The Canadian television comedy program "The Kids in the Hall" is a new generation of Canadian humour which *Rolling Stone Magazine* proclaimed in 1987 "would change the face of comedy for the 1990's" (Simons, 1988). In 1994, the series began its fifth season. Broadcast first on the CBC, The Kids moved into the American market with a three-year run on the U.S. pay channel HBO and in the fall of 1992 moved to CBS and a 12:30 a.m. time slot. Once again, even as Canada recognizes her own offspring with prestigious Gemini awards for the Kids, they, and Canadian humour, successfully penetrate America. They draw six million viewers in the United States (Chidley, 1993). Like successful Canadians in America before them, the comedy team of Mark McKinney, Bruce McCulloch, Kevin Macdonald, David Foley, and Scott Thompson have had the professional and creative advantage of comic apprenticeship in Canada at Calgary's Loose Moose theatre where Theatresports, invented by Keith Johnstone, depends on teams improvising immediate comic antics based on a zany concept. McKinney is reported as saying, "Loose Moose...presented very few borders or walls. In contrast...it's almost impossible for young performers in New York to create and present original material" (quoted in Simons, 1988). It seems that the Kids have developed their original comic style with a Canadian sensibility that goes beyond Loose Moose. In contrast to the American convention of highly individualized stand-up comedy that is compatible with the Hollywood star syndrome, the Kids perform with the communalism that has often been associated with the Canadian character; they operate like a comic collective with no leadership, no one in charge. Even the writing process is a group effort (Simons, 1988), and in performance, it is not always easy to distinguish them, to put a name to the comic. Theirs has also been a marginalized Canadian underdog psychology, one which has contributed, suggests Lorne Michaels, to their "detached ironic style" (quoted in Lacey, 1993). Their name, however, which also betrays the psychology of the outsider, is rooted in the history of popular comedy in the United States. Jack Benny was reported to have occasionally used jokes from those aspiring writers who hung around studios waiting for a break; these were the kids in the hall. Nonetheless, the humour of the Canadian kids in the hall emerges from a much more liberal television environment for humour than that of the United States. In 1992 they had to adjust to a different set of standards at CBS, sometimes creating "two versions of the same skit—the unexpurgated one for Canadian television and a sanitized one for the U.S. audience" (Lacey, 1994)

The humour of the Kids, presented in a one-hour show format as a collection of skits, has been characterized as being "closer to Monty Python's Flying Circus than to 'Saturday Night Live,' which tends to media narcissism, to parody of television, media celebrities and the news" (Lacey, 1994).The ethos of the Kids in the Hall is absurdist in the style of Monty Python, but it moves beyond the Flying Circus, projecting a world of comic dream scape, peopled by the likes of the highly sexed Chicken Lady (offspring of a chicken and a lusty farmer), bearded wedding party (female), digitless waiters, a character with an Oompah band in his head, and even the body of God (which, once discovered, shocked the world with its small size). Dream scape also verges on bizarre nightmare as, for example, when a businessman bothered by his heart, which is interfering with his busy schedule, takes it out of his bloody chest to adjust it. The Kids, in fact, constantly test the limits of their audience's comfort zone about acceptable language and comic material. In one sketch, two young men are out for a good time with girls, and one is seduced by an aggressive bear-like man in a homosexual encounter that features in one frame the victim's bare backside. Other sketches don't even make it to the television screen. In the first season, CBC would not run a skit called Dr. Seuss's bible in which Christ is killed to Dr. Seuss verse, or a skit about AIDS in 1993 (Chidley, 1993).

This bizarre and absurdist comic universe inhabited by the Kids in the Hall is unique, singularly their own: "it's a place that is similar in shape to the world we know but not identical—more desperate but also more bleakly funny. It has a certain internal logic. It makes sense to them" (*Newsweek*, 1989).

The 1990s humour of the Kids in the Hall also has a strong vein of social satire. *Rolling Stone* acknowledges this dimension in its description of the Kids' early form: "The whole structure is new, sort of like jazz, with a Sixties-like conscience" (Handleman, 1988). Notably, homosexuality is a recurring topic. Through the ironic observations of a stereotypic gay character, the barfly Buddy Cole, and through skits that focus on gay characters and homosexual themes, the kids promote acceptance of homosexuality and gay rights. Although traditionally, homosexual jokes trade on the status quo, on the comic incongruity of sexual acts that are different from normative standards (Wilson, 1979, 228), the presentation of gay culture by the Kids is a sympathetically drawn mini-universe that has the effect of challenging the audience to accept its realities. Buddy is a charming and lovable person and a delightful entertainer in his many witty monologues delivered to the audience from a homoerotic point of view. In a discussion of virtual reality, he explains that he has just been auditioning a dancer for virtual reality, pauses pregnantly, and goes on to say, "He's hired. I thought that he was *really* sexy for a cartoon." "Virtual sex," he ponders, "that should be easy. Gays have been having virtual sex for years now." Undoubtedly, the Kids in the Hall are taking a risk that their mass audience of the 1990s will share their sentiments about sexual identity and behaviour.

"The Kids in the Hall" also demonstrates latent television content of the kind that "reflects symbolically, the structure of values, and relationships beneath the surface" of society (Fiske, 1978, 24). One aspect of the series' latent content is the message about gender that is transmitted through the cross-dressing of the actors (who play women's parts regularly, with variety and extremely convincingly). In Canada, this is arguably part of the comic tradition inherited from the Dumbells (an all-male troupe who entertained soldiers during the First World War and later toured the country), Monty Python, and even Wayne and Shuster, who delightfully played the Mothers of Confederation. It nonetheless remains latent television content that takes on a new significance in the gender-sensitive nineties.

An obvious interpretation of the male domination of the comic stage is one that any student of humour knows, that in patriarchy where men have social and political power and women have no voice, the traditionally male humorist reflects the reality of masculine authority, of the male as agent and the female as his audience. Female comics, of course, have begun to upset this status quo. The female masquerade of "The Kids in the Hall" would seem to go beyond this symbolic expression of social reality, however. Most certainly they undermine traditional sexual definitions. One critic discovers in them "a perverse androgyny" (Handleman, 1988, 14), while *Chatelaine* describes the Kids' women as "subtle postfeminist portrayals with character counting more than gender." It may be that the Kids' gender-blending through their assumption of female identities reveals an implicit North American preoccupation with, and perhaps acceptance of, some freedoms from stereotypic sexual roles in the 1990s. If this is so, then as Canadians they are well equipped to symbolically reflect this reality. It would seem that they have, in effect, internalized the "feminine" sensibilities of the national identity. In their assumptions of female roles, McKinney says, "We call it femming out—getting in touch with our feminine sides" (Lyall, 1994). In this comedy of the 1990s coming from Canada, a country, which like the Kids, thinks of itself as small and on the margins, the humour is largely subversive, both of the current conventions of American popular television comedy and the norms of sexual identity.

Importing the Simpsons

Despite the relative success of the "Kids in the Hall" in America, it is unlikely that they will appeal to prime-time America. That slot is reserved for the likes of "The Simpsons," an anti-utopian cartoon about family life in America. "The Simpsons" is brilliant satire that demonstrates the authority of both media culture and a commercialism that originates largely in the United States. These are the strong forces that help shape the audience and determine the parish for the humour of "The Simpsons."

In many ways, "The Simpsons" is all that Leacock feared about the future of humour in modern technology: the humour of malice predominates in quickly paced animated antics that refer back to real life. What he did not foresee is the extent to which media humour is self-reflexive. A significant portion of the humour of "The Simpsons" rests on the humour of media parody; television viewers of this cartoon often find themselves watching the Simpsons, who are watching television cartoons. Bart Simpson, the comic delinquent child, is perpetually and maliciously delighted with the cartoon programs of "Itchy and Scratchy" or "Krusty the Klown," which are parodied as violent and sadistic fantasies. This twinned comic fantasy of a cartoon within a cartoon imaginatively locates and locks the viewer into a closed-circuit television culture, a culture that by now has a history of generational audiences that includes the baby boomers who were weaned on cartoon humour: "Boomers who grew up on 'The Flintstones' and 'The Jetsons,' the last cartoon families to make it into prime time, undoubtedly harbor a soft spot for animated antics" (Watters, 1990).

Media self-referencing can, and increasingly does, command a historiography of media culture through allusions to past and passing media figures, events, and products; these allusions both assume and reaffirm a body of common knowledge with the audience. In "The Simpsons," media culture is substantiated and its "reality" authenticated by continuous references to media celebrities, television programs, and movies. Most of these are instantaneous, a quick comic fix, to those who happily know themselves to be "in the know." For example, a man in a motel room in bed with a woman is incidental to the main action, but he has one line to say—in a John Kennedy voice imitation. In a few mega-seconds, Bart looks out his window with binoculars to see a man looking back at him with binoculars who utters a few words in a Jimmy Stewart accent—and the reference to the movie *Rear Window* amuses the happy viewer as he or she catches it. Not surprisingly, comic books and television programs were the inspiration for Matt Groening, creator of "The Simpsons," which he admits was a "decidedly perverse take" on some of the most popular shows of his childhood like "Leave It to Beaver" (Kolbert, 1993). Groening's TV cartoon parody of a TV comedy underlines a recent sardonic comment about America and its culture by a broadcaster on CBC Radio's "Definitely Not Ballet," that is, that America is a plagiarized comic strip.

The electronic parish for humour obviously crosses national, and perhaps even linguistic borders, with Canadians, in fact, having been innovators in addressing this audience. SCTV was a parody of television, "Saturday Night Live," created by a Canadian, the same. In December 1994, a humorous French-Canadian film about man and the media, *Louis 19, King of the Airwaves*, was released in English Canada, with subtitles. The film *Wayne's World*, born of "Saturday Night Live" skits, also tunes into this audience when it takes as its subject the media. Produced by Canadian Lorne Michaels, and starring the Canadian Mike Myers as the adolescent hero, *Wayne's World* attacks the hand that feeds it with more clearcut satire than does "The Simpsons." Wayne and his sidekick Garth have an "amazing" cable access show, which is periodically presented to the audience on public access TV. A communications executive wants to buy it for commercial TV, having convinced an owner of a video arcade to be a sponsor. Although the satire of the communications industry is obvious, there is also the electronic comedy of slipping out of the conventions of narrative "realism." Wayne, a little-guy hero of right values and heavy metal mythology, drawn from the actor's Toronto experience (Marin and Hustak, 1993), speaks to the audience outside the story, and adjusts the conclusion of the film's plot several times as quick as the flick of a remote control.

Self-parody, satire, and mimicry of the media in "The Simpsons" and *Wayne's World* is clearly an expression of a media-wise and media-saturated community that is coming to learn media-speak. In the case of "The Simpsons," this language is also promoted through media-sell. "The Simpsons" are promoted via the media in a mass merchandising campaign and consumer sell of gross proportions. All manner of items, including key chains, watches, bubble gum, bed sheets, pinball machines, Nintendo games, mugs, towels, chess sets, cheese balls, pasta, and bread, are imprinted with the Simpson image and aggressively marketed. "The Simpsons" have demonstrated that humour of the 1990s, addressed to the electronic parish that knows no national boundaries, can be highly profitable.

Conclusion

In the past, Canadian colonial literary humour and satire have had audiences both within and without the country. More recently, television comedy and our comic talents have also been exported. Some of this humour and these humorists have been refined in Canada; others have been absorbed directly into the American media mainstream. It is clear that Canadian humour has a history of export because Canadians, as well as having a talent for comedy, have been adept at articulating the tastes and interests and cultural context of the larger, increasingly homogeneous North American, and electronic, parish. Partly, this understanding has come from *being* a Canadian, from observing from the margins and noting the differences between the Americans and us, eh. In the face of a pending massive electronic expansion, however, one of the questions that Canadians need to be asking themselves is whether humour created by Canadians for Canadians is becoming irrelevant. Of course, Canadians continue to tell jokes and create humour locally, but what of the necessity of retaining a national parish, of giving Canadians a sense of their own country through humour? More importantly, what of its continuing possibility?

By now there is no question that much of the media humour created in the United States has successfully vaulted over national fences, appealing to a majority of Canadians, even if the humour is located in the culture of America. The current popular comedy series "Seinfeld" provides a good example. "Seinfeld," who is a stand-up comedian within a sitcom, emerges out of the stage tradition in the United States where Irish and Jewish, and later Afro-American, performers have been urban comic oracles for well over 150 years (Rourke, 1931, 141). The program's locale, too, is rooted in the urban mythology of the United States; the urban backdrop, as well as the characters' lifestyles, are suggestive of the New York fantasy of the "big apple." Nonetheless, there is enough commonality of lived experience in Seinfeld's observational humour to appeal to Americans and Canadians alike. Would it matter, then, if Canadians were placed on an exclusive comic diet of the likes of Seinfeld? What if Canadians rarely, or never, saw Canadian politics, experience, history, locations, and traditions reflected back through humour in print or in the media? Is it important to foster comic programs like "CODCO," a television comedy delight that regularly expanded the Canadian Newfie joke to sublimely absurd heights of humour for a national parish?

We know that humour articulates the values of a group and cements its identity. It seems reasonable, then, that if we believe in our own identity, in Canadian standards, and in a Canadian value system that humour—while it can continue to be exportable—should also continue to be expressed to the nation about the nation in the Canadian media. Humour that shows Canada itself promotes national community and, logically, should be supported by national agency. It is obvious that the CBC both on radio and television has been the major vehicle for bringing Canadians laughingly together. To destroy the CBC's national mandate and to further diminish its capabilities is likely to cut the country's comic lifeline. Similarly, a healthy Canadian publishing industry is important to humour in print. A final argument in support of Canadian humour is one that many artists and intellectuals have given for other creative cultural expressions.

Humour that gives us back ourselves is integral to our imaginative life and fundamental to our "necessary awareness of the authenticity of our own lives." Otherwise, as writer Robert Kroetsch explains, himself no stranger to Canadian comic fiction, we will feel ourselves to be invisible (1993, 430). Canadians need to see themselves in their own backyards, or in the large country field presented by the "Kids in the Hall" as a place crowded full of like-minded, ordinary-looking women named Helen; this is a Canadian place where *thirty Helens agree* that Canadians need to know themselves *first,* before they can become humorous North American little men, or serious citizens of the world.

Note

I am indebted to the research assistance of Marie Rajic in the preparation of this article.

References

Allen, R.T. (1967). *A Treasury of Canadian Humour.* Toronto: McClelland and Stewart.

Barol, Bill. (1989). *Newsweek*, October 2.

Bergson, H. (1956). "Laughter." In *Comedy*, edited by W. Sypher, 61–190. New York: Doubleday.

Chatelaine. (1991, November). "What's So Funny About the Kids in the Hall?" pp. 119–21, 139.

Chidley, J. (1993). "Kids on the Ball." *Maclean's*, July 26, p. 41.

Curry, R. (1957). "Robert Benchley and Stephen Leacock: An Acknowledged Literary Debt." *The American Book Collector* 7:11–15.

Desbarats, P., and T. Mosher. (1979). *The Hecklers*. Toronto: McClelland and Stewart.

Ferguson, M. (1983). "Rawhide: Radio's Unrepentant Rascal." *Reader's Digest*, May, pp. 54–58.

Fiske, J., and J. Hartley. (1978). *Reading Television*. London: Methuen and Company.

Gzowski, P. (1994). "Morningside," September 9.

Handleman, D. (1988). "Hot Comedy." *Rolling Stone*, May 19, pp. 114–18, 152.

Johnson, B., and A. Gregor. (1994). Obituary, "Candy's Sweet Legacy." *Maclean's*, March 14, p. 67

Kolbert, E. (1993). "Simpson Creator Carries No Grudge." *The Vancouver Sun*, June 2, p. C4.

Kroetsch, R. (1993). "On Being an Alberta Writer." In *A Passion For Identity*, edited by D. Taras et al., 436–39. Toronto: Nelson Canada.

Lacey, L. (1993). "There's These Guys...." *The Globe and Mail*, January 29, p. C2.

Leacock, S. (1937). *American Humour.* London: Methuen and Company.

Lee, D. (1981). "William Lyon Mackenzie King." In *The Maple Laugh Forever*, edited by D. Barbour and S. Scobie, 23. Edmonton: Hurtig Publishers.

Legate, D. (1970). *Stephen Leacock*. Toronto: Doubleday

Lyall, S. (1994). "Troupe Pushes at Boundaries." *Winnipeg Free Press*, January 13, p. D6.

Manning, F.E. (1993). "Reversible Resistance: Canadian Popular Culture and the American Other." In *The Beaver Bites Back*, edited by D. Flaherty and F. Manning, 3–28. Montreal and Kingston: McGill-Queen's University Press.

Marin, R. (1993). "Trying to Remember When America Wasn't Canadian." *The Globe and Mail*, June 29), p. D3.

Marin, R, and A. Hustak. (1993). "The Funniest People in America Are...Canadian." *Montreal Gazette*, July 11, P. F1.

McCann, W. (1994). "The Kids Leaving TV for Movies." *The Globe and Mail*, February 19, p. C11.

McDougall, L. (1958). "Introduction" in Thomas Haliburton, *The Clockmaker*. Toronto: McClelland and Stewart.

Nicol, E. (1986). *The U.S. or US—What's The Difference, Eh?* Edmonton: Hurtig Publishers.

Rourke, C. (1931). *American Humor*. New York: Harcourt Brace.

Rutherford, P. (1993). "Made in America: The Problem of Mass Culture in Canada." In *The Beaver Bites Back*, edited by D. Flaherty and F. Manning, 260–80. Montreal and Kingston: McGill-Queen's University Press.

Salutin, R. (1984). *Marginal Notes: Challenges to the Mainstream.* Toronto: Lester & Orpen Denys.

Simons, P. (1988). "Rise of the Kids in the Hall." *Alberta Report*, July 14, pp. 44–45.

Sypher, W. (1956). "The Meanings of Comedy." In *Comedy*, edited by W. Sypher. New York: Doubleday.

Watters, H.F. (1990). "Family Feuds." *Newsweek*, April 23, pp. 58–62.

Watters, R. (1960). "A Special Tang: Stephen Leacock's Canadian Humour." *Canadian Literature* (Summer), 21–32.

Wilson, C. (1979). *Jokes: Form, Content, Use and Function*. Toronto: Academic Press.

Yates, N. (1964). *The American Humorist*. Iowa: Iowa State University Press.

AND ALWAYS WILL BE: THE CANADIAN FILM INDUSTRY

Seth Feldman

"Brazil," according to its weary cynics, "is the country of the future and always will be." To the equally weary cynic, the same might be said of Canadian cinema. For Canadians, the promise of a viable film industry is usually met with a well-weathered incredulity. Both the private and public sectors have promised us Hollywood North. And they have done so far too often. But have we really gained nothing? The question we ask here is not: Has Canada succeeded, or can Canada succeed, in creating a Hollywood North? Rather, it is the question of the relevance of that criterion as a measure of what has been accomplished. Similarly, the reality of Canadian cinema today must be measured against what it—or indeed any national cinema—can be. There is a second question: Have we built a cinema culture in which Canadian audiences are used to taking Canadian cinema seriously?

Parallel Histories

The answers to both questions are best found in historical context. Because cinema itself is part industry, part public policy, and perennially the product of changing social and artistic norms, the standards for judging Canadian cinema have evolved over time. During the medium's first decade, the potential for an indigenous Canadian film industry was taken for granted. There was no question of having to establish a Hollywood North because there was very little in the way of a Hollywood South. As the American industry developed, it became the model against which other national cinemas were measured. Yet that model has always been a moving target, subject to internal and external demands.

The several stages of cinema's invention came to fruition in the 1890s, the Lumière Brothers public screening of December 28, 1895, being the convenient if somewhat apocryphal date usually cited. In reality, work on the new medium had taken place simultaneously in a number of industrialized nations. The earliest stages of film dissemination mirrored its global origins. Typically, a French, American, or British crew arrived both to shoot and screen filmstrips lasting barely a minute. The event would catch the attention of a local photographer, showman, or other entrepreneur. In some nations—most notably Japan—the new medium was venerated as a technological wonder. In most places, it was soon submerged into the general run of novelties and entertainments. Either way, one of the selling points of the earliest cinema was its ability to present moving pictures from all over the world. Films from the original producing nations and the local offshoots circulated globally, their intertitles (when they had intertitles) easily replaced with local translations.

In Canada, the emergence of cinema fits well within this paradigm. The first screenings took place on June 27, 1896, in Montreal and on July 21 of that year in Ottawa. Before the turn of the century, foreign and Canadian cameramen had shot footage throughout the country. By 1914, American companies alone had shot more than 100 films here. The consolidation of that footage into longer productions also kept pace with world trends. In 1903, Joe Rosenthal of Desbarats, Ontario, made *Hiawatha, The Messiah of the Ojibway Indians*, one of a number of works that make up a body of early Canadian narrative films. In 1908, Ernest Leo Ouimet produced the first of a long series of newsreels and documentaries in Montreal. Other independent filmmakers followed.

If anything distinguished Canadian cinema during this period, it was the relative sophistication with which the medium was being used as an informational tool. In 1903–04, the Canadian Pacific Railroad (CPR) hired the Edison Company to produce 35 short travelogues and thirteen short dramas to lure immigrants and tourists to the Canadian West. Beginning in 1915, the federal government, as well as the governments of Ontario, Quebec, Saskatchewan and British Columbia, sponsored documentaries with increasing frequency.

The end of this first period of cinema history came with the emergence of the feature film. By 1905, the development of acting, filming, and editing techniques allowed filmmakers to sustain audience interest in increasingly longer films. Canada was part of this international trend, most notably in the Canadian Bioscope Company's production of the feature *Evangeline* in 1913. But the breakthrough film was D.W. Griffith's 1915 American epic, *The Birth of A Nation*. The unprecedented success of that work upped the ante of commercial filmmaking. Profitable filmmaking would now require substantial capital, teams of specialists working in elaborate production facilities, and large theatre chains.

Southern California, with its good weather, varied topography, and far remove from the supervision of New York investors, seemed like the ideal location for the newly centralized industry. By the 1920s, Hollywood attracted the best film talent in the world, a process that drained the pool of human resources available to national cinemas. Mary Pickford and Mack Sennett were among the first Canadian contributions. Hollywood was also a blender of international styles, successfully domesticating German Expressionism, Soviet Constructivism, and French Surrealism. Canada's contribution was less a style than it was subject matter: the Mounties, bush pilots, and indeed the entire array of what Pierre Berton calls "Hollywood's Canada" (1975). During the interwar period, Canada was in the avant garde of cultures that came to know themselves through their Hollywood (mis)representations.

Partly because of resentment at this cultural abuse and largely through their underestimation of Hollywood's mushrooming hegemony, a small number of Canadians attempted to create their own feature film industry. In 1919, Adanac Films of Toronto built a permanent studio in Trenton, Ontario. That same year, "Ten Per Cent Ernie" Shipman, an Ottawa-born entrepreneur with some experience in the American entertainment industry, sold Calgary investors on the idea of establishing a filmmaking centre. In the next four years, Shipman also brought the concept to Winnipeg, Ottawa, Sault Ste. Marie, and Saint John. These various Hollywood Norths financed seven films, some taken from the works of Canadian authors. The first of these, *Back to God's Country*, was an unqualified success. Subsequent titles fared less well, the last films not being distributed. Shipman left Canada altogether in 1923. The following year, Adanac's Trenton studio was sold to the Ontario Government Motion Picture Bureau.

Shipman and Adanac served to prove the limitations of the Hollywood North strategy. What success they had was more the result of an alternative production system, a model of regional, locally financed production, which, flawed as it was, led to the production of a few feature films. This model would be used again in 1927 to produce Canada's only First World War epic. *Carry On, Sergeant*, financed entirely by private investors, was the most ambitious Canadian film prior to the creation of the Canadian Film Development Corporation in 1967. However, the regional model's greatest success (as measured by number of films produced) came in Quebec between 1944 and 1953 when two companies, Renaissance Films and Quebec Productions, made some nineteen feature films.

The production of locally made feature films was, at best, sporadic. The filmmakers worked in isolation. Because movie-theatre chains were either owned or dominated by American studios, few Canadians ever saw the films. By 1930, Famous Players alone owned nearly one-third of the nation's screens. They and the other Hollywood studios forced theatre owners to show nothing but a single studio's films if they wanted to show any. At the same time, the American industry's relentless publicity machine ensured that even the relatively few independent theatres also screened Hollywood productions.

While the Radio League won its battles for the Canadianization of its medium, the federal government backed down on the issue of foreign control of the film industry. In 1930, Famous Players was cited under the Combines Investigation Act. The following year, the studio was found to have contravened the Act and yet nothing was done. Nor did the federal government show any interest in subsidizing feature film production. By the end of the 1920s, the Weimar Republic had underwritten the mammoth UFA studio, and the Golden Age of Soviet Cinema had been sponsored by the new Communist government. But beyond the creation of the Canadian Government Motion Picture Bureau in 1923, there was no desire to use federal funds to make movies.

The federal government's apathy toward the industry went so far as to subvert the one piece of legislation during the interwar period that did encourage Canadian feature production. In 1928, the British Parliament established a quota on the screening of foreign films. Thanks to Westminster's inclusion of Commonwealth films under the scheme, 21 "quota quickies" were produced in Hollywood branch plants in Western Canada. Made for the least possible money by skeleton crews and third-rate actors, most of the quota quickies were ultimately screened during the morning hours in empty

British cinemas. Canada did nothing to discourage these abuses. In 1938, the British, disgusted by Canadian quota quickies, specifically excluded Commonwealth productions from the theatre quotas. The branch-plant studios closed overnight.

PURPOSE AND STYLE

At the end of the interwar period, Canada had only one successful cinema strategy. Building on the early documentaries and the publicly financed informational films, the tiny Canadian industry began to attract some notice for its nonfiction films. The Canadian Government Motion Picture Bureau had a growing catalogue of practical if not terribly glamorous information films. By the end of the period, the Bureau had also produced two widely screened feature-length documentaries: Frank Badgley's *Lest We Forget* (1935), and his film *The Royal Visit* (1939). Private-sector filmmakers also produced notable work. Beginning in 1925, Albert Tessier shot 70 ethnographic films of life in rural Quebec. In 1932, Gordon Sparling made the first of his 85 newsreels under the title *Canadian Cameos*. And throughout the 1930s, Bill Oliver earned an international reputation for his wildlife films.

On the eve of the Second World War, Canada was ripe for John Grierson. He had coined the term "documentary" in 1926 and had gone on to produce and influence hundreds of British films. In the late 1930s, he had also pioneered what would later be called "the non-theatrical circuit," a means of distributing documentaries and special-interest films outside movie houses. Grierson was invited in 1938 to review the state of Canadian government filmmaking. The result of his investigation was the National Film Act establishing a National Film Board (NFB) as a coordinating agency for all public involvement with the medium. In October 1939, Grierson became the first Film Commissioner. The wartime need for propaganda and Grierson's own skill as a bureaucrat transformed the new agency into a documentary studio employing nearly 800 people, including a stellar collection of American, British, and refugee European filmmakers. During the war years, the Film Board produced more than 500 films and distributed them throughout Canada, the United States, and Britain. In 1942, it even won an Oscar for its newsreel *Churchill's Island*.

Grierson contributed not only quantity but also purpose and an aesthetic to Canadian filmmaking. The generation of young Canadians employed by the wartime Film Board learned to think of the medium as a pulpit to be used in the service of precisely defined social objectives. The Film Board's in-house style was a complex juxtaposition of image, narration, and music working at a tremendous pace to produce the impression of irrefutable logic. The world in front of the camera surrendered its identity to a metaphorical meaning (the shot of a city skyline, for instance, was defined by narration describing "the new horizons of adventure"). Whether they focused on global or domestic issues, the Film Board's bombastic documentaries were made to transform reality into saleable ideas.

The Griersonian aesthetic coupled with the new importance of film per se, gave Canadians their first hint of continuity in the development of a national cinema. After the war, Parliament would question the need for a Film Board. The Board would become a prime target in the Canadian Red Scare. But the quantity and sense of purpose of the Board's productions, as well as masterful lobbying by Grierson and his successors, kept it intact.

In the late 1940s, with the maturing of the first generation of Canadians at the Board, the authoritarian voice-over documentary gave way to experiments with less assertive, more contemplative work. The best films of the Board into the early 1960s represented a calculated dismembering of the authoritative voice in favour of a more ambiguous cinematic view of the world. Works like *Paul Tomkowicz; Street Railway Switchman* (Roman Kroiter, 1954); *City of Gold* (Wolf Koenig and Colin Low, 1957); *The Days Before Christmas* (Terrence Macartney-Filgate and Wolf Koenig, 1958); *Back Breaking Leaf* (Terrence Macartney-Filgate, 1959) *Universe* (Roman Kroiter and Colin Low, 1960), and *Lonely Boy* (Roman Kroiter and Wolf Koenig, 1962) insisted upon the vulnerability of the filmmaker's perception and, cumulatively, drew a portrait of reality as open text, free of any geopolitical preconception. The critic Peter Harcourt concluded: "There is in all these films a quality of suspended judgement, of something left open at the end, of something undecided....There is something rather detached from the immediate pressures of existence, something rather apart" (1977).

While the Film Board was developing its documentary aestheticism, it was also pursuing other avenues in Canada's strategy of alternative filmmaking. The animation unit achieved a growing recognition as Norman McLaren's *Neighbours* won the NFB's second Academy Award in 1952. Nontheatrical distribution expanded and came to include television. The Film Board's in-house laboratory was in the forefront of developing lightweight, portable filmmaking equipment. By the 1960s, this would make possible not only cinema verité documentaries but community-based filmmaking and low-budget feature films.

All of these developments took place during a hiatus in Canadian feature film production. At the end of the war, with the exception of Renaissance Films and Quebec Productions, there were no Canadian companies willing to compete with a Hollywood studio system at its zenith. The federal government would acknowledge as much in 1948 by secretly agreeing to what the Motion Picture Association of America called "The Canadian Cooperation Project." In exchange for some location shooting, mention of Canada in Hollywood scripts, and American distribution of NFB shorts, Canada agreed to do nothing that would interfere with the dominance of American features on Canadian screens. This included a guarantee that it would provide no federal support for a feature film industry.

The Canadian Cooperation Project was not a bad idea given the priorities of the immediate postwar period. Ottawa traded something it didn't have (i.e., a viable feature film industry) for the good will of Canada's major trading partner. The deal would last until 1958. But what no one could have predicted was the change in the structure of Hollywood that would take place during those ten years. No sooner was the Canadian Cooperation Project enacted than the American studios lost an antitrust suit that forced them to divest themselves of their theatre chains. The industry's prestige suffered as Hollywood personalities were dragged before The House Un-American Activities Committee. Most importantly, the advent of television cut deeply into

Hollywood's well-established distribution and marketing system. By the late 1950s, weekly movie attendance in the United States was less than half of what it had been a decade earlier.

At the same time, the very idea of Hollywood's hegemony was beginning to slip. The postwar generation of film goers and film critics became increasingly interested in the work of non-Hollywood directors such as Ingmar Bergman, Federico Fellini, and Akira Kurosawa. When the French studio system faced near collapse in the late 1950s, more than 60 new directors (including Jean-Luc Godard, Francois Truffaut, and Claude Chabrol) proved they could make highly successful, individualistic, low-budget features. In the 1960s, this New Wave model was repeated throughout Europe.

Canada returned to feature filmmaking with its own New Wave. The most important manifestations were in post-Quiet Revolution Quebec, where a number of young filmmakers had completed their apprenticeships with the National Film Board's French Unit. The unit had already made six features when Claude Jutra made his feature film debut with *À tout prendre* in 1963. The next year, Gilles Groulx directed a minor masterpiece of Separatist angst, *Le chat dans le sac*. Also in 1964, Gilles Carle was asked by the Film Board to produce a documentary on snow removal in Montreal. He turned the project into his first feature, *La vie heureuse de Leopold Z.* Jean Pierre Lefebvre launched his career with *L'homoman*. In 1965, Michel Brault, the cinematographer for much of the Quebec New Wave, produced his own first feature, *Entre la mer et l'eau douce*.

Compared to the charged political atmosphere in which Quebec viewed its New Wave features, the English-Canadian films of the period went virtually unnoticed.

English-Canadian features were hampered by the perennial problems of American competition and continued disinterest of film theatres. In Quebec, films could recoup their investments in a small number of urban cinemas. Theatre owners and their audiences recognized the work as part of an important—and marketable—cultural dialogue. Outside Quebec, neither the dialogue nor the recognition existed. Sympathetic theatre owners were few and widely scattered. And Hollywood was quick to respond to any proposal that would limit access to the Canadian theatres *Variety* counted in its totals of the American domestic market. At the same time, the NFB was wary of feature film production and amateurish in its efforts at distribution. The CBC had problems with the production values, language, and sexual content of the English-Canadian New Wave. The first feature was Don Haldane's *The Drylanders*, made at the Film Board in 1963. But the best known work of the period was a film which, like *La vie heureuse de Leopold Z*, grew out of an NFB documentary assignment. Don Owen's *Nobody Waved Goodbye* (1964), was an improvisational drama of teenage alienation in suburban Toronto. Even that film had to prove itself in a New York "art house" theatre before the NFB distributed it in Canada (where one Canadian theatre owner described it as "amateur night in Hicksville"). Still less exposure was given to micro-budgeted first films of directors who would go on to better things: Larry Kent (*The Bitter Ash*, 1963, and *High*, 1967); David Cronenberg (*Stereo*, 1969); Ivan Reitman (*Cannibal Girls*, 1970); Jack Darcus (*The Great Coups of History*, 1969); and Peter Rowe (*Buffalo Airport Visions*, 1967). Other promising English-Canadian directors had their careers stalled or stymied altogether by public disinterest. These included David Secter (*Winter Kept Us Warm*, 1965); John Hofsess (*The Palace of Pleasure*, 1966, and *The Columbus of Sex*, 1967); Robert Fothergill (*Countdown Canada*, 1970); and Clarke Mackey (*The Only Thing You Know*, 1971).

For English Canada, the great loss of the New Wave period was more than the obscurity of its own films. There was also a tragic lack of resources and foresight that left much of the Quebec New Wave untranslated. As the nation moved toward the October Crisis, there was little access in English Canada to these films' meticulously drawn picture of the mood and aspirations of a restless Quebec. Unfortunately, it was a mistake that continues to be repeated.

The First Age of Subsidy

Despite the difficulties inherent in feature film production, by the mid-1960s there was a growing consensus that Canada was ready for a feature film industry. The federal government's response was the creation of the Canadian Film Development Corporation (CFDC) in 1967. In theory, the CFDC was a bank whose job it was to loan seed money to projects whose profits would then replenish the fund to provide seed money for yet more films. In practice, the agency often found itself investing far more than seed money and seldom receiving any return on its investment. Potential filmmakers complained of arbitrary or politically motivated funding decisions and endless red tape. Policy analysts wondered whether the CFDC's first priority was to fund commercially or artistically viable proposals. Quebec producers complained of a bias toward anglophone filmmaking. And the CFDC did little to address the ongoing problem of distribution.

Augmenting the CFDC initiative was the establishment of the 100-percent Capital Cost Allowance in 1974. This generous tax shelter was meant to attract private capital that would match the government's seed money. The CCA generated the mythical figure of the upscale citizen eager to exchange his or her savings for the opportunity to appear under the klieg lights on opening night. The reality was that most investors found themselves lured into projects that had little chance of succeeding—or even of being completed. The glamour of Canadian cinema was soon replaced by embarrassment at the resulting product and no small degree of anger at producers, lawyers, and accountants who grew quite wealthy manipulating the system. There was also a good deal of discussion as to how Canadian these films really were. Despite an elaborate point system used to "certify" Canadian content, it was often hard to see how the resulting product advanced the national ethos.

But if the goals of the CFDC and the CCA were to convert a small but promising New Wave into a permanent institution, they did stumble onto some degree of success. In Quebec, the emerging directors matured. Gilles Carle made a dozen feature films during the 1970s, while Jean Pierre Lefebvre made eight. Michel Brault, who continued as cinematographer on (seemingly) everyone else's films, directed the definitive film about the October Crisis, *Les Ordres* (1974). Denys Arcand grew tired of censorship battles over his Film Board documentaries and turned to feature filmmaking. His *Rejeanne Padovani*

(1973)—in which actors bearing a striking resemblance to the provincial premier and mayor of Montreal end a shady construction deal with a murder—furthered his bad boy image. A very short list of other important Quebec feature filmmakers to emerge in the 1970s would have to include Mireille Dansereau (*La vie revée*, 1972); Francis Mankiewicz (*Le temps d'une chasse*, 1972); André Forcier (*Bar salon*, 1973), and Micheline Lanctot (*L'homme à tout faire*, 1979). The overall highlight of the decade, though, was the result of one of the Film Board's periodic efforts to join the feature film boom. Claude Jutra made his (and perhaps the nation's) greatest film, *Mon Oncle Antoine*, in 1971.

As it was from the beginning, the work of the Quebec auteurs was characterized by an ethos of entre nous. The films were thoughtful, wry, political, full of references to the events and personalities of Quebec culture. Even soft-core pornography, like Claude Fournier's enormously popular *Deux femmes en or* (1970), played upon common perceptions of a well-formed culture. In Quebec, the screen reflected a sizable and thoughtful audience participating in a cultural dialogue. Films caused scandals, sparked public debate, and served, on the whole, as proof of the reborn society's coming of age.

Quebec films attracted little attention in English Canada. This is one of the few things they had in common with anglophone Canadian features of the 1970s. Perhaps as a result of being made and screened in a vacuum, the films themselves tended to be self-pitying, immature, culturally vacuous, and often bereft of any reason for existence other than as an exercise in feature film production. Robert Fothergill, who as a CFDC script reader and film critic in the 1970s, saw an inordinate amount of this work, wrote: "it is very rare indeed to find an English Canadian film in which a male character of some worth and substance is depicted as growing towards self-realization, achieving or even working towards a worthwhile goal, playing a significant part in any kind of community, or establishing a mature loving relationship with a woman" (1977). It almost goes without saying that female characters were marginal at best, the losers' victims.

Despite this low-grade existential crisis (on and off screen), genuine talent did emerge and develop in English-Canadian feature films during the 1970s. The breakthrough film of the period was Don Shebib's *Goin Down the Road* (1970), whose naive Maritimers seem in retrospect to have been prototypes for SCTV's "Great White North" and fodder for Margaret Atwood's *Survival*. Among the most commercially successful of these films were Ted Kotcheff's *The Apprenticeship of Duddy Kravitz* (1974), and Richard Benner's *Outrageous* (1977). Peter Pearson made his fine realist drama, *The Best Damned Fiddler from Calaboogie to Kaladar* (1968), at the Film Board. He went on to the private sector to direct *Paperback Hero* (1973), and to CBC for the twin political dramas, *The Insurance Man From Ingersoll* (1975), and *The Tar Sands* (1976). In the latter work, the likable loser is Peter Lougheed (who responded with the very un-Canadian gestures of suing and winning his case). Other classics of the loser subgenre included Don Owen's *The Ernie Game* (1967); William Fruet's *Wedding in White* (1972), Jack Darcus's *The Wolfpen Principle* (1974); Zale Dalen's *Skip Tracer* (1977), and Clay Borris' *Alligator Shoes* (1980).

Of those who tried to break away from the loser film, the most notable was Paul Almond, a longtime CBC director, who attempted a self-consciously artistic triology: *Isabel* (1968), *Act of the Heart* (1970), and *Journey* (1972). Joyce Wieland tried to merge the experimental and feature traditions in her work, *The Far Shore* (1975). Two of the most commercially successful filmmakers of the 1970s were David Cronenberg and Ivan Reitman. Cronenberg's horror films (*Crimes of the Future*, *The Parasite Murders*, *Scanners*) and Reitman's *Meatballs* (1979) provided work for the infrastructure of the fledging industry while having very little to do with anything Canadian. And when the balance sheets were finally tallied, the box office champion of the first age of subsidy was Bob Clark's *Porky's* (1981), a teen film in which American lads come of age in a Southern brothel.

The Second Age of Subsidy

The mixed results of the 1970s and early 1980s brought about a re-examination of federal film policy. Unhappiness with the abuses of the Capital Cost Allowance led to a series of amendments to the tax legislation enacted in 1976, 1978, 1982, 1983, and 1987. The objective of each of these reforms was either to increase Canadian content or to tighten the means by which the tax credit could be claimed. Each initiative brought a jolt to the industry by both threatening its sources of capital and disturbing the sense of continuity necessary to attract investors. After 1987, the CCA became an insignificant incentive.

A similar unhappiness with the track record of the CFDC resulted in that agency's 1983 metamorphosis into Telefilm Canada. The change was aimed directly at the stalemate in film distribution. Most of Telefilm's budget went to a Broadcast Program Development Fund of $254 million over five years. The money was to provide one-third of the budgets of Canadian programs (not necessarily films) with guaranteed prime-time "windows." This move coincided with the licensing of Pay-TV services which, it was hoped, would use the funding in partnership with film producers.

As the CCA regulations tightened, and as Telefilm turned more toward mini-series and other television formats, provincial governments attempted to take up the slack in feature-film production incentives. The first provincial agency was Quebec's La Société générale des indépendant culturelles, created in 1977. It was followed by The Alberta Motion Picture Development Corporation (1981), Manitoba Film (1984), The Ontario Film Development Corporation (1986), Film B.C. (1987), and Saskfilm (1989). Including grants by the government of Nova Scotia, these provincial agencies by 1988–89 accounted for 27 percent of the public funding expended on feature filmmaking (Ontario Film Development Corporation, 1990). During the 1980s, Quebec also experimented with its own 150-percent and 166-percent tax writeoffs.

Public support for feature filmmaking was, by the end of the 1980s, only one part of the incentive for development of the industry's infrastructure. Federal and provincial arts councils provided support for small-budget narrative films, experimental films, and documentaries. Provincial and municipal film offices donated free services to film crews. Public funding also increased for ancillary activities and institutions: film festivals, cinémathèques, film publications, and training programs. In the late 1980s and early 1990s, private funding sources such as the Rogers Telefund, the Maclean Hunter Television Fund, and the Canadian Independent Film and Video Fund began to provide substantial sums for film development.

What Canada bought for all its film incentives was a ticket to the worldwide infrastructure that "Hollywood" had become. The lines between film and television production (not to mention cable, video, and merchandising) had blurred. Both capital and markets were as international as they had been at the beginning of cinema history. Japanese corporations were less interested in the Japanese film industry than they were in acquiring Hollywood studios. These studios, in turn, paid less attention to their own back lots than they did to the product (films, television series, made-for-TV films) they commissioned from independent companies which, in turn, shot the product wherever it was most economical to do so.

In English Canada, one of the most frequently cited icons of 1980s filmmaking was the imported garbage used to disguise Canadian cities as New York or Los Angeles. American style television series like *Night Heat* or the very American escapades of Reitman's *Police Academy* films were the most visible manifestations of a growing number of crossborder deals. Supporters argued that the people spreading garbage on the streets of Toronto and Vancouver were surrounded by ever growing numbers of Canadians in increasingly responsible positions. Canadian cameramen, editors, and sound technicians won the respect of their Hollywood counterparts. The American expenditures in Canada also generated an impressive multiplier effect through a wide range of specialty services—from entertainment-industry lawyers and financial services to laboratories, caterers, and equipment rental agencies.

During the 1980s, independent Canadian film companies were able to take advantage of this increasingly sophisticated filmmaking infrastructure. The most successful of these companies was Alliance Communications which, between its founding in 1985 and 1992, produced fifteen feature films and more than 200 hours of television programs. Atlantis Films, the creation of young Queen's University graduates, spent the first half of the decade making its reputation with documentaries like John Walker's *Chambers; Tracks and Gestures* (1982), and with adaptations of short stories. It went on to succeed in a variety of film and television formats sold in Canada and abroad. Rhombus Media, the creation of young York University graduates, won international recognition for its extraordinary films on the performing arts. Nelvana Films specialized in television series and theatrical animation. Playing With Time sold its "Degrassi" television series to CBC, PBS, and television networks around the world.

The independent companies as well as the institutional producers took advantage of the increasing internationalization of the film industry. The 1989, Canadian feature-film output included eleven international co-productions (Canadian Film Yearbook, 1990). Television movies like Kevin Sullivan's *Anne of Green Gables* (1985); Eric Till's *Glory Enough for All* (1988); and Francis Mankiewicz's *Love and Hate* (1989) cracked international markets—an achievement made all the more satisfying by their Canadian subject matter. Canadian features—most notably Denys Arcand's *Decline of the American Empire* (1986), and *Jesus of Montreal* (1988), and Patricia Rozema's *I've Heard the Mermaids Singing* (1987)—enjoyed respectable theatrical runs outside (and even inside) Canada.

The 1980s boom produced a new generation of feature filmmakers. Phillip Borsos's *The Grey Fox* (1982) was the first such work of this new generation. It earned him a ticket to Hollywood—and a ticket back to make the big-budget feature *Bethune* (1990). Atom Egoyan stayed in the Greater Toronto Area to direct seminal postmodern dramas: *Next of Kin* (1986), *Family Viewing* (1987), and *Speaking Parts* (1989). Sandy Wilson released her autobiographical *My American Cousin* in 1985, a film that did well enough to permit a sequel, *American Boyfriends* (1989). Wilson's very British Columbian tales were emblematic of the rise of regional filmmaking during the decade. Alberta-based Anne Wheeler directed two important works: *Loyalties* (1985), and *Bye Bye Blues* (1989). In Nova Scotia, Bill MacGillivray made the features *Aerial View* (1979), *Stations* (1984), *Life Classes* (1988), and *Understanding Bliss* (1990). Winnipeg produced a neosurrealist school of animation highlighted by films like Richard Conde's *The Big Snit* (1985), and Cordell Barker's *The Cat Came Back* (1988). A similar sensibility produced startling short films by John Paisz and Arthur Kroeker as well as Guy Maddin's midnight cult film, *Tales From the Gimli Hospital* (1988).

If Canadian filmmaking in the 1980s owed its prosperity to the decade's cult of free enterprise, it is not surprising that Canada's two largest public filmmaking agencies, the CBC and the National Film Board, found themselves under attack. Even before the Conservative government introduced its own version of Reaganism/Thatcherism, both institutions were encouraged to farm out more of their work to private-sector filmmakers. After the 1984 Conservative victory, the CBC was forced to do so amid continuing budget cuts. The Corporation's large overhead (increased in 1992 with the opening of the Toronto Broadcast Centre) left less room to manoeuvre. The situation came to a head in December 1990, when the Corporation was forced to choose between its ambitious drama program and its presence in local television markets. In a move that recognized the new importance of television in the production of Canadian drama, the CBC in fact chose to close its local news outlets.

The National Film Board faced a far more serious challenge. Private-sector filmmakers had always seen the Board as unfair competition. With the rise of a viable independent film industry, they argued that the civil service filmmakers were an inefficient anachronism. In 1982, the Federal Cultural Policy Review Committee (Applebaum/Hebert) bought the argument. For the first time, a federal task force recommended that the NFB be divested of all production. The Committee suggested that a much reduced Board remain only as a research and training centre. Predictably, the Board responded with considerable indignation. However, in 1984, it underwent a massive restructuring that cut a number of peripheral activities and aimed to reallocate resources in order to provide greater support for private-sector filmmakers. This did not protect it from cutbacks that further constrained its own production. As a result of the cutbacks, the Board's in-house filmmakers found themselves making fewer films. Some of the best left the Board entirely. In 1988, even the Film Commissioner, François Macerola, quit in mid-term to pursue more lucrative prospects in the private sector. The general gloom was such that the 50th-anniversary celebration of the Film Board—the cornerstone of a larger homage to Canadian cinema—was cancelled.

The filmmakers who remained at the National Film Board found themselves increasingly discouraged. In the early part of the decade, the women of Studio D made the Board's most popular film to date, Bonnie Sherr Klein's *Not a Love Story* (1981), as well as another Oscar winner, Terri Nash's *If You Love This Planet* (1982). Under the new policy, Studio D's directors were reassigned while the Studio itself became a conduit for funding to independent women filmmakers. In the same way, the Board chose to invest heavily in independent feature films. Its $5-million drama fund went only to outside producers. Far less support was forthcoming for the in-house Alternative Drama Programme that nevertheless released three popular theatrical features: Giles Walker's *90 Days* (1985), John H. Smith's *Sitting in Limbo* (1986), and Cynthia Scott's *Company of Strangers* (1990).

The transformation of the NFB from the centre of Canadian documentary to a support mechanism for the genre did little to interfere with the high quality of Canadian documentary as a whole. Donald Brittain, the most urbane and literate of Canadian filmmakers, had from the mid-1960s used the Board as a resource. Packaging deals between the NFB and the CBC, he made superb films like *Fields of Sacrifice* (1963), *Memorandum* (1966), *Dreamland* (1974), *Volcano* (1976), *The Champions* (1978), and *Canada's Sweetheart* (1988). By the time of his death in 1989, Brittain was the closest English Canada had come to producing a cinematic sage.

Despite the boom and the increasingly high quality of work being produced, the 1980s ended with a sense of foreboding. Tax incentives were largely gone. Telefilm Canada had overextended itself and, shades of the old CFDC, had sunk its money into a number of questionable projects. In 1989, the 85-cent dollar that followed Free Trade frightened off American production companies. The next year, as if in response to Canadian cinema's rapidly diminishing prospects, *Cinema Canada*, the industry's longest running and most influential journal, folded. And, as the new decade dawned, it became increasingly clear that the upcoming recession would be every bit as pervasive as the boom which preceded it.

Into the Nineties

Seen from the perspective of the mid-1990s, what is most important about the recession's challenges to the Canadian film is that the industry survived. Much of this durability may be credited to its size and diversity, much of which was generated by the unprecedented boom of the late 1980s. Between 1986–87 and 1990–91, by Statistics Canada's rather conservative definition, the total number of theatrical features had more than doubled, from 26 to 54. The total number of Canadian titles produced (films for television, nontheatrical films, short films, industrial films, commercials, etc.) had risen by 32 percent. In all, film and audio-visual production in Canada had gone from a $400-million to a $700-million-per-year enterprise, while distribution revenues exceeded $1 billion (Statistics Canada, 1992). Less conservative estimates produced far higher figures. The Ontario Film Development Corporation put the revenue generated by distribution and exhibition of all film and video in Ontario during 1988–89 at more than $2.7 billion (1990). Indirect economic output was seen as nearly doubling that figure.

Like other mature industries, Canadian film responded to the recession by downsizing and restructuring. Between 1990–91 and 1992–93, the number of people identified by Statistics Canada as full-time employees of Canadian film-production houses fell by one-tenth, from 33 000 to 30 000. (Statistics Canada, *Focus on Culture*, Winter 1994). But at the same time, the industry made far more extensive use of freelancers. Having bottomed out in 1991–92, the salaries paid by the industry jumped by almost 50 percent in 1992–93. The total salary figure was still below 1990–91 levels, as was the number of titles produced. Yet restructuring yielded a considerable increase over the 1990–91 profit margin. As of 1992–93, Canadian film and television production remained a $700-million-per-year industry in terms of its revenues. The significant change was that its expenditures dropped by ten percent to $637 million. (Statistics Canada, *Film and Video Culture Statistics*, 1994).

If there is one aspect of the Canadian film industry that has not undergone serious restructuring, it is its dependence on public subsidy. The late 1980s boom was to a large degree fuelled by an increase in public investment. Between 1987–88 and 1991–92, federal and provincial governments increased their direct support of the industry from $231 million to $341 million (Statistics Canada, 1993). Given the increase in production during the same period, public investors had succeeded in generating three dollars in economic activity for each dollar spent (a figure which excludes any multiplier effect). By the mid-1990s, the relationship between government investment and economic activity had stablized at two to one.

Given the deficit panic of the mid-1990s, it is unlikely that the public sector will sustain even so profitable an investment. In 1993, the Ontario government renewed its $28-million film investment program administered by the Ontario Film Development Corporation. However, Telefilm's Canadian Broadcast Program Development Fund—the largest single fund for Canadian production—slipped from $76 million to $65 million between 1990–91 and 1993–94. Ongoing cuts at the CBC threaten future production. Nor is it likely that other sources of public funding for film will escape the Chrétien government's determination to achieve major cutbacks. The first hint in this regard was a 1994 report commissioned by the federal government which reiterated the Applebaum/Hebert Committee's advice that the National Film Board's production function be given to the CBC and the private sector.

Certainly, the test of Canadian cinema for the remainder of the 1990s will be its ability to maintain its development despite inevitable cuts in government support. It is unclear how much (or if) the size of the industry will shrink in proportion to vanishing public incentives. In mid-decade, the impact of government cutbacks is mitigated by a persistently weak dollar. American films and television programs continue to be shot in Canadian cities; Toronto doubles as Chicago in the co-produced hit series "Due South," while the UBC bus was seen cruising through "Minneapolis" on an episode of "X-Files." But as trade barriers crumble and other nation's currencies become yet weaker, Canadian film, like all Canadian industries, will be challenged by the twin realities of a declining public presence and the growth of the global economy.

The least disputable fact about Canada's film and television production industry is that in the future, it will rely less on government incentives or protection and more on the established strength of its production and distribution companies. In recognition of this, private film companies are lobbying for a public funding system that would shift remaining public support away from individual films and toward the companies themselves. At the same time, the industry's traditional dependence upon protectionist legislation is shifting toward a reliance on co-production. As of this writing, Canada has signed 23 co-production treaties with other nations. Foreign, mostly American, production in Canada remains a significant contributor to the maintenance of the production infrastructure. Canadian film producers have been increasingly successful in exporting television series and made-for-TV movies to overseas markets. The internationalization—or "Canadianization"—of European television networks has accelerated (Ontario Advisory Committee, 1994), opening up new markets for Canadian as well as the ubiquitous American products. At the same time, the French success in protecting their film industry in the 1993 GATT talks, has signalled a determination to place limits on the hegenomy of the American-dominated international industry. Whether that stance will serve to keep film off the table at future free-trade talks remains to be seen.

Canadian filmmakers will continue to cross another sort of border, that between cinema and television. Increasingly, the Canadian film industry is, in fact, a television industry. Home video rentals and broadcast revenues have long since overtaken theatrical screenings as sources of revenue for filmmakers and production companies. Alliance Communications, still the industry's success story, has maintained its regular feature film production through television sales of both its features and the television series. And, possibly cognizant of the symbolism, the CBC in 1992 revived *Cinema Canada*—not as a journal but as a weekly showcase for Canadian feature films.

Proliferation of new cable networks and both cable and satellite pay-per-view services can only increase the importance of electronic distribution as a source of revenue for the Canadian film industry. The CRTC's 1994 decision to allow telephone companies to transmit programming over a proposed fibre-optic network may well produce a second cable system. Direct Satellite Broadcasting promises to become a significant distribution outlet by the end of the decade. Other new technologies will also have an impact not only in expanding the industry but in redefining it. Alias Research, a Toronto-based industrial software developer, has become one of Canada's major film producers through its sales of computer-generated special effects. In 1995, Alias was purchased by the American computer manufacturer, Sun Systems, with a view toward releasing home computing versions of its software. That event was evidence of Canada's participation in the new technologies of moving image entertainment. Hollywood is creating links with video game producers (whose revenues exceed that of the American film industry), and it might be expected that similar links will be developed here.

The net result of these trends is to define the Canadian industry's strengths as the services it provides foreign (largely American) producers, its television and industrial film production, its co-productions, and its small-scale niche filmmaking in areas such as documentary and animation. Seen from another perspective, Hollywood North—if measured by Canadian feature film output—is likely to remain as elusive as ever. Companies specializing in the production of theatrical features continue to lose money (Statistics Canada, 1992). From 1991–92 to 1992–93, the number of feature film titles declined sharply from 56 to 31 (Statistics Canada, *Film and Video Culture*

Statistics, 1994). Ironically, this comes at a moment when the Canadian feature film has reached an unprecedented level of artistic maturity. Art house, film festival, and limited electronic distribution, while not providing a dependable return on investment, have guaranteed a reliable flow of critical feedback and international exposure. Canadian feature films and their directors may be no closer to challenging the Hollywood hegemony (particularly in Canada), but they are becoming ever more familiar to the international community of serious film audiences.

In terms of both artistic and commercial success, David Cronenberg remains at the high end of the Canadian art house feature. Cronenberg is the only Canadian director shooting in Canada whose production budgets come close to Hollywood norms.

Beyond Cronenberg, the enduring if somewhat quixotic urge to produce Canadian theatrical features is exemplified by a number of gifted directors. In the early 1990s, Atom Egoyan built a strong international reputation with his films *The Adjuster* (1991) and *Calendar* (1993). His sixth feature film, *Exotica*, won the International Film Critics Award at the 1994 Cannes Film Festival. Other films receiving critical acclaim and limited theatrical releases in Canada and abroad included Richard Bugajski's *Clearcut* (1991); the Australian director Bruce Beresford's *Black Robe* (1991); Jean-Claude Lauzon's *Leolo* (1992); John H. Smith's *The Boys of St. Vincent* (1993), and Denys Arcand's *Love and Human Remains* (1994). Guy Maddin entertained his cult audience with *Careful* (1992), while an entirely new cult following formed around Bruce McDonald's wry youth films *Highway 61* (1992), and *Dance Me Outside* (1994). Quebec's most widely screened film of the nineties is Pierre Falardeau's *Octobre* (1994), yet another revisiting of the October Crisis. Other promising new directors from Quebec include Michel Poulette (*Louis 19, King of the Airwaves*); Charles Biname (*C'était le 12 du 12 et Chili avait les blues*); Michel Jette (*Le lac de la lune*); and François Delisle (*Ruth*). The 1990s have also seen the debut of promising ethnic films such as Srinivas Krishna's *Masala* (1991); Deepa Mehta's *Sam and Me* (1991) and *Camilla* (1994); and Ging Wee Dere's *Moving the Mountain* (1993). There was even room for a film about the Canadian film industry itself, Paul Donovan's merciless satire, *Paint Cans* (1994).

Documentary films have also continued to play a role in the national ethos. Despite Ottawa's growing impatience with it, the Film Board produced two of the most widely discussed documentaries of the early 1990s, Mark Achbar and Peter Wintonick's *Manufacturing Consent* (1992), and Alanis Obomsawin's *Kanehsatake; 270 Years of Resistance* (1993). It co-produced with the CBC an even more contentious work, Brian and Terrence McKenna's revisionist history of Canadians in the Second World War, *The Valour and the Horror* (1991). An independently produced theatrical documentary, Simcha Jacobovici's *Deadly Currents* (1991), provided a compelling personal account of the Arab/Israeli conflict. Ron Mann pursued his survey of popular culture with *Twist* (1992), while Rhombus Media released its most imaginative and widely screened work, François Girard's *Thirty Two Short Films About Glenn Gould* (1993).

As all these films, and the films which follow them, win their international awards and their day on the entertainment page, it becomes ever more certain that we will continue to see a Canadian film cum television cum electronic entertainment industry whose scope and products will be of at least moderate interest both within Canada and within the world's other Canadianized cultures. But is that enough? Or can Canadian cinema play a more central role in the national culture? In 1985, Bruce Elder, the most prolific and outspoken experimental filmmaker in Canada, published a manifesto entitled "The Cinema We Need." In it, he condemned narrative film per se (and to a lesser extent, documentary) as the manifestations of a broader acceptance of technological causality. For Elder, the structure of narrative cinema—from its corporate producers to the design of each film's shooting and editing—mirrors the values of a culture that habitually narrows its options to meet the dictates of predetermined ends. Certainty becomes the essential value.

Elder's way out is a recognition that Canada need not accept the teleological bias of Hollywood's use of technology. Citing Canadians such as Innis, McLuhan, and Grant as humanist alternatives to technological determinism, he argues that we deserve better:

> The makers of the cinema we need will be those who have the strength to abide with doubt and uncertainty and still open themselves up to unfolding situations, allow themselves even to be remade by experiences the destiny of which they cannot foresee. It is only through this process that truth will arrive.... (Elder, 1985)

Elder writes from within the third tradition in Canadian cinema: experimental filmmaking. During the 100 years of the medium's existence, experimental filmmakers have explored alternatives to cinema's prevailing trends and formats. They have forged a direct link between cinema and the changing sensibilities of the artistic avant garde. Experimental cinema is "experimental" not in the sense of providing new material for mainstream narrative and documentary filmmaking—though that indeed does happen (e.g., the use of experimental cinema techniques in music videos). Rather, the role of the genre within the larger practice of moving image-making is to remind viewers of the broader possibilities that lie beyond conventionalized practices. It is, in short, a way out.

The recognition of a role for experimental cinema in Canada can be traced back to John Grierson's grudging admission that the NFB could afford one animator. In 1941, Norman McLaren (and his much underrated assistant, Evelyn Lambart), began the Film Board's production of unconventional animation and experiments with cinematic formats. The tradition has continued into the 1990s with the work of new filmmakers such as Garine Torossian (*Girl From Moush*, 1993 and *Drowning in Flames*, 1994), and Erik Meade (*Warm*, 1992, and *Homebelly*, 1994). For the practice as a whole, the 1990s have seen an ever more intricate mix of narrative, documentary and experimental styles. Fleming's *New Shoes* (1991), Longfellow's *Gerda* (1992), Hoolboom's *Valentine's Day* (1994), and Zwieg's *The Darling Family* (1994), were all ventures into feature-length experimental narrative. These and other blurrings of conventional distinctions led to the Ontario Arts Council's 1994 decision to merge its experimental film funding with the funds set aside for documentary and narrative.

While they too will likely be impacted by future government cutbacks, Canada's experimental filmmakers retain a degree of public funding generally superior to that enjoyed by their counterparts in other nations. In art museums, festivals and cinémathèques around the world, their work has rewarded that support several times over. Hence, from a strictly aesthetic prospective, Elder's "The Cinema We Need" and his 1989 book, *Image and Identity*, are not entirely fanciful in positing experimental filmmaking as a model for the industry as a whole. Not surprisingly, the call for a reallocation of resources away from narrative filmmaking was forcefully rebutted in a collection of articles appearing in *Cinema Canada* (the entire exchange has since been reproduced in *Documents in Canadian Film*, see bibliography). Nor was it a particularly realistic proposal given the economic interests at stake. But what remains important in Elder's manifesto is its public declaration that Canadian cinema be planned as a proactive assertion of a national ethos rather than as a reaction to the prevailing trends in industrial development—that there be a purpose to finding its purpose.

References

Berton, Pierre. (1975) *Hollywood's Canada; The Americanization of Our National Image*. Toronto: McClelland and Stewart.

Elder, Bruce. (1988). "The Cinema We Need" in *Documents in Canadian Film*, edited by Douglas Fetherling, Peterborough, Ont.: Broadview Press. 260–71.

————. (1989). *Image and Identity; Reflections on Canadian Film and Culture*. Waterloo, Ont.: Wilfrid Laurier Press.

Film Canada Yearbook, 1990, edited by Patricia Thompson. Toronto: Cine-Communications.

Fothergill, Robert. (1977) "Coward, Bully or Clown: The Dream-Life of a Younger Brother," in *Canadian Film Reader*, edited by Seth Feldman and Joyce Nelson, Toronto: Peter Martin Associates. 234–50.

Harcourt, Peter. (1977). "The Innocent Eye: An Aspect of the National Film Board of Canada," in *Canadian Film Reader*, edited by Seth Feldman and Joyce Nelson, Toronto: Peter Martin Associates. 67–77.

Morris, Peter. (1978). *Embattled Shadows; A History of Canadian Cinema, 1895–1939*. Montreal: Queens-McGill University Press.

Ontario Advisory Committee on A Cultural Industries Sectoral Strategy. (1994). *Report*. Toronto: Government of Ontario.

Ontario Film Development Corporation. (1990). *Socio-Economic Impact Assessment of the Ontario Film and Video Industry, Phase I*, June 29.

————. Press Release, "Ontario Film & TV Production Sets Another Record in 1993." December 31, 1993.

Statistics Canada. (1992). *Film and Video 1990–91 Culture Statistics*. Ottawa: Statistics Canada.

————. (1993). *Government Expenditure on Culture 1991–92*. Ottawa: Statistics Canada.

————. (1994). *Film and Video 1992–93 Culture Statistics*. Ottawa: Statistics Canada.

————. (1994) *Focus on Culture* 6, 3 (Autumn).

————. (1994). *Focus on Culture* 6, 4 (Winter).

PART II

MEDIA, LAW, AND REGULATION

THE MEDIA AND DEFAMATION LAW IN CANADA

Mary Gerace Gold

The Defamation Debate

In recent years, particularly since the advent of the Charter of Rights and Freedoms, a renewed debate has emerged on whether Canada's law on defamation should be reformed.[1] The media regard the law as a serious impediment to their ability to cover important political, economic and social matters. The high degree of protection the law accords an individual who is defamed, it is argued, is out of step with the needs of a modern democracy that requires the press to be vigilant in its reporting of the wrongdoing of the influential and powerful. The proponents of expanded press freedom maintain that the press enjoys a special position in society because its primary task is to ensure that the public is informed of important matters. In so doing, the press participates in the democratic process and promotes the participation of an informed electorate.

Because of this important role, the argument proceeds, the press needs greater latitude in deciding what it can report. The existing law is weighed too heavily in favour of the defamed individual and, consequently, holds the media to a level of accountability beyond that required of other actors in other areas of the law. This often results in the press killing stories in which the public has an interest because of publishers' fear of expensive and protracted litigation.

Nonetheless, many have argued for no, or only modest, reform to the defamation laws. Canadian media organizations have become more and more concentrated in the hands of a few owners, who wield enormous financial clout and political power. These institutions shape the context for debate on controversial issues. Moreover, they often espouse points of view which support their own financial interests. Furthermore, many argue that the press has less interest in acquainting the public with the complexities inherent in most controversial issues than in attracting audiences and, consequently, revenues. The media are primarily in the business of entertaining the public through the portrayal of human drama, in the hope of increasing their market share. The competition this creates does not result in the emergence of "truth" but in sensational and titillating stories that focus on the drama of individual citizens rather than on the controversial issues in which they are involved.

Even if it were conceded that the defamation laws favour the claimant, most individuals who have been defamed by the press have no real recourse. Launching a defamation action is extremely expensive, and only those with extensive financial resources can match the deep pockets of media enterprises. Few prospective plaintiffs can afford to use the law as the means of restoring their reputations or seeking compensation for the injuries they suffered.

Few have gone so far as to suggest that defamation law reform should centre on whether the press ought to be completely immunized from defamation litigation. Agreement exists that the press should be legally and ethically accountable for what it reports. Differences of opinion arise as to whether the current law appropriately balances the protection of an individual's reputation with the media's right to freedom of expression. To address this concern, many reforms have been suggested. For example, some advocate that the plaintiff in a defamation action should have a more stringent burden of proof; that the media defendant should have available more precise, and thus more reliable, defences: that courts should be limited in terms of the amount of money they can award successful plaintiffs so as to ensure that defendants do not either suffer economic hardship or cease to report on important matters.

In this essay we examine the current debate on defamation law within its specific legal context of, first, the burden of proof which the law places upon the plaintiff; second, the defences available to the defendant; third, the remedies the court can provide; and fourth, the possible reforms to the law. The cases discussed include public figures involved in matters of public interest, as well as private individuals and business enterprises thrust upon the public stage because of their involvement in controversial or newsworthy events.[2]

It should be noted at the outset that, with the exception of criminal libel, which is a federal matter articulated in the Criminal Code, the civil side of defamation is within the jurisdiction of the provinces. While defamation has its genesis in the common law made by judges, a number of provinces have enacted statutes which have varied the common law. Furthermore, it is important to note that defamation law does not accord the press any special rights or privileges. The press is treated in the same manner as any other party sued for defamation.

The Plaintiff's Case

Central to any discussion of defamation law is an understanding of why the law would choose to protect the individual's reputation. The words of Shakespeare in *Othello* are frequently cited as a poetic statement of the law's protective principle, "Who steals my purse steals trash— ... But he that filches from me my good name [r]obs me of that which...makes me poor indeed."[3] As we all know and feel, how we are regarded by our peers and others has a profound effect on our self-worth and self-esteem. Aspersions are not only emotionally hurtful; they are frequently damaging to a person's psychological well-being. Furthermore, a good reputation often has a commercial value. For example, reputation can help secure and maintain employment, customers, or clients. Similarly, the loss of a good reputation can adversely affect a person's credibility and the assessment by others of his or her knowledge and skills in the marketplace. The law, then, seeks to protect persons from the psychological, emotional, and economic harm that defamation can cause.[4]

Defamation law, therefore, protects individuals' reputations from the harm caused by the dissemination of false information that could lower their standing in the community. While the law recognizes that every individual may be subject to scrutiny and criticism for their words and actions, it protects them from false statements that adversely affect their social position as well as their personal and professional relationships.[5]

A plaintiff who sues for defamation must be able to establish three main points: 1) that the statement was communicated ("published") by the defendant to someone other than the plaintiff, that is, to a third party (the term of art used for "communication" in defamation law is "publication"); 2) that the statement was "of and concerning" the plaintiff; 3) that the plaintiff's reputation was injured by the defendant exposing him or her to the hatred, contempt, or ridicule of the community.

This burden of proof placed upon the plaintiff has been criticized as too lenient, resulting in the plaintiff's being accorded an unfair advantage vis-a-vis the defendant. A comparison with the proof required in two types of personal injury cases illustrates this criticism. First, in certain circumstances, plaintiffs have to establish the defendant's intent in inflicting injury, that is, prove that the defendant intended to cause harm. For example, if the plaintiff claims that the defendant knocked him or her down, the plaintiff would have to prove not only that the act took place but also that the defendant intended to cause harm. Second, in many circumstances, there is legal liability if an individual while behaving in a negligent or reckless manner inflicts an injury on another person. For example, if the driver of an automobile hits and injures a person who darts in front of the vehicle, the injured party must prove to the court that the driver did not exercise reasonable care in driving the vehicle. If the plaintiff is unable to do so, he or she has no case.

In defamation actions, unless certain defences are raised by the defendant, the plaintiff does not have to prove that the defendant had what the law calls a wrongful intent or that the defendant recklessly or negligently made a defamatory statement. Thus, in defamation cases, intent to cause harm is irrelevant. The defendant is liable for the damage caused by a defamatory expression even if it is made innocently, and even if that innocence can be proved. Neither the making of an innocent mistake nor having an honest belief that the statement is true constitutes a defence.[6]

In addition to this fact that intent is irrelevant, the law also presumes that the injurious statement is false. The rationale most commonly given for the existence of this presumption is that requiring a plaintiff to prove a negative statement, that is, the falsity of a statement, is too onerous and consequently unfair. Consequently, the burden of proving that a statement is true, and thus not defamatory, is placed on the defendant.

The law is replete with examples of how the burden of proof that seems to favour the plaintiff can place a high level of accountability on the press. In the famous English case of *Cassidy* v. *Daily Mirror Newspapers, Ltd.,*[7] decided in 1929, the newspaper ran a picture of a Mr. Cassidy posing with a woman. The accompanying caption identified the two of them and stated that their engagement had been announced. Cassidy, in fact, told the photographer that he was engaged to the woman and gave him permission to announce it in the newspaper. The newspaper did not inquire further into the matter. Cassidy, however, was married to a different woman, the plaintiff,

Mrs. Cassidy. Although the couple did not live together, Cassidy visited his wife frequently. For most people, the announcement of Cassidy's "engagement" was irrelevant. The effect of the announcement on Mrs. Cassidy's friends was completely different. They believed her claims that she was married to Mr. Cassidy. Upon seeing the photograph and the caption, they concluded that the Cassidys were not married, that Mrs. Cassidy misrepresented their relationship, and that Cassidy's visits to his wife were most inappropriate. Mrs. Cassidy sued successfully for libel on the ground that the caption accompanying the picture imputed immoral behaviour to her for cohabiting with someone to whom she was not married. The newspaper was strictly liable for the defamatory statement regardless of the fact that it was misled by Mr. Cassidy's statements about his engagement.[8]

In an equally famous English case, *E. Hulton & Co.* v. *Jones*,[9] the defendant used the name Artemis Jones for a fictional character through whom he gave a humorous, but defamatory, account of the morals of certain English visitors in Dieppe, France. This name was the same as the plaintiff's. Even though the newspaper did not know of the existence of the plaintiff, who lived in a remote part of Wales, the court found the newspaper liable because those reading the account could reasonably believe that it referred to the plaintiff. Here the court stated that if a person, possessed of excellent intentions, were to publish a statement honestly believing it to be true but it is false, he would have no defence to a defamation action. Both cases illustrate how liability without fault places a heavy responsibility on the defendant. In the *Cassidy* case, the court stated, "To publish statements first and inquire into their truthfulness afterwards may seem attractive and up to date. Only to publish after inquiry may be slow, but at any rate it would lead to accuracy and reliability."[10]

Repeating a defamatory statement that originated with someone else also constitutes legal liability. In fact, every repetition of a defamatory statement is considered a new publication giving rise to a separate cause of action. The fact that it is a current rumour and those repeating it think it is true does not relieve them of liability. Nor is an individual protected from liability by naming the original source or by expressly disavowing the truth of the statement.

If a plaintiff succeeds in proving libel, the law presumes that he or she was injured and is therefore entitled to damages in the form of monetary compensation. During the past few years, the amount of such awards has been increasing. In 1988, the Supreme Court of Canada restored a jury award of $135 000 even though the Court admitted that it appeared high.[11] In 1992, the British Columbia Court of Appeal decided an award of $400 000 was excessive.[12] The largest award to date was one for $1.6 million that was affirmed by the Ontario Court of Appeal in 1994.[13]

A plaintiff and defendant in a case will often disagree as to whether the offending statement is defamatory. In making a determination on this issue, the court will take into consideration the ordinary and natural meaning of the words and the effect they would have on a reasonable person of average intelligence and experience. It will consider all the surrounding circumstances including the publication as a whole, the context and setting in which the words were published, and the audience to whom they were addressed. Articles will be considered together with any illustrations; pictures will be viewed with captions; and stories will be read with their headlines. When the defamation is contained in a television broadcast or a film, the court will examine the impression created by the juxtaposition of shots and the interplay among the visual content, the dialogue, and the voice-over.[14]

The following examination of two contemporary cases in which plaintiffs were successful in their defamation claims will illustrate the kinds of statements that constitute defamation and will describe the injuries sustained by the plaintiffs.

The case, of *Vogel* v. *CBC, Bird and Good*,[15] tried by the British Columbia Supreme Court in 1981, provides a good example of what constitutes a defamatory communication. It also illustrates how a reporter's zeal to expose corruption in the Ministry of the Attorney General resulted in his exercising inexcusably bad judgement and inflicting irreparable harm on the claimant. Mr. Vogel, the claimant, was the Deputy Attorney General of British Columbia. Complaints had been made that he had acted improperly in his dealing with a judge of the Provincial Court. An inquiry into the matter found that Vogel engaged in some inappropriate communications with a judge and "displayed an attitude inconsistent with the independence of the judiciary." The inquiry concluded, however, that these communications "were not made with an evil intent."[16] The inquiry recommended that no disciplinary action be taken.

When the report was made public, the CBC decided to investigate the matter further. One of the Corporation's investigative reporters, relying upon a source within the Ministry of the Attorney General who had a personal motive in seeing Vogel dismissed from his position, produced a story which accused Vogel of "trying to influence the course of justice... for the purpose of protecting his friends." [17] The CBC carried the story both regionally and nationally. As a result of the report, the opposition party in the B.C. House demanded that the Attorney General's offices be "padlocked and that the Chief Justice of British Columbia take immediate control"[18] of the Ministry of Justice. Newspapers picked up the story and demanded Vogel's resignation. Vogel was suspended from his post for two weeks until the completion of an investigation. He was quickly exonerated and returned to his job.

The court analyzed at length both the investigative techniques used by the reporter and the editorial oversight exercised by the CBC staff. It found that the reporter was so intent on breaking this sensational story that he lost all objectivity in the matter. He ingenuously believed everything his source told him. Despite interviewing many people who would have been aware of the alleged wrongdoing, the reporter could not find anyone able to corroborate his source's story. Even the source's own letters, written to superiors within the ministry, contradicted his own accusation of Vogel's wrongdoing. The reporter ignored all of the evidence inconsistent with the premise that Vogel engaged in corrupt behaviour. The CBC editorial staff, although it was aware of the reporter's lack of objectivity on the matter, did not inquire into the reporter's sources or subject the story "to scrutiny by someone who could view it objectively."[19]

The effects of the defamation upon Vogel were both immediate and lasting. Members of the press, some accompanied by camera crews, positioned themselves outside his home. This situation made it impossible for Vogel and his family to enjoy any respite from the controversy. The court noted that the plaintiff seemed to become depressed, finding it difficult to do his job effectively while the controversy raged.

Vogel also felt that he had lost the confidence and respect of those with whom he worked. Even the morale within the ministry was affected.

The court, in ruling that the CBC story constituted defamation, commented on how Vogel's reputation was damaged. It noted that Vogel was a lawyer and that one of the qualities the public expects of lawyers is integrity. The false accusation constituted a massive attack on his integrity and, as a result, created a stigma that would never be erased, even though Vogel was exonerated. The court held that, in addition to causing significant emotional distress to Vogel and his family, the stigma could very well affect his earning power should he decide to seek employment outside the ministry. The cloud of alleged wrongdoing would never disappear.

Yet critics of the present law maintain that the public has a right to know of allegations that have been made against public officials, even though these allegations may turn out to be unfounded. They claim that the interest in a free and vocal press should outweigh the protection of individuals from hurt feelings caused by false allegations and even the damage to a career such statements might cause[20] those in the public eye should be made of sterner stuff and learn to tolerate relentless press scrutiny.

The recent Ontario case *Color Your World* v. *Canadian Broadcasting Corporation et al.* [21] provides another example of a successful defamation claim. The case concerned a segment on the television program "Market Place" that discussed the health risks created by the use of mercury in latex paint. Color Your World was identified as one of three manufacturers (eleven were surveyed) whose paints contained the highest levels of mercury. The dangers of mercury poisoning were illustrated with archival footage depicting fish being caught in the waters of Minamata Bay in Japan and Grassy Narrows in Ontario. The shots of the two locations were juxtaposed with shots of paint cans being filled. The voice-over stated that fish from Minamata Bay and Grassy Narrows were contaminated with mercury. Some of those who ate the fish died while others suffered from tunnel vision, a lack of coordination, and other symptoms of mercury poisoning. No mention was made that the type of mercury used in latex paint was different from and significantly less toxic than that which caused the health problems in Japan and Ontario. Furthermore, the program did not state that the mercury used in latex paint did not appear to cause a health hazard once the paint had dried. These facts were, however, known to the CBC. Finally, the CBC was aware that Color Your World was phasing out the use of mercury in latex paint.

The repercussions of the program on the plaintiff were immediate. Competitors used the information to stress the superiority of their paints. Customers complained about being put at risk, and retailers expressed fear that they were unknowingly selling a highly toxic product. Color Your World lost a number of lucrative contracts because of the bad publicity it had received on the "Market Place" segment. The plaintiff had to engage in extensive damage control to protect its name and its product.

The CBC asserted that the statement was not defamatory because Color Your World paint did contain mercury. The plaintiff, conceding that it did use mercury in some of its latex paint, argued that the broadcast had to be looked at as a whole. The inclusion of the segments on mercury poisoning in Japan and Ontario created the impression that the plaintiff was knowingly selling paints that caused a significant health risk to customers.

Audiences would conclude from the presentation that the Color Your World paint contained the same kind of mercury caused poisoning and death in Ontario and Japan.

The court held in the plaintiff's favour, finding that Color Your World was defamed. In concluding its analysis of the broadcast, the court noted that the CBC saw as its priority the creation of a program which would have "a more dramatic impact."[22] Information that would dilute this impact was omitted. The CBC in choosing to stress the dramatic failed to meet its "duty to produce a balanced show."[23]

The courts that decided the *Vogel* and *Color Your World* cases engaged in painstaking analysis of not only the final programs containing the defamations but also of the entire production process from initial research to final form. In the *Color Your World* case, for example, the court examined all of the raw material for the program including various research memoranda on the topic, the shooting script, the editing script, and the out-takes of the interviews conducted. This information enabled the court to better understand the editorial process and to determine how the defamation arose.

The press would prefer that such information remain confidential. The rules for discovery in civil litigation cases, however, give the plaintiff the right to obtain access to such information when the truthfulness of the alleged defamatory statement is at issue or when other defences are raised. Critics of the defamation laws contend that liberal discovery rules enable disgruntled prospective plaintiffs to engage in "fishing expeditions" in order to determine the nature of and potential harm caused by the information that has been collected. This tactic is said to intimidate press organizations and make them less willing to cover important stories about powerful individuals who would be quick to file vexatious claims.[24]

Furthermore, reporters have an interest in protecting the identity of sources and informants who have been assured anonymity. Such sources can be indispensable to the reporter's investigation of sensitive stories relating to wrongdoing on the part of government officials or corporate enterprises. The confidentiality of sources frequently serves the free press interest by enabling the media to function as a check on the abuses of government and private enterprise alike. To deprive defendants completely of the ability to protect confidential sources during the discovery process might constitute too great an incursion on the free press interest. The amount of protection the courts now provide for confidential sources will be discussed later in the essay.

Some also express concern that the discovery process can be used to call into question the credibility of the media organization. When the news gathering process is held to intense scrutiny, the flaws in the process are likely to be revealed. One can argue, however, that media accountability is an important dimension of a free press. Furthermore, if members of the public are aware of circumstances in which the media's manipulation of facts in the interest of producing a compelling story can result in defamation, they are more likely to approach press reports with a healthy scepticism.[25]

The Defences

That a plaintiff can establish the fact that he or she has been defamed does not mean that a resolution in the plaintiff's favour will automatically follow. Several defences exist that support the right of free speech. These are justification, consent, absolute privilege, qualified privilege, and fair comment. The scope courts and legislatures have given to these defences provide a good indication of the relative importance accorded to the right of free expression. It should be reiterated that Canadian law does not accord to the press any special status with respect to defamation law; the press is subject to the same strict liability standard as any defamation defendant and is not protected by any defences unavailable to any other litigant.

In some instances, defamatory statements are protected by what is called an absolute privilege. In limited circumstances, a person making a defamatory statement is immunized from liability because the law recognizes the overriding importance of certain societal rights. Such defamatory statements are protected by what is called an absolute privilege. There are also instances in which a defamatory statement will be tolerated in the interests of society so long as the court is convinced that the person making the statement is not motivated by malice. This type of protection is known as a qualified privilege.

a) Justification

The most important defence, known as an affirmative defence, is that of justification, that is, proving that the publication is true. The statement is presumed to be false and only false statements are actionable. Proof that the statement is true or substantially true defeats absolutely the plaintiff's claim regardless of the motive that prompted the accusation or the fact that it is harmful to the plaintiff's reputation. The law will not permit a person to recover damages with respect to an injury to a character that he or she does not possess.

Yet proving truthfulness can at times be difficult. In the *Color Your World* case, the court found that many statements in the program were statements of true fact. For example, it was true that some Color Your World paint contained mercury. More specifically, the paint sold in Eastern Canada contained mercury while that sold west of Saskatchewan did not. The defamation, however, arose out of the fact that the CBC omitted important details necessary to give the audience a balanced view of the problem. The audience was neither told that the mercury used in the paint was not the type that caused the health hazards in Japan and Ontario nor that mercury was eliminated from the paint in Western Canada because of environmental and not health concerns. The omissions permitted negative and defamatory conclusions to be drawn.

The court also took into account the fact that the defamation occurred in a broadcast. Compared with print media, a broadcast has an ephemeral and transitory quality. A television news story is typically composed of visual material, narration and dialogue. Words can be used that taken out of context, are true. However, when the component parts of the broadcast are edited into the whole, the meaning can be altered to such an extent that "what has been said has been given a defamatory meaning."[26] The court's analysis in both the *Vogel* and *Color Your World* cases indicate that narrow interpretations of what constitutes truth or falsity will not prevail. When relevant facts are omitted,the meaning of the stated facts, even though they are true, can be distorted. This places a great responsibility on reporters and editors to be sensitive to the reality that true facts can be juxtaposed in a way that creates a defamatory imputation.

b) Consent

The defendant is also absolutely protected from an action for defamation if the plaintiff consents to the defamatory statement. But the defence will be lost if the defendant exceeds the scope of the plaintiff's permission. Thus, in *Syms* v. *Warren*,[27] the plaintiff was invited to participate in a radio program to discuss and explain some defamatory remarks that had been circulated about him. After the plaintiff left the studio, the talk-show host took calls from listeners. One of the callers, to whom the host had first spoken off air about the purpose of her call, repeated the defamation on air. The court held that, in accepting this invitation, the plaintiff had implicitly consented to the publication of this defamatory information contained in questions directed to him for the purpose of eliciting his clarification and denials. However, the plaintiff's consent did not extend to the subsequent remarks made by the caller and broadcast by the station.

c) Absolute Privilege

The law also recognizes that in certain circumstances the defamation of an individual must be tolerated in order to advance more important public policy goals. Thus statements made, for example, in the proceedings of a court or quasi-judicial body, or in a federal or provincial parliament, are protected by an absolute privilege. Defamatory statements made during these proceedings cannot give rise to any claim. These proceedings share a common purpose. Courts and other tribunals frequently must weigh competing claims and interests and set policy which affect the public at large. Free and open debate is essential to the fact-finding process and thus all statements, true or false, malicious or negligent, are protected from legal action.[28]

d) Qualified Privilege

The press will often defend itself in a defamation action by raising defences that offer the protection of a qualified privilege. These defences are especially attractive because, by raising them successfully, the defendant is no longer held to the strict liability standard. The making of a defamatory comment is protected so long as it is not made maliciously. Furthermore, the onus is on the plaintiff to prove the malicious intent of the defendant. If the plaintiff is unable to do so he or she loses the case.

Communications that take place within the context of specific types of relationships are protected by a qualified privilege. This defence has been traditionally used in very specific and narrow circumstances. If the court can identify the existence of a special relationship in which one party has a private or public duty to communicate information and the party to whom it is communicated has an interest in receiving it, a defendant is protected unless the plaintiff can prove malice. Privileges are recognized if the person is acting in the protection of his or her personal interest, the interest of a third person, an interest shared in common with someone else, or a public interest. A teaching assistant, for example, who believes that a student has plagiarized an assignment has a duty to inform the professor in charge. If the information were untrue, it would be defamatory. Nonetheless, once the existence of the qualified privilege was established by the defendant, the student who was defamed would have to prove that the teaching assistant acted maliciously. In many circumstances that would be quite difficult to do.

The press has argued that it has this type of special relationship with the members of the public that places on the press a public duty to inform its audience on matters of public interest. The law does recognize that there are occasions when the public interest in obtaining information sometimes requires that the press be insulated from liability unless it acts maliciously.

In *Camporese* v. *Parton*,[29] it was held that a newspaper consumer-affairs columnist was protected by a qualified privilege in informing the public generally about the risks associated with the use of the plaintiff's canning lids, since the public generally had an interest in knowing about the adverse characteristics of such products. The defendant, Ms. Parton, initially published an article commending a line of canning lids distributed by the plaintiff, Mr. Camporese. She informed her readers both that the Consumer Association of Canada had tested the lids and had concluded that the seal was inadequate and that Camporese disagreed with the results of the test. After her newspaper received complaints from readers about the performance of the lids, Parton decided to investigate the problem. Her anonymous questioning of Camporese led her to conclude that he was selling the lids despite the fact he knew they were defective. Further research, characterized by the court as superficial and incomplete, resulted in Parton concluding that the faulty seal could result in the formation of a deadly strain of botulism. Her newspaper article on the matter accused the plaintiff of selling a product that was life threatening. Expert evidence introduced at trial established that it was highly improbable that the use of defective canning lids could result in the formation of the deadly toxin. The court found that Parton's statements defamed Camporese.

Parton was, however, able to establish that she and her readers had a common interest in the adequacy of the canning lids and that she had a special duty to report on the fact that they were defective. The duty arose from her initial endorsement of the lids, which caused readers of her newspaper article to purchase a defective product. Other prospective purchasers who might rely on her endorsement had to be warned of the danger. The plaintiff tried to defeat the defence by proving that Parton acted maliciously. The court was persuaded that her research on the topic was reckless because she relied solely on an opinion she solicited rather hurriedly from one home economist. In her rush to publish the story, Ms. Parton did not further test the accuracy of this opinion. The court stated that a more in-depth investigation into the botulism claim would have been in order. Such recklessness does not, however, constitute malice. Because Ms. Parton was able to prove that she honestly believed that the opinion expressed by the home economist was true, she was able to succeed in her defence.

e) Fair Comment

It is the right of every citizen to express his or her opinions on matters of public concern. It is also one of the essential freedoms of the communications media. In the law of defamation, this right is reflected in the defence of fair comment. To satisfy the requirements of this defence, it must be shown that the words are comment based upon facts that are true, and that the comment is made honestly and fairly, without malice, on a matter of public interest.

Fair comment is the defence on which the press most relies. It gives the media the latitude to express opinions on a range of topics including the review of government actions, the evaluation of consumer products, and the review of art exhibitions, film, and television programs. Fair comment recognizes that the press serves an important role in providing information on matters of concern to the public and that it should be protected when stating an opinion. The only limitation on the press is that the statements of opinion must be made fairly and honestly, without malice, on a matter of public interest.

One of the more interesting libel actions in which the defence of fair comment was used successfully involved a political cartoon that appeared in B.C.'s *Victoria Times* and featured then Human Resources minister William Vander Zalm.[30] The British Columbia Court of Appeal described the cartoon in the following way:

> [T]he cartoon exaggerated the facial features of the plaintiff. It depicted Mr. Vander Zalm smiling, seated at a table, and engaged in plucking the wings from a fly. Other flies, without wings, were shown moving on the table. On plaintiff's lapel were inscribed the words, 'Human Resources.'[31]

Mr. Vander Zalm claimed that the cartoon libelled him in that it depicted him as a "person of cruel and sadistic nature who enjoys inflicting suffering and torture on helpless beings who cannot protect themselves."[32]

The defence, in asserting that the cartoon constituted valid commentary, established the political context which prompted its publication. Vander Zalm in his capacity as Minister of Human Resources had made numerous statements and implemented controversial policies. For example, he had "cut off funding for a number of community groups that had been providing assistance to the poor," had tightened regulations so that fewer persons could qualify as disabled for the purpose of collecting benefits, and had stated that Native Canadians living in Vancouver should return to reserves because there was more opportunity for them there. Mr. Bierman, the cartoonist, testified at trial about his opinion of Vander Zalm's statements and policies. He believed that the minister had a cruel attitude toward those in society who were defenceless and underprivileged. Beirman used as an example Vander Zalm's comment that Native Canadians, attracted by the bright lights of the city, should return to their reserves if they wanted to collect welfare payments.

When asked to explain the meaning of the cartoon, Beirman responded that it identified Vander Zalm as the Minister of Human Resources. "[T]he fly depicts the helpless Indians that were in his words, 'Attracted to the big city lights'...[H]e is more or less clipping their wings. However, he is pulling them out which is different from clipping, but he's clipping their wings so they can't roam around any longer or fly to the bright lights, not realizing the pain he causes."[33]

The defence of fair comment acknowledges that individuals in the public eye should expect press scrutiny. As the court in *Vander Zalm* succinctly stated, "the act of putting oneself in the public arena tends to invite appraisal of one's public conduct."[34] For some, the Vander Zalm case represented an example of a politician using the defamation laws to silence critics on matters of public concern. The comment provided in Beirman's cartoon served the democratic process by highlighting policies which were, in his opinion, insensitive and unjust. The public has a right to know not only the policies articulated by elected officials but also reasonable assessments of these policies. It is argued that politicians should have to seek redress, not by pursuing a legal action but by responding to their critics from the public platform their offices provide.

The concern has been expressed that the defence of fair comment, although successful in the *Vander Zalm* case, does not always offer sufficient protection for the press. As stated previously, the fair comment defence can only be raised in situations in which a comment is made, or an opinion given, that is based on true facts. Critics contend that a grey area exists in what constitutes a statement of opinion as opposed to a statement of fact. The press has expressed concern that the court might characterize as fact a comment that the press clearly viewed as opinion, and thus inappropriately subject the defendant to liability. The media argue that the uncertainty this creates results in their exercising self-censorship even in the expression of opinion on important public interest matters. The biggest loser, the argument goes, is the public itself.[35]

In summary, the press argues that the strict liability nature of a defamation claim places them in a disadvantageous position. Defendants cannot always be sure that a court will accept their interpretation as to the truth of the statement. If possible, defendants must attempt to characterize the circumstances of the case in a manner that will raise a qualified privilege. This is the only mechanism that will protect the press from liability for statements which they do not make maliciously. The press, and hence the public interest, it is argued, would be better served if the plaintiff were required to prove malicious intent in all circumstances rather than only when the defendant successfully raises a qualified privilege. The defendant would be protected when making an honest and inadvertent error. Furthermore, the public would have greater access to information because the press would not have to engage in needless self-censorship.

The Remedies

The law recognizes that when a person's reputation has been injured by a defamatory statement, the damage can never be fully remedied. There is a need, therefore, for some alternative means of correcting the wrong and compensating the plaintiff. As stated earlier, the law presumes that a libelous statement results in injury. A successful plaintiff is automatically entitled to a money award as compensation for the injuries suffered by the defamatory publication. He or she may also recover for any mental pain, suffering, distress, insult, wounded feelings, anguish, anxiety, embarrassment, and humiliation that may have been caused. In determining the amount of the award, the court will also take into account such factors as the plaintiff's employment or profession, reputation, prominence, standing in the community, the nature and character of the defamation, and the extent to which it was disseminated to the public. The court will also consider the stature of the publication, television or radio station that communicated the libel—a bigger damage award is likely if the defamation emanated from a credible media outlet, for example, the CBC, than from a poorly regarded tabloid newspaper. In addition, the plaintiff is recompensed for any specific monetary loss caused by the defamation. This type of remedy is called the specific or actual damages. For example, in the *Color Your World* case, the plaintiff had to employ a firm to provide crisis management services to restore the plaintiff's reputation and sales. The court required the defendant to pay an amount compensating the plaintiff for the cost of these services.

Courts will also consider whether the defendant published a retraction; if it did, most provincial statutes provide a mechanism by which the defendant may mitigate damages, that is, limit the amount of money the defendant must pay to the actual damages the plaintiff suffered. Finally, in cases where the defamation and the behaviour of the defendant are particularly egregious, and merit the condemnation of the court, the court may award punitive or exemplary damages. This final type of monetary award does more than just compensate the plaintiff for his or her loss: it punishes the defendant for unacceptable behaviour. In the *Vogel* case, for example, the court noted that the CBC "showed no sign of feeling any real concern about the harm caused by the irresponsible abuse of its great power."[36] Punitive damages in the amount of $25 000 were awarded.

Damages awards for defamation cases in Canada are generally much lower than those in the United States. However, recent awards in Ontario have led some observers to be concerned that excessive awards could have a negative impact on the freedom of the press. Critics contend that the payment of large damage awards coupled with the high costs of protracted litigation make libel actions too expensive for the press and, hence, contrary to the public interest.[37] In addition, the courts in Canada have the discretion to award costs to the winning party in a defamation action. This means that the losing party may be ordered to pay these costs in addition to his or her own costs. This creates a burdensome economic risk for both plaintiffs and defendants, and only those with substantial financial resources can reasonably pursue defamation actions.[38] Insurance funds have been created to protect the media,[39] but plaintiffs generally do not have similar protection.

Is There a Need for Reform?

As stated earlier, the press is on the same footing as any individual in defending a defamation claim. The argument has been made that the press should be granted a special status in recognition of its role in promoting the values of democracy by keeping the public informed on matters of public interest. As we have seen, unless a defendant can successfully raise the fair comment defence or seek the protection of a qualified privilege, he or she is strictly liable for defamatory statements regardless of how innocently made. For example, investigative journalists, even though they check their sources carefully, may be in error. Although they can avail themselves of the defence of qualified privilege and fair comment, these defences have limited application.

Reformers have looked to the United States for guidance on making the defamation laws in Canada more responsive to the free speech interests of the press.

Reform of the defamation laws began in the United States in 1964 with the landmark Supreme Court decision *New York Times* v. *Sullivan*.[40] In this case, the court held that in order for debate on public issues to be "uninhibited, robust, and wide open," accommodation must be allowed for the occasional erroneous statement. Therefore, when public officials brought actions against critics of their official conduct, they had to prove actual malice with convincing clarity. The court defined actual malice as a statement made "with knowledge that it was false or with reckless disregard of whether it was false or not."[41] Where the issue was recklessness, it was subsequently defined as a statement made under circumstances where there was a high degree of probable falsity, or where a defendant entertained serious doubts about the truth of the statement.

Following *Sullivan*, the court imposed a comparable burden of actual malice on those who were considered public figures.[42] A person achieved that status by reason of the notoriety of his or her achievements, or the vigour or success with which he or she sought public attention. This led the court to define two classes of public figures. The first class contains those persons who, over a period of time, have become well known to the public, either because of their fame or notoriety. Such persons are deemed public figures for all purposes. The second class contains those persons who may find themselves at the forefront of a particular public controversy in order to influence the resolution of that controversy. Rodney King, the Los Angeles motorist whose beating by the police was the subject matter of a videotape, is an example of such a public figure.[43] King would be considered a public figure for the issues connected with this police beating.

Where a person was a private rather than a public figure, liability against the communications media could be imposed only where there was a finding of fault.[44] The plaintiff must prove that the words are false,[45] and presumed or punitive damages could not be imposed against the media unless there is a finding of actual malice,[46] at least where the issues involved are matters of public concern.[47] Finally, while the Supreme Court has refused to find a wholesale exemption for words that might be labelled as opinion, the court held "that a statement on matters of public concern must be provable as false before there can be liability under state defamation law."[48] The effect of this decision, however, is to exempt from liability under the law of defamation all expressions of opinion, however harsh, insulting, distasteful, or pejorative, unless they imply facts that can be proved to be false and defamatory.

Another constitutional doctrine has emerged, formulated in some American jurisdictions, that greatly assists the communications media in publishing newsworthy stories. This is referred to as the "privilege of neutral reporting" and was first articulated by Chief Judge Kaufman in *Edwards* v. *National Audubon Society Inc*.[49] Under this doctrine, the media is privileged to report fairly, accurately, and dispassionately any newsworthy charges directed against public officials or public figures if they are made by responsible or prominent persons or organizations.

The Canadian press has tried to convince Canadian courts to adopt the American approach. The Supreme Court of Canada, however, made it clear in *Dolphin Delivery*

Ltd. v. *Retail, Wholesale & Department Store Union, Local 580*[50] that the Charter of Rights does not apply to private litigation between private parties involving the common law unless an element of government intervention is involved that infringes some fundamental right or freedom. In the few preliminary Charter skirmishes involving actions for defamation, media defendants have been uniformly unsuccessful in bringing challenges under the Charter. In many instances, there is evidence that, even if the Charter were applicable, Canadian judges would not be inclined to view favourably the constitutional protection afforded the media articulated by the American courts. This view is reflected in the opinion of Judge Wood in *Westbank Indian Band* v. *Tomat*[51] who said:

> The rule in the *New York Times* case leaves vulnerable the reputation of all who are or would be in public life, by depriving such people of any legal recourse from defamatory falsehoods directed against them, except in those rare cases where "actual malice" can be established. Such a rule would be likely to discourage honest and decent people from standing for public office. Thus the rule destroys, rather than preserves, the delicate balance between freedom of expression and protection of reputation which... is vital to the survival of our democratic process of government. For that reason I would be opposed to introducing such a rule in this country.

There is yet another area in which the media in the United States often have greater protection than their Canadian counterparts. As stated previously, the rules for discovery require that the litigants to a claim make available to each other documents pertinent to the action. Media defendants have complained that rules requiring them to turn over their raw material operate as a "chill" inhibiting their ability to speak. Of equally great concern to the press is the request that they reveal the names of confidential sources. In Canada, where a publisher or broadcaster has entered a plea of privilege or fair comment, there is a division of authority in the provinces as to whether they can be required to reveal the names of confidential informants or sources at discovery in advance of the trial. In England, there is an established practice that disclosure should not be ordered in the absence of any special or exceptional reasons to do so.[52] In Canada, while it is recognized that there is no common law privilege for the press to maintain the confidentiality of its sources, there is a division of opinion as to whether to follow the English practice. Ontario has embraced the English rule, and courts refuse to order the disclosure of the name of an informant before trial. British Columbia, New Brunswick, and Saskatchewan have rejected the rule. Of course, eventually the name will have to be disclosed if it is relevant and pertinent to the issue of the presence of malice that might defeat a qualified privilege.

In the United States, the courts have attempted to balance freedom of the press with the right of a person to vindicate his or her reputation by having access to sources of defamatory information. This has led some states to enact statutory provisions shielding the media from forced disclosure of confidential sources whether at the discovery stage or during the course of litigation. In other states, in deciding whether to order the production of names, courts will consider the nature of the litigation, whether a reporter is named as a party in the dispute, whether there is a compelling need for the information, whether the case is frivolous in character, and whether the information is relevant and necessary.

Reform in Canada will not likely follow the American approach. Instead, our courts may limit the amount defendants are required to pay in damages to a successful plaintiff. In his dissenting opinion in *Snyder* v. *The Montreal Gazette Ltd.*,[53] Chief Justice Dickson expressed concern about courts granting excessive monetary awards to compensate the plaintiff for the general damages they had suffered. This would include the damage to their reputation as well such injuries as humiliation, embarrassment, and mental pain. The Chief Justice stated that courts find it difficult to calculate what constitutes an appropriate amount. As a result, the amount of compensation can be arbitrary in nature. The Chief Justice would not preclude successful plaintiffs from collecting compensation for actual and calculable damages, that is, such items as lost profits, lost income, and so on. The danger exists that large general-damages awards might do more than compensate the plaintiff. They might contain a concealed punitive award although punitive damages should only be awarded if the court found specifically that the defendant's actions were so egregious that punishment was required. The Chief Justice continued,

> In coming to the rescue of a defamation victim, the courts must not overlook the fact that the written and spoken press is indispensable and is an essential component of a free and democratic society. Moreover, both the Quebec and Canadian Charters recognize the importance of a free press.... If information agencies are ordered to pay large amounts as the result of a defamation the danger is that their operations will be paralyzed, indeed, in some cases, that their very existence may be endangered. Although society undoubtedly places a great value on the reputation of its members, that value, as it is subjective, cannot be so high as to threaten the very existence of the press agencies which are essential to preserve a right guaranteed by the Charters.[54]

Similar sentiments have been expressed in the United States. The American courts have recognized that responsible government is best served by an informed citizenry, and that a free and independent press is a fundamental requisite for the vitality of a democratic society, and the best assurance of a responsible and representative government. Fear has been expressed that the threat of libel actions may gradually erode journalistic independence. There is, therefore, a national recognition of the constitutional "right to vehement, caustic, and unpleasantly sharp criticism of government and public officials."[55] While the courts continue to acknowledge a moderating role for the law of defamation, they also recognize that it must not be pursued at the expense of a free press. The principle was stated by Thomas Jefferson many years ago.

> The remedy of libel judgments has a role in our democracy; it compensates individuals for their injured reputations. But only free expression can preserve a democratic nation. Money awards are a medium of financial recompense. But free speech is the national currency. Our legislatures have advanced this country's goals by protecting the press even at the cost of reducing their own protection against its attack. Their action would have stirred the former president of this country who said that "were it left to me to decide whether we should have government without newspapers, or newspapers without a government, I should not hesitate a moment to prefer the latter."[56]

In the United States, therefore, the balance has been tipped in favour of a free press. In theory, the American approach appears laudable. Closer examination of press practices in the United States reveals another reality. One questions whether the level of political debate now evident in the United States still warrants the priority given to the right of free speech at the expense of the individual's reputation. The current popularity of talk radio and television programs, in which informed debate has been replaced by mindless name-calling and intolerance, is alarming. Commentators have noted with equal alarm that the sensational reporting techniques once relegated to the print and television tabloids are now practised by highly regarded media outlets. Invariably, audience share increases when "scandals" are revealed about well-known figures. Serious political, social, and economic debate are revenue losers. These trends cannot be attributed wholly to the changes in the defamation laws in the United States. Nonetheless, one cannot help but speculate whether the tabloid press, which continues to skirt the liberal defamation laws, has had a profound effect on the declining interest in and capacity for a responsible debate. The very purposes of a free press have themselves been undermined.

The most vocal proponents of defamation reform are frequently the media enterprises themselves. They do so, supposedly, in the interests of free speech, arguing that the public gains immeasurably from a system that protects free speech. Yet those who clearly benefit from such a system are those who have the greatest power and the best resources to exercise their rights.[57] With rapidly developing technology coupled with worrisome economic concentration, the media's ability to influence public opinion expands continually. In this context, media enterprises have the ability to irretrievably destroy the reputations, and consequently the credibility, of those on the public stage. This does not always serve the interests of democracy. The public then must be assured that the media exercise their power responsibly and that they are held to a high level of accountability for shoddy or reckless reporting. Perhaps the free speech interests of the public are best served by a media operating within the confines of the existing defamation laws in Canada. If there is to be reform, it should be openly and thoroughly debated in a manner which permits input from the media as well as potential and actual defamation victims.[58] After all, if the media control the debate, they effectively close the debate. Only in this way can the needs of a democratic society be met.

NOTES

The author wishes to thank Professor Raymond Brown, Faculty of Law, University of Windsor, for his helpful criticisms.

1. M. David Lepofsky, "Making Sense of the Libel Chill Debate: Do Libel Laws Chill the Expression of Freedom of Expression?" *National Journal of Constitutional Law* 4 (1994): 196–206. This article presents a detailed analysis of many of the arguments presented in this chapter.
2. In Canada, see Raymond Brown, *The Law of Defamation*, 2nd. ed., (Toronto: Carswell, 1994); Jeremy Williams, *The Law of Libel and Slander*, 2nd ed. (Toronto: Butterworths, 1988). In the United States, see Bruce Sanford, *Libel and Privacy*, 2nd ed (New York: Prentice Hall Law and Business) (looseleaf); Rodney A. Smolla, *Law of Defamation* (New York: Clark Boardman Callaghan, 1986) (looseleaf).
3. William Shakespeare, *The Tragedy of Othello, The Moor of Venice*, Act III, Scene iii.
4. Lepofsky, "Making Sense," 197.
5. The common law draws a distinction between slander (an oral, and hence transitory, defamatory statement) and libel (a defamation in a permanent form), although in a number of provinces, statutory provisions have provided for the treatment of slander as the same as libel. In those jurisdictions retaining the common law distinctions, damages are presumed in all libel actions, but special damages must be proved in all slander actions except in those cases where the imputation reflects adversely on persons in their trade, office, profession, or occupation; accuses them of a criminal offence; charges them with having a particularly loathsome or contagious disease; or accuses a woman of unchastity. This latter exception may be in conflict with the Charter of Rights. For this reason, the exception has been deleted from the Ontario statute.

   Special damages include any pecuniary loss, or any material or temporal disadvantage that is capable of being measured in money, that are the natural and direct result of the defamatory words.

   Most provincial statutes categorize defamatory statements made by the electronic media as libel. (See, for example, Section 2 of the Ontario Libel and Slander Act, R.S.O. 1990, c. 237.)
6. The only instance in which the plaintiff must prove wrongful intent arises where there is a dispute as to whether the defamation was published. Here the plaintiff must prove that the defendant intended to communicate the defamatory statement to a third party or that his or her negligence resulted in the communication.
7. [1929] 2 K.B. 331 (C.A.).
8. Because the defamation originated with Mr. Cassidy, the newspaper could seek indemnification from him.
9. [1910] A.C. 20 (H.L.).
10. *Cassidy* at 342.
11. *Snyder* v. *Montreal Gazette* [1988] 1 S.C.R. 494.
12. *Derrick* v. *Tomat* 74 D.L.R. (4th) 453. (B.C.C.A.)
13. *Hill* v. *Church of Scientology of Toronto* 18 Ontario Reports (3d) 385 (C.A.); leave to appeal to the Supreme Court of Canada granted; see Stephen Bindman, "Scientology Spurs Check of Libel Laws," *The Vancouver Sun*, February 20, 1995, p. 1.
14. Where the action is for slander, a court will consider the expression on the defendant's face and any accompanying gestures, the intonation of the voice, and the accent or emphasis placed on particular words or phrases.

15. [1982] 3 W.W.R. 97 (B.C.S.C.).
16. Ibid. at 104.
17. Ibid. at 97.
18. Ibid. at 105.
19. Ibid. at 132.
20. D.G. Crawford, "The Big Chill: Are Libel Laws Killing Free Speech? Or Should They Be Made Tougher?" *Canadian Lawyer* 18, 3 (1992):14–20.
21. (1994) 17 O.R.(3d) 308 (Gen. Div.)
22. Ibid. at 348.
23. Ibid.
24. Lepofsky, "Making Sense," p. 173.
25. Ibid. at 201.
26. *Color Your World* at 336.
27. (1976), 71 D.L.R.(3d) 558 (Man. Q.B.).
28. The press has an absolute privilege to report on these proceedings so long as the report is fair and accurate. It must not misstate the facts, although relatively minor inaccuracies will not defeat the privilege if the report is otherwise substantially correct. An abstract, abridgement or abbreviated summary, or excerpt of the proceeding may be reported if nothing is added, edited, or deleted that would tend to misrepresent the nature of the proceeding or create an erroneous impression of what occurred.
29. (1983), 150 D.L.R. (3d) 208 (B.C.S.C.).
30. *Vander Zalm* v. *Times Publishers* (1980) 109 D.L.R. (3d) 531 (B.C.C.A.)
31. Ibid., at 534, per Nemetz C.J.
32. Ibid. at 534.
33. Ibid. at 534.
34. Ibid. at 536.
35. D.G. Crawford "The Big Chill," p.
36. *Vogel* at 186.
37. In *Hill* v. *Church of Scientology of Toronto* (1994), 18 O.R. (3d) 385 (C.A.).
38. Douglas A. Alderson, "The Constitutionalization of Defamation: American and Canadian Approaches to the Constitutional Regulation of Speech," *Advocates' Quarterly* (1993) 15: 385.
39. D.G. Crawford, "The Big Chill," p. 18.
40. 376 U.S. 254 (1964).
41. Ibid., 376 U.S. 280.
42. *Curtis Publishing Co.* v. *Butts*, 388 U.S. 130 (1967).
43. Lepofsky, "Making Sense," p. 204.
44. This is a minimum requirement established by the Supreme Court. While most states have adopted a negligence test to meet this standard, some states have adopted a more rigorous standard of actual malice. New York has bridged the differences with a test of "gross irresponsibility."
45. *Philadelphia Newspapers, Inc.* v. *Hepps*, 475 U.S. 767 (1986).
46. *Gertz* v. *Robert Welch, Inc.*, 418 U.S. 323 (1974).
47. *Dun & Bradstreet, Inc.* v. *Greenmoss Builders, Inc.*, 472 U.S. 749 (1985).
48. Per Rehnquist C.J. in *Milkovich* v. *Lorain Journal Co.*, 110 S. Ct. 2695 at 2706 (1990).
49. 556 F. 2d 113 (2d Cir. 1977).
50. [1986] 2 S.C.R. 573.
51. (1992), 63 B.C.L.R. (2d) 273 at 294 (C.A.).

52. See, for example, *Georgius* v. *The Vice-Chancellor and Delegates of the Press of Oxford University*, [1949] 1 K.B. 729 (C.A.).
53. (1988) 49 D.L.R. (4th) 17 (SCC).
54. Ibid. at 28.
55. Per J. Sutin in *Ammerman* v. *Hubbard Broadcasting, Inc.*, 91 N.M. 250, 572 P. 2d 1258 at 1261 (1977).
56. Per J. Pashman in *Maressa* v. *New Jersey Monthly*, 89 N.J. 176, 445 A. 2d 376 at 389 (1982), quoting from *The Life and Selected Writings of Thomas Jefferson* edited byAdrienne Koch and William Peden (New York: Modern Library, 1944): pp. 411–12
57. Frederick Schauer, "Free Speech and Its Harms," *Constitutional Forum* (1991) 2: 80–81.
58. Lepofsky, "Making Sense," p. 206.

MIMICKING BLUEBEARD: FEMINISM AND THE PORNOGRAPHY PANIC

Janice Dickin

INTRODUCTION

Since the personal is the political,[1] let's get right down to it. As a child growing up in the fifties, as a girl trying to stake her claim in the sixties, and as a woman insisting on making up my own life as I went along in the seventies, I frequently remarked that women were put on earth to tell me No. Feminist in my bones, I was nonetheless suspicious of feminism because I had never been comfortable with women in groups. The only girl in a family that runs to males, I had developed strategies which had allowed me to do most of what I wanted by functioning as an "exception female," asserting my own rights without asserting those of my sex in general. It took pregnancy in the eighties to make me seek out women and to struggle to interact with them on an equal basis.

Given how hard I had to work to achieve sisterhood and given my depth of understanding of the power structure that puts women unfairly into positions of policing themselves and other women, it is painful for me in the nineties to find myself once again writing against the sincere and committed work of sisters. I hope, for more than one reason, I never feel called upon to write about pornography again.

When I began writing my first piece on pornography for a law journal in 1988—regarding the fifties campaign against crime comics[2]—I thought I was in favour of something I imagined as a selective censorship, a censorship that would control or abolish or at least criminalize "works of no worth" while allowing "works of worth" to thrive. That article is of most interest to me now for the fact that it is the only one I have ever written in which I thought I was arguing one thing, only to find myself in my conclusion forced to address the humbling fact that my evidence pointed inevitably in the other direction. Although I had to go back and write a new head for it, the body remained the same. Unknowingly, I had joined a growing league of anti-censorship feminists.

I had also quite unknowingly joined a league of scholars employing "the notion of 'moral panic'... to account for developments in widely diverse areas."[3] In a footnote to an article on the nineteenth-century English bar, I found myself cited along with a slew of other scholars writing on prostitution, prohibition, mugging, garotting, and "moral enterprise" in general. It was exceedingly interesting to find out that my empirical work had a theoretical basis. As well as pointing me the way home, the author of this article introduced me to "Stanley Cohen's now-classic description" of moral panic, a cathartic set of reflexes gone through by a society in the grasp of a "condition, episode, person or group of persons [which emerges] to become defined as a threat to societal values and interests."[4] The article also introduced me to the concept of "moral entrepreneurs," those who highjack such panics for their own purposes.

As a feminist, I feel the implications of moral panic in my gut. I have personally been a direct target for blame; I have seen independent women both as individuals and in groups attacked, or worse, quarantined into ineffectuality; I have sat in front of the old man at the school play who states loudly that the young girls on stage are "feminist bitches." I have much to fear from moral panic. How distressing, then, to be forced to consider whether some of my sisters have become moral entrepreneurs.

Sirens, after all, seduce: that is their job. The sirens who sing to feminists are the same ones who sang to the women who told us no. They sing of the ability to be able to make a difference, the chance to protect those who can't or won't protect themselves, self-empowerment through action. But, since we are also overwhelmingly middle class, the sirens who sing to us also sing of getting ahead, making a name, finding a niche. It is much easier to do any of these things if the system in general stays stable. Hence, we harbour a fantasy that meaningful jobs will be found for all women (when the system can't even provide them for men), that men will meekly move into the roles we seek to leave behind (without feeling the insecurity that has caused us to flee them), that tinkering will suffice (rather than the full-scale revolution the sixties antifeminist panic preternaturally predicted).

How delightful for all of us should the problem turn out to be singular, diagnosable, susceptible to social surgery! How wonderful to find the cause, trace the effect, apply the tourniquet! How those sirens do sing!

In her book, *The Politics of Domesticity. Women, Evangelism and Temperance in Nineteenth-Century America*, Barbara Epstein explores the attraction to middle-class women reformers of prohibition and/or temperance as cures to the ills of the body politic.[5] If the problems are all due to booze, they can be solved by drying it up. Who is hurt by this? Saloon-keepers and brewers, easily hived off from the rest of us, few enough in numbers to be reformed and absorbed into the economy without causing a great deal of harm to their wives and families. There are also the "victims" of alcohol who will now be saved and sent home. Of course, there are the barmaids and brewmaids, but they suffer from false consciousness and will be able to make better choices now that they have had this pointed out to them. Also, you can expect the support of those middle-class males close to you who are probably as horrified at pain inflicted on innocent children and helpless women as they are at ideas of making any real change in their own assumptions of position and possibility. The isolation and chastisement of a few bounders is a small matter to them.

Reforms of this type are so irresistible. They bring such contentment. They make you feel like you're accomplishing something while leaving your own life largely secure. Alas, that they should also be so dangerous.

Moral panics are about scapegoating. They legitimize scapegoating. While it may feel like power to be allowed to choose the scapegoat for a while, it is unlikely to have much lasting advantage. And it is likely to have much more disadvantage: because the damage done not only by you but in your name will be laid at your feet, you run the risk of being scapegoated yourself. The feminist movement is seriously divided over the question of pornography. I described this schism in a chapter ("Chilling Expression: Obscenity Law and the Halo Zone") of the first edition of this book.[6] On a thumbnail, the point of difference has to do with the question of what is more dangerous to women, pornography or censorship. Antipornography feminists feel that pornography is an important factor in preventing equality for individual women (because it encourages attacks by individual men) and for women as a group because it encourages the victimization of women generally. The slogan is "rape is the practice, pornography is the theory." Anticensorship feminists basically are motivated by the conviction that it is simply too dangerous for women to be supporting state-imposed silence at a time when women should be encouraged to say any damned thing they want.

In "Halo Zone," I described in some detail the regulatory measures in which antipornography feminists have taken part, as well as two unsuccessful attempts to have the Criminal Code revised in such a way that "morality" in the form of "obscenity" would cease to be the issue, to be replaced by "harm" in the form of "pornography." Two bills, both of which were introduced by the Mulroney government, both of which died on the order paper, tried to effect this by removing the old term of obscenity entirely from the Code and instead trying to find some sort of serviceable definition for pornography, even breaking it down into various types of pornography according to such factors as degradation, violence and physical harm. Antipornography feminists had as allies in these attempts not only religious and moral crusaders but politicians who would have been sincerely happy to be able to satisfy a constituency in such a straightforward, low-cost manner. Nonetheless, while the concept was simple enough, effecting it was not. "Pornography" turned out to be a very slippery term to define, and, in the end, replacing one vague and hard-to-enforce law with a newer and equally vague one didn't seem to merit the legislative effort.[7] Among other things, any new term would have to be considered and given a meaning by the courts.

Interestingly, this failure to pass new legislation put initiatives firmly back into the courts, busily trying out their enhanced ability to create law granted them by the Charter of Rights and Freedoms. Not surprisingly, it was to the courts that antipornography feminists would turn after the failure of Bills C-114 and C-54. Through the offices of LEAF (The Women's Legal and Action Fund), they made use of funds available under the federal Court Challenges program by defining pornography as an equality issue and arguing against it under the Charter. The culmination in terms of this tactic came when the Supreme Court of Canada handed down its decision in *R.* v. *Butler* (1992) 70 C.C.C. (3d) 129, just as the first edition of this book was going to press. I referred to it very briefly in a postscript. I could not have known at the time that LEAF at least, and possibly antipornography feminists in general, consider it such a victory that they have now decided to turn their attention to other issues. Certainly anticensorship feminists will no doubt welcome the fact that we will no longer have to spend time "writing against" sisters. We certainly have other issues we wish to address, most importantly the self-empowerment of women. Unfortunately—partly because self-empowerment by definition necessitates women's exploration of their own sexuality, partly because the antipornography campaign has left behind a legacy of "woman-as-victim," and partly because censorship has been, is, and will continue to be, used against women's expression—we are forced to concern ourselves with the damage done to women, not by pornography but by the pornography panic.

Obscenity Law

The facts of the *Butler* case look modest enough on the face of it. Donald Butler ran a video store in Winnipeg. In August 1987, police seized his entire inventory and laid charges under the obscenity section (s. 163) of the Criminal Code. Eventually, the case wound its way to the Supreme Court of Canada, where LEAF sought and received the right to intervene to argue "equality." It should be noted that the right to intervene is not easily won and is granted only to allow representations from groups that successfully argue that their legitimate rights will be directly affected by the outcome of the case. In this case, LEAF convinced the Supreme Court that it spoke for women as a "class" and that women as a "class" are harmed by pornography.

In order to explain why *Butler* set precedent, it is necessary to review briefly the way "obscenity" has been dealt with heretofore in Canadian courts. The most important provisions from the Criminal Code (R.S.C. 1985, c. C-46) read:

> 163(1) Every one commits an offence who,
>
> > (a) makes, prints, publishes, distributes, circulates, or has in his possession for the purpose of publication, distribution or circulation any obscene written matter, picture, model, phonograph record or other thing whatever;
> > (3) No person shall be convicted of an offence under this section if he establishes that the public good was served by the acts that are alleged to constitute the offence and that the acts alleged did not extend beyond what served the public good.
> > (5) For the purposes of this section, the motives of an accused are irrelevant.
> > (8) For the purposes of this Act, any publication a dominant characteristic of which is the undue exploitation of sex, or of sex and any one or more of the following subjects, namely, crime, horror, cruelty and violence, shall be deemed to be obscene.

Subsection (8) is important in that it is the sole definition offered of the term "obscene," as outlawed in subsection (1). This definition was added in 1959, in an attempt to make more clear law which had theretofore existed only in case reports. It could not, however, bear the freight and soon fell prey to case law interpretation itself. The argument, as I have already explained at some length in "Halo Zone"[8] has mostly to do with what poet and civil rights lawyer F.R. Scott dubbed "that dubious word 'undue'."[9] The concept of "undue exploitation of sex" of course begs the question of what constitutes "due exploitation."

This is where antipornography feminists find themselves at odds with other proponents of censorship of sexual expression. Feminists, on whatever side of the pornography issue, are not comfortable arguing sexual morals, for the simple reason that we have too often been the scapegoat in such discussions.[10] Antipornography feminists have therefore quite sensibly and quite insistently sought to distance themselves from "moral" aspects of obscenity. They instead wish to concentrate on what they have decided are the "harmful" aspects of pornography. Note that they try to avoid as much as possible the use of the term "obscene," the only term used in the Criminal Code itself. Clearly some creativity is in order and that is what LEAF offered the Supreme Court in *Butler*: a creative way out of an old, old problem. And, I will argue, a creative way into more new ones than we can yet identify.

Over years, Canadian courts evolved a method of deciding "undueness" through what is called "the community standards test." This is meant to be an objective test to be decided not on the grounds of what the judge or jury would *personally* tolerate reading, seeing, hearing, etc., but what they would be willing to tolerate other members of the community reading and so on. This test has built into it a valuing of questions of "harm" over those of "morals," in the sense that other people's morals are their issue so long as they do not harm you or the rest of the community in any way. In other words, the door already gaped open for antipornography feminist argument. What was needed was a way of getting a foot in.

If the question is to be one of harm, its existence must be proved in some manner to support a finding of "undue exploitation." To prove something in court, you need evidence. If you have a dead or injured body, you can prove harm. If you have stolen money or property, you have proof of harm. But how do you prove harm from obscene materials? To pin this wave upon the sand, recourse has traditionally been made to what are called "expert witnesses." These are people, properly credentialled in some manner, who can speak to the issue. In the case of obscenity trials, experts have generally been psychologists or sociologists who testify for either the prosecution or the defence as to whether pornography incites users to commit harmful acts on others. Antipornography feminists have for some time been unhappy with these experts, arguing that they represent the (male) power structure and by definition cannot represent the greater community. Such feminists grew frustrated that the research literature upon which they base their assertions of "proven" harm are countered by equally respectable research literature that goes against such assertions. Unable to get all "experts" to accept their reading of the literature, the obvious option was to get the court to de-credential the expert evidence it had theretofore relied upon. In *Butler*, LEAF succeeded in doing just that.

THE BUTLER CASE

In *Butler*, the Supreme Court to large extent completed the task Parliament had failed to achieve; it shifted the eye of the law off "obscenity" and onto "pornography," and defined that last term in such a way as to separate portrayals into two categories it found to be "harmful" and a third it found in general not to be. The first two categories are "explicit sex with violence" and "explicit sex without violence but which subjects people to treatment that is degrading or dehumanizing." In the case of these two categories, the Supreme Court basically issued orders to assume "harm." Gone is the need to show that the depictions on trial actually made someone do something harmful or that they can be counted on to actually make someone do something harmful. That put to rest years of evidentiary madness, and no doubt the nine judges were delighted to be presented with an ingenious way out, especially one that they were assured represented the wishes of Canadian women, a large part of the community, after all, not to say the majority!

What was offered to the Supreme Court and what it adopted is not a way of proving harm but rather a way of proving people *feel* harmed. As the headnote in *Canadian Criminal Cases* summarizes the Court's thinking:

> Whether material falls within the definition depends on a determination of what the community would tolerate others being exposed to on the basis of the harm that may flow from such exposure. Harm in this context means that it predisposes persons to act in an antisocial manner as, for example, the physical or mental mistreatment of women by men. Antisocial conduct for this purpose is conduct which society formally recognizes as incompatible with its proper functioning. The stronger the inference of risk of harm the lesser the likelihood of tolerance.[11]

"May flow," "predisposes," "incompatible," "inference," "likelihood"—the Supreme Court is settling for some pretty inconclusive wording here. One case comment discussing the decision cynically characterizes the new test for obscenity as "whatever offends women" and attributes this attitude to an undifferentiated "feminism."[12] An opposing view gushes that *Butler* is "a milestone not only for its clarification of obscenity law, but for the advancement of equality rights in Canada."[13] Why is it an advancement of equality rights? Because that is basically what LEAF argued, using section 15 of the Charter, and what the court means when it talks about "conduct which society formally recognizes as incompatible with its proper functioning." Basically, the thinking runs like this: if women don't feel equal, they can't be equal. That pornography, in the form of violent and degrading images in which women are often the targets, is accepted by Canadian society means that the equality of women is not accepted. If equality is not accepted, then equality (as guaranteed by the Charter) cannot exist. Therefore, the Criminal Code provisions on obscenity—which must be read in light of the Charter—are properly used to ban such images. To underline that this is about equality and not about morals, the third category of "pornography" legally created by *Butler* is found not to be proscribed by law. That category covers "explicit sex without violence that is neither degrading nor dehumanizing."

It is important to understand that *Butler* pertains not simply to judicial reading of the Criminal Code obscenity provisions but to judicial reading of the Charter itself. As the first case to be tried by the Supreme Court on the tension between censorship of obscenity and freedom of expression as guaranteed by section 2(b) of the Charter, it speaks not simply to criminalization of "pornography" but to limits on freedom of expression generally. *Butler* is not simply about censorship writ small; it is about censorship writ large. Section 1 of the Charter has been used repeatedly by the courts to uphold limits on a variety of the "rights" granted elsewhere in the Charter. This section holds that it is valid to do so so long as it is done by "a reasonable limit, prescribed by law." Assuming that pornography is rightfully brought in under the obscenity umbrella of the Criminal Code, it is by definition "prescribed by law." The question then shifts to definition of "reasonableness," in essence an exercise not unlike coming to a definition of "undue." Two "tests" that the Supreme Court has devised to assess "reasonableness" are the proportionality test and the minimal impairment test. The first has to do with whether the object of the law being set in place over the right is sufficiently important to warrant such protection. The second has to do with whether there is a less onerous way to achieve the same results. In *Butler*, the Supreme Court found both of these tests to be satisfied.

The court found the objective of section 163 to be of "sufficient importance" to warrant overriding freedom of expression. It did so by characterizing the obscenity section as being not about moral disapprobation but about avoidance of harm to society. If nothing else, this reasoning demonstrates how old laws, written for different reasons, can have second lives. Like the Bible, some written law achieves a timeless status that allows it to survive change through re-interpretation by successive societies. In stating that section 163 is not about morals but about harm, the court upheld an old law by giving it a new meaning. Let's accept for argument that the society of the time that produced the original obscenity law was also directly concerned about harm, just that they had a different definition of it, one that carried moral overtones we now wish to shed. Let's accept that we have a right as a society which has "developed" to redefine old laws to make them useful to us. But let's not kid ourselves that our definition of what causes the ills of society will be any less vulnerable to reinterpretation in turn. Therefore, to argue that freedom of expression is rightfully limited because a set of images will cause "harm" is to give up a long-term liberty for the sake of a short-term victory.

The "minimal impairment" test looks not to whether the law under examination might be too frivolous but rather to whether it might be too sweeping. This, too, the Supreme Court found to be satisfied, and here it pointed directly to the excision of its new third category, sexually explicit erotica without violence, from sanction under the obscenity section. This of course harks back to the proportionality test in that such material is deemed to cause no harm, an interesting shift from the mores that created the obscenity laws in the first place. Now narrowed to material which it accepts as causing harm to society, the Supreme Court claims that it is proscribing only material which "lies far from the core" of the expression meant to be protected under the Charter. In other words, the court is saying, don't worry, we're just shutting up the bad guys.

There are two more aspects of the case that must be touched on before I proceed to talk about the dangers of sucking solace from ephemeral victories. The first has to do with the defence of artistic merit as provided for in subsection (3) of the obscenity provisions. I have discussed this before in "Halo Zone."[14] In arguing that section 163 passes the "minimal impairment" test, the Supreme Court referred directly to the fact that materials of scientific, artistic, or literary merit are not "captured" by the provision. This is only partly so. The so-called artistic merit defence is only that, a defence. What it grants you is an opportunity—in court—to argue that your expression does indeed fall within "the core of the guarantee of expression." The key phrase here is of course "in court." To have your case heard, you must plead not guilty, put forward your case, spend time, spend money. At the end, the material you felt you created in good faith (remember section 163 provides that your motives are irrelevant) may still be found obscene. This means that you will bear the penalty and your court costs, including your lawyer's fees. If you are fortunate enough to win your artistic merit argument, you need only pay your costs, often large enough to discourage you from the tenuous life of the artist. Hence, the "chilling effect" of such laws—the protection offered the artist may still be too expensive to allow the embarking on the adventure. Artists argue that this cost is too high. Anticensorship feminists make the same argument, particularly when it comes to the degrading and dehumanizing part of the test. We are not sure what the edges are here, and we hate to see a scenario where feminists as well as artists are going to find themselves hedged in by a law we are supposed to be hailing as a victory for "the women of Canada."

The other difficulty with the *Butler* decision has to do with its reading, or rather rereading, of "legislative intent." In arguing that its shift to violent pornography from obscene erotica falls within the original "legislative intent" of that section of the Criminal Code, it sets out a broad permission to read law as convenient, a permission that can only tell in the long run against marginalized groups in the society, a designation to which women in general and feminists in particular still belong. To say that those who drafted the obscenity provisions did so because they were concerned about the harm caused to society by attitudes that work against the interests of women is balderdash. The idea of equality rights—the rights LEAF employed in argument to uphold this proscription of freedom of speech—was not the motivating force behind this legislation. *Immorality* was the motivating force and that had directly to do with keeping in the ascendancy the very class-specific, gender-specific, and age-specific power structure that worked so well for the legislators and the (by definition, white) male property owners they represented. So, what we have is an old law, originally drafted not to be in our best interests now defined in a way that we are assured is in our best interests but surely open for use to the next entrepreneur who comes along seeking to seize hold of the tale of a panic and turn it to her—or his—own purposes.

Implications for Feminist Expression

This is precisely what anticensorship feminists fear: that obscenity will again be redefined and that in the meantime we will have sold our birthright of freedom of expression and will not be able to access it to protect our own expression, expression which may very well be "found" by some court to be harmful to our society. Lesbians in particular have expressed concern that their right to expression will be curtailed by the

Butler case, not only in undermining as it does freedom of expression in general but in highlighting the concept of "degrading and dehumanizing" portrayals, an area into which many people would argue lesbian sexual expression naturally falls. It should also be noted that both lesbian and gay pornography, just like heterosexual pornography, seeks sometimes to explore the nexus between sex and violence.

That LEAF is sensitive to lesbian criticisms of the position it put forward as being of benefit to all women is indicated by the amount of space it spends trying to counter those concerns in its more or less official statement on the outcome of the case.[15] *Butler*, it contends, is of long-term benefit not only to lesbians but to male homosexuals. It sets up for itself such questions as "Did LEAF appeal to homophobia in the *Butler* case?" and "Is LEAF's position on pornography antilesbian?" and spends a considerable amount of space arguing No.[16] Basically, the argument of the lesbian arts community is that its work in the exploration of women's sexuality stands to suffer from this reaffirmation of obscenity as a concept and this derogation of expression as a freedom. They find ludicrous the arguments of antipornography feminists that violent, degrading, or dehumanizing depictions are not really the business of women anyway, but are only aberrations of the white male power structure. How are we to know the truth about women and sexuality, they argue, unless we search for answers? To tell girls to be good and to not look for answers in ugly places is to mimic Bluebeard, who promised his new wife that her life would be a happy one so long as she did not use the key that opened the door to the room where he had locked away the mutilated bodies of his past wives. Really, the lesbian community argues, it is not *we* who are acting as pseudo-males here, in our explorations pushing the borders of sex, but *you* who have just taken over from the male power structure the job of patrolling the borders of what is acceptable for women to even *think* about, let alone do.

Clearly a great deal of lesbian imagery does not fall under the violent category. The greater danger is presented by the "degrading and dehumanizing" head. As LEAF admits in its own apologia, one of the first reactions of a police force to the *Butler* case came in Toronto, where the force staged its first raid in years on a gay and lesbian bookstore. Glad Day Bookshop was convicted at trial. LEAF does not intend to intervene because it only does so "when no one else will be making equality arguments."[17] It also feels that the trial judge misused the *Butler* decision and that this will be remedied on appeal. LEAF also seems disinclined to do anything about the fact that Canada Customs is also still stopping gay and lesbian material at the border, including materials destined for Glad Day again.

LEAF may have decided that it is an organization involved only in the making of law, not in dealing with the social implications of law, but it is hardly fair to set the pendulum in motion and walk away. It is dishonest to credential oneself by arguing one speaks for all women and then to ignore criticisms from that constituency. And as yet we have no idea of just how much damage will be done. Just as it proved too difficult to achieve a sensible limitation of the term "pornography" or even "violent pornography" in the two pieces of proposed legislation that failed to find approval, the terms presented to the court as definitive in *Butler* will have to be sorted out year after year, case after case. In the meantime, people stand to have their material seized if they look like they're even in the region of Bluebeard's locked room.

The best discussion I have seen of the implications of *Butler*—interestingly enough, in an American legal journal—says that "pornography" is so vague a term that it will be modified throughout the article with quotation marks. Nadine Strossen's interest in the case has to do with its implications for the attitude of the U.S. Supreme Court. This may seem a flight of fancy, but, in some sense, Canada and its Charter have been used by American antipornography feminists as a proving ground for their own legislative and judicial ambitions. Catharine MacKinnon, along with University of Calgary law professor Kathleen Mahoney and Calgary lawyer Linda Taylor wrote the LEAF factum for the *Butler* case "in three intensive weeks."[18] MacKinnon, a figurehead of the American feminist antipornography movement, has long expressed her hopes for the Canadian Charter in terms of having international, specifically American, impact.[19]

Strossen notes that MacKinnon expected the United States Supreme Court to follow the lead of the Supreme Court of Canada in *Butler*. Strossen considers this unlikely, since to do so that court would have to reverse itself.[20] However, she is concerned about other types of damage caused by the antipornography movement in general, especially its insistence (as accepted by the court in *Butler*) of MacKinnon's general theory that women's consent, either *in* pornography or *of* pornography, should not only not be taken as prima facie evidence of consent (i.e., you accept it as a starting point to argue against) but that it should instead be taken as evidence of degradation and dehumanization. The idea here is that "no good girl would, after all." Strossen finds the idea that women—either in fact or in depiction—are incapable of giving meaningful consent to be degrading and dehumanizing in its own right.[21]

Strossen argues instead that feminism should be getting on with the business of empowering women and spends the bulk of her essay discussing ten "important reasons for concluding that women's rights are disserved by censoring 'pornography'."

1. Any censorship scheme would inevitably encompass many works that are especially valuable to feminists;
2. Any such scheme would be enforced in a way that discriminates against the least popular, least powerful groups in our society, including feminists and lesbians;
3. Censorship perpetuates the disempowering notion that women are essentially victims;
4. Censorship distracts from constructive approaches to countering antifemale discrimination and violence;
6. Censorship would harm women who voluntarily work in the sex industry;
7. Censorship would harm women's efforts to develop their own sexuality;
8. Censorship would strengthen the power of the religious right, whose patriarchal agenda would curtail women's rights;

9. By undermining free speech, censorship deprives feminists of a powerful tool for advancing women's equality; and
10. Sexual freedom, and freedom for sexually explicit expression, are essential aspects of human freedom; denying these specific freedoms undermines human rights more broadly.[22]

Given the strong influence of American thinking on Canada's antipornography feminists, it is interesting to note that one of Strossen's main philosophical sources for her article is a paper given by Thelma McCormack, Director of Feminist Research at York University. Professor McCormack made her comments at a public forum held at York on November 7-8, 1992, in response to the *Butler* decision. The forum was called "Refusing Censorship: Feminists and Activists Fight Back."

It is Strossen's point about "victimhood" that I find most telling here. This is something that a lot of feminists have not wanted to hear. Feminism has for too long been fuelled by its own moral panic, one that concentrates on "bad" men who somehow "prevent" us from getting on with our lives. It is very important that we do not simply replace "bad men" with "good women." It is important that we position women to take charge of their own existence. It is important that we offer them true freedom rather than just another blueprint—or another Bluebeard.

It is indisputable that feminism has offered some women freedom. The title of the York conference is full of action and refusal, the forum itself allied to a major institution, public, defiant, stand-taking. It bespeaks empowerment and the refusal to be disempowered, even by sisters. Another example of empowerment flowing directly from the *Butler* case is that of a group of Calgary law students (who identified themselves with LEAF), who spent months renting and viewing some 200 videos from local outlets to ascertain whether they failed the *Butler* test. The students turned their findings over to the police, who some time later laid charges.[23] This is an exact copy of the sort of activity followed by at least one Alberta group in its attempt to eradicate crime comics in the fifties.[24]

It is also, in spirit, a direct copy of the sort of sisterly, earnest collaboration evident in the antipornography feminist movement, not least of all in its "three intensive weeks" of collaboration on the *Butler* factum. It is therefore disingenuous of LEAF to disclaim any connection with this indulgence in what has been called "the sport of the timid."[25] LEAF claims that:

> No one has ever proposed that LEAF take on this project and it has never been approved for adoption by LEAF. Nonetheless, many now believe that LEAF is behind the project. LEAF National Office only heard about the project when the newspaper report was brought to our attention.[26]

Maybe so, but this is a lawyer's argument, the sort of thing one would argue in a factum. The fact is that these students consciously took their lead from a women's group they looked up to, were students at a university where the antipornography movement has found a secure home, were even emulating the tactics of mission-motivated, action-oriented use of the law. LEAF may have decided that it has now done all it wishes regarding pornography with its *Butler* intervention, but to deny that there will be damage or to deny responsibility for damage is irresponsible.

Anticensorship feminists like myself find ourselves left in a position where, in order to defend freedom of speech, we must defend material that would appear to fall rather short of being socially beneficial. It would be much easier were we arguing in favour of the sort of material that might stand a chance under the "artistic merit" defence. But unlike F.R. Scott, who "...went to bat for the Lady Chatte / Dressed in my bib and gown. / The judges three glared down at me / The priests patrolled the town,"[27] we are not talking about exempting "literature" but about outlawing censorship, and the irate crowd waiting for us outside includes our own sisters!

And it's not like the problem is going to go away, either. Despite the claims made for *Butler*, the reasoning of the court is simply too convoluted for it not to be revisited, likely again and again. It is a legal truism that "hard cases make bad law." Politically inspired though they may have been to do what they could for "women," all the judges nine managed to do was to send argument off down a side-tunnel. Unfortunately, they also laid down so broad a definition of harm and so devious a way of defining it that the case will no doubt also find its way into other areas of the law.

Child Pornography

Just as the first edition of this collection was going to press in 1992, the *Butler* decision came down and I had to end with a brief note on its possible outcome. As I began this essay, another precedent-setting case was being argued in Ontario in the area of pornography law. In a hearing before Mr. Justice David McCombs of the Ontario Court, General Division, the question of whether the work of Toronto artist Eli Langer should be forfeited was being considered. This case set precedent for the simple reason that it was the occasion for the first court consideration of the child pornography section (s. 163.1) of the Criminal Code brought in by Kim Campbell as Justice Minister. Aversion to "kiddie porn" has a motherhood aura about it, which no doubt accounts at least partly for this amendment to the code being accepted when attempts to shift Criminal Code focus generally from "obscenity" to "pornography" failed, twice.

The child porn law resembles the obscenity section, which it follows in the Code. It provides for a maximum of ten years' imprisonment for making, printing, publishing, or possessing for publication "child pornography," which is defined as

> (a) a photographic, film, video or other visual representation, whether or not it was made by electronic or mechanical means,
>
> (i) that shows a person who is or is depicted as being under the age of eighteen years and is engaged in or is depicted as engaged in explicit sexual activity, or
>
> (ii) the dominant characteristic of which is the depiction, for sexual purpose, of a sexual organ or the anal region of a person under the age of eighteen years; or

> (b) any written material or visual representation that advocates or counsels sexual activity with a person under the age of eighteen years...

Anomalously, it also provides for up to five years imprisonment for simple *possession* of what the court agrees is child porn. Arguing that you didn't know the person being depicted was under 18 is no defence unless you take "all reasonable steps" both to ensure that the person was over 18 *and* was not depicted as being under 18. Artistic merit or educational, scientific, or medical purposes do qualify as defences.

Guess what was being argued before the Ontario court? Harm, of course, and artistic merit. The case involved five paintings and 35 sketches seized in a police raid on the Mercer Union gallery in December 1993. The Crown proceeded with prosecution under the Criminal Code on the grounds that the work portrayed persons under the age of 18 engaged in sexual activity. The question of harm was—as it always is in such cases—addressed by competing psychologists who testified that (1) yes, the pictures will incite pedophiles to molest children or (2) no, the pictures will not incite pedophiles to molest children. This testimony pertains to harm, which pertains to community standards, which pertains to more cases than just *Butler*, but certainly is reaffirmed by *Butler*.

Testimony under the artistic merit defence is of a different kind. Basically, art witnesses are unconcerned with whether such works will or will not incite but rather whether this is serious work. Doris McCarthy, at 84 one of Canada's foremost artists, testified that Langer's work was "important, serious, passionate, and interesting" and that an observer would realize the message was "condemnatory," as evidenced by the black and red colour scheme. Another witness for the defence, Christopher Hume, art critic for *The Toronto Star*, agreed that the images were troubling but pointed out that artists often seek to express anger, disapproval, or outrage "and therefore the images they create are sometimes very disturbing."[28] In the end, the artistic merit defence won the day: the judge upheld the constitutionality of the child pornography law but ruled that Langer's paintings escaped sanction on the grounds that they were "art."[29]

The Langer case concerns me, not simply as someone who believes that it is often an artist's job to consider precisely those things we would rather not think about but also directly because of the fact that I am on the editorial board of a press which recently brought out the memoirs, in poetic form, of a sexual abuse survivor. The book is disturbing and certainly it is peopled with persons under 18. The press is proud of the book and certain of the decision to publish it. However, we could arguably face criminal prosecution of the author and the press, confiscation of the material, and legal fees. The question is whether this book might be read as somehow advocating or counselling child sex. Thank God, there are no sketches, in which case mere depiction without counselling is sufficient to attract prosecution. Is the cover safe? Of course, we would have open to us the defence of artistic merit, which was successful for Langer, but that can only be made in a court room, with all the attendant costs.

Should we just have asked this woman to shut up because telling her story might be inconvenient or unsettling or offensive to other people? Somehow I balk at joining the legions always willing to tell women no. And what about psychotherapists who encourage patients to create written and verbal depictions of their experience to try to overcome child sexual abuse? Might these not fall under the child porn section as showing "a person who is or is depicted as being under the age of eighteen years and is engaged in or is depicted as engaged in explicit sexual activity"? Remember, this section is unusual in that mere *possession* can net you five years. If a psychotherapist consulted me as a lawyer on using such techniques, I would have to advise written over pictorial methods under this new law and I would have to advise on the dangers of both. Surely this is just another way of telling people who have been damaged by the shortcomings of our society to be more convenient in the way they express their suffering.

Conclusion

Which brings me back to the problems of trying to tidy up the messiness that is women's lives by imposing the values of what after all is middle-class feminism. It would be so convenient for us all if women would choose "good" careers, would not marry or would leave "bad" men, would act in ways that are "best" for them. But they don't. Prostitutes have accused feminists of trying to "pimp" them—that is, to use them to further feminists' own agenda to credential themselves within the power structure[30]—in short, to turn the moral panic against prostitution to entrepreneurial advantage for feminism. Surely, "women" in general have the same complaint to make regarding the pornography panic. Strossen points out that labelling women as victims is unlikely to bring them any advantage, though it may bring the labeller advantage when she rides in on the white horse. Lesbians have objected loudly that they are women too and that they have been undermined, not supported by this campaign. LEAF's statement that its activities were not aimed at women, but aimed at helping them, is simply not enough.

The business of any women's movement should be the empowerment of women. The antipornography movement, no matter what its intentions, has moved to disempower them. Perhaps this is the fault of law—a system of little imagination or grace—but one on which feminism has relied heavily. We have sucked great contentment from a case here, a statute there, and middle-class women have indisputably managed to move up the ladder because of them. However, for the large number of women, the fruits of feminism have been less noticeable. The antipornography movement has noble ambitions, insofar as it really does have an underlying wish to protect women from the violence thought to be caused by portrayals of violence, degradation, and dehumanization. But closing off corridors of expression works against everything feminism stands for in terms of empowering women to fulfil their individual destinies. What is needed to allow that to happen is a lighter, not a heavier, hand.

Furthermore, we must proceed in faith that help will come to us from places where we least expect it. Consider, for example, Angela Carter's concept of the "moral pornographer," developed almost two decades ago.

> The moral pornographer would be an artist who uses pornographic material as part of the acceptance of the logic of a world of absolute sexual

> license for all the genders, and projects a model of the way such a world might work. A moral pornographer might use pornography as a critique of current relationships of the flesh and the subsequent revelation, through the infinite modulations of the sexual act, of the real relations of man and his kind. Such a pornographer would not be the enemy of women, perhaps because he might begin to penetrate to the heart of the contempt for women that distorts our culture even as he entered the realm of true obscenity as he describes it.[31]

In other words, the "moral pornographer" would encourage searching for Bluebeard's charnel-house. Surely that is at foundation a more feminist act than hiding its existence and inviting the young girl or naive woman to take refuge in incuriosity and innocence.

Notes

1. "A major slogan of feminist theory and politics which argues that personal and intimate experience is not isolated, individual, or undetermined, but rather is social, political, and systemic." Cheris Kramarae and Paula A. Treichler, *Amazons, Bluestockings and Crones: A Feminist Dictionary* (London: Pandora Press, 1992), p. 333.
2. Janice Dickin McGinnis, "Bogeymen and the Law: Crime Comics and Pornography," *Ottawa Law Review* 20 (1988):3–22. Crime comics fall under the obscenity section. See R.S.C. 1985, c. C–46, s. 163.
3. W. Wesley Pue, "Moral Panic at the English Bar: Paternal vs. Commercial Ideologies of Legal Practice in the 1860s," *Law and Social Inquiry* 15 (1990):49–118.
4. Stanley Cohen, *Folk Devils and Moral Panics: The Creation of Mods and Rockers* (Oxford: Oxford University Press, 1980), p. 9. Quoted in Pue, *Moral Panic*, p. 50.
5. Barbara Epstein, *The Politics of Domesticity: Women, Evangelism and Temperance in Nineteenth-Century America* (Middleton, Conn.: Wesleyan University Press, 1981) p. 103.
6. Janice Dickin McGinnis, "Chilling Expression: Obscenity Law and the Halo Zone" in *Seeing Ourselves. Media Power and Policy in Canada*, edited by Helen Holmes and David Taras (Toronto: Harcourt Brace Jovanovitch, 1992), pp. 270–86.
7. Ibid., pp. 273–75.
8. Ibid., pp. 275–78.
9. F.R. Scott, "A Lass in Wonderland" in *The Collected Poems of F.R. Scott* (Toronto: McClelland and Stewart, 1981), pp. 264–65.
10. I have argued this in Janice Dickin McGinnis, "Whores and Worthies: Feminism and Prostitution," *Canadian Journal of Law and Society* 9 (1994):105–22.
11. Headnote, *R. v. Butler* (1992) 70 C.C.C. (3d) 129 at 129–30.
12. Ian A. Hunter, "Feminism Trumps Morality" *Criminal Law Quarterly* 35 (1993):147–52 at 147.
13. Debra M. McAllister, "*Butler*: A Triumph for Equality Rights," *National Journal of Constitutional Law* 2 (1992–93):118–31 at 130.
14. McGinnis, "Halo Zone," pp. 278–80.
15. See Karen Busby, "LEAF and Pornography: Litigating on Equality and Sexual Representations," *Canadian Journal of Law and Society* 9 (1994):165–92. I believe we are allowed to take this article as more or less the official position of LEAF. According to Busby: "The 'we' in this paper is LEAF. Writing this paper has been a collective process." (p. 165n.)
16. Ibid., pp. 179–87.

17. Ibid., p. 185n.
18 Ibid., p. 165n.
19 Catharine A. MacKinnon, "Charter of Rights and the Possibilities of Women's Equality." The Ronald Martland Lecture, Faculty of Law, University of Calgary, January 17, 1989.
20. Nadine Strossen, "A Feminist Critique of 'The' Feminist Critique of Pornography," *Virginia Law Review* 79 (1993):1099–1190 at 1126.
21. Ibid.
22. Ibid., pp. 1111–112.
23. Rick Mofina and Monte Stewart, "Video Stores Face Obscenity Charges," *Calgary Herald* (October 22, 1993), p. B3. My information also comes from students involved in the exercise. More than a year later, two of the three stores charged were acquitted. Bob Bealy and Monte Stewart, "Stores Acquitted of Obscenity," *Calgary Herald* (December 15, 1994), p. B1.
24. McGinnis, "Bogeymen," p. 19.
25. Jan Bauer, "Comment on Crime Comics and Pornography" *Ottawa Law Review* 20 (1988):46–48 at 48. Bauer at the time was Executive Director of The Canadian Centre (English-speaking) of International P.E.N., a group which deals with writers' rights.
26. Busby, "LEAF and Pornography," p. 191n.
27. Scott, "A Lass in Wonderland," p. 264.
28. Accounts of the hearing taken from "Gallery Chose Disputed Pictures Over Many Entries," *The Globe and Mail* (October 8, 1994); and "Artists Back Right to Paint Sexual Work," *The Toronto Star* (October 8, 1994), p. A16.
29. Tracey Tyler, "Artist's Sexual Images Ruled Legal," *The Toronto Star*, April 21, p. A1.
30. L. Bell, ed., *Good Girls/Bad Girls: Sex Trade Workers and Feminists Face to Face* (Toronto: The Women's Press, 1987) p. 114.
31. Angela Carter, *The Sadeian Woman and the Ideology of Pornography* (New York: Pantheon Books, 1978), pp. 19–20, as quoted in Kramerae and Treichler, *Amazons*, p. 348.

LINGUISTIC DUALITY IN BROADCASTING POLICY: A MICROCOSM OF CANADA'S CONSTITUTIONAL POLITICS[1]

Marc Raboy

INTRODUCTION

Short of the radical alternative of Quebec sovereignty, there is no question that Canadian communications policy will continue to be marked by the need to reconcile the "two solitudes" of linguistic duality.

Canada can only work to the extent that all participating partners recognize the valid claims of each of the distinct components that make up the country. In communications, particularly broadcasting, we have a long history of vacillation between recognition and denial of this basic fact. As a result, it can be variously argued that communication policy has contributed to holding the country together as much as to splitting it apart. But perhaps this is the essence of Canada: an amalgam of discrete components held together by centrifugal force.*

From the origins of public broadcasting in the 1930s through the free trade talks of 1988, communication policy has been seen as a central bulwark of Canadian cultural and even political sovereignty vis-à-vis the United States. At the same time, and especially from the mid-1960s through the Quebec referendum of 1980, a second layer of policy objectives specifically aimed at lessening the fragmenting pressures coming from Quebec. In the Meech Lake and Charlottetown accords, however, there was nary a whimper about the cultural goals of policy; if anything, communication policy has been increasingly set up as an economic and industrial issue, particularly in the framework of economic globalization and frontier-busting communication technologies. At best, cultural imperatives have taken a backseat to these issues.

*"Canada," as used in this chapter, refers to the set of political institutions that have evolved from 1867 to the present, and includes Quebec. "Quebec" is used somewhat more ambiguously as, depending on the context, its meaning can range from referring to an unproblematic component part of Canada to a putative separate state. Most of the time it is somewhere in between. My use of these terms reflects the tension of the unresolved aspects of the national question as of summer 1995 and is not intended to be read as a political position.

In Quebec, meanwhile, the federal policy stranglehold on culture is one of the strongest metaphors for characterizing the constitutional dilemma. If Quebec cannot control the policy framework of culture and communication, the argument goes, it loses one of the crucial levers for defining and orienting its distinct society. The problem is that the pan-Canadian and the Quebec views are mutually exclusive, insofar as each one is premised on the crucial importance of culture and communication in defining nationhood.

Increased globalization, meanwhile, requires us to rethink the idea of nationhood in the late twentieth century. Accordingly, the state, and particularly public policy in culture and communication, is defined in terms of development, rather than national identity. We must all function in a global marketplace. Communication policy thus aims to allow a favourable positioning for national cultural industries which, it is hoped, will help bolster indigenous culture. Policy is aimed outward rather than inward, and Canada is seen only as the domestic market.

At the same time, however, policy has at least implied sociocultural goals. One sees this most clearly expressed in general policy statements emanating from both Ottawa and Quebec City, and also in specific policies that aim to take account of the political realities of the country. In this respect, be it in a Canadian or a Quebec perspective, policy objectives tend to be the same.

Thus, questions surrounding a range of contemporary issues, from the political framework for introducing the "information superhighways" and the regulation of telecommunications to the role and financing of the CBC and other national cultural institutions, tend to be distorted in Canada by considerations coloured by the national question.

The extent to which this is so can best be illustrated by recalling the history of broadcasting in Canada, as reflected in the evolution of Canadian broadcasting policy.[2]

1928–1945: Creating a System...and Its Problems

Although broadcasting in Canada actually began in 1919 (Vipond, 1992), the basic framework of the Canadian broadcasting system was laid out by the Royal Commission on Radio Broadcasting (chaired by Sir John Aird) that reported in 1929 (Canada, Royal Commission on Radio Broadcasting, 1929). Remarkably, the central issues in Canadian broadcasting today are essentially the same as they were then.

The Aird Commission recommended wholesale nationalization of the then largely commercial radio system, and creation of a national, publicly owned monopoly to operate all broadcasting in Canada on a basis of public service for the information, enlightenment, and entertainment of the Canadian people. Even before its report was tabled, however, the Quebec government of Louis-Alexandre Taschereau passed legislation authorizing Quebec to erect and operate its own radio station, as well as produce programs for broadcast by existing commercial stations.

Before acting on the recommendations, Ottawa asked the Supreme Court to determine whether jurisdiction over broadcasting lay with the Dominion or with the provinces, and in 1931 the Court ruled in Ottawa's favour. An appeal to the Judicial Committee of the Privy Council in London took another year to resolve, and so it was only in 1932 that Ottawa had a clear signal to legislate.

The Canadian Radio Broadcasting Act of 1932 created a national public broadcaster, the Canadian Radio Broadcasting Commission (CRBC), which had the additional responsibility of regulating the activities of the private broadcasters. This double mandate would be transferred to the CRBC's successor, the Canadian Broadcasting Corporation (CBC), when it was created in 1936.

Aird had proposed that broadcasting content be overseen by assistant commissioners in each of the provinces, but this interesting recommendation was not followed. Instead, the CRBC set out to create a single national radio service in English and in French, using both languages alternately so that both English and French audiences heard the same program. In other words, the CRBC took the view that there was only one radio audience in Canada, made up of members of two different language groups.

As the CBC reflected in its submission to the Royal Commission on Bilingualism and Biculturalism some 30 years later: "Obviously, such an alternative was only workable as long as the program needs of both groups could be met by a single network." Indeed, as the demands of each group for a more complete service continued to grow, "the Corporation [was presented] with a situation which could only be met adequately by duplicate networks, English and French" (CBC, 1964, 5).

The most compelling factor for the CRBC to begin moving away from a single service using two languages to "parallel services" in each language as early as 1934 was the absolute, militant refusal of anglophone communities in the Maritimes, Ontario, and Western Canada to accept the presence of French on the air. This has been documented in the memoirs of Canadian radio pioneers such as E.A. Corbett, Hector Charlesworth, and Austin Weir, according to whom French programming on national radio sparked "a queer mixture of prejudice, bigotry and fear" (Weir, 1965, 151).

By 1941, separation of the two services was complete—although the original CBC news service, created to meet the demands of covering the Second World War, operated bilingually. Paradoxically, yet to be expected, the institution of separate services was welcomed by French-Canadian nationalists, who had feared becoming the marginalized minority within a single, nominally bilingual service. The French network achieved a degree of administrative autonomy because of "the need for national unity raised by the war," but no sooner was it in place than it became the focus of a national crisis (Lamarche, 1960).

In January 1942, the government announced it would hold a plebiscite on conscription. In the ensuing campaign, the Quebec-based Ligue pour la défense du Canada, a broad front of political and social leaders opposed to conscription, sought to use the public airwaves in order to urge their fellow citizens to vote No. The CBC, by order of the government, denied the No voice access to its stations. The opponents of conscription were able to promote their cause by purchasing paid advertising on commercial stations, however, resulting in another paradox: the identification of "public" broadcasting as an oppressive agent of centralized federalism, and of French-Canadian entrepreneurial capital as a progressive force (Laurendeau, 1962).

1945–1963: Consolidating the System...and the Syndrome

Citing the educational nature of broadcasting, as "a powerful medium of publicity and intellectual and moral training," the government of Quebec under Maurice Duplessis claimed that Quebec had the constitutional authority to create a provincial broadcasting service, and passed legislation setting up Radio-Québec in 1945 (Quebec, Statutes, 1945). This legislation was never put into effect, however, after the federal minister responsible for broadcasting, C.D. Howe, announced in the House of Commons that, "since broadcasting is the sole responsibility of the Dominion government, broadcasting licences shall not be issued to other governments or corporations owned by other governments" (Canada, House of Commons, 1946, 1167).

Meanwhile, outside Quebec, the "parallel services" of public broadcasting were developing unequally. While the CBC's English- language radio service extended from coast to coast by 1938, the same could not yet be said for French-language service, even in the 1950s. The Royal Commission on National Development in the Arts, Letters and Sciences (chaired by Vincent Massey) reported in 1951 that French-speaking communities outside Quebec were still poorly served by the CBC (Canada, 1951, 297). Six years later, another Royal Commission on Broadcasting (chaired by Robert Fowler) found that many parts of Canada were still unserved in French, and suggested that this was more than a question of available resources: "It remains a moot question, however, whether Canada has yet reached the stage of complete national maturity where the introduction of French on the airwaves of Ontario... would not be regarded by a substantial majority as an intolerable intrusion rather than the cultural complement that in truth it would be" (Canada, Royal Commission on Broadcasting, 1957, 242).

The Conservative government elected in 1957 sought to build up the commercial side of Canadian broadcasting, and paid little attention to its role in the complexities of the national dilemma. This was most apparent in its response to the historic Radio-Canada producers' strike of 1958–59, which saw, among other things, the rise to political prominence of René Lévesque. Then a well-known television journalist, Lévesque became an outspoken supporter of the producers, who were seeking their first collective agreement with the corporation. He would often say that if the strike had shut down English television instead of French—there was only one Canadian channel in each language at the time—the government would have forced a settlement in half an hour. As it turned out, Radio-Canada was paralyzed for 68 days, and the producers' strike took on mythical proportions as a main reference point of Quebec nationalism.[3]

1963–1980: National Unity and Struggles for Power

When the Liberals returned to power in 1963, the Pearson government publicly identified cultural policy in general and broadcasting in particular as strategic weapons in its struggle against the rising and increasingly radical nationalist movement in Quebec. In the House of Commons on November 13, 1964, Secretary of State Maurice Lamontagne announced the government's intention to rationalize and centralize the activities of all federal cultural agencies under the jurisdiction of his office, and to create a cabinet committee on cultural affairs. Under the new policy, the national broadcasting service, the CBC, would play a central role:

> The CBC is one of Canada's most vital and essential institutions at this crucial moment of our history. The CBC must become a living and daily

> testimony of the Canadian identity, a faithful reflection of our two main cultures and a powerful element of understanding, moderation and unity in our country. If it performs these national tasks with efficiency, its occasional mistakes will be easily forgotten; if it fails in that mission, its other achievements will not compensate for that failure (Canada, House of Commons, 1964–65, 10084).

This was the clearest enunciation of the CBC's mission, in the government's eyes, since the war. It became clearer still during the next few years. At parliamentary committee hearings in 1966, Liberal backbenchers from Quebec and Radio-Canada middle management executives sparred over their respective views of the CBC's role vis-à-vis the emerging question of "separatism." When a new broadcasting act was introduced in October 1967, it contained a clause that read as follows: "The national broadcasting service [CBC] should…contribute to the development of national unity and provide for a continuing expression of Canadian identity" (Canada, Statutes, 1967–68, art. 3.g.iv).

In the House, Secretary of State Judy LaMarsh said the national unity clause was "perhaps the most important feature of the CBC's mandate in the new bill" (Canada, House of Commons, 1967–68a, 3754). But the NDP's R.W. Prittie expressed the fear that the clause could be used as an excuse for a witch hunt against Radio-Canada journalists who did not toe a strict federalist line. Gérard Pelletier, then chairman of the parliamentary committee on broadcasting and soon to join the Cabinet at the side of his lifelong friend Pierre Elliott Trudeau, admitted he had doubts about it "lead[ing] some people to believe that it is not a matter of promotion but of propaganda" (Canada, House of Commons, 1967–68, 6017). And an important observation on the clause's implications came from Conservative MP David MacDonald, a future minister of communications:

> When we begin to move into areas such as…national unity, we are in effect moving away from the concept of public broadcasting toward the idea of state broadcasting whereby the broadcasting system of the country becomes an extension of the state (Canada, House of Commons, 1967–68, 6025).

After some vigorous debate, the broadcasting act passed, with the controversial clause intact. Radio-Canada's interpretation of its mandate to promote national unity led to bizarre incidents such as keeping its cameras trained on the parade at the 1968 Saint-Jean Baptiste Day celebrations in Montreal, while police and demonstrators fought a bloody battle on the sidelines. During the October Crisis of 1970, the federal cabinet closely oversaw what was and was not broadcast by Radio-Canada, and a few months later a string of management "supervisors" appeared in the corporation's newsrooms, with no apparent function other than political surveillance (Raboy, 1990, 204–08). The former head of Radio-Canada news and public affairs, Marc Thibault, remembers one official whose job was to monitor all news programs and count the number of times the word *Québécois* was used (Thibault, 1988).

The situation culminated with Prime Minister Trudeau's instruction to the federal regulatory agency, the Canadian Radio-television and Telecommunications Commission (CRTC), to inquire into CBC news coverage in the wake of the election of a Parti Québécois government in Quebec in November 1976.

The CRTC dutifully investigated and reported, in July 1977, that the CBC had indeed failed "to contribute to the development of national unity"—but not in the sense meant by the prime minister. The problem was not a bias in favour of separatist politics, the CRTC said, but deficient representation of Canada's "two solitudes" to one another. In English and in French, the CBC did not pay adequate attention to the regions of Canada; it was too centralized and aloof, too influenced by commercial pressures, too bureaucratic. "In the modern world," reported the CRTC, "political and economic developments tend to centralize; cultural developments, on the other hand, tend to be regional, arising in much more sharply delimited areas" (1977, 9).

The 1977 CRTC inquiry appears to have been a turning point in the Liberal government's view of the role of media in Canada's constitutional struggle. Political expectations of the CBC diminished, and in the important run-up to the Quebec referendum of 1980, the corporation was left to establish and carry out an internal policy of news coverage according to rigorous journalistic standards and the principle of "the public's right to be informed" (CBC, 1979, 377-424). Ultimately, the referendum campaign was covered by the CBC as a straight news event, while the government sought to mobilize the federalist constituency directly, particularly through advertising (Johnson, 1983; Stark, 1983).

The role of the CBC aside, political struggles surrounding the national question continued to mark the evolution of Canadian broadcasting in the 1960s and 1970s. From 1968 on, renewed demands from Quebec for constitutional powers in broadcasting highlighted the constitutional debates of the day and marked the evolution of communications in Canada. In its brief to the constitutional conference convened by prime minister Lester Pearson in February 1968, Quebec claimed the right to play the role of a national state in matters pertaining to language and culture, including broadcasting. As instruments of education and culture, radio and television rightfully belong under provincial jurisdiction, the Quebec brief argued. The court ruling of 1932 was "unacceptable"; federal agencies like the CBC should be made to reflect the "bicultural reality" of Canada; jurisdiction over broadcasting should not be the exclusive domain of the federal government (Quebec, Brief, 1968).

In the coming months, debate focussed on the question of "educational broadcasting." The new broadcasting act stated that "facilities should be provided within the Canadian broadcasting system for educational broadcasting" (Canada, Statutes, 1967, art. s.2.i.). Yet, education was clearly under provincial jurisdiction. Returning to Quebec from the constitutional conference, Premier Daniel Johnson declared that his government had decided to apply the province's 1945 law establishing Radio-Québec (Quebec, Legislative Assembly, 1968, 3). By the end of 1969, Ottawa and the provinces had settled on a definition of educational broadcasting under which, in the 1970s, provincial public broadcasting agencies would begin operating in four provinces.

In the early 1970s, negotiating a strong role for Quebec in communications policy became one of the hallmarks of Quebec Premier Robert Bourassa's program for achieving "cultural sovereignty." In a series of important policy statements, Quebec proposed "to promote and maintain a *Québécois* system of communications" (Quebec, Ministère des communications du Québec, 1971), and to become "master craftsman of communications policy on its territory" (Quebec, 1973).

The cornerstone of Quebec's policy was to be the Régie des services publics, an agency regulating utilities falling under the province's jurisdiction, which Quebec saw as equivalent to the CRTC. In 1973, the Régie began to regulate the 160 cable companies then operating in Quebec, although they were already subject to the regulation of the CRTC. Within a year, the inevitable occurred: in applications to serve a community in the lower St. Lawrence region near Rimouski, the Régie and the CRTC awarded licences to two different applicants. It took until November 1977 for the Supreme Court to decide the case in favour of the CRTC, ruling that Ottawa had exclusive jurisdiction over cable (Canada, Supreme Court, 1978, 191–210).

Under the Parti Québécois government of the 1970s, Quebec did not directly engage with Ottawa over communications policy. The PQ carried over the policy thrust of the Bourassa government but basically abdicated in view of its lack of power over communications under the existing system. When pressed, PQ politicians would state that political sovereignty was the only solution to Quebec's communications problems (Quebec, National Assembly, 1977, B-2095). Paradoxically, the PQ was thus a lot less aggressive than its predecessors in seeking concrete gains from Ottawa in this area. It concentrated instead on developing the programs and policies begun by previous Union Nationale and Liberal governments: Radio-Québec, now a full-fledged broadcaster, and the particular Quebec form of participatory communication known as "community" media.

1980–1990: The Triumph of the Market

Both in Ottawa and Quebec, communication policy took on a new, yet strangely familiar, shape after the referendum of 1980.

In Ottawa, as we saw earlier, the view of the CBC as the centrepiece of Canadian cultural policy had begun to shift in the late 1970s. With the referendum out of the way, the entire cultural sphere took on a distinctly economic vocation. In July 1980, the arts and culture branch of the Department of the Secretary of State and ministerial responsbility for culture were transferred to the industry-oriented Department of Communications. The diffusion of culture would henceforth depend increasingly on its industrial base, and the DOC would be concentrating on the growth of "cultural industries," communications minister Francis Fox told the parliamentary committee (Canada, House of Commons, 1980–83, 2/9).

The new orientation was underwritten by the Federal Cultural Policy Review Committee (chaired by Louis Applebaum and Jacques Hébert) that reported in 1982, and was spelled out in detail in a series of policy statements signed by Fox in 1983–84 (Canada, Federal Cultural Policy Review Committee, 1982; Canada,

Department of Communications, 1983a; 1983b; 1984). Since then, federal policy has been marked notably by a gradual withdrawal of fiscal responsibility for public-service broadcasting (CBC budget cuts), privatization of television production (through the Telefilm fund), and the introduction of a wide range of new commercial cable-delivered television signals (pay-TV and both optional and nondiscretionary subscriber-funded specialty services). In general, the 1980s marked a shift from the political to the economic, and the eclipse of the traditional sociocultural objectives of broadcasting in Canada.

The Quebec government's new approach was strangely similar; as in the postreferendum context of the early 1980s, Quebec appeared to lose interest in the sociocultural possibilities of communications altogether, and placed its emphasis on industrial development. Ottawa and Quebec City thus found themselves on the same wavelength, as the PQ discourse on communications became increasingly economically oriented, and its policy industrially oriented. Instead of making jurisdictional demands, Quebec in the early 1980s seemed determined to outpace Ottawa in shifting the accent in communications from the cultural and political to the industrial and economic spheres (Quebec, Ministère des communications du Québec, 1982; 1983).

A historic shift occurred with the election of the Mulroney Conservatives in 1984. In general, the government's early initiatives with respect to broadcasting coincided with its general thrust toward reduced public spending and expanding the role of the private sector in the Canadian economy (Canada, Task Force on Program Review, 1986). But broadcasting, and communications generally, quickly emerged as one of the sectors on the cutting edge of the government's plan for "national reconciliation" after the institutionalized antagonism of the Trudeau years.

Brian Mulroney's choice of Marcel Masse to be his minister of communications was an astute one in this regard. Masse was not only a loyal Tory but a well-known Quebec nationalist who had been a cabinet minister in the Union Nationale government that had fought, in the 1960s, for more provincial power through agencies such as Radio-Québec. He was the ideal minister for thawing relations with Quebec, while applying broad government policy to communications.[4]

Tendering the olive branch to Quebec in communications was also a move to deflect criticism from the Tories' attitude toward national public broadcasting. Even as his government was administering crippling surgery to the CBC budget, Masse was fond of reminding audiences of the Liberals' attitude toward public broadcasting: "We're not the ones who threatened to put the key in the door of the CBC because we didn't like its news coverage," he told a meeting of Quebec journalists in Montreal in December 1984 (Masse, 1984).

In February 1985, Ottawa and Quebec City signed their first agreement in communications since creating their respective communications ministries a few months apart in 1969. The industrial thrust of the accord was evident, aiming at technical innovation and support for the production, development, and marketing of communications goods and services, especially in export markets (Canada/Quebec, 1985a; Tremblay, 1988). The two governments also set up a permanent joint committee, chaired by the two deputy ministers of communications, to pursue further areas of collaboration.

The committee's first effort produced an important report on the future of French-language television, whose central recommendation was crucial to the developing federal policy with respect to broadcasting. It proposed "that the special nature of the French-language television system be recognized within the Canadian broadcasting system, and that government policies and regulations be adapted accordingly" (Canada/Quebec, 1985b, 2).[5] Such a proposal would recognize, for the first time, the historic reality of parallel development of Canadian broadcasting since the 1930s. It would also mark a major shift in Ottawa's official attitude, which had always been that there is but one policy for Canadian broadcasting, not two.

In addition to a series of specific proposals, the report proposed general ongoing consultation between Ottawa and Quebec. A "harmonization" agreement for the development of French-language television was signed soon thereafter (Canada/Quebec, 1986). Since then, areas of federal-provincial cooperation have included working groups on cable television, children's advertising, and computer software (Tremblay, 1988, 83); and the idea of tailoring policy to meet the distinct needs of different markets has been reflected notably in CRTC decisions (CRTC, 1987), and in the functioning of the Telefilm fund.

Quebec public opinion welcomed the new distribution of resources in communications, which was seen as a move away from the traditional approach of massive, and exclusive, federal involvement in cultural affairs (Bissonnette, 1985). This, it was recalled, had begun as a kind of benevolent state intervention in the 1950s in the wake of the Massey Report, only to be transformed into a strategic weapon for the promotion of national unity under the Pearson and, particularly, the Trudeau governments.

The Mulroney government's first term in office was also marked by a series of formal initiatives with respect to broadcasting policy: a comprehensive review by a Task Force on Broadcasting Policy (chaired by Gerald Caplan and Florian Sauvageau, Canada, Task Force on Broadcasting Policy, 1986), lengthy hearings and a report by the parliamentary Standing Committee on Communications and Culture (Canada, House of Commons, 1988), a ministerial policy statement (Canada, Communications Canada, 1988), and, finally, a new broadcasting act (Canada, Unpassed Bills, 1988a).

The Caplan-Sauvageau task force welcomed the proposals of the federal-provincial committee on French-language television (Canada, Task Force on Broadcasting Policy, 1986, 157), and reiterated many of its key proposals. It proposed "that the distinctive character of Quebec broadcasting be recognized both in itself and as the nucleus of French-language broadcasting throughout Canada" (p. 223). French- and English-language services within the CBC should be recognized as serving "distinct societies," and should be allowed to take "different approaches to meeting the objectives assigned to public broadcasting" (p. 217). The CBC's French network budgets should be reviewed to bring hourly production costs for television more into line with the higher amounts allocated to English production (p. 253). As for the CBC's national unity mandate, the task force found it "inappropriate for any broadcaster, public or private.... It suggests constrained attachment to a political order rather than free expression in the pursuit of a national culture broadly defined" (pp. 283–84). The task force proposed to replace it with "a more socially oriented provision, for example, that the service contribute to the development of national consciousness" (p. 285).

The parliamentary committee that studied the Caplan- Sauvageau recommendations made two pertinent proposals of its own. One concerned making the law reflect the CRTC practice of "tak[ing] into consideration the distinctive characters of French and English broadcasting when implementing broadcasting policy" (Canada, House of Commons, 1988, 418). The other extended the task force proposal on CBC budgets, specifying that production costs be established "so that the quality of the Canadian programs of the English and French networks would be comparable" (p. 363).

The government's position was formalized in the policy statement *Canadian Voices Canadian Choices*, signed by Flora MacDonald and made public a few days after the report of the parliamentary committee in June 1988. Here it was recognized that

> The problems and challenges for English-language broadcasting and French-language broadcasting are not the same...[and that] these differences between the English and French broadcasting environments necessarily require different policy approaches for each (Canada, Communications Canada, 1988, 6–7).

The legislation tabled at the same time (Bill C-136) featured a half-dozen clauses referring to the linguistic duality of the system. The key clause specified that "English and French language broadcasting, while sharing common aspects, operate under different conditions and may have different requirements" (Canada, Unpassed Bills, 1988a, art. 3.1.b.). The CBC's mandate was changed to read that "the programming provided by the Canadian Broadcasting Corporation should...contribute to shared national consciousness and identity" (art. 3.1.n.iv.). An amendment introduced at third reading added that it should "strive to be of equivalent quality in English and in French" as well (Canada, Unpassed Bills, 1988b, art. 3.1.k.iv.).

Bill C-136 died in the Senate on September 30, 1988, as Parliament was dissolved for the national elections (Raboy, 1990, 329–34). It was reintroduced virtually intact, however, as Bill C-40 in October 1989 (Canada, 1989).

While the debate on Bill C-136 had generated almost no controversy over its constitutional implications, this was not the case with Bill C-40. When the new bill went to legislative committee in January 1990, the minister—now once again Marcel Masse—was compelled to reiterate the general thrust of the legislation as it had been expressed in Flora MacDonald's policy statement of June 1988, and to explain the rewording of the CBC's national unity mandate (Canada, House of Commons, 1990, 11).

The semantic soul-searching culminated in a highly partisan parliamentary debate only months before the collapse of the Meech Lake Accord in 1990. In legislative committee, New Democratic Party critic Ian Waddell accused the government of "Meeching" the CBC, before asking minister Masse point blank if he was a "separatist" (Canada, House of Commons, 1990, 17–18). Liberals peppered CBC and CRTC spokespersons with leading questions about the CBC's ability to serve the country if the wording of its mandate was changed. But the government's majority in the House of Commons proved more reliable than its constitutional deal with the provincial premiers, and the Act passed essentially intact (Canada, Statistics, 1991).

The 1990s: Broadcasting, Culture, Communications, and Nation-Saving

For about 70 years, as we have seen, broadcasting policy has been one of the main arenas for playing out the paradoxical issues of Canada's constitutional politics. Royal commission reports from Aird (radio broadcasting) to Massey (arts and culture) to Laurendeau-Dunton (bilingualism and biculturalism) have included some of the best efforts at making Canada work. Resulting legislation, funding programs, and regulatory policies have reflected more mundane, sometimes partisan concerns.

Inevitably, the institutions and practices of Canadian communications have reflected the inconsistencies of Canada rather than the national unity designs of their architects. In one sense, they have fostered a dualistic view, but instead of tapping this as a source of strength, the Canadian policy apparatus continued to struggle against it during the 1990s.

The federal government was still spending close to $3 billion per year in the area of culture and communication, much of it explicitly earmarked to efforts at promoting national unity. In 1991, in the wake of the collapse of the Meech Lake Accord, the House of Commons Standing Committee on Communications and Culture undertook an investigation aimed at exploring the role of culture and communications in Canada's constitutional future, in the belief "that the constitutional issue is as much cultural as it is political" (Canada, House of Commons, 1992, ix). The Committee sought to establish the relationship between cultural identity, cultural diversity, and political unity, and the role of communications systems in this process.

Characteristically, the Committee identified the CBC as a critical institution, and, regarding regulation, proposed "...the continuation of a single, federal authority over broadcasting and telecommunications [the CRTC], with provincial and regional consultation in the national application of a comprehensive communications policy" (Canada, House of Commons, 1992, xi). In general, it recommended that...the federal role in both culture and communications must be maintained and, indeed, strengthened" (p. xiii).

This conventional federal position was, to say the least, somewhat incompatible with the view the Quebec government was then articulating in every possible venue regarding jurisdiction, to the point that it could be seen as a virtual exercise in noncommunication.

In keeping with the Mulroney government's constitutional position, however, the multiparty committee endorsed "the recognition of Quebec in the charter as a distinct society within Canada, based on its French-speaking majority, its unique culture and its civil law tradition..." (Canada, House of Commons, 1992, app. B), while recognizing the problem of limiting this to Quebec and thus ignoring or negating other aspects of Canadian distinctiveness. The Committee's report elicited a formal response from the government (Canada, Communications Canada, 1993), but nothing in the way of concrete action.

Quebec, meanwhile, was insisting on full repatriation of powers in culture and communication—while remaining characteristically vague about just what that might mean in any context short of full-blown sovereignty. Beginning with testimony from the arts community before the Bélanger-Campeau commission on Quebec's political and constitutional future (Quebec, Commission, 1991), and the Quebec Liberal Party's Allaire Report (Quebec Liberal Party, 1991) in 1991, forces in Quebec civil society persistently and consistently re-articulated a "cultural sovereignty" position first developed in the early 1970s and, in some respects, dating back to the Taschereau government's abortive attempt to outflank Ottawa in the radio field in the late 1920s. A blue-ribbon committee chaired by Musée de la civilisation director Roland Arpin[6] (Quebec, Gouvernement du Québec, 1991) recommended Quebec seek full powers in 1991, and the ministry for cultural affairs tried to flesh out what this might look like in a document that became Quebec's official cultural policy the following year (Quebec, Gouvernement du Québec, 1992).

Quebec's cultural policy would be concentrated in four main areas: 1) affirmation of cultural identity (promoting the French language, heritage activities, and reinforcing dialogue between cultural groups in Quebec); 2) support for the creative arts; 3) access and popular participation in cultural life; 4) new instruments of support (a ministry of culture, an arts and culture council modelled after the Canada Council, partnership with municipal authorities).

Looking at specific proposals in terms of dollars and cents provided a clearer view of the problem, however; under the existing constitutional arrangement, Quebec simply did not have the power to exercise significant influence in this sphere. Its strategy for development of cultural industries, for example, was based on a funding agency called SOGIC (Société générale des industries culturelles), which had provided a total of $118 million in loans, guarantees, and subsidies across the range of the cultural industries between 1979 and 1991—about 10 percent of what Ottawa spends on the CBC alone in just one year.

Conflicting interpretations of who spent how much on what in culture and communication provided some of the less edifying material in the constitutional debate, but at least gave some indication of the scope of the issue. Thus, according to a study done for the Quebec ministry of cultural affairs (Samson et al., 1990), Quebec financed arts and culture to the tune of $482 million in 1990, while in the same year, Ottawa spent $283 million in Quebec, *excluding* the part of CBC operations that could be attributed to Quebec. When one factored in this amount—an estimated $450 million—one can begin to appreciate both the nature of such *guerres des chiffres*, as well as the centrality of broadcasting to federal cultural strategy with respect to the national question.

As we have seen, the mechanics of dualism in Canadian broadcasting constituted an important aspect of the broadcasting policy review of 1985–90. In the framework of reduced available public funding, attention in Quebec was now drawn to the need to close the gap between money earmarked for French- and English-language CBC production. In the process leading up to the new broadcasting legislation, Quebec-based lobby groups had succeeded in including a provision that CBC programming should "strive to be of equivalent quality" in English and in French—a neat peg on which to hang arguments for more money. Taken together with the emphasis on linguistic asymmetry that was equally part of the new context, however, the *textual* provisions of the new policy did not prevent the creation of new aberrations, such as the informational inequality that resulted from introduction of the CBC's cable television all-news service, "Newsworld," in English only.[7]

Here, the full essence of the Canadian dilemma could be appreciated. Does "programming of equivalent quality" imply an equal distribution of resources? Where do you distinguish between "distinct characters" and "different policy approaches"? Is symmetrical programming an imposition, or is asymmetry a smoke screen for discrimination? The CBC budget is an opaque document that begs for interpretation, but no matter how you read it, the linguistic breakdown indicates that budget allocation is based neither on demographics nor on strict application of the principle of dualism—oscillating around 37 percent spent on French language programming, it is a solution characteristic of the compromise that is Canada: at one and the same time fair and sure to please no one.

The historic ambiguity of Canadian cultural policy with respect to duality was evident in the text of the agreement signed by federal, provincial, territorial, and aboriginal leaders in Charlottetown on August 28, 1992, In a single paragraph under the rubric "Culture," the accord managed both to give exclusive jurisdiction over cultural matters *within* provinces to the provincial authorities, and to assert the continuing responsibility of the federal government in "Canadian" cultural matters. Furthermore, the federal government would retain responsibility for national cultural institutions, including grants and contributions delivered by these institutions (Canada, 1992a).

The document contained what the Toronto *Globe and Mail* (Godfrey, 1992) described as "the makings of a minefield." On the question that captured the most public attention—Which level of government would henceforth be expected to patronize the arts?—no clear answer was forthcoming. Were governments proposing to divide the turf, or share it? How precisely could one reconcile such clearly contradictory notions as "exclusive jurisdiction over cultural matters within the provinces," "continuing responsibility of the federal government in Canadian cultural matters," and "responsibility for national cultural institutions, including grants and contributions delivered by these institutions"? While a film documentary on the James Bay hydroelectric project or local radio in the Gaspé were quite arguably "cultural matters within a province," *funding* the documentary or *regulating* radio would most likely continue to fall under the responsibility of "national cultural institutions." Establishing the hierarchy of authority in such affairs could keep the wheels of the constitution industry turning for a long time indeed.

In fact, the new arrangement would have eliminated none of the ambiguity or policy overlap in the cultural sector (Julien, 1992). More to the point (from a Quebec perspective), it would have enshrined Ottawa's legitimacy in an area that had traditionally been the provinces', *constitutionally, if not in fact*.

In short, the Charlottetown Accord would have constitutionalized the structural imbalance in the pragmatics of cultural dualism in Canada—unlike the Meech Lake Accord, which would have validated the symbolic goal that drives cultural and communication policy in Quebec. What we have instead is a most uncomfortable status quo, still struggling to find a suitable alternative to both centralized federalism and the breakup of the federation.

Conclusion

A country's communication system, it has often been said, closely follows the chief characteristics which define the country in space and in time. In this respect, to paraphrase Alphonse Ouimet, former president of the CBC, the problem of Canadian broadcasting is "the problem of Canada itself" (1979, 149). His words were echoed by a more recent successor, Gérard Veilleux, who was quoted in 1993 as stating that "managing the CBC is like managing federalism" (Lemay, 1993, 16).

The problem continues to emerge around symbolic issues. Debating the bill to create the new federal Department of Heritage in October 1994, minister Michel Dupuy characterized the new department as "the flagship of Canadian identity" (Canada, 1994, 6416). For Bloc Québécois critic Suzanne Tremblay, however, "This bill shamelessly infringes on what so far has been considered provincial jurisdiction: culture" (Canada, House of Commons, 1994, 6419).

Both were correct. In the context in which communication policy is made, the idea of "two solitudes" refers more to divergent visions of Canada and Quebec than it does to language. There are two separate but obviously related issues here. One concerns the division of cultural resources between two predominant linguistic groups, sharing a political space called Canada. The other concerns the relationship and division of powers between two states, Canada and Quebec. Up until now, communication policy has focussed on the first issue, for better and for worse. For Canada, the second issue is a nonstarter. For Quebec, however, it is the only one, and as long as this is so, communication and culture will continue to be a flash point.

Make no mistake about it: the issue is sovereignty. Increasingly, in the context of globalization, political and economic sovereignty will be tied to the capacity to make policy and rules regarding communication. In parallel to the tendency toward a reduced role for the national state, the flourishing of local and national cultures will depend on a given population's capacity to use its state for the promotion of culture (Raboy et al., 1994).

In a country like Canada, where the complexities of nationhood overlap in an uneasy relationship with the state, the most intelligent policy approach would seem to indicate strong public support for national cultural institutions, which should then be allowed a maximum of autonomy from state interference, so that they can appropriately reflect the complexities of a multinational federation (Resnick, 1994).

This is already partly the case with institutions such as the CBC, the CRTC, and Telefilm, whose own operational logics have evolved out of their relationships with their constituencies rather than the grand designs of federal policy. It is also reflected in the struggles surrounding the emergence of provincial educational broadcasting, community broadcasting, and at least in the far north, native broadcasting. The first principles governing Canadian broadcasting and telecommunications legislation, for example, are basically sound and valid for the different constituencies that make up Canada. Where we run into trouble is when the imperatives of defining the parameters of the state turn to dictating the framework of policy, when the struggles to maximize the authority of the state spill over into communication policy.

The question of public broadcasting, for example, is not clarified by arguments that a national public broadcaster should be a vehicle for promoting national unity. Cultural development is not well served by programs whose main aim appears to be to purchase the political loyalty of artistic communities. Information highways cannot be developed in the public interest through policies designed to centralize control in one jurisdiction rather than another.

But, as is often the case in politics, public discourse regarding the relationship of culture and communications to Canada's constitutional problems usually generates more heat than light.

Thus, it is impossible, in the perspective of a fundamental political struggle over the future of Canada, to look seriously at the role of communication. As we see most clearly in broadcasting, notions of culture and politics are continuously conflated in a strange and often confusing mix. As Tremblay has argued perceptively, on the one hand, if Canada is to continue as a sovereign country, "one must accord the central government some power of intervention in the areas of culture and communications." On the other hand, "a renewed federalism should very much lead to shared jurisdictional authority over communications" (1993, 241–42). But, as Tremblay concludes, this is the least likely scenario at the moment. On the federal side, the trend is toward greater centralization of authority, as was underscored by the April 1994 Supreme Court decision declaring telecommunications to be an exclusive federal jurisdiction. In Quebec, at time of writing, a Parti Québécois government was moving toward full sovereignty.

Just what would the communications environment look like in an independent Quebec? Just how it would differ from the present one is not at all clear. Cultural policy was not a high-profile item in the September 1994 election campaign—a "warm potato" was how one journalist described it (Baillargeon, 1994). Short of promising to spend one percent of the Quebec budget on cultural subsidies, the PQ's electoral program on culture was paper-thin. Otherwise, there was no indication of what precisely Quebec would do with the new powers it would acquire. Paradoxically, as the otherwise pro-péquiste publisher of *Le Devoir*, Lise Bissonnette, wrote in a pre-election editorial, the Quebec Liberals actually had a better track record on culture than the PQ (1994). "While they had literally carried the PQ to power by providing it with a soul and a driving force," Bissonnette wrote, "the artistic milieu was left emptyhanded at the end of the PQ era in 1985." The Liberals, meanwhile, brought in legislation on the status of the artist, an umbrella cultural policy, a cultural funding agency (Conseil des arts et des lettres du Québec—CALQ), and a new crown corporation for providing grants to cultural industries (Société de développement des entreprises culturelles—SODEC).

In broadcasting, there has not been a word on PQ plans. In all likelihood, Quebec broadcasting legislation and regulation would closely follow the Canadian model, in which, as we have seen, Quebec has had a prominent hand. However, it is difficult to avoid thinking that the net shift would be to more power over less resources. Would a sovereign Quebec maintain public funding of broadcasting at present levels? In the only public indication to date of government thinking in this area, the PQ's first culture minister, Marie Malavoy, commented ambiguously that in the event of repatriation of Quebec's share of the CBC budget, "we would have to see. I am not sure that Radio-Québec could absorb all that" (Des Rivières, 1994).[8] It is also unclear whether a Quebec with full jurisdiction over communication would have a single public broadcaster or would continue to support both a repatriated CBC and Radio-Quebec, as public interest groups have recommended (ICEA, 1992). It is indeed paradoxical, given the vast attention paid to communication in the ideology of Canadian nation-building, to note how little specific place it occupies in the iconography of Quebec nationalism.

So, we have come full circle as we stand on the brink of the precipice. A degree of uncertainty and the possibility of a lower level of material good is the price of self-determination—more control over less resources—for Quebec as it is for Canada. But this should not obscure the reality that in culture and communications, as in other areas, both Canada and Quebec, francophone and anglophone culture, have been well served by the tensions inherent in the existing system, often, as we have seen, in spite of itself. As Canada searches for a place in the sea of global culture, its linguistic duality is one of the most unmistakeable, irreducible forms of Canadian distinctiveness. The challenge remains to try to find an institutional arrangement that turns this into a source of strength.

NOTES

1. This chapter is an updated version of Marc Raboy, "Canadian Broadcasting, Canadian Nationhood: Two Concepts, Two Solitudes and Great Expectations," which appeared in the first edition of Helen Holmes and David Taras, eds., *Seeing Ourselves: Media Power and Policy in Canada* (Toronto: HBJ-Holt Canada, 1992), pp. 156–73. Parts have appeared as well in Marc Raboy, "Broadcasting Policy, Nationbuilding and Constitutional Politics in Canada and Quebec," *Quebec Studies* 18 (1994).
2. This chapter deals only with issues related to broadcasting and the national question. For a broader and far more extensive treatment of the history of Canadian broadcasting policy, up to 1988, see Raboy, 1990.
3. Gérard Pelletier, also a Radio-Canada personality at the time and later a federal cabinet minister, has pointed out that much of the problem was attributable to the fact that the French network executives in Montreal lacked the authority to negotiate on behalf of the corporation, while the head office in Ottawa did not bother to take it seriously (Pelletier, 1983).
4. After leaving federal politics in 1992, Masse resurfaced to chair one of the PQ's consultative commissions leading up to the sovereignty referendum of 1995.
5. According to a senior official of the ministère des Communications du Québec interviewed by the author in June 1990, a few days before the collapse of the Meech Lake Accord, this proposal was "Meech before its time."
6. Later named deputy minister of culture by the Parizeau government.
7. The problem was finally corrected when the CRTC approved the CBC's application for an equivalent French-language service, le Réseau de l'information (RDI), which began broadcasting in January 1995.

8. Malavoy had to resign in disgrace soon after taking office when it was revealed that she had voted illegally in several elections before becoming a Canadian citizen. Her equally short-term successor, Rita Dionne-Marsolais, was removed after alienating the arts community by excluding them from consultations about a Quebec policy on information highways, and attempting to name a campaign contributor as head of Radio-Québec (Lesage, 1995). Premier Parizeau then took over the culture portfolio himself.

References

Baillargeon, Stéphane. (1994). "Culture: PQ et PLQ se lancent la patate tiède." *Le Devoir*, August 29.

Bissonnette, Lise. (1985). "L'envers du décor." *Le Devoir*, March 23.

————. "Le choix." *Le Devoir*, August 27.

Canada. (1989). 34th Parliament, Second Session, *Broadcasting Act*, Bill C-40, First Reading, October 12.

Canada. (1992). *The Consensus Report on the Constitution*. Ottawa: Government of Canada.

Canada, Communications Canada. (1988). *Canadian Voices Canadian Choices: A New Broadcasting Policy for Canada*. Ottawa: Minister of Supply and Services Canada.

————. (1993). *Unique Among Nations*. A Response by the Government of Canada to the Recommendations of the Standing Committee on Communications and Culture as presented in the report "The Ties That Bind." Ottawa.

Canada, Department of Communications. (1983a). *Towards a New National Broadcasting Policy*. Ottawa: Minister of Supply and Services Canada.

————. (1983b). *Building for the Future: Towards a Distinctive CBC*. Ottawa: Minister of Supply and Services Canada.

————. (1984). *The National Film and Video Policy*. Ottawa: Minister of Supply and Services Canada.

Canada, Federal Cultural Policy Review Committee. (1982). *Report*. Ottawa: Minister of Supply and Services Canada.

Canada, House of Commons. (1946). *Debates*.

————. (1964–65). *Debates*.

————. (1967–68). *Debates*.

————. (1994). *Debates*.

Canada, House of Commons. (1990). Legislative Committee on Bill C-40. *Minutes* (31 January 1990 and ss.).

Canada, House of Commons (1980–83). Standing Committee on Communications and Culture. *Minutes* (1980–83).

————. (1988). *A Broadcasting Policy for Canada (Report)*. Ottawa: Minister of Supply and Services Canada.

————. (1992). *Culture and Communications: The Ties That Bind*. Ottawa.

Canada/Quebec. (1985a). *Canada-Quebec Subsidiary Agreement on Communications Enterprises Development 1984–1990*. Ottawa and Quebec: Government of Canada/Gouvernement du Québec.

————. (1985b). Federal-provincial Committee, *The Future of French-Language Television*. Ottawa and Quebec: Government of Canada/Gouvernement du Québec.

————. (1986, 13 February). "Canada-Quebec Memorandum of Understanding on the Development of the French-language Television System." Ottawa and Quebec: Government of Canada/Gouvernement du Québec.

Canada, Royal Commission on Broadcasting (1957). *Report*. Ottawa: Queen's Printer.
Canada, Royal Commission on National Development in the Arts, Letters and Sciences. (1951). *Report*. Ottawa: King's Printer.
Canada, Royal Commission on Radio Broadcasting. (1929). *Report*. Ottawa: King's Printer.
Canada, Statutes. *Broadcasting Act*. (1967–68). SC 1967–68, c. 25.
————. (1991). 38–39 Elizabeth II, 1991, c. 11.
Canada, Supreme Court. (1978). *Supreme Court Reports*, vol. 2.
Canada, Task Force on Broadcasting Policy. (1986). *Report*. Ottawa: Minister of Supply and Services Canada.
Canada, Task Force on Program Review. (1986). *An Introduction to the Process of Program Review*. Ottawa: Minister of Supply and Services Canada.
Canada, Unpassed Bills, Broadcasting Act. (1988a). Bill C-136, First Reading, June 23, 1988.
Canada, Unpassed Bills, Broadcasting Act. (1988b). Bill C-136, Third Reading, September 28, 1988.
Canadian Broadcasting Corporation. (1964). *Submission to the Royal Commission on Bilingualism and Biculturalism*. Ottawa.
————. (1979). *The CBC—A Perspective*. Ottawa.
Canadian Radio-Television and Telecommunications Commission. (1977). Committee of Inquiry into the National Broadcasting Service, *Report*. Ottawa.
————. (1987). *More Canadian Programming Choices*. Ottawa: CRTC, 30 November.
Des Rivières, Paule. (1994). "Marie Malavoy entend amadouer les artistes." *Le Devoir*, October 15.
Godfrey, Stephen. (1992). "The Constitution and Culture: The Makings of a Minefield." *The Globe and Mail*, Toronto, August 29.
ICEA, Institut canadien d'éducation des adultes. (1992). *Éléments pour une politique québécoise des communications*. Montréal: ICEA.
Johnson, A.W. (1983). "The Re-Canadianization of Broadcasting." *Policy Options* 4, 2:6–12.
Julien, Germain. (1992). "L'accord constitutionnel n'éliminera pas le chevauchement." *Le Soleil*, Quebec, August 30.
Lamarche, Gérard. (1960). "Radio-Canada et sa mission française." *Canadian Communications* 1, 1:6–15.
Laurendeau, André. (1962). *La Crise de la conscription*. Montreal: Éditions du Jour.
Lemay, Daniel. (1994). "The Veilleux Years." *SCAN*, January-February, 14–17.
Lesage, Gilles. (1995). "Radio-Québec sous influence." *Le Devoir*, February 3.
Masse, Marcel. (1994). Comments to a meeting of the Fédération professionnelle des journalistes du Québec, Montreal, December 10.
Ouimet, Alphonse. (1979). "The Communications Revolution and Canadian Sovereignty." In *Gutenberg Two: The New Electronics and Social Change*, edited by David Godfrey and Douglas Parkhill, 131–50. Toronto: Porcépic Press.
Pelletier, Gérard. (1983). *Les années d'impatience (1950–1960)*. Montreal: Stanké.
Quebec. (1968). "Ce que veut le Québec," submitted by Daniel Johnson to the Constitutional Conference, first meeting, Ottawa, February 5–7.
Quebec, Commission sur l'avenir politique et constitutionnel du Québec. (1991). *L'avenir politique et constitutionnel du Québec* (Bélanger-Campeau). Quebec: Gouvernement du Québec.
Quebec, Gouvernement du Québec. (1991). Groupe-conseil sur la politique culturelle du Québec (présidé par Roland Arpin). *Une politique de la culture et des arts*. Québec.
Quebec, Gouvernement du Québec, ministère des Affaires culturelles. (1992). *La politique culturelle du Québec*. Québec.

Quebec, Legislative Assembly. (1968). *Journal des débats.*

Quebec, ministère des Communications du Québec. (1971). *Pour une politique québécoise des communications*. Quebec: MCQ.

————. (1973). *Le Québec, maître d'oeuvre de la politique des communications sur son territoire*. Quebec: MCQ.

————. (1982). *Bâtir l'avenir*. Quebec: Gouvernement du Québec.

————. (1983). *Le Québec et les communications: Un futur simple?* Quebec: Gouvernement du Québec.

Quebec Liberal Party. (1991). Comité constitutionnel du Parti libéral du Québec, *Un Québec libre de ses choix* (Allaire Report). Quebec: PLQ.

Quebec, National Assembly. (1977). *Journal des débats.*

Quebec, Statutes. (1945). Loi autorisant la création d'un service de radiodiffusion provinciale. SQ 1945, c. 56.

Raboy, Marc. (1990). *Missed Opportunities: The Story of Canada's Broadcasting Policy.* Montreal and Kingston: McGill-Queen's University Press.

Raboy, Marc, Ivan Bernier, Florian Sauvageau, and Dave Atkinson. (1994). "Cultural Development and the Open Economy: A Democratic Issue and a Challenge to Public Policy." *Canadian Journal of Communication* 19, 3/4:291–315.

Resnick, Philip. (1994). "The Crisis of Multi-National Federations: Post-Charlottetown Reflections." *Review of Constitutional Studies* 1, 2:189–202.

Samson, Bélair, Deloitte & Touche. (1990). *Étude sur le financement des arts et de la culture au Québec*. Prepared for the ministère des Affaires culturelles du Québec, Montreal.

Stark, Frank. (1983). "Persuasion, Propaganda, and Public Policy." Paper to the fourth annual conference of the Canadian Communication Association, Vancouver, June 1983, typescript.

Thibault, Marc. (1988). Comments at the National Archives of Canada conference, "Beyond the Printed Word," Ottawa, October 1988.

Tremblay, Gaëtan. (1988). "La politique québécoise en matière de communication (1966–1986): 'De l'affirmation autonomiste à la coopération fédérale-provinciale." *Communication information* 9, 3:57–87.

————. (1993). "The Constitutional Debate and Communications Policies." *Canadian Journal of Communication* 18, 2:237–43.

Vipond, Mary. (1992). *Listening In: The First Decade of Canadian Broadcasting*. Montreal: McGill-Queen's University Press.

Weir, E. Austin. (1965). *The Struggle for National Broadcasting in Canada*. Toronto: McClelland and Stewart.

NORTHERN VOICES AND MEDIATING STRUCTURES: FIRST PEOPLES' TELEVISION BROADCASTING NORTH OF 60

Lorna Roth

The development of indigenous Canadian media policies, discourses, and practices is an important subject to examine toward the end of the twentieth century as aboriginal self-government is closer than ever to being achieved. First, as a direct result of the development of indigenous media over the last three decades, there has been a restructuring of the Canadian broadcasting system to include aboriginal broadcasting as an integral element. Second, First Peoples' broadcasting lobbies have influenced the development of new mediating structures in Canada through new policies and funding programs, a new broadcasting channel (Television Northern Canada), and closer working arrangements with existing channels. Third, First Peoples' broadcasters have used television as an emancipatory tool. They see television as a vehicle for social and cultural action, for education, and for building their national identity.

The use of media as a tool for self-empowerment in Canada was pioneered by John Grierson, the first Commissioner of the National Film Board, (NFB) and its now defunct Challenge for Change Program. It is within this tradition of using media as a process tool rather than as an end product that First Peoples have begun using broadcasting innovatively, in an alternative fashion (Roncagliolo, 1991, 207), as a vehicle for transformation. Two kinds of transformations are the subject of First Peoples' television broadcasting history: first, the ways in which television has been used to reinforce indigenous languages and cultures and to build and promote stronger cultural and national identities; second, the negotiation of a national status for aboriginal broadcasting within federal broadcasting legislation.

As television producers and broadcasting administrators have become leaders in Northern community and cultural life, their reshaping of the public media has enabled new forms of producer/community audience relationships to develop. These are different from those which generally exist within large metropolitan areas. Rooted as they have been in sociocultural movements, First Peoples have turned to those organizing and receiving Northern and, more recently, Southern media to align their diverse communities with one another. Finally, given that Canada's Northern broadcasting infrastructure has been recognized, to date, as the most advanced aboriginal broadcasting system in the world, First Peoples' media initiatives, such as those described in this essay, can provide insights into the ways in which other Fourth World communities might chart the courses of *their* broadcasting development.

First Peoples' demand for state financial and regulatory support for native-controlled broadcasting and for fairer portrayal and employment practices has resulted in a new, more inclusive public discourse. The potential and actual roles that indigenous and other minority-group communications have played in the process of Canadian self-definition have become highly valued.

In Canada, a multiplicity of less-than-national, less empowered identity groups have struggled for recognition of their interests against the dominance of a one-dimensional Canada, and it is, in fact, their efforts that have maintained the Canadian difference against the overwhelming forces of continental integration in North America (Raboy, 1990a, 8).

Through the opening up and management of (cross)cultural discursive spaces and mass-mediated public spheres in the North, First Peoples are combining the forces of postmodernity with their own particular cultures. This process has taken three decades and the dedicated commitment by First Peoples broadcasters and lobbyists. Their work has resulted in the legal recognition and acceptance of aboriginal voices within the Canadian public and private broadcasting spheres, as integral participants in the developing fabric of a pluralistic community of communities—Canada.

The Canadian North

The North as a general category has been geographically defined by Louis-Edmond Hamelin, a well-known Quebecois geographer, as being North of the 60th latitude line. Hamelin divides the north into three categories or zones. The first is called the "Middle North": the northern areas of the ten provinces, Labrador, and much of the Yukon where road access is possible (Hamelin, 1979, 333). Beyond the Middle North lies the "Far North," which takes in "mainly the Northwest Territories and corresponds in part to the Arctic climate," and the "Extreme North," which consists of the "Northern part of the Arctic archipelago" (332).

Mythical notions of the North have made powerful inroads in the imaginations of the Canadian population. The symbolic North has been imagined and defined predominantly in terms of Southern interests. Since crosscultural contact, notions of the North have been fabricated by non-natives who have talked about it, analyzed it, made statements about it, settled it, ruled it, authorized certain views of it, managed it, and even produced it for Southern commodity and "exotic" touristic consumption (Said, 1979).

Ideas and fictions about the North have shifted focus throughout history as various Southern-based institutions set up outpost organizations to extract resources or impose authority. (Valaskakis, 1979). Among these controlling agents/agencies have been the early explorers (from Frobisher's 1576 voyage onwards), the missionaries (from 1578 onward); the whalers (beginning in the early part of the fifteenth century); the traders (1880s); the North West Mounted Police followed by the Royal Canadian Mounted

Police (since 1903); the U.S. and Canadian military (1940s); and finally externally controlled media institutions (since the 1950s) (Valaskakis, 1979). Southerners' descriptions of the North and its peoples, as exemplified in the discourses of the various change agencies, have affected the ways in which the idea of the North has been defined by and to populations in the South. Indeed, Hamelin and others have suggested that present-day texts still reveal an echo of Voltaire's opinion of the Northerner as "the miserable Canadian settler, squatting 'in the snow between the bear and the beaver'" (Hamelin, 1979, 1). These mediated ideas, in turn, have found their way back to the North and have had effects on Northern peoples' identities.

Images of the North have oscillated between images of a frozen wilderness, a resource rich hinterland, and a hotly defended cultural heartland. The "mysterious" North is often treated as a beautiful "paradise which has temporarily lost its charm" (Hamelin, 1984, 167). However, it is also characterized as "inhospitable—such beauty as is only to be experienced with the comfort of the best survival equipment" (Shields, 1991, 173). It is hard to be indifferent to the North, its peoples, and the ways in which it has been depicted in the media.

First Peoples' Television Broadcasting History

Accounting for a little less than 2 percent of the Canadian population, First Peoples have been historically located outside of the Canadian national project on many levels—territorially, socially, politically, economically, culturally. Lacking access to their own means of social definition and authority until the mid-1970s, First Peoples slipped easily into the position of being "subjects," not "citizens." Treated in an objectified manner, their absences and stereotypical portrayals in media in the first two-thirds of the twentieth century rendered First Peoples somewhat akin to landscape imagery, savages, or exotic representations of the ethnographic "Other."

First Peoples' energetic participation in the media as producers only began systematically *after* the Anik satellite commenced live broadcasting service in the North in 1973. At this time, the world brought to them via television was one in which they rapidly became aware of their apparent nonexistence as living and historically evolving cultural communities. In recognizing this absence, they began to demand a presence in all aspects of media production and distribution. It was, therefore, only *after* the intrusion of Southern media into the North that First Peoples began to contest their exclusion from Canadian print and media representations. They called for compensatory histories and anthropologies, ones which would fill in the gaps, highlight their experiences and perspectives, and which would transform them from being positioned as passive objects to being active subjects of history (Northern Quebec Inuit Association, 1974; Inuit Tapirisat of Canada, 1976).

From the vantage point of the mid-1990s, it is apparent that First Peoples have achieved remarkable changes in their media status. One might recall, for instance, that in 1901 Thomas Edison filmed several Inuit running amongst plaster icebergs in temperatures of up to 90° for the amusement of visitors at the Buffalo exhibition (Raymont, 1981, *Magic in the Sky*). At present, almost all of the thirteen Northern regional Native communications societies produce twenty hours of radio and at least four hours of television weekly—from a native perspective. These productions, along with other Northern-theme programming, are distributed within the thirteen Northern regions via Television Northern Canada, a Pan-Northern satellite service begun in 1992, which airs 100 hours of Northern-oriented programming per week to 94 communities.[1]

Northern indigenous broadcasting has moved through several organizational phases. At first, aboriginal peoples had very little opportunity to represent themselves. This was followed by a stage characterized by protests and attempts to seize control by bypassing or ignoring federal regulatory procedures. As a result of this turbulent period, they eventually gained access to a fairly broad range of federally sponsored media projects (i.e., radio, television, and community video), which allowed them a means of self-representation. More recently, First Peoples in the North have gone beyond portraying themselves to their immediate communities. They now represent themselves to other native and non-native audience members. There are now redistribution arrangements that Northern Native Broadcasting, Yukon has established with CBC "Newsworld."

Phase 1. Early Northern Broadcasting: First Peoples' Representations by Outsiders

When CBC public radio was transplanted into the North in 1958, it presented itself as a fairly open medium to which First Peoples turned for information about their own lives in the North. Partly because of lower costs, and because the technology is simpler than television, the languages and content of radio were well suited to the information needs of aboriginal listeners. Emphasis was on local and national news, weather, road and flying conditions, flood and fire warnings, and personal messages, such as health reports on relatives who were hospitalized down South (Government of Canada, 1965, 190). Native staff were recruited and trained in radio production techniques, and quickly reached managerial positions within the CBC Northern Service. Accustomed to listening to relevant messages that conformed to their information needs, Northern residents expected a television service which would do the same.

The early demand for television in the North did not come from the permanent native population, whose basic information needs required other kinds of communication facilities: telephone, trail radio, and community radio in their native language (North Quebec Inuit Association, 1974; Inuit Tapirisat of Canada, 1976). Rather, television broadcasting facilities in the North were developed in settlements that were of military, economic, or administrative significance to the South and were introduced for two dominant reasons: to stabilize transient Southern workforces in Northern mining towns and to visibly/audibly demonstrate Canadian sovereignty in the North. Local native populations were not consulted by the CBC in its decision to expand service. Indeed, the federal authorities bypassed First Peoples entirely because they did not yet constitute a formidable lobby group.

In 1967, the CBC introduced the "Frontier Coverage Package" (FCP) to seventeen remote communities in the North.[2] The FCP was designed to be a temporary, presatellite television system, making use of reliable, inexpensive, and easily available videotape technology. It consisted of a "four-hour helical-scan videotape recorded in the South and bicycled on a one, two, three or four-week delay basis to various locations in the North for playback over local television transmitters" (CBC, 1978b, 3). Programming for the Frontier Coverage Package consisted of a cross-selection of Southern programs. Although the CBC approved native content programming in principle, no financial accommodation was made for the inclusion of native-language programming. Nor were relevant Northern subjects given particular importance in the schedule.

The establishment of a domestic satellite policy for Canada in the late sixties (1968–69), and the launching of Anik A-1 in 1972, precipitated a new phase in First Peoples' development in the North. In 1973, the satellite became operational, bringing telephone service, live television, and radio broadcasting to the same seventeen communities hitherto receiving the Frontier Coverage Package. In 1974, the Accelerated Coverage Plan was approved, bringing live television to all Northern and remote communities with a population of 500 or more. In most cases, these communities were anxious to receive programming. In some (Igloolik in the Baffin region and in Northern Quebec Inuit communities), there was reticence, framed by discussions of the right to cultural privacy. For instance, with no funding allocated for the production of culturally and linguistically relevant programming, Joseph Padlayat, then Communications Officer for the Northern Quebec Inuit Association, protested the intrusion of foreign Southern broadcasting into their community priorities (1974). Padlayat had become aware of communications research documenting the negative impact of Southern programming on Inuit culture and felt that unless there was to be a first-service in the Inuktitut language, television would act as a potent factor in eroding the culture and language of his people.

Concurrent with this protest, Southern communications researchers began to undertake longitudinal media impact studies. The gathering of data was followed by open criticism of the federal government's use of Northern television programming as an "alien culture socialization agent" (Coldevin, 1977, 34). A Native community influence in broadcast decision-making, and in the production of relevant cultural and linguistic television programming, was strongly recommended as a method for mediating the potentially overwhelming impact of Southern programming (Valaskakis, 1979: Coldevin, 1977; Caron 1977; O'Connell, 1974; Northern Quebec Inuit Association, 1974, Inuit Tapirisat of Canada, 1976). The establishment of production, training, and resource centres in the North and the formal encouragement of a lateral communication flow were considered necessary steps in this process by all interested parties preoccupied with television's impact (Valaskakis, 1976; Coldevin, 1977a and 1976).

In the process of evaluating their communication needs, First Peoples (mostly the Inuit) came to recognize that the academic data generated about media effects on individuals and cultural communities would not provide enough fuel for desired changes within the broadcasting system. A means of engaging federal government policy-makers and bureaucrats in a critical dialogue would have to be found and initiated by First Peoples' representatives. "Bridge discourses," which would mediate the relations between the unilingual aboriginal communities and the federal government, would have to be developed.[3] "Go-betweens"—native people who could speak both their own and at least one of the official languages of Canada and/or non-native "interested parties" (activists, media researchers) who were acceptable to the native community leadership—would soon begin to play a valuable bridging role, situating themselves "between" the two worlds and attempting to knit together the disparate discourses of governmental regulatory policies and native cultural concerns (Fraser, 1989, 11).

Phase II. The Impact of the Inuit Lobbies on Northern Communications

Two Inuit organizations were critical in researching and publicizing Inuit perceptions of Northern communication needs. The Inuit Tapirisat of Canada (Eskimo Brotherhood of Canada) and the Northern Quebec Inuit Association worked persistently and systematically to alter federal government communications priorities in the North so that they would be more consistent with those of the Inuit themselves. Through legal and political channels, interventions at CBC/Bell Canada licence-application hearings at the CRTC, through confrontations and negotiations with the CBC Northern Service, and with the CBC's corporate management, and through publications, they promoted a new vision of Northern broadcasting.

As early debates about the potential social impact of satellite communications entered the public domain, efforts to broaden and improve understanding of media applications in the North took shape in a series of projects, experiments, and field tests using conventional and satellite technology: HF two-way radio, FM radio broadcasting, portable VTR, and 16 mm. and Super 8 film. These experiments were generally designed to test the technical and social parameters of community-oriented media usage and control patterns. They represented a strategic way to provide media services to the North and became the acceptable method of mediating the divergent policy goals of the federal government (including those of the CBC) and those of the First Peoples (Roth, 1983a).

Northern media projects have generally fallen into three broad categories: (1) field tests and experiments to test the viability of new technologies and to explore alternative forms of communications for the North (for example, the Anik-B experimental projects—Inukshuk, Naalakvik—and other interactive media projects); (2) projects designed to mitigate the potential negative effects or influences of Southern programming on native cultures (NFB film support projects of the early 1970s and a variety of community radio and television projects); and (3) projects associated with the use of community media for organization and development purposes (community media projects) (Roth, 1983b).

These media projects provided both the First Peoples and government sponsors with empirical data to support the First Peoples' readiness to take on the full network operations. As Gail Valaskakis and I observed some years ago,

> These projects were successful in training staff, in producing culturally-relevant, native-language programming, and in establishing the technical infrastructure to link several aboriginal communities laterally so that

> local residents could participate in inter-community discussions. Through federally sponsored projects, Inuit have historically (re)constructed traditional folklore and heritage through programming which reclaims active use of native languages and promotes lived cultures.... The Northern native media project...demonstrated their [First Peoples'] competence as broadcasters to funding agencies as they met the basic communications needs in their communities (Roth and Valaskakis 1989, 225–26).

Evidence of project successes repeatedly documented the point that First Peoples' broadcasting could be a legitimate undertaking, and helped to chip away at government resistance to the subsidization of Northern broadcasting through public funding.

Phase III. Policy-ing the North

Until the early 1980s, the federal, provincial, and territorial governments tended to react to each new First Peoples' media initiative in an ad hoc, and sometimes, post hoc manner.[4] In 1980, a CRTC committee under the direction of the Vice-Chairman, Real Therrien, undertook an extensive Northern CRTC and remote community consultation to assess possible options, and to establish a set of fundamental principles governing the fair expansion of television and pay-TV services to the North. The resulting report, "The 1980s—A Decade of Diversity: Broadcasting Satellites and Pay-TV," laid out a comprehensive and supportive framework for a Northern Broadcasting Policy, which was to be formalized in 1983. In 1981, the Inuit Broadcasting Corporation was incorporated and licensed by the CRTC in recognition of achievements and management potential demonstrated in the interactive audio and video Inukshuk Anik-B satellite experiment (1978–81). By 1982, the Applebaum-Hébert Cultural Policy Committee Report acknowledged that native peoples had gained a "special place in cultural policy" (Applebaum-Hébert, 1982, 11).

In March 1983, after years of aboriginal lobbying and both formal and informal consultations, the federal government announced a Northern Broadcasting Policy (NBP). This policy, the most important document in aboriginal communications development to date, enunciated five basic principles, establishing a significant measure of native participation in both media programming and the regulatory process:

1. Northern residents should be offered access to an increasing range of programming choices through the exploitation of technological opportunities.
2. Northern native people should have the opportunity to participate actively in the determination by the CRTC of the character, quantity, and priority of programming broadcast in predominantly native communities.
3. Northern native people should have fair access to northern broadcasting distribution systems to maintain and develop their cultures and languages.

4. Programming relevant to native concerns, including content originated by native people, should be produced for distribution on northern broadcasting services wherever native people form a significant proportion of the population in the service area.
5. Northern native representatives should be consulted regularly by government agencies engaged in establishing broadcasting policies which would affect their cultures (Government of Canada, 1983a, 2).

The policy vehicle designed to operationalize the five principles was called the Northern Native Broadcast Access Program (NNBAP). Administered by the Department of the Secretary of State, Native Citizens Directorate (Canada), it was mandated to distribute $40.3 million over a four-year period to thirteen regionally based Native Communications Societies so that they could produce twenty hours of radio and five hours of television programming per week.[5] This programming was "expected" to be transmitted by either the CBC Northern Service or Cancom (a Northern satellite distribution service). NNBAP funding was provided to produce and distribute programming that enhanced native culture and the use of native languages.

Two key aspects of previous discussions were missing from the NNBAP, which rendered the policy even more problematic in the initial implementation phases. These included the lack of funding to provide employment training and the assumption that CBC Northern Service and Cancom would embrace their new "expectations" without hesitation. With respect to training, it was assumed that Canada Manpower and Employment would assume the responsibility of providing monies on an annual basis. This might have been a realistic expectation during the first four years, but as time wore on, as personnel changed, and as cutbacks were instituted, negotiations for this and other funding requirements became exceedingly difficult. The issue of adequate funding remains increasingly problematic as federal budget allocations for Northern First Peoples' broadcasting continue to decrease annually.

As far as carriage of programming was concerned, the antiquated Broadcasting Act of 1968 did not *obligate* the CBC to comply with the CRTC expectation of donating its satellite transponder for distribution of aboriginal broadcasting. Nor did Cancom have any legal obligation to comply with the CRTC's policy statement. As a result, native broadcasters had to rely on moral suasion and "amiable negotiations" for program and scheduling arrangements.

The question of First Peoples' access to broadcasting distribution facilities was as much a moral as a political one for the two networks involved. From the perspectives of the CBC Northern Service and Cancom, carriage of First People's programming involved infrastructure, scheduling, and financial difficulties. Because of these difficulties, the new imperative became the enshrinement of aboriginal broadcasting in legislation. In the view of First Peoples, enshrinement of aboriginal broadcasting in legislation was a necessity. Without this legal recognition, funding for training and distribution would remain unstable, erratic, and might eventually disappear.

As a result of these and other struggles, the Northern Broadcasting Policy has been modified several times. In 1986, an otherwise positive program evaluation, undertaken by Lougheed and Associates, identified further problems with what were seen as fuzzy notions of "native culture" and "native languages," and an initial lack of realistic planning around questions of distribution became apparent rather soon after its implementation period. In 1988, the CRTC undertook a study (Smith and Associates, 1988) to clarify the definition of native cultural programming. This was also in response to several complaints from private radio stations in Yellowknife and Whitehorse that the publicly subsidized native radio stations were intruding on their audience niches by playing Bruce Springsteen and heavy metal music, and by advertising in the English language. Northern First Peoples argued that they had just as much a right to call Bruce Springsteen's music "theirs" as did the private, non-native stations, and that because of budgetary constraints, it was necessary to sell advertising in English as well as in the native languages. This, in addition to the other programs of NNBAP, impelled the CRTC to clarify what constituted native cultural programming and to resolve the difficulties of Northern television-programming distribution.

In 1990, the Department of the Secretary of State imposed a severe budgetary cutback on native communications funding. Federal funding of native newspapers (financed under another program called the Native Communications Program) was cut 100 percent, funding for NNBAP television and radio services chopped by 16 percent. These cuts were sharply criticized, and in significant contrast to the federal government's attitude in the 1980s when it had been fairly generous in its support of Northern aboriginal broadcasting. This was likely due to the impressive lobby efforts that Northern First Peoples had undertaken at the time.

There is some speculation that the cuts also concerned Elijah Harper, an aboriginal Member of the Manitoba Legislative Assembly, who in 1990 had refused to ratify and thus contributed to the defeat of the Meech Lake Constitutional Accord—the proposed new constitution for Canada. Furthermore, 1990 was the year in which a land conflict between the Mohawks of Kahnesetake and a neighbouring municipality, Oka, had begun to escalate into what would become a 78-day armed confrontation between the Mohawks and local and Quebec provincial police and the Canadian army. A native journalistic voice, documenting each of these mounting crises, would have added a very important perspective to the national debates surrounding these turning points in Canadian history. But because of financial cuts, First Peoples' journalists could not afford the costs of on-site coverage. Was this distancing and silencing process a conscious strategy on the part of federal bureaucrats, or was it just an incidental part of an ad hoc decision-making process? I do not suggest a conspiratorial theory here. What I am suggesting, though, is that it is important to place the budget cuts within the political context of the time.

It is interesting to note that the fiscal cutbacks of 1990 were just as much of a surprise to those administering the NNBAP and NCP as they were to native broadcasters themselves.[6] None of the evaluations undertaken to assess the quality of the programs had ever suggested the possibility that they could be terminated. On the contrary, independent evaluators had suggested fortifying them with increased budgets and expanding their range of services.

Since the events of 1990, aboriginal peoples seem to have received a more empathetic hearing in Ottawa. This increased sympathy, however, has not meant generous subsidization of media development. The effects of the cuts have been and continue to be devastating. Native communications societies have had to lay off employees; the number of hours of production have been cut; programs have been cancelled; production values have suffered in some cases. The disruption and damage caused to the relations of trust between the civil servants involved in the administration of native communications programs and the First Peoples have been immeasurable and can only be compared to the politicization effects that occurred around the Trudeau White Paper on Indian Policy in 1969. This breach of trust reinforced an even stronger commitment on the part of First Peoples' broadcasters to figure out a way to not only diversify their funding sources but also to expand their audiences in an effort to build both a political support group and an advertising base outside of their immediate regions.

While all of this was going on, the CRTC has been collecting comments on their Proposed Native Broadcasting Policy (CRTC, 1990a), based on the results of the study undertaken by Greg Smith and Associates, and were about to announce a new policy to the public.

On September 20, 1990, toward the end of the Oka crisis, the CRTC released its Native Broadcasting Policy (CRTC, 1990b) with a notable shift in title from its previous one of 1983 (the Northern Broadcasting Policy). Calling its new approach "flexible" and "minimalist," the Commission took into consideration the effects of government budget cuts by relaxing its advertising restrictions on native stations (CRTC, 1990b). Borrowing from its Community Radio and Broadcasting Policy Reflecting Canada's Linguistic and Cultural Diversity, the Commission clarified what it meant by an aboriginal broadcasting undertaking and native programming. It is to be:

> owned and controlled by a non-profit organization whose board members are drawn from the aboriginal population of the region it serves. Its programming can be in any aboriginal language or in either or both of the two official languages, but should be specifically oriented to the aboriginal audience it is licensed to serve. It also has a distinct role in fostering the development of aboriginal cultures and, where possible, the preservation of ancestral languages. An aboriginal program is a program in any language directed specifically towards a distinct aboriginal audience, or a program about any aspect of the life, interests, or culture of Canada's native people (CRTC, 1990b, 2).

For communities with more than just the native station, native broadcasters were given permission to advertise for up to an average of four minutes per hour each day, with a maximum of six minutes in any given hour. However, should the service be the sole broadcasting undertaking in a given community, all advertising restrictions were to be waived (CRTC, 1990b, 1–2).

The Native Broadcasting Policy freed the notion of culture and language from its heritage containment framework and allowed for the potential development of programming based on other considerations. First Peoples were satisfied with the Native

Broadcasting Policy in principle. But there were still several policy and program tasks left—the need to secure necessary program funding and the enshrinement of aboriginal communications rights within the Broadcasting Act. The former is still in danger of continuous erosion; the latter was accomplished in 1991, though aboriginal language rights are still not mentioned in the Act.

Legislation prior to 1991 specified that "all Canadians are entitled to broadcasting service in English and French as public funds become available" (Broadcasting Act, 7 March 1968, 16 & 17 Eliz. 2, c. 25; S.2(e)), and that the national broadcasting service should "be extended to all parts of Canada, as public funds become available" (S.2 [g] [ii]). Native peoples had the right to receive programming in English and French, but not to transmit broadcasts in their own language.

Between 1968 and the passing of the current Broadcasting Act on June 4, 1991, the Northern broadcasting infrastructure had developed to include thirteen regional native communications societies in the North, CBC's Northern Service, CBC's Northern Quebec Service, several private radio stations in Yellowknife, Whitehorse, and Iqaluit, 117 First Peoples' community radio stations across the country, and the TVNC-dedicated Northern satellite transponder service. As a result, there had been intense lobbying and new alliances formed. Aboriginal broadcasting is now addressed specifically in the Broadcasting Act, 1991, Section 3(1)(d)(iii), which states that

> (d) the Canadian broadcasting system should:
>
> (iii) through its programming and the employment opportunities arising out of its operation, serve the needs and interests, and reflect the circumstances and aspirations of Canadian men, women and children, including equal rights, the linguistic duality and multicultural and multiracial nature of Canadian society and the special place of aboriginal peoples within that society…

These changes mark a turning point in Canada's official recognition of collective over individual rights in broadcasting. The 1991 Broadcasting Act takes Canada's existing commitment to equality rights inscribed in the Charter of Rights and Freedoms (1982), the Multiculturalism Act, 1988, the Human Rights Act (1976–77) and the Employment Equity Act (1986) and applies it to the broadcasting field. These equality rights include the right to be and express multicultural and multiracial differences; the prohibition of discrimination on the basis of race, national, or ethnic origin, colour, religion, sex, age, or mental or physical disability; and the right to equitable job opportunities.

In the native broadcasting policy case, the federal government has demonstrated at least two parallel and contradictory policy tracks—that of positively responding to the aboriginal demands for broadcasting, on one hand, and that of pulling cultural funding from aboriginal peoples on the other.

More specifically, earlier on in the 1980s, the federal government had demonstrated its good will by financially supporting cultural broadcasting services within regions with significant aboriginal populations.[7] By the 1990s, these native broadcasting systems were operating smoothly and perhaps as a result were no longer as much a priority on the federal agenda as they had once been. There were other concerns of greater import to those in government, such as the Meech Lake constitutional discussions, and the political/national questions about the role and place of First Nations' within a reformed federal system. Aboriginal peoples had sharpened and made their demands for self-government more coherent; land claims treaties were in various stages of negotiations around the country. As communications became more sophisticated within native communities, First Peoples became more articulate about their demands on the federal, provincial, and territorial governments. They did not take the 1990 cuts sitting down and organized a national protest campaign as well as private meetings with the Minister of Native Affairs.

Ironically, it was the minister himself who informed aboriginal broadcasters of the strategy that was needed - they had to build alliances with non-natives and have them demonstrate to the government that *they* supported native broadcasters. Only then might the minister listen to *their* and *the native broadcasters'* messages. The minister's suggestions were taken even more seriously than *he* expected. Indeed, activities with this goal in mind were already underway in the late 1980s, when Northern Native Broadcasting, Yukon had struck an arrangement with CBC's "Newsworld" for its half-hour program "Nedaa" to be aired on a weekly basis, to an "imagined" Southern audience interested in Northern First Nations issues and entertainment. Television Northern Canada was also in the works, preparing for its launch in 1992, with the eventual possibility of becoming a third national television service in the future.

Phase IV. Emergent Trends in Northern First Peoples' Television Broadcasting

The essence of broadcast (microwave and satellite) technology is its capacity to cross great distances. In Canada, in the past, state communications policies and regulations have restricted the number of broadcast licences and their audience reach because of scarce resource and competition arguments. Government broadcasting policies and programs have supported native projects and have licensed undertakings which were intended for local community or regional broadcasting only. There were no exceptions to this restrictive policy until 1988. This was the year the federal government allocated $10 million to a national consortium to research and begin organization of a Pan-Arctic satellite channel-distribution service. There is still no nationally received aboriginal broadcasting service. Television Northern Canada, subsidized by federal funding, serves 94 communities in the North exclusively. A national cross-cultural audience reach was unforeseen in the official policies or funding formulae of Northern Broadcasting Services. Local and regional priorities have taken precedence in the context of Northern cultural development objectives for the obvious reason that, until local and regional strategies are in place, national considerations would not be paramount.

Recently, several factors have shifted regional Native Communications Societies' perceptions about the potential for national broadcasting. First, native audiences are fairly satisfied with their aboriginal services, as documented in the mandatory Native Communications Societies' surveys every few years. Second, a multiplicity of channels is becoming available through more sophisticated technology offered by signal compression. Third, having become aware that "the institutions and processes of public communication are themselves a central part of the political structure and process" (Garnham, 1986, 37), professional native broadcasters realized that access to technology depended on government financing, government ministers, and private capital investors. With new satellite technologies and increased pressure on the communications industry for multiplication of its services, it is no longer possible for politicians and regulators to argue that there are too few frequencies available to allow for an expansion of native broadcasting. Thus, because of new technological developments, the potential exists for First Nations to develop transregional networks that could influence a wide range of native and non-native audience members.

In the Canadian Northwest, Northern Native Broadcasting, Yukon (NNBY) utilizes English as its broadcasting language. Because there are so many native languages in the Yukon that have become eroded in their use (Garnham, 1986, 6), English has become the lingua franca. This factor is not incidental to the service's cross-cultural broadcasting potential. The adoption of English has enabled Yukon First Nations broadcasters to communicate cross-culturally with greater facility than most of the other twelve native communications societies that utilize a spoken native language for broadcasting. English has thus become their main broadcasting language in which programs reflecting a native perspective are transmitted. The NNBY's flagship program, "Nedaa" (Your Eye on the Yukon), covers a variety of subjects including land claims discussions, traditional story telling, hard-core news stories and documentaries pertinent to Yukon development, social issues, spirituality, music, and "Mission School" syndrome, among others. English carriage of these discussions on CBC's "Newsworld" has enabled First Nations broadcasters in the Yukon to use modern technology to convey both traditional and current indigenous issues across cultural and racial borderlines in Canada.

The expansion of Yukon regional broadcasting services across previously impermeable cultural, regional, and technological borderlines may have a profound impact on the potential of Northern broadcasting to play a role outside of the traditional one allotted by government-sponsored aboriginal broadcasting programs, that is, that of the reinforcement of First Nations cultures, languages, and native identities.

Television Northern Canada, the North's primary distribution system, which became operational on January 21, 1992, spans five time zones and covers an area of over 4.3 million square kilometres. It broadcasts a selection of programs from seven native communications societies, as well as CBC Northern Service, Government of the Northwest Territories, Yukon College, and Kativik School Board of Northern Quebec. TVNC exists as an exemplar of Pan-Arctic cross-cultural broadcasting. Broadcasters, as well as audiences, can see and evaluate their own and others' programs on a scheduled basis, thus having access to a variety of cultural productions originating from outside of their specific regions. The quality and range of program subjects carried by TVNC is impressive. Wrapped around Broadcast News and weather reports supplied by Environment Canada, programs from each of the contributing native communications societies and governmental entities cover cultural, political, social, and economic topics targeted at a diversity of age groups. National Film Board films are screened as are other independent productions; documentary and children's programming are distributed; and local soap opera-like segments are popular. In the "most appreciated" category is the Inuit Broadcasting Corporation's "Super Shamou" feature, which has become compelling viewing to youngsters and adults alike across the North. A blend of the South's Superman and the North's Magic Man, or Shaman, Super Shamou wears a cape, winks at the audience, and flies in the skies above Iqaluit on Baffin Island, overseeing the moral behaviour of the town's residents. Like Clark Kent, he intervenes when he sees people about to get into or make trouble for themselves. The "Super Shamou" segments are fascinating broadcasting strips, showing a way in which Inuit broadcasters have indigenized a social "comic" narrative of North American popular culture—to make it more relevant and appealing to Northern aboriginal viewers.

In general, TVNC's programs are fairly sophisticated. Unfortunately, however, many remain accessible only to those who speak the program producers' language. To directly address the issues of narrow casting, there are tentative plans to subtitle native programs so that language will not remain a barrier for TVNC's network-wide audience and, eventually, for a Canadian national audience. Due to budgetary constraints, however, this option remains unviable at the moment. If and when funding for versioning becomes available, carriage by Southern cable operators will most likely be TVNC's next stage of development—to expand their audiences "to include aboriginal and non-aboriginal viewers in Southern Canada" (CRTC Public Notice 1992-13., TVNC Presentation, March 1, 1993, 1).

Television Northern Canada has already had the occasion to bring together an audience of native and non-native viewers that spans the Arctic. This fact, in itself, has enormous implications for influencing public opinion. Moving South would expand TVNC's potential to become an active participant in national dialogues. In the future, international Fourth World connections may further extend possibilities for TVNC to become a key opinion-maker on a more global scale.

I believe that existing extensions of NNBY and TVNC into the South are motivated by First Peoples' recognition that in order to maintain a stable presence within Canadian broadcasting and Canadian society, they must expand their influence by constructing new social, political, and cultural alignments. They are aware that using media as a tool for identity and nation-building might not be adequately empowering if there is not also a venue through which to address issues of broader (Canada-wide) common interest to a wider audience. In the words of George Henry, one of the founders of Northern Native Broadcasting, Yukon and Television Northern Canada:

> We have to have the ability to give our messages a modern-day voice by our own people in order to promote and effect social change such as the misconceptions that Canadians have about the aboriginal people in terms of their languages, cultures, and customs. If you look at the last ten years, Indian people have been fighting to change the minds of the Canadian middle class or the middle ground. They're not really dealing with the politicians. They're not really dealing with the ethnic communities.

> They're trying to change the views of the middle ground in Canadian society. They've carved out their allies and that's where communications comes in. The more understanding and education you give people, the more tolerant a society you have (Personal interview with George Henry, August 7, 1990).

There may be interesting and important, though yet unacknowledged, ramifications when minority broadcasters gain access to nationwide audiences, and with it the ability to persuade, to lobby, and to electronically constitute regional/Pan-Arctic or national publics, and to building cross-cultural bridges and social alignments.

A presence within mainstream broadcasting menus in the South, as promised in the 1991 Broadcasting Act, would no doubt provide First Peoples' broadcasters with the potential for influencing Southern-based public opinion about aboriginal issues.

Funding is clearly the key challenge. Ideas for fundraising have included the development of a native broadcasting lottery, the creation a fund based on a Southern cable-service tax to subsidize Northern program production, and the establishment of a Native Broadcasting Program Fund, such as that of Telefilm (MacPherson and Campbell, 1993). To date, none of these ideas have been tried or adopted.

THE SYMBOLIC DEMOCRATIZATION OF THE CANADIAN BROADCASTING SYSTEM

Gaining control over the production and distribution of their own culture through local and regional venues has involved First Peoples in negotiations with various levels of civil servants, cabinet ministers, and other groups with common interests. This has ensured that those in authority have taken seriously the paradigmatic discourses on cultural and racial pluralism amd that these are reflected in the making and implementation of important native broadcasting decisions.

The enshrinement of aboriginal broadcasting in the 1991 Broadcasting Act did not end the narrative. The Northern case goes beyond redress of imbalances and oppression to something like national self-determination. First Nations are seeking a new place within Canada. They are seeking a new social contract, a reconfiguration of power relations in Canadian society—a recognition that they, too, are founding nations.

Insofar as this manifests itself in communications spheres, it tells us that what First Peoples are essentially seeking is a *national* status, as opposed to a *cultural* status. In broadcasting, it has not been enough to enshrine communication rights in legislation, while leaving aboriginal broadcasters on the financial and political peripheries of Canadian society. First Peoples want to be an integral part of the national media. They want a Canada-wide (inclusive of the North and South) national aboriginal service, complementary to the French Radio Canada and the English CBC—a central presence on a nationwide basis (MacPherson and Campbell, 1993).

What might a national First Peoples' channel mean in actual terms? For instance, would some view such a development as the institutionalization of media reservations,[8] or would it be viewed as a positive development on par with the broadcasting of English- and French-language television throughout the country? A great deal more thinking and research is needed on what it might mean for Fourth World frontier nations to achieve such a status in Canada and in other countries which "encompass" their peoples.

Seeking a national media status in broadcasting parallels political movements in self-government, territorial and environmental rights, among others. It goes beyond a repairing mode of thinking, that is, repairing the damages of colonialism, and represents a national self-affirmation. It calls for the recognition of First Nations peoples as *national*, not just cultural *citizens*.

NOTES

1. Beginning in 1983, with the introduction of the Northern Broadcasting Policy and its accompanying program, the Northern Native Broadcast Access Program, the federal government sponsors 13 regional Native Communications Societies, which are mandated to produce 20 hours of radio and/or 4.5 hours of television per week reflecting native perspectives and in the First Peoples' languages, where possible. Television Northern Canada was provided $10 million in 1988 by the federal government to develop and establish a dedicated Northern transponder in order to provide a reliable means of distributing television programming in the North, without having to piggyback First Peoples' programming on existing services.
2. No plans for the addition of FM radio service developed until 1974.
3. The term "bridge discourse" comes from the work of Nancy Fraser (1989).
4. Although it is not the subject of this paper, we must note here that since the early seventies (1974), the Native Communications Program, sponsored alternately by the federal Department of Communications and the Secretary of State, had provided community media (mostly radio) support monies to enable native communities to develop some grass-roots information sources. This money was drawn upon for all local media projects up until the 1983 Northern Broadcasting Policy was announced. After this period, the division between North and South and funding principles became much clearer.
5. It is interesting to note how these figures were conceived. In a study of minority languages in Europe, it was determined that in order to preserve a lesser-used language—one spoken by less than one million people (Alcock and O'Brien, 1980, 1.122), it would be necessary to broadcast the language for a minimum of 40 hours of radio and 20–25 hours of television per week, at peak viewing hours (p. 3.120). The Alcock and O'Brien study was one to which the federal government referred in the design of the NBP and NNBAP for background information. Obviously, the Canadian government could not afford the costs involved in such an undertaking and, therefore, reduced the number of hours for native-language broadcasting production support on the assumption that it was better to fund a portion of this amount than nothing at all.
6. In the eighties, the federal government was fairly generous in its support of Northern aboriginal broadcasting. This was likely due to the impressive lobby efforts that Northern First Peoples undertook at the time. After seven years of active developmental spending, budgets were cut in 1990. It is significant that during this year, Elijah Harper, an aboriginal Member of the Manitoba National Assembly, refused to ratify and, therefore, defeated the Meech Lake Constitutional Accord for Canada. Furthermore, 1990 was the year of the Oka conflict. Since 1990, aboriginal peoples have commanded increased respect from federal circles.

This respect, though evident in political relations, has not meant generous subsidization of media development.

7. While in the Yukon in the summer of 1990, I interviewed a former federal bureaucrat who strongly believed that the decision to cut the budgets was made on the basis of bureaucratic expediency rather than on concerted strategy. He believed that the Minister had received a total amount which he was compelled to cut from his overall program budget. This person suspected that the Minister just scanned his Directory of sponsored programs and found that if he cut the two Native Communications Programs and the Women's Program, it was the simplest way to equal the overall figure which had to be chopped. So he did this without deliberation. After receiving approximately 14 000 protest letters from women's groups and individuals, the Women's Program was reinstated. A similar number of letters did not have the same effect with Native Communications.
8. This term was suggested by Thierry Le Brun.

References

Alcock, Antony and Terence O'Brien. (1980). "Policies to Support Radio and Television Broadcasting in the Lesser Used Languages of the European Community." (Consultative Draft). Northern Ireland: University of Ulster.

Applebaum, L., and J. Hébert, (1982) (Department of Communications). Federal Cultural Policy Review Committee. Summary of Briefs and Hearings. Ottawa: Minister of Supply and Services.

Berton, Pierre. (1975). Hollywood's Canada: The Americanization of Our National Image. Toronto: McClelland and Stewart.

Canada. (1965). *Report of the Committee on Broadcasting—Fowler Committee*. Ottawa: Queen's Printer.

———. (1967–68). *Broadcasting Act*. 1968, c. 25, s. 1.

———. (1982). *Federal Cultural Policy Review Committee. Summary of Briefs and Hearings*. Ottawa: Minister of Supply and Services.

———. (1983a). News Release. "The Northern Broadcasting Policy." March 10.

———. (1983b). *Discussion Paper: Northern Broadcasting*. Ottawa: Minister of Communications, Minister of Indian and Northern Affairs, Secretary of State, February 18.

———. (1991). *Broadcasting Act*. June 4.

Caron, Andre. (1977). "The Impact of Television on Inuit Children's Cultural Images." Paper presented at the International Communications Association Conference, Berlin, June.

CBC. (1978a). "Background and Historical Mileposts in the Operations of CBC Northern Service." Ottawa: CBC Northern Service.

———. (1978b). "The CBC—A Perspective: Submission to the CRTC in Support of Applications for Renewal of Network Licenses." Ottawa: CBC.

Churchill, Ward. (1992). "I am Indigenist: Notes On The Ideology Of The Fourth World." *Z Papers* 1, 3 (July/September): 8–22.

Coldevin, Gary O. (1977a). "Anik I and Isolation: Television in the Lives of Canadian Eskimos." *Journal of Communication* 27, 4: 145–53.

———. (1977b). "Developmental Effects of Television Via Satellite on Canadian Inuit Heads of Households." Research Paper. Montreal: Concordia University, June.

CRTC. (1979). Renewal of the CBC's Television and Radio Network Licenses. Decision CRTC 79–320 dated April 30.

———. (1990a). "Review of Native Broadcasting—A Proposed Policy." Public Notice CRTC 1990–12 dated February 2.

————. (1990b). "Native Broadcasting Policy." *Public Notice CRTC* 1990–1989 dated September 20.

————. (1991). Television Northern Canada Incorporated. Decision CRTC 91–826 dated 28 October.

————. (1980). *The 1980's—A Decade of Diversity: Broadcasting Satellites and Pay-TV. Report of the Committee on Extension of Service to Northern and Remote Communities.* Ottawa: Canadian Government Publishing House.

————. (1985). "A Broadcasting Policy Reflecting Canada's Linguistic and Cultural Diversity." Public Notice CRTC 1985–139 dated July 4.

————. (1989). "Review of Northern Native Broadcasting: Call for Comments." Public Notice CRTC 1989–53 dated May 26.

Feaver, Charles. (1976). "The Politics of the Introduction of Television in the Canadian North: A Study of the Conflict Between National Policies and Needs of Native People in the North." M.A. thesis. Ottawa: Carleton University.

Fraser, Nancy. (1989). *Unruly Practices: Power, Discourse and Gender in Contemporary Social Theory*. Minneapolis: University of Minnesota Press.

————. (1990). "Rethinking the Public Sphere." *Social Text* 25/26, 8, 3., and 9, 1: 56–80.

————. (1993). "Television Northern Canada Position Paper on Northern Native Broadcasting." Public Notice 1992–13 dated March 1.

Garnham, Nicholas. (1986). "The Media and the Public Sphere." In *Communicating Politics: Mass Communications and the Political Process*. Edited by Peter Golding, Graham Murdock, and Philip Schlesinger, 37–53. New York: Leicester University Press.

Hamelin, Louis-Edmond. (1979). *Canadian Nordicity: It's Your North, Too*. Montreal: Harvest House.

————. (1984). "Managing Canada's North: Challenges and Opportunities: Rapporteur's Summary and Comments." In *Canadian Public Administration/Administration publique du Canada* 27 2 (Summer): 165–181.

————. Inuit Tapirisat of Canada. (1976). *Inuit Today* 4, 9; 5, 7.

————. (1981). "ITC Project." List of Events in Northern Broadcasting, February. Ottawa: ITC.

Lougheed and Associates. (1986). *Report on the Native Communications Program and the Northern Native Broadcast Access Program*. Ottawa: Secretary of State.

MacPherson, Lorne W., and Wil Campbell. (1973). "The Creation of a Canadian Aboriginal Film and Video Production Fund and a Canadian Film and Delivery System as an Economic Development Strategy." Unpublished proposal.

Northern Quebec Inuit Association. (1974). *The Northerners*. Quebec: NQIA.

O'Connell, Sheldon, (1974). "Television Impact on Eskimo People of Canada." M.A. thesis. Montreal: Concordia University, Department of Educational Technology.

————. (1977). "Television and the Canadian Eskimo: The Human Perspective." *Journal of Communication* 27, 4: 140–44.

Peers, Frank W. (1979). *The Public Eye: Television and the Politics of Canadian Broadcasting 1952–1968*. Toronto: University of Toronto Press.

Raboy, Marc. (1990a). "From Cultural Diversity to Social Equality: The Democratic Trials of Canadian Broadcasting." *Studies of Broadcasting* (Japan Broadcasting Corporation), 26: 7–41.

————. (1990b). *Missed Opportunities: The Story of Canada's Broadcasting Policy*. Montreal: McGill-Queen's University Press.

Roncagliolo, Rafael. (1991). "Notes on 'The Alternative.'" In *Video: The Changing World*, edited by Nancy Thede and Alain Ambrosia, 206–8. Montreal: Black Rose Books.

Roth, Lorna. (1983a). "The Role of Communication Projects and Inuit Participation in the Formation of a Communication Policy for the North." *M.A. Thesis*. Montreal: McGill University.

———. (1983b). "Inuit Media Projects and Northern Communications Policy." Monograph on Northern Native Communications. Montreal, Concordia University.

———. (1994). "Northern Voices and Mediating Structures: The Emergence and Development of First Peoples' Television Broadcasting in the Canadian North." Doctoral dissertation. Montreal: Concordia University.

Roth, Lorna and Gail Valaskakis. (1989). "Aboriginal Broadcasting in Canada: A Case Study in Democratization." In *Communication For and Against Democracy*, edited by Marc Raboy and Peter A. Bruck, 221–34. Montreal: Black Rose Books Ltd.

Said, Edward W. (1979). *Orientalism*. New York: Vintage Books.

Shields, Rob. (1991). "The True North Strong and Free." In Places on the Margin: Alternative Geographic Modernity. London: Routledge.

Smith, Greg and Associates. (1988). *Review of Native Broadcasting. A Study Commissioned by the CRTC*. Ottawa: CRTC.

TVNC. (1987). *Television Northern Canada: A Proposal for a Shared Distribution Service in Northern Canada*, June.

———. Presentation. *Response to CRTC Public Notice 1992–13*. March 1.

———. (1992). "The Dawn of a New Era." Publicity Pamphlet.

Valaskakis, Gail Guthrie. (1979). "A Communicational Analysis of Interaction Patterns: Southern Baffin Eastern Arctic." Doctoral dissertation. Montreal: McGill University.

Weir, E. Austin. (1965). *The Struggle for National Broadcasting in Canada*. Toronto: McClelland and Stewart.

Personal Interview

George Henry. Whitehorse, Yukon, August 7, 1990.

Films

Raymont, Peter, Director. *Magic in the Sky*. Producers: NFB and Investigative Films Production.

THE RAVELLED SLEEVE: ADVERTISING POLICY IN CANADA

Stephen Kline and William Leiss

Not so very long ago, Dallas Smythe called advertising the "blind spot" in our understanding of contemporary communication because no one recognized the significance of this "free lunch" in the commercial media (Smythe, 1977). Yet in the 1990s, advertising has become an increasingly controversial aspect of the Canadian communications system. Restrictions on the language of commercial signage; the fairness of comparative and ambush advertising; a ban on all tobacco print advertising; the emergence of program length commercials for children; the restrictions on television alcoholic beverage advertising; the funding of referendum and third-party political advertising; the stereotyped portrayals of women and ethnic minorities; and the problem of negative political and advocacy campaigns are but a few of the contentious developments in advertising that have figured prominently. It is clear that as the role advertising plays in Canadian society expands, the questions concerning an appropriate framework for its regulation will reappear on the public agenda.

Unfortunately, as a field of communication enquiry, advertising has tended to be situated in one of two camps: either as a pragmatic business communication technique used by marketers to promote their wares, or as a practice chastened by ideological critics as the mechanism of manipulating consumer demand by making us buy what we don't really need. Unfortunately, neither of these perspectives took advertising seriously as an important sociocultural enterprise; nor did they study in detail how advertising plays a role in mediating between commerce and media, within the broader cultural system.

Advertising's methods and applications have been transformed significantly since the turn of the century when it served primarily as a means of introducing new products into the market with florid announcements in magazines or newspapers. Advertisements are now the most visible evidence of a new promotional infrastructure (i.e., market-oriented) that manages the broader mobilization of product design, research, and communication resources in most organizational domains of our culture (Wernick, 1988). We now conduct our major political debates and encourage our children's learning through commercial forms. In this market-oriented environment, advertising agencies have become an important institutional force. They have helped to break down the assumed autonomy between the domains of commerce and popular culture, and, in so doing, have transformed older cultural traditions and practices which sought to balance information, entertainment, and education.

The agencies have created, tested, and managed the development of a panoply of communication tactics that now compose the key protocols for exerting social influence in our society. As advertising has also become a privileged funnel for public speech in which various interests conduct broader moral and social debates about the environment, spousal abuse, and violence in media, these protocols are becoming as integral now to the perpetuation of democracy as they are to the marketplace.

Clearly, the expansion of advertising as the pre-eminent model of persuasion has influenced our society in a number of important ways: 1) as a key element of marketing strategy, advertising plays an increasingly important role in the battles of market expansion and positioning within a global market; 2) as the economic engine of broadcast enterprise, advertising has important consequences for program decision-making and quality, and for the performance of our democratic media; and 3) as a model for social communication among public relations, political, and social advocacy practitioners, advertising has become an important communicative venue for public education and debates about morality.

Advertising has expanded its range of application because its practitioners have learned some important lessons about effective communication. Far from dull and meaningless harangues about goods, advertisers speak of our most private and psychologically significant experiences of daily life—our emotional bonds with the world of goods, with each other, and with the values, sense of hope, purpose, justice, and risks in our society. In their practice of persuasive communication, no distinction need be made between political, social, and commercial communication problems, for they are speaking in a language of our "essential" humanity. This is why Benetton sells its products with shocking images of strife; Calvin Klein sells perfume with ambiguous scenes of sex; or why the federal government promoted its constitutional deal through images of batters at the plate. The designer's task is to express an idea simply, in a compelling way, to increase the social influence of the message.

Advertising messages result from a complex mobilization of fiscal and creative resources. Funds are allocated to various components of the communication design process which typically includes segmentation analysis and psychographic research profiling target groups in terms of their attitudes, behaviours, and media use; positioning of the product or idea relative to competing ideas and messages; development and execution of a creative strategy in a style appropriate to the communication task; a media buy that ensures optimal exposure of the message to the target audience; and an evaluation to measure campaign impact and to provide feedback for the next phase. Advertising then, must always be understood as a strategic communication activity because it is purposefully designed to achieve specific goals of persuasion.

We believe advertising's contribution to contemporary communications is largely rooted in this perfection of the communication model for social influence through persuasion. An ever increasing circle of corporate, governmental, and advocacy groups employ the strategic communication model because it is simply the most effective way of influencing others. Yet as a wider range of social interests turn to advertising, they also broaden the picture of modern social life that it provides, the issues it discusses, and the means by which it communicates. For this reason, we have seen a change in the arguments and appeals of advertising as oil companies urge us to "think environmentally"; clear-cutting foresters promise us "forests forever"; government committees glorify the wonders of Canada in a referendum year; the Brewer's Association encourages us to "Please Drink Responsibly"; and the Canadian Association of Broadcasters fills the television screen with blood to encourage us to "speak out against violence," while member broadcasters continue to show violent and sexist programming. One can't help but notice either that the Canadian government is one of the country's leading advertisers (spending approximately $44 million in 1993 according to the Advertising Management Group, Public Works and Government Services Canada), or that such expenditures are protected from budget cuts, if not actually increased, in election years. Yet, ironically, despite the Canadian government's extensive use of advertising, it appears that Canadian policy-makers have failed to appreciate the breadth of advertising's impact or the centrality of its social role in mediating between the marketplace and modern communication systems. Indeed, the ideas conveyed in advertising should not be confused with myths and folkloric narratives that emerge organically and therefore "reflect" the national culture and its sensibilities. It is because advertising is a persuasive form of social communication that it cannot be regulated only in terms of the information role it plays in the economy. "Advertising is more than a mechanism for communicating product information to individuals: it is a cultural system. The primary field of content in modern advertising is contemporary culture itself, and advertising is a contested discourse precisely for this reason" (Leiss et al., 1990).

PUTTING ON OLD CLOTHES: THE CANADIAN FRAMEWORK FOR ADVERTISING POLICY

Advertising is a unique communication activity located in the interstice between the market's mediation of the spheres of production and consumption, and the democratic state's mandate to promote open democratic communication and culture in public media. And though the Constitution Act (1982) does not address advertising per se, it does weave the rights of media and business to free expression into the fabric of Canadian communication policy.

Under the Canadian Charter, Part I of the Act, every citizen or group has the fundamental right to free thought, belief, opinion, and expression. Under the Constitution, special collective rights have also been established to ensure the freedom of expression of specific kinds of organizations. They include the freedom of the press granted to publishers and broadcasters as specified in the Broadcasting Act (1991); the freedom of political expression for the media and official parties as articulated in the Elections Act (1991); and the freedom of commercial expression that was granted to businesses by a Supreme Court of Canada ruling in December 1988.

But these rights to communication are not the only provisions of the Charter. Other sections of the Charter recognize the need to simultaneously protect and limit these fundamental rights of expression to ensure fair and equal treatment and provide peace, order, and good government for all Canadians. Section 15(1) establishes that "every individual has the right to the equal protection and equal benefit of the law without discrimination, in particular discrimination based on race, nationality or ethnic origin, colour, religion, sex, age or mental or physical disability." Section 26 also provides that no right or freedom outlined in the Charter shall be construed as denying the existence of any other right or freedom that exists in Canada under the Charter. These rights are also subject to laws of general application which impose limitations on communications which are slanderous, libellous, pornographic, or promote hatred.

The Constitution had the predictable effect of using the right of commercial speech to launch new legal challenges, for example, in cases against prostitutes for soliciting or in reaction to bans on street vendors who have challenged bans on their commercial endeavour under the Charter. The rights of expression have also been invoked in three rather significant cases of paid advertising in which Supreme Court judges have had to rule on whether "third party" political ads can play a role during election campaigns; whether the limitations imposed on tobacco advertising are legal; and whether a consumer protection law in Quebec banning advertising directed at children is legitimate.

Yet because advertising inhabits a complex niche in our society, no single principle or framework has emerged for its satisfactory regulation. For example, product advertising must meet standards for honesty that political and advocacy advertising don't. Indeed, the regulation of advertising is a patchwork quilt of arguments, a set of loosely connected policy rationales, which have been established each with its own definitions of advertising and view of its social consequences, institutional mandates, organizational actors, and regulatory traditions. The following brief review explores the complexity of regulating advertising by tracing three very different debates that have taken place around

1) those connected with business and its practice of fair communication with consumers;
2) those connected with the operation of an open and democratic media system;
3) and those related to the problem of articulating and maintaining the values of Canadian culture.

The Canadian Framework for Advertising Policy

As Figure 1 illustrates, the regulation of advertising communication in Canada must be characterized by a fragmented set of laws and provisions and modes of regulation. Legislation referring to advertising includes advertising bans (e.g., Tobacco Products Control Act); monitoring and registration (e.g., Food and Drug Act); licence review and certification (e.g., Broadcasting Act); reporting and arbitration (e.g., Elections Act); complaints procedures (e.g., Competition Act, Broadcasting Act); professional codes of conduct and self-regulatory guidelines (e.g., Canadian Advertising Foundation, Canadian Broadcast Standards Council). Indeed, one of the hallmarks of Canadian

FIGURE 1

The Canadian Framework for Advertising Policy

FUNDAMENTAL RIGHTS UNDER THE CONSTITUTION ACT

Freedom of political and commercial expression
Equality before and under the law and equal protection and benefit of the law
Other rights and freedoms not affected by the Charter

MODES OF REGULATION	TRADITIONS OF SOCIAL POLICY	
Bans (Tobacco Products Control Act) Monitoring & Registration (Food & Drug Act, CCA, CRTC) Licence Review & Certification (CRTC) Reporting & Arbitration (Elections Act) Pre-clearances (CRTC, CCA) Industry Codes of Conduct and Self-Regulatory Guidelines (CAF, CBSC) Watchdog Organizations (MediaWatch) Complaint Procedures (CCA, CRTC)		Fair Business Practice Misleading advertising, dangerous products, language laws, trademark infringements Democratic Media Libel and slander, third party expenditures, election spending restrictions, language restrictions Defending Canadian Culture Diversity, gender representation, protection of special needs and interests, linguistic duality, sovereignty

approaches to advertising regulation (in contrast with the cycles of regulation and deregulation in the United States) is the persistence of multiple approaches to regulation and the inconsistency of rationales applied.

Advertising as Commercial Speech

In Canada, commercial speech has been historically regulated for three reasons:

1) preventing competitive advantage to any firm willing to use deceptive, comparative, or otherwise unfair advertising tactics;
2) protecting the young, unwary, or credulous consumer against false claims and other misleading advertising practices;
3) restricting the advertising of risky or hazardous products (alcohol, tobacco) where public health and safety are concerned, and monitoring of the information provided

about complex products (food and drugs, financial services) where the ability of all consumers to fully understand the nature of the claims is questioned.

The first and second rationales underwrite a set of provisions in the Competition Act (1987), administered through Corporate and Consumer Affairs, intended to eliminate deception for consumers and to ensure fair competition among businesses in the marketplace. The third is a set of restrictions on the promotion of products that may be harmful or addictive to consumers (e.g., alcohol, tobacco, drugs), or where a reasonable consumer cannot be expected to know about the appropriate use of a product (e.g., prescription drugs).

With regard to the restrictions necessary for fair business practice, many commercial advertisers recognize that the seemingly cumbersome system of restraints on commercial speech in these areas works in favour of maintaining competitive business practices while helping to ensure that advertising remains a responsible, accepted, and legitimate part of society (Esbin, 1979). Most advertisers recognize that their constitutional guarantees of free commercial speech must be accompanied by broader responsibilities to society and to the consumer. As Brian Philcox (1989), president of the Association of Canadian Advertisers wrote, "commercial free speech simply means the right to inform the consumer of what is for sale. It is also the right of the consumer to be informed. At no time does an advertiser have license to misinform. Let's not forget that advertising, along with all other facets of marketing communication, is a deeply rooted part of our cultural heritage."

In fact, the restrictions on general commercial advertising are not that onerous. Complaints procedures have been favoured as the means of reducing the frequency of unfair and misleading advertising practice. Established under the Department of Consumer and Corporate Affairs mainly to deal with infractions under the Competition Act, the Marketing Practices Branch reports regularly on the complaints it receives (Marketing Practices Branch, 1989; Director of Investigation and Research, 1990) both making the infractions public and analyzing trends in complaints.

By far the largest number of complaints are lodged by competing businesses and concern false and misleading pricing. Recent court cases would suggest that the trend in comparative advertising laws may be moving toward a more restrictive approach that benefits market leaders and leaves consumers short of valuable information. A number of market leaders (e.g., Maple Leaf Foods; Church & Dwight, distributor of Arm & Hammer baking soda) successfully restrained their competition from publishing comparative print ads on the basis of false and misleading information (Tackaberry and Musgrove, 1994). The concern here is that market leaders may use preliminary injunctions as a matter of course, to prevent comparative advertising. Currently, a simple allegation of misleading advertising is enough to restrain the ad until the case is heard by a judge, which could take years. Unless the recent cases of Maple Leaf Foods and Church & Dwight are successfully appealed, the use of comparative ads will be significantly restricted; competitors will avoid the risk of having their ads restrained by not using comparative techniques, which will ultimately reduce the ability of consumers to make informed decisions.

Although many magazine and television ads make few "falsifiable" claims concerning the performance, utility, or pricing of a product any more, the issue of dramatic visualization and implied claims in television advertising such as the Volvo "monster truck" spot have demanded some rethinking of the notion of deceptive practices of representation. In the Volvo ad, it was the unseen reinforcement of the car and the "editing in" of a hand-rolled monster truck tire that made the ad deceptive (the controversy had nothing to do with stated claims). Such cases reveal the need to specify more clearly what is meant by "misleading" given the ways contemporary advertisers can now communicate ideas with imagery as well as language. U.S. regulators have explored the notion of defining misleading in terms of "implied" claims as tested not by their truth but by their interpretation by consumers.

The Competition Act defines violations of fair advertising practice concerning "any representation to the public that is false or misleading in any material respect." The criteria for "material reflects on the degree to which the purchaser is affected by the words." The Crown does not, however, have to show that "someone was actually misled by the representation." These prohibitions apply to goods and services and include "representations by any and every means whatsoever." The test for what is misleading rests on the general impression created and not whether the representation is technically or literally accurate. The intention to mislead or the lack of such intention is immaterial. An advertisement can be misleading because it "fails to reveal certain essential information; or because it is partially true and partially false; or the representation is capable of two meanings one of which is false."

It is precisely such limitations on their persuasive techniques that some commercial interests see as restrictive. Most vocal have been the alcohol beverage advertisers, who have been subject to restrictions on their commercial speech for over 50 years because their product falls into a "restricted" category considered to pose a health risk, to be potentially addictive, or otherwise pose adverse social impacts. Spirit alcohol advertising is limited to the print media, while wine and beer products cannot depict consumers either consuming the product, or doing something which could be construed as illegal (e.g., driving). This is why all guests walk or take the bus to the never-ending parties of television beer commercials.

Opposition to restrictions placed on execution style rests on the view that advertising has a limited role. Alcohol beverage manufacturers, for example, maintain that their advertising is designed solely for brand switching and is not likely to induce young people to drink more: "Marketers can only promote a brand that fulfils a consumer demand.... The sole objective of advertising is to gain brand share at the expense of the competition" (Mehr, 1986). Yet when the CRTC addressed the system of regulation by seeking a voluntary code in 1986, the divergent interests in the alcohol products market were unable to develop a self-regulatory code (CRTC, 1990).

Alcohol advertisers are not the only ones to find themselves restricted in what and how they can communicate about their products. The strictures on unfair and misleading advertising have led to an elaborate system of regulation laid out in the Food and Drug Act (1986). Medicinal advertising has long been one of the most controversial areas of advertising, resulting in very early calls among advertising and media professionals for restraints on the excesses of "quacks." In our current Food and Drug Act, a list of drugs (narcotic drugs, controlled drugs, etc.) are banned from the use of advertising to the general public. Only those drugs intended to treat symptoms that can be self-diagnosed and self-treated can be advertised to the general public. This ruling is maintained because correct diagnosis is "exceedingly difficult...advertisements to the general public must be both informative and realistic with respect to the condition being treated and the effectiveness of the drug...vague lists of common symptoms whose purpose is to induce the public to diagnose their condition as one which will be alleviated by a particular drug have no place in drug advertising."

To guard against false and misleading advertising, all advertisements both for the purpose of promoting drugs "directly and indirectly" must get pre-clearance. The Act additionally provides that "No person shall label, package, treat, process, sell or advertise any drug in a manner that is false, misleading or deceptive or is likely to create an erroneous impression regarding its character, value, quantity, composition, merit or safety." The Act prohibits practices that make a product appear to "resemble, in a manner likely to deceive."

The Act goes on to specify in detailed words and phrases the types of advertising appeals that are considered misleading (i.e., professional endorsement, quotations from media, testimonials, and certificates of approval). Indeed, the provisions of the Act are spelled out in exacting specificity for a number of troublesome advertising practices including competitive comparisons which are considered to be misleading when they are "incomplete, exaggerate the importance of an alleged advantage, and fail to disclose a difference of opinion among qualified experts." The Act specifically mentions troublesome words in the description of potency like "rich in," "high," or "low," and goes on to advise against dangling comparatives. It also discourages the use of negative terms, scientific and technical terms, accepted opinion, questionnaires, qualifying statements, undue emphasis, inferred claims, scare advertising, illustrations, and abbreviations in comparative advertising.

Fair Business Practice and the Ban on Tobacco

Indeed the arguments about free commercial speech and the role of advertising have been brought to a head recently with the government's imposition of a ban on tobacco product advertising. When the Department of National Health and Welfare announced its ban on tobacco advertising for all media in 1989, it elicited a quick protest based on a fear that such bans are precedent-setting. Bob Foss of the Association of Canadian Advertisers immediately saw it as a threat to other advertising sectors: "What will be next? We know there are many places people would like to see it [an ad ban]. Numerous products have been targets, like tobacco and children's toys and alcoholic beverages....We're afraid [an ad ban] could come about if a precedent is set" (Strauss, 1989).

Until recently, restrictions on the content and placement of tobacco advertising—for example, its exclusion from radio and television—were the result of voluntary agreements between governments and the industry. Such voluntary restraints had prevented tobacco advertising from being regulated under the Food and Drug Act. This cosy arrangement was changed when the federal government's Bill C-5I became law on June 28, 1988, through the Tobacco Products Control Act, "an act to prohibit the advertising and promotion and respecting the labelling and monitoring of tobacco products." Section 3 defines the purposes of the Act as follows:

> (a) to protect the health of Canadians in light of conclusive evidence implicating tobacco use in the incidence of numerous debilitating and fatal diseases;
> (b) to protect young persons and others, to the extent that is reasonable in a free and democratic society, from inducements to use tobacco products and consequent dependence on them; and
> (c) to enhance public awareness of the hazards of tobacco use by ensuring the effective communication of pertinent information to consumers of tobacco products.

Section 4 states: "No person shall advertise any tobacco product offered for sale in Canada"; this includes advertisements by anyone in Canada that are placed in foreign publications or broadcasts for the purpose of promoting tobacco products specifically in Canada, but Section 4 also contains a blanket exemption for the contents of foreign media distributed in Canada, which means that Canadians would continue to be exposed to tobacco advertisements in foreign magazines.

The ban became effective January 1, 1989, for magazines and newspapers, while the prevailing voluntary ban on broadcast ads became mandatory on the same date. Outdoor ads were banned as of January 1, 1991, with a provision for gradually reducing expenditures on the same beginning in 1989. Retail signs were banned as of January 1, 1993. Promotional sponsorships of cultural or sporting events were also banned as of the beginning of 1989, excluding contractual arrangements that were in place on the date (January 25, 1988) when the final version of Bill C-5I was introduced in the House of Commons. However, no product logos or cigarette depictions are allowed in publicity for events, and monetary expenditures for the same are frozen at 1987 levels. Tobacco manufacturers have cleverly circumvented this provision by forming subsidiary companies bearing the name of certain cigarette brands, which has essentially allowed them to continue promoting their products at special events (e.g., the DuMaurier Jazz Festival).

Other provisions in the Tobacco Products Control Act include bans on free distribution of product samples; on rebates, contests, prizes, etc.; and on use of cigarette trademarks or brand names on nontobacco goods such as clothing. The Act also tries to limit access to tobacco products by obligating store owners who sell tobacco products to display a "no cigarette sales to minors" sign. Section 9 of the Act requires a health-effects warning (to be defined by regulation), including a list of toxic constituents in the products and the smoke produced by burning them, and gives authority for the requirement of an informational insert for product packages.

Thus, the passage of the Tobacco Products Control Act marked the first time in Canada that the health-hazard warnings appearing on tobacco packages had the force of law. The warnings, which must be placed prominently on the front of tobacco packages, appeared toward the end of 1989, replacing voluntary practices in effect since

1971, under which a single English and French text ("Warning: Health and Welfare Canada advises that danger to health increases with amount smoked—avoid inhaling") appeared, in small print, on the side panel of cigarette packages. Section 9(3) of the Act states: "This section does not affect any obligation of a distributor, at common law or under any Act of Parliament or of a provincial legislature, to warn purchasers of tobacco products of the health effects of those products." Thus, the Act attempts to prevent tobacco firms from using the hazard-warning requirement as a defence against civil liability claims.[1]

Finally, the Tobacco Products Control Act contains elaborate stipulations on reporting by manufacturers to the Minister of National Health and Welfare on such matters as sales, product constituents (including prescriptions on testing methods), and controlled expenditures (e.g., for sponsorships). Almost immediately upon passage of the Act, Canadian tobacco manufacturers—Rothmans, Benson & Hedges, RIR-Macdonald, and Imperial Tobacco—filed lawsuits against the federal government, claiming, among other things, that the prohibition on advertising and promotion in the Act is a violation of the Charter of Rights and Freedoms in the Canadian Constitution, which contains protection of freedom of speech and expression similar to those guaranteed in the First Amendment to the U.S. Constitution.

In the case of tobacco product advertising, the federal government's legislation is based on its understanding of the very serious health risks incurred by users of tobacco products. The government's position may be stated as follows: even though the effects of advertising and other promotional activities cannot be identified with precision—because human behaviour is complex, and there are so many influences (such as peer approval) on a person's attitudes and behaviour—advertising must be presumed to have some persuasive effect on consumers. These presumed effects are helping to encourage young persons to begin using tobacco products; encouraging them to continue doing so, even when tobacco users become aware of the associated health risks; and, finally, promoting the erroneous belief that switching to brands that are lower in tar and nicotine content will significantly reduce those health risks. Due to such effects, consumption of tobacco products and the consequent health risks are higher than they would be if people were not exposed to promotional activities (including advertising) on behalf of tobacco products.

In responding to the government's position, the tobacco industry has made three basic points. First, selling tobacco products remains a legal activity, and it is therefore unfair and unwarranted to ban outright promotional activities on their behalf. Second, there are many other products, such as alcoholic beverages and motor vehicles (especially off-road vehicles and motorcycles), whose use and misuse give rise to serious health risks, and yet the government has not imposed a total advertising and promotion ban on these product groups. Third, it is not the intention of tobacco-product marketing to attempt to persuade nonusers to begin using their products; rather, tobacco-product advertising is aimed at encouraging existing smokers to switch brands, either among competing manufacturers or among product lines by the same manufacturer.

From this perspective, the government's prohibition will not, therefore, have the desired effect of lowering health risks. Nor does it recognize the difficulties posed for

Canadian publications, which already have trouble competing with those American magazines that cross the border fattened with American cigarette ads. If the Canadian government's position is to be consistent on the relationship between advertising and demand, some argue, then it must extend the ban to all tobacco advertising in Canada. The case opened before a single judge in Quebec Superior Court in October 1989, and nine months later the judge ruled in favour of the tobacco companies on all arguments. The government immediately appealed, and early in 1992 the three-member Quebec Court of Appeal unanimously reversed this judgement; the only disagreement was that, in the opinion of one justice, the government should regulate the content of tobacco advertising rather than banning it outright. The tobacco companies appealed to the Supreme Court of Canada, whose final judgement is expected in mid-1995. Yet the battle will surely not stop there; Health Canada is currently preparing new legislation requiring all tobacco products to be sold in plain packaging, in the hope of reducing their appeal, especially to young adults, at the point of purchase.

Democratic Media, Advertising, and Political Speech

Product advertising is sometimes called "commercial free speech," in order to distinguish it from the rights of the press and of individuals and groups to freedom of "political speech." Freedom of political speech is, in fact, a central concern of most democracies, which try to promote the conditions that ensure fair and open discussion of all social, moral, and political issues. In Canadian society, the fair and open discussion of matters of public concern is established through a number of means including edict of freedom of the press, and provisions in the Broadcasting Act intended to guarantee the fair and responsible performance of broadcasters who rent the public airwaves.

Advertising is a restricted class of political speech largely to prevent wealthier segments of the population from acquiring unfair influence over public debate through their unfettered ability to purchase media time. Although there is growing evidence of businesses choosing to engage in corporate interest and advocacy campaigns, there are no provisions within the Broadcasting Act that regulate corporate or advocacy groups from using advertising for influencing public debate; nor are there restrictions on political party advertising outside of the election umbrella. Several broadcast organizations (most notably the CBC) have voluntary guidelines for "controversial" advertising, but these are mainly used to suppress fringe groups such as Adbusters'[2] attempt to air its Mr. Tubehead campaign rather than corporate PR campaigns like the Council of Forest Industry's controversial "Forests Forever."

But this same concern about the power of particular interests in our society to control public discussion through advertising has lead to an elaborate system for regulating the political speech of political parties during elections under the Elections Act 1991. As it now stands, this Act concerns itself with the allocation of paid and unpaid political broadcasts of registered parties during the election period (29 days before polling day). Although there is no detailed specification of what distinguishes "political" advertisements from other forms of commercial and political speech (such as institutional, advocacy, government advertising, social marketing, public service announcements, and product advertising), the Act implicitly defines political advertising narrowly through its restrictions on expenditures to registered parties or their agents for the purposes of "promoting and opposing parties and candidates."

The primary regulatory thrust of this Act concerns the issue of fairness in party access to broadcast advertising and the maintenance of an equitable distribution of political influence in media through the election period. To achieve the goals of fair and equitable campaigns, the Act requires each broadcaster to make available a quota of hours of paid time. The Act also sets out allocation rules based on several factors (percentage of seats, percentage of popular vote in the previous election, and number of candidates running), and also defines a 50-percent maximum of the total broadcast time that may be purchased on behalf of any party.

To oversee the media buy, the Act mandates a broadcast arbitrator to ensure fairness in the allocation of time by specifying the manner in which parties negotiate their broadcast spots from broadcasters. This ensures that it is done "fairly throughout prime time," although the arbiter must take into account the idea that parties should have freedom and flexibility in their media buys. The Act also prohibits broadcasters from making inequitable charges for equivalent prime-time spots and from charging more than the standard rate for prime time. The Act states that paid spots may be considered "election expenses," and the government allows refunds for certified claims of 22.5 percent of total election expenses.

Similarly, it is the owners or managers of the television networks who must take responsibility for allocating the required number of political broadcasts that are to be made available free of charge to candidates. The total amount of free time broadcasts must be not less than that allocated in the previous electoral campaign. Each registered political party must be granted two minutes of air time, and the remainder must be allocated in proportion to the number of ads paid for by the various candidates and parties. Any free time allocations are not considered to be election expenses or donations to the parties themselves by the broadcasters.

Yet there is considerable concern that control of election spending by political parties is not an adequate way of assuring equity and fairness in the use of advertising during elections. In the case brought to the Alberta Court of the Queen's Bench (1984) by the Attorney General concerning advertisements in newspapers undertaken during the pre-election period by the National Citizens Coalition, the judge found that "there should be actual demonstration of harm or a real likelihood of harm to a society value" before a limitation can be said to be justified. This judge stated that he had not been satisfied "that the limit is reasonably or demonstrably justified in a free and democratic society."

In addition to these spending, allocation, and arbitration rules concerning the media buying practices of parties during election, Boyer (1983, 325) also noted several other factors necessary for equitable and fair elections. The first factor concerns the question of content restrictions such as matters of privilege, copyright, libel, and slander, untrue statements that reflect on a candidate's character, and limitations on "theatrical" or highly dramatized advertising. In light of increasingly negative election campaigns, concern has been expressed about the need to control excesses of attack "rhetoric," deception, and outright lies in political advertising (Romanow et al., 1990).

The second factor necessary for equitable and fair elections concerns source restrictions, such as the use of government advertising by the party in power, the potential use of advertising broadcast from outside Canada that circumvents allocations, and "third party" advertising, that is, organizations not registered under the Elections Act who engage in advertising "promoting or opposing" a party or candidate or who attack or advocate a key policy during a campaign (e.g., signage that was displayed during the last federal elections by free trade advocates). As Seidle (1985, 126-28) notes, the Alberta decision still leaves open the issue of whether "third party" interest-group advertisements that neither promote nor oppose parties or candidates but advocate policies ("for the purpose of gaining support on an issue of public policy and done in good faith") are to be excluded during the election period. The Elections Act of 1991, however, remained silent on the issue (1) of whether third party interests should be granted the unfettered ability to purchase broadcast time during the election period for addressing issues of public importance; (2) whether the criteria of fairness and equity that apply to party political broadcasts should also be extended to them; and (3) whether the tax writeoff as a "business expense" could be claimed by third party advertisers.

Hook Them While They're Young: Defending Canadian Culture against Commercialization

Advertisers are also subject to regulations that govern the broadcast industries and their performance in the public interest. The Canadian Radio-television and Telecommunications Commission (CRTC) regulates and supervises all aspects of the Canadian broadcasting system subject to the Broadcasting Act (1991) and the Radiocommunication Act. Subsection 3(1) of the Broadcasting Act, mandates the CRTC to "serve(s) to safeguard, enrich and strengthen the cultural, political, social and economic fabric of Canada"; and "serve(s) the needs and interests, and reflect(s) the circumstances and aspirations, of Canadian men, women and children, including equal rights, the linguistic duality and multicultural and multiracial nature of Canadian society and the special place of aboriginal peoples within that society." In keeping with this mandate, the CRTC has attempted to ensure a strong Canadian component in the cultural industries under its regulatory umbrella through the Canadian-content guidelines, although these guidelines were never applied to advertising and prove hard to administer in the transnational context of the contemporary cultural industries.

In the service of maintaining the Canadian social fabric, the CRTC supervises and monitors television advertising through a system of logging and pre-clearance procedures intended to maintain provisions of the Act that limit the amount of advertising in prime time to 12 minutes per hour; prohibits the use of subliminal messages; and seeks to maintain Canadian standards and values by preventing demeaning, insulting, or offensive representations. Pre-clearance involves the striking of committees of appropriate expertise or representativeness that consider matters of taste, scientific fact, or violations of established standards. The Canadian Advertising Standards Council, the Telecaster Committee, and the Canadian Broadcast Standards Council add a self-regulatory dimension to this process of vetting advertising. The intent of all this extensive monitoring and pre-clearance is to ensure, without infringing on the freedom of commercial speech, that media buying and advertising design practices are transparent to the public, and that the standards and values applied in advertising design reflect those of the public.

All this is based on a clear distinction between advertising and programming. But this distinction is thrown into question by current marketing communication and public relations practices. Increasingly, news stories contain clips from corporate video press releases (which confuses the division between corporate and advocacy), and promotional messages are increasingly blended into the media environment—masquerading as programming. For example, why is a product placement in a film or sponsor identification at a sporting event shown on television not counted as advertising time? What is the home shopping network as a broadcast enterprise—why is it not regulated as advertising?

The abandonment of the "arms length" distinction between advertising and programming interests is evident in the way the CRTC has dealt with the infomercial, a form of program length advertisement increasingly shown on U.S. television in which the broadcaster shares in the revenue from the sales of the product. The infomercial is defined as "the combining of entertainment and information together with the selling and promoting of goods and services into a virtually indistinguishable whole." The CRTC recognized that infomercials may be construed as deceptive because they look like programs and "consumers should be protected from disguised advertising messages." Yet the CRTC had experimented with infomercials on Canadian networks, allowing them to air between midnight and 6 a.m. by viewing them as "programming" and not commercial time. Then the CRTC called for public debate on a new proposal to air infomercials during the broadcast day where, "a stand-alone infomercial would not be counted as part of the maximum 12 minutes of advertising per hour permitted by regulation" (CRTC, News Release, March 29, 1994).

Yet on November 7, 1994, Keith Spicer (then head of the CRTC) announced that infomercials will be allowed at all times in the broadcast schedule, and that private television stations can apply for a change in their condition of licence to broadcast more than 12 minutes of advertising each hour (Enchin, 1994). The motivation for this change in policy is meant to give, "greater flexibility in scheduling infomercials, and this should help to repatriate significant advertising dollars from the U.S. which can then strengthen Canadian programming of a more culturally worthwhile nature" (CRTC, November 7, 1994). Spicer made his announcement at a convention of the Canadian Association of Broadcasters. While this new source of revenue may help to provide much needed funds to develop Canadian programming, the move is also an indication of a gradual drift in Canadian advertising regulation toward an American approach which deregulates the marketplace without concern for social and cultural consequences. In doing so, the CRTC is overturning the historical legacy of Canada's strong public sector and refashioning policies that have created a protective buffer between commercial interests and the "sacred trust" of culture.

As this example reveals, the powers of the CRTC lie in its ability to regulate the amount and character of broadcast advertising; and to issue, suspend, and revoke broadcast licences; put forward new regulations; support research; and conduct hearings on matters under the jurisdiction of the Broadcasting Act. But if the CRTC is unwilling to enforce its broad mandate to maintain Canadian standards in advertising through the revoking of licences or pressure brought to bear on broadcasters, the regulatory guidelines are of little value. In this light, the CRTC was harshly criticized recently, in a Special Joint Senate-Commons Committee Reviewing Canada's Foreign Policy, for allowing private broadcasters and cable networks to thrive on American fare. The report argued that:

> The CRTC has the power to regulate the level of Canadian content in broadcasting and it does so, but so weakly that it gives the impression that it prefers to let private Canadian broadcasters enjoy the benefits that result from distributing foreign, largely American, cultural products that they buy at artificially low prices. In a similar vein, Canada is the most cabled country in the world, but the CRTC again imposes only weak content requirements on cable networks. As a consequence, on the English language cable networks 96% of drama and entertainment is foreign (Canada, 1994, 68).

The difficulties of regulating transborder commercial communication are crucial for understanding the current debates about Canadian regulation of children's advertising and the capacity of young consumers to "defend themselves" against the persuasive force of advertising. Increased commercialization of children's television, the depiction of gratuitous violence, sexual stereotyping (Trimble, 1990), ethnic representation, and the transborder flow of American commercial messages challenge broadcasters and regulating bodies to re-evaluate the framework of Canadian advertising policy.

The longstanding "rationale for regulatory codes for children's advertising is based on the principle that children are incapable of identifying advertising as commercial persuasion, and moreover, do not have the experience and conceptual abilities to evaluate advertisements" (Roberts, 1983). For this reason, in 1974 the Federal Communication Commission (FCC) limited Saturday-morning network television to nine and one-half minutes of advertising per broadcast hour. But in 1980, after intensive hearings, the FCC reversed this ruling, reasoning that market forces and industry self-regulation would prevent the "over-commercialization" of media. The regulatory agency assumed that both the limited demand for children's advertising and self-regulatory codes established for children's broadcasting would restrain children's advertisers.

Contrary to this expectation, expenditure on children's marketing increased dramatically between 1982 and 1987 in the United States, particularly among toy advertisers, who not only became the leading children's advertisers but also used the de facto deregulation implied by the suspension of children's guidelines to launch product-based animated programs, dubbed the "30-minute commercial." The new opportunities for children's merchandising afforded by the deregulation also decreased the role of network broadcasters in children's advertising. The syndicates also encouraged a dramatic increase in the production of low-cost, tie-in programs that are indirectly subsidized by the toy manufacturers (e.g., Teenage Mutant Ninja Turtles, Mighty Morphin Power Rangers). By using the syndicates of television stations, toy-marketing consortia were able both to compete with network children's programming and to short-circuit the broadcaster-based guidelines for the self-regulation of children's advertising that had been developed independently of the FCC.

The children's market was not only the first to be inundated with infomercials, but by a style of advertising long held unacceptable under the broadcast industry codes. These codes had restricted the use of children's TV heroes in advertisements and required that children's advertisements not take advantage of children's inability to distinguish fantasy from reality, or advertising from programming. Many of the advertisements for the character toys, however, blend scenes from the animated TV series with images of children playing with their character toys. In one ad, for example, a young boy is shrunk, climbs into a toy plane, and flies off into a GI Joe program (Kline, 1993). Such ads are clearly misleading in ways defined under the Canadian Competition Act. By reorganizing the economic basis of children's television in the United States, toy marketers have been able to circumvent the system of self-regulation set up by network broadcasters. These changes in American children's programs and advertising crossed the border into Canada through satellite and cable in spite of the CRTC and Advertising Standards Council guidelines.

As long ago as 1978, the FTC staff had proclaimed concern about children's advertising under the misleading advertising provisions: "It is both unfair and deceptive, within the meaning of Section 5 of the Federal Trade Commission (FTC) act, to address advertising for any product to young children who are still too young to understand the selling purpose of, or otherwise comprehend or evaluate, the advertising. If it is unfair and deceptive to seek to bypass the defenses which adults are presumed to have when they are aware that advertising is being directed at them, then it is unfair and deceptive to advertise to children in whom these defenses do not yet even exist." This FTC paper was the first to clearly articulate the widely accepted notion that children's advertising had to be separately regulated because of the special vulnerability of children. This same principle of "the capacity to recognize an advertisement" was confirmed as providing reasonable grounds for limiting broadcast advertising for children in Quebec, where a ban on advertising directed at children under age thirteen has been in place since 1976.

The Quebec ban was upheld in a Canadian Supreme Court (1989) ruling as a reasonable limitation on commercial speech under the Charter, because it accords with consumer protection legislation that strives to "protect a group that is most vulnerable to commercial manipulation." The Court stated that "in sum, the evidence sustains the reasonableness of the legislature's conclusion that a ban on commercial advertising directed to children was the minimal impairment of free expression consistent with the pressing and substantial goal of protecting children against manipulation through such advertising." Notwithstanding children's vulnerability, these "30-minute commercials" were also problematic because they and their advertising campaigns also violated the Canadian Advertising Standards Council's code for children's ads. This code states in its preamble that because children sometimes do not distinguish between fantasy and reality, "advertisements should respect and not abuse the power of the child's imagination … or stimulate unreasonable expectations of product or premium performance."

The code has a number of important provisions, including the provision that advertising must not exaggerate service, product, or premium characteristics such as performance, speed, size, colour durability, etc. (1b); also "puppets, persons and characters (including cartoon characters), well-known to children or featured on children's programs, must not be used to endorse or personally promote products" (4a); and echoing the Broadcasting Act states "advertising must not encourage a range of values that are inconsistent with the moral, ethical or legal standards of Canadian society" (8a).

Yet, for all these well-stated intentions, this code has no authority over either the character toy programs or advertisements that were both fanciful and sometimes violent. And although Canadian broadcasters were at first reluctant to run what were in effect 30-minute commercials, in order to attract children's advertising, they were forced to find cheap programming that could compete with the popular fare offered on cable. Moreover, the toy industry found it hard to understand why they should place ads with Canadian stations who were forced to vet their ads through the standards council when they could reach larger audiences of Canadian children by advertising on American border stations carried into Canadian markets by cable.

The impossibility of this situation obviously also struck the members of the Canadian Advertising Standards Council, so that by 1990 they approved a Teenage Ninja Turtle ad that not only used a cartoon character, cut back and forth between animated sequences and children's play sets, but ended with the invocation to "reach out and crush somebody." Susan Birk of the Council explained that the committee felt this incitement to violence did not violate Canadian moral or legal standards because it was said in humour. The "Turtle" who speaks this line in the ad was thought to be smiling, so kids would know he didn't really mean it.

In reaction to the mounting concern that children's promotional television programs were excessively violent, the CRTC supported a move by the Canadian Association of Broadcasters (CAB) to implement a self-regulatory code for violence on children's programs, in 1993. The new code created a 9 p.m. watershed (i.e., ensuring that no violent programming would be shown before 9 p.m.) and encouraged its members to eliminate "gratuitous" violence in children's shows by ensuring that 1) violence will not be the central theme; 2) animated programming will not invite dangerous imitation by children or that violence will be shown as a preferred way of solving problems; and that 3) the consequences of violence will be portrayed in animated programs. The CRTC stated in its announcement of this new self-regulatory solution that "Dealing with this complex issue demands that we walk a tightrope: trying to achieve a delicate but indispensable balance between protecting children and protecting free speech … we believe this code provides a realistic starting point that will help eliminate gratuitous violence from our TV screens without handcuffing program creators" (CRTC, News Release, October 28, 1993).

A recent news story would suggest that at least some of the CAB members are taking the code seriously—YTV and TVA took "The Mighty Morphin Power Rangers" off the air in reaction to a Scandinavian broadcaster which pulled the program after a news story alleged that two children kicked a third to death after watching "Power Rangers." Although there was no proven link between the killing and the program, YTV has not reinstated the program because it is sensitive to the claim that it violates the guidelines established for the industry. Global Television, a third broadcaster, has said that it will not withdraw the show "directly"; rather it will attempt to work with the American producers, Saban International, to see if the program can be modified to meet Canadian violence standards (Lacey, November 2, 1994). The Canadian Broadcast Standards Council, which monitors Global, has ruled there is too much violence in the program (approximately 25–35 percent of the show is violent) and that there is no alternative means of problem-solving presented in the program (Interview with chair of the CBSC, Ron Cohen, on "Canada AM," November 3, 1994). What is lost in this debate, however, is that "Power Rangers" is not so much a television program but an infomercial which should be subject to advertising standards as well as programming codes. As the Toys'R Us President Elliott Wahle notes, "there are millions of dollars involved" in lost sales of toys and pyjamas if the program is banned (Doyle, 1994).

But here we return to the real dilemma of regulating Canadian advertising and marketing practices. What good is a code that restricts Canadian advertisers and programmers without applying to U.S. programs and ads carried across the border by cable? To add to this self-regulatory confusion, the cable industry was supposed to be developing its own self-regulatory code for violence in children's television. However, cable operators are not permitted to meddle with programming decisions made by U.S. stations carried on their systems: "we are legally not allowed to alter or curtail a signal" (Lacey, 1994). As in the case of tobacco products, regulating advertising in the interests of all Canadians demands a totally different approach to transborder communication flows.

Darning the Ravelled Sleeve

Given the complexity of advertising's social role, the major problem that confronts policy-making is the danger of oversimplification: advertising is a policy issue that ties economic, media, and cultural questions into a tight weave, and only a framework of analysis able to recognize the complexity of advertising's cultural and institutional location will be adequate for addressing future issues. Based on past, often well-intentioned, attempts to deal with the cultural issues engendered in advertising, one must conclude that Canada's record is not a good one. Canadians see tobacco ads in American magazines they read, and at sporting events sponsored by brand-tobacco companies. They watch infomercials because they are available on U.S. stations; and children (even in Quebec) watch violent "30-minute commercials" and advertisements that don't meet Canadian standards for violence, thanks to cable and satellite technologies. Although the regulatory mechanisms are diverse and multilayered, their mandate and effectiveness are increasingly being called into question by both industry and advocacy groups, and by new approaches to advertising which blend commercial persuasion with programming.

Recognizing that the current modes of promoting, providing access to, and regulating Canadian culture are insufficient, the Special Joint Committee Reviewing

Canada's Foreign Policy recommends that, "the Government of Canada with the collaboration of interested provinces, give high priority to developing a strategy for Canada's International cultural, scientific and educational relations." Indeed, advertising, as part of a larger culture industry that includes publishing, music, arts, sports, television, motion pictures, and theatre, together with broader indicators of science and education which define culture, "should be regarded as a fundamental dimension of foreign policy."

Current Canadian policy appears to be "darning the ravelled sleeve" of communication regulation without understanding the threads that pull economic, media, and cultural influences into a tight "weave": the situation will get no simpler as changes in advertising tactics confront policy-makers. The first dilemma awaiting policy-makers derives from advertising's success as a form of communication. Advertising is a discursive practice that has emerged from an enormous investment of capital and creative resources: many regard its 30-second visions of life as the most interesting and creative feature of television. Marketers have pioneered ways of compressing and presenting ideas, as well as ways of engaging audiences and producing evocative messages, that are now becoming the standard for effective communication in all spheres. Increasingly, messages about social issues including public health, political programs, and corporate relations are adopting the approaches, techniques, and forms of expression from marketing, bringing with them a whole range of social policy matters into the debates about advertising and communication strategies. These questions demand a radical rethinking of the role of advertising in our society including the assumed distinction between commercial, corporate, advocacy, and political speech.

We must do this before we confront the next and greatest challenge of advertising policy which, like the issues of tobacco and children's culture, arises from new cultural conflicts. The rapid globalization of marketing networks, and the introduction of "free" market economic policies throughout the world, forces us to confront some complex questions about the continuation of democratic media systems and the implications of a consumer culture. We suspect that current trends in global markets will intensify the controversies over advertising as the key link between production and cultural autonomy, and will force many nations to rethink advertising's social role and responsibilities within the changing global communication context. Are commercial media systems the only "democratic" solution for financing an "independent" press? Is advertising, as conducted in the developed West, destined to become an international cultural practice creating a homogeneous, global consumer culture?

In spite of Canada's unique situation, which has forced us to wrestle longer than most nations with the issues of intensive government advertising and social marketing, environmental advocacy campaigns, and the preservation of cultural identity in a free market society, there is no indication yet that Canadian public policy-makers deal effectively with these matters. There is growing evidence only that acceptance of the "free market" as the foundational economic institution in Canada gradually brings with it the acceptance of American marketing communication as a cultural reality.

Canada has a unique history with regard to advertising regulation. A succession of issues in health promotion, social marketing, governmental and political advertising, and environmental and social advocacy advertising have forced successive governments to wrestle with the question of advertising's role in a democratic market society. Canadian public policy-making has yet to develop either a more comprehensive conception of advertising's cultural role or the legislative tools to deal effectively with these as matters of public policy. Without this understanding, Canada seems poorly placed to deal with the challenges to transnational and blended advertising that lie ahead.

Notes

1. In September 1994, a set of "tougher" hazard warnings, required by Health Canada, began to appear, including the statements "Smoking can kill you" and "Tobacco is addictive." These are among the strongest tobacco hazard warnings to be required anywhere in the world. Whereas before, manufacturers tried to blend the warnings into the design of the cigarette box, warnings are now required to be in black and white in order to heighten their legibility.
2. The Adbusters Media Foundation is a nonprofit group providing media analysis and education, often satirizing popular ad campaigns through *Adbusters Quarterly: Journal of the Mental Environment*.

References

Note: In addition to new materials, this essay draws freely upon Chapter 12, "Issue in Social Policy," in W. Leiss, S. Kline, and S. Jhally, *Social Communication in Advertising,* 2nd ed. Toronto: Nelson Canada, by permission of the publishers, 1990.

Addiction Research Foundation. (1986). *Response to CRTC Public Notice No. 1986–68.*

Boyer, J.P. (1983). *Money and Message: The Law Governing Election Financing, Advertising, Broadcasting and Campaigning in Canada.* Toronto: Butterworths.

Canada. (1982). *Constitution Act.*

Canada. (1986). *Food and Drug Act.*

Canada. (1987). *Competition Act.*

Canada. (1991). *Broadcasting Act.*

Canada. (1991). *Elections Act.*

Canada, Special Joint Committee of the Senate and House of Commons Reviewing Canada's Foreign Policy. (1989). *Projecting Canadian Culture and Learning Abroad* (report).

CRTC. (1994). "CRTC Seeks comments on Proposed Regulatory Changes Concerning Infomercials." News Release dated March 29.

CRTC. (1993). "Protecting Children While Protecting Creative Freedom: CRTC Accepts Private Broadcasters' Strengthened TV Violence Code." News Release dated October 28.

CRTC. (1994). "Broadcasters Who Listen: New Opportunities in a Consumer-driven Marketplace." Notes for an address to the Canadian Association of Broadcasters, November 7.

Director of Investigation and Research, Consumer and Corporate Affairs. (1990). *Misleading Advertising Bulletin*, 2. Minister of Supply and Services Canada.

Doyle, John. (1994). "Why Their Plug Was Pulled." *The Globe and Mail*, November 7, A9.

Enchin, Harvey. (1994). "Infomercials Get Better Time Slot," *Report on Business Magazine*, November 8, p. B1.

Esbin, S. (1979). "A Compliance Test for False or Misleading Ads." *Marketing*, May 21, 18–19.

The Globe and Mail. (1990). "CRTC Urged to Ban Alcohol Ads." *The Globe and Mail*, October 26.

Kline, S. (1989). "Limits to the Imagination." In *Cultural Politics and Contemporary America*, edited by I. Angus and S. Jhally, 299–316. New York: Routledge.

————————. (1993). *Out of the Garden: Children, Toys and Television in the Age of Marketing*. London: Verso Press.

Kline, S., R. Deodat, A. Shwetz, and W. Leiss. (1991). "Political Broadcast Advertising in Canada," under "Election Broadcasting in Canada," Volume 21. In *Reforming Electoral Democracy, Volume 4, What Canadians Told Us*, Royal Commission on Electoral Reform and Party Financing.

Lacey, L. (1994). "Power Rangers Suffers Body Blow to Programming." *The Globe and Mail*, November 2, p. A14.

————————. (1994). "Cable Operators Won't Take Power Rangers Off the Air." *The Globe and Mail*, November 9, A12.

Leiss, W., S. Kline, and S. Jhally. (1990). *Social Communication in Advertising*, 2nd ed. Toronto: Nelson Canada.

Marketing (1986). "Look what the winds will blow in." *Marketing*, January 13, p. 10.

Marketing Practices Branch. Selected articles from the Misleading Advertising Bulletin, 1976–1989.

McLuhan, M. (1951). *The Mechanical Bride: Folklore of Industrial Man.* New York: Vanguard Press.

Mehr, M. (1986). "CRTC Pondering Codes for Booze Advertising: CAB Awaits Verdict on Self-regulation." *Marketing*, June 2.

Philcox, B. (1989). "The Public Has a Right to Know What's for Sale." *The Globe and Mail*, January 16.

Roberts, D. (1983). "Children and Commercials: Issues, Evidence, Interventions." In *Rx Television: Enhancing the Preventative Impact of TV*, edited by J. Sprafkin, C. Swift, and R. Hess. New York: Hawthorne Press.

Romanow, W., Walter Soderlund, and Richard Price. (1990). "Negative Political Advertising: An Analysis of Research Findings in Light of Canadian Practice." A Report to the Royal Commission on Electoral Reform and Party Financing, November, p. C2.

Seidle, P.L. (1985). "The Election Expenses Act: The House of Commons and the Parties." In *The Canadian House of Commons: Essays in Honour of Norman Ward*, edited by John C. Courtney, 113–34. Calgary: University of Calgary Press.

Singer, B. (1986). *Advertising and Society.* Don Mills, Ont.: Addison-Wesley.

Smythe, D. (1977). "Communications: Blindspot of Western Marxism." *Canadian Journal of Social and Political Theory* 1(3).

Strauss, M. (1989). "Tobacco Firms Start Challenge of Ad-Ban Law." *The Globe and Mail*, September 25, B1.

Tackabery, Paul and James Musgrove. (1994). "Give Freer Rein to Comparative Advertising." *Financial Post*, October 29.

Trimble, L. (1990). "Coming Soon to a Station near You." Unpublished dissertation, Queen's University.

Wernick, A. (1988). "Promotional Culture." *Canadian Journal of Social and Political Theory* 12, 1–2.

Suggested Readings

Holbrook, M.B. (1987). "Mirror, Mirror, on the Wall, What's Unfair in the Reflections on Advertising?" *Journal of Marketing* 51, 3 (July):95–103.

Kline, S. (1988). "The Theatre of Consumption: On Comparing U.S. and Japanese Advertising." *Canadian Journal of Social and Political Theory*, November.

Leiss, W. (1976). *The Limits to Satisfaction.* Toronto: University of Toronto Press.

Leiss, W., S. Kline, and S. Jhally. (1986). *Social Communication in Advertising.* Toronto: Methuen.

Marketing. (1986). "Globalization," *Marketing*, January 13, pp. 9–10.

——————. (1986). "Supra-national Forces Conspiring Against Advertisers: WFA president." *Marketing*, June 9, p. 7.

Pollay, R.W. (1977). "On the Value of Reflections in 'The Distorted Mirror.'" *Journal of Marketing* 51, 3 (July):104–10.

Pollay, R.W. (1985). "Images of Ourselves: The Good Life in Twentieth Century Advertising." *Journal of Consumer Research* 11, 4 (March):887–97.

PRIVACY POTHOLES ON THE INFORMATION HIGHWAY

Ray Straatsma and Catherine Murray

> *Protecting privacy in the computer age is like trying to change a tire on a moving car.*
>
> *C. Hibbert, Computer Professionals for Social Responsibility*

Unwanted telemarketing and junk mail are already the bane of the consumer's existence. As the Canadian "Information Highway" carries more commercial traffic, mere nuisance may escalate into infringements on consumer rights and privacy. These forms of targeted marketing communication are already finding their way onto the Internet, a public telecommunications network linking computers in Canadian homes, businesses, universities, governments, and social agencies. As additional communication networks involving cable and radio communication are extended and become more "intelligent," they involve computers in managing and routing two-way traffic of video, voice, and text information at higher speeds in compressed digital form. Growing "intelligence" brings greater capability for these network "highways" to become new sites for economic production, distribution, and exchange.

Information networks have already proved essential for firms in the transformation of manufacturing. They are now also changing the nature of consumption and exchange for Canadian consumers, providing the opportunity to shop, bank, or order specific entertainment and news services from their homes. Each remote transaction involves the exchange of some personal information, usually a telephone number, name, address, postal code, or credit or debit card number. No transaction can be anonymous until software developments such as encryption provide some type of "blinder" over transactional information.

This article explores the technology and practice of marketing communication as it moves on the information highway. Will the era of the information highway end privacy as we know it? Probably. The majority of Canadians (64 percent), in a national survey conducted by Equifax in 1993, agreed that "consumers have lost control over how their personal information is used by companies." They may be right. What can be done to protect privacy? Responses so far from the private and public sectors have been sporadic, tentative, and only marginally effective.

The argument presented here is that with so many potholes on the information highway, the concept of privacy as we know it needs radical revision. Effective consumer protection will require not just a changing of the tires, but an overhaul of the entire vehicle. Most importantly, effective consumer protection requires that Canadians emerge from what Bruce Phillips, Canada's Privacy Commissioner, has called a "technological trance" in which citizens and consumers let technology drive the interpretation of individual privacy rights on the information highway rather than taking the wheel themselves.

THE RISE OF DATABASE MARKETING

The biggest challenge to individual privacy is rooted not in the technology itself but in the attendant changes in marketing communication. General advertising is becoming less strategically important to companies interested in selling products; instead, they want to address or target consumers individually. More marketing budgets are being spent on "direct marketing," or promotional and advertising messages customerized for individual tastes and buying habits.

"Customerizing" involves the creation, storage, and exchange of consumer data for marketing purposes. Such data can now be collected at almost every conceivable point of market transaction and exchange (except those where only cash changes hands), and packaged to use or resell through the implementation of software programs or relational databases. Once the preserve of direct mail-order houses or catalogue sellers, the boundaries of direct and database marketing are expanding. The Canadian Direct Marketing Association (CDMA) now defines its activities widely:

> a range of activities designed to offer information, goods or services to members of the public and the business community by mail, telephone or other direct means, based on prior knowledge, or assumptions about, the addressee[']s interests, so as to elicit a direct, measurable response and establish a mutually beneficial relationship (CDMA, 1993, 14).

Why has the marketing communication system changed? Because businesses are finding these changes cost-effective. Obtaining new customers can cost three to five times more than getting a repeat customer—even if that repeat customer is only a sporadic one. Marketers increasingly plot the life cycle of a consumer—that is, the yield over time (Blattberg and Deighton, 1991). Leading marketing experts such as Theodore Levitt and Philip Kotler forcefully proclaim the importance of "relationship marketing and management" and insist "customer retention is far more important than customer attraction." Post-sale customer communications and service, what marketing professor Terry Vavra calls "after-marketing," is now recognized by marketers as a key path to long-term, profitable survival.

Such change in the economic incentives that structure marketing communication explain recent innovations such as "loyalty" and "affinity" cards. Retail and grocery outlets such as Zellers, IKEA, Price Club, and A&P provide customers with these membership cards, which provide discounts on goods.[1] Air Miles programs adopted widely by grocery chains such as Safeway or Zehrs, and credit-card affiliations like GM with

MasterCard or Ford with Visa, also encourage long-term customer-company relationships. The advantage of such customer information-management techniques is the capture of "direct measurable response." Transactionally generated marketing information provides instant gratification to a marketer in a way that TV, radio, or newspaper advertising cannot. The speed of the informational transaction is important. In electronic consumer goods, for example, the product life cycle has telescoped from 36 months to 18, and now to 9 months. As the formulation period for the research and development of new consumer products shortens, so too does the lifetime of the marketing plan. Every consumer response—negative, positive, or indifferent—to a promotional offer, coupon, or TV ad must be tallied immediately and layered on top of information about the individual, household, or neighbourhood available from credit agencies or other commercial databases. In the view of modern business enterprise, the collection, storage, and manipulation of information about consumers and their behaviour has become central to the continuing success of contemporary capitalist economies.

Growing trade in personal information by private-sector businesses is based upon enhanced telephone services such as automatic call identification; 1-800 or 1-900 numbers; and credit, debit, and affinity cards, which all enable ever more precise monitoring of business-to-customer exchange. When the call comes in, or before it is answered, many 1-800 operations can routinely combine the incoming telephone number with a file on household information collected from other sources. Firms that use these services—typically direct marketers like infomercial or mail-order operators—are able to amend their sales pitch according to the characteristics of the caller. Such use of *data matching* and *transactionally generated information* to construct consumer profiles has become routine.[2]

If a consumer buys running shoes over the phone, and later purchases a sports event on pay-per-view TV, both consumer facts could theoretically be joined by matching the originating phone number. Currently, data matching is most often done by an individual manufacturer or retailer over time. As concentration of ownership and vertical integration of the corporate landscape increases, so can the potential size and depth of information contained in a vertical network of databases. For example, in the United States, Blockbuster Video's 50-million-person database is being used to direct market to new subscribers to Showtime, and potential visitors to Paramount theme parks. All three companies are owned by Viacom.

In Canada, acquisitions of Maclean Hunter and Unitel by Rogers Communications Inc. give the cable giant an advantageous position in the emerging era of communications convergence. The merging of technology and content in telecommunications, computers, entertainment, and broadcasting will bring new interactive and information services—pay-per-view video, electronic newspapers, phone signals, home shopping—into your home via fibre-optic wire. Information will flow both ways; the feedback of information on purchases and viewing choices will allow the tracking of most consumer transactions and choices made through interactive networks. The multimedia companies scrambling to build these information highways—such as Rogers—will be more than just program distributors and providers; they will also be the collectors and managers of personal information and preferences.

But such information practices are not restricted to the big media players. Increasingly, firms buy and sell information from one another across different ownership groups. The result has been a veritable explosion in information-oriented marketing and research companies in the United States and Canada. This sector includes specialized firms such as list brokers (over 100 in Canada alone), direct marketers, mailing houses, telemarketing agencies, software producers and users of database and geographic information systems, plus a myriad of consultants and in-house firms. A *Maclean's* magazine report (April 23, 1993), estimated that the revenues from the collection, compilation, and tracking in personal data, one component of the revenues of database marketing, are as much as $300 million per year.

Sizing the scope of database and direct marketing in the economy is very difficult. The boundaries between direct sales, mail order, manufacturers' or credit databases, list brokers, and direct-response radio or TV selling are blurred in both definition and activity. Many observers agree that marketing activities using software and relational databases are now incorporated into traditional marketing methods for many consumer-goods sectors such as catalogues and media sales. Most marketers currently design a campaign to include an experimental mix of traditional and nontraditional media. Consequently, many database marketers know more about the finances of Canadians than we know about theirs.

Nonetheless, some preliminary figures can be cited. Revenue from Canadian-based direct marketing activities in 1991 was more than $8.5 billion, up 7 percent from 1990, and almost double the 1984 figure. Direct mail alone made up a 23.9 percent share of net advertising revenues in Canada in 1990, up from 21.1 percent in 1980 (see Table 1), and greater than net revenues from television advertising. Managers indicate they are shifting their budget allocations toward direct response selling (Figure 1), but such techniques still do not command the majority of marketing budgets as they do in the United States. "Technology and database planning," says Peter Case, Vice-President of advertising for the Royal Bank of Canada, "will do to advertising what television did for it 40 or 50 years ago."[4]

TABLE 1

Net Advertising Revenues for Canada (in $ millions)

	Direct/ Cat.	% of Total	TV	% of Total	Radio	% of Total	Other*	Total
1970	217.3	20.5	139.3	13.1	113.7	10.7	589.8	1060.1
1975	386.6	19.9	265.6	13.7	207.7	10.7	1078.6	1938.5
1980	742.1	21.1	610.3	17.4	392.0	11.2	2019.0	3763.4
1985	1413.6	23.8	1046.5	17.6	566.2	9.5	2913.2	5939.5
1990	2204.2	23.9	1536.5	16.7	787.1	8.6	4677.7	9205.5

*includes newspapers (daily, weekly, controlled distribution), outdoor, directories, etc.

Source: Statistics Canada actuals 1970–1980; Maclean Hunter actuals 1985; estimates 1990

FIGURE 1

Allocation of Spending in Marketing Budget

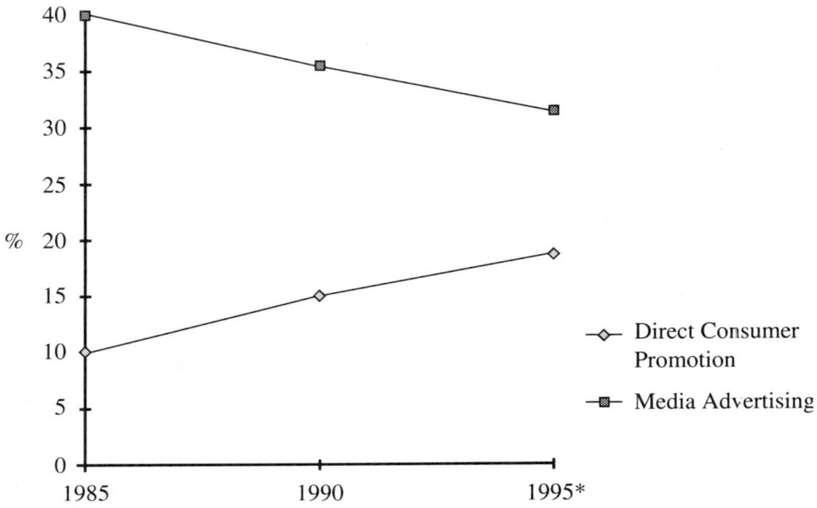

*projected

Base: Top 37 Canadian Advertisers

Source: International Surveys Limited (ISL).

In the United States, a recent survey by Donnelly Marketing Inc. revealed that 85 percent of manufacturers and retailers believe they will need database marketing to become competitive past the year 2000; 56 percent are currently building databases; and 10 percent plan to do so.[5] Some of the databases of Canadian consumers built by Canadian businesses are profiled in Table 2.

The most intensive databases—such as Air Miles—which track purchases over a number of retail channels and over time reach some 40 percent of households. Transactionally generated information via debit or credit cards or other methods is even more difficult to aggregate. An estimated 46 million credit cards are in circulation in Canada, or about 2.3 for each person over 18 years of age (Finlayson and Martin, 1993). In Canada, the market data collected from grocery-store checkout counters alone is estimated to be worth $70 million.[6] Traditional advertising media like television now engage heavily in direct response techniques. Canadian broadcasters derive revenues of $220 million from direct selling methods.[7] Direct response advertising has also generated its own TV genre: the infomercial, a category of offering that the Canadian Radio-telecommunication and Television Commission (CRTC) is in the

TABLE 2

Canada's Larger Customer Databases

Consumers Distributing Inc.	Purchase orders	8 million
Zellers Inc.	Club Z	7 million
Radio Shack	Point of sale	5 million
Air Miles Promotions Ltd.	Air Miles	4* million
Royal Bank of Canada	VISA card members	4 million
Bank of Montreal	MasterCard members	4 million
Toronto-Dominion Bank	VISA card members	1.7 million
Reader's Digest Magazines Ltd.	Subscribers	1.5 million

*households

Total number of households: 10.0 million
Total number of adults (18 & over): 20.5 million (*Statistics Canada/1991 Census*)

Source: Adapted from John Southerst, "Customer Crunching," *Canadian Business* (September 1993): 30. Data from Statistics Canada, 1991 Census.

process of opening up. Such infomercials feature extended product or service ads and a 1-800 number to call for more information or for an immediate order.

THE EMERGENCE OF THE DATA SHADOW

Systems to collect, store, and traffic in consumer information have their origins in early market research and behavioural sciences in North America in the 1920s and 1930s. Alfred Sloan of General Motors used primitive "market feedback" techniques at the time of the purchase transaction to collect data on automobile buyers and to coordinate production or refine product design or pricing elements (Robins and Webster, 1988, 334; Beniger, 1986, 310-11). In *The Control Revolution*, James Beniger has documented the development of other market research techniques, from ad testing (1906), to door-to-door surveys (1911), and circulation audits (1914).[8] However, these were relatively marginal activities until the sixties when more or less similar products were sold on a mass scale to customers perceived to have more or less the same characteristics.

In its most primitive form of intelligence gathering, market research simply attempted to survey the basic characteristics of consumers. How old were they? How many children were there in the household? How much discretionary income was available? The precision of such basic demographic information about consumers was radically enhanced when government census departments began to regularize information about markets, and make such data available to private market researchers in manufacturing companies or independent research or advertising firms. In many ways, the assembling of such information grew out of the state's need to collect tax revenue and to monitor social programs more effectively. But increasingly, the collection and expansion of the types of information gathered were intended to serve the orderly organization of markets at a time of rapid social change, and to improve the efficiency of marketing, performing, in short, what Leo Panitch has called the "capital accumulation" function of the state. Various government departments at provincial or federal levels sell access to data.[9] Such databases are often purchased on CD-Rom or other electronic forms and repackaged and sold by companies such as Compusearch or Dun and Bradstreet, using postal codes as a data-fusion tool.

Street addresses and telephone numbers can be matched via reverse directories from the White or Yellow Pages of your telephone company, also easily available on CD-Rom for a fee. Thus, the capacity to purchase this data, and to match and load it into other publicly available government sources, is easily available even to the smallest business. When blended with account or billing records from private companies or credit information, or matched with data from lists of, say, magazine sellers, a firm can begin to add information about media consumption or other lifestyle interests. The strategic value of integrating such demographic, behavioural, and lifestyle information has been recognized in commercial audience research since the early 1980s, when Nielsen people-meter households were given special cards so that the diary of their purchases could be matched against their viewing behaviour and compared to their exposure to certain ads. In the world of list exchange for direct marketing, or database matching, the boundaries between public and private information are difficult to find.

This process of *data matching* allows the construction of remarkably comprehensive *data shadows* of consumers. The biggest risk to the concept of the data shadow is that the data on which it is based may not be complete or accurate. The shadow may or may not accurately follow the past history of a consumer, or his or her needs and wants. Databases contain mistakes that get passed on; certain information becomes outdated and irrelevant; competing or related firms can easily have quite different and contradictory profiles of the same person, gathered from separate sources. And all information, no matter how complete, is prone to subjective inferences and interpretations. For instance, most transactional and other personal information is skewed by its emphasis on consumerism, or its tendency to define persons primarily by their relationship to the marketplace. Huge boundaries of activity—in the so-called grey or alternative economy, or in voluntary or not-for-profit activities—generally lie outside of the world of database shadows constructed by market information-management techniques.

The Political Economy of Database Marketing

These trends in database marketing communication may be understood from different perspectives. The standard neoclassical economic argument in favour of such an "improvement" in the techniques of marketing communication will turn on the increased efficiencies, reduced marketing costs, and increased choice and convenience afforded the consumer. If the availability of better data lowers the cost of reaching niche markets, then products can be launched that might otherwise never have been brought to market. More radical pro-business positions underline the increased control this gives the consumer in the marketplace. For example, the trend to specially targeted affinity marketing suggests that consumers will find advertising, direct mail, or telemarketing less of an annoyance, since such communication is particularly targeted to their interest. An ad for fly fishing in a targeted mailout or on a nature channel is not annoying to the avid fisher.

Somewhat different arguments about marketing communication are made from a more liberal perspective. The emergence of mass marketing techniques and the rise of advertising as the dominant mode of marketing communication were key factors in what economist J.K. Galbraith called "demand-management," co-ordinating and balancing supply to demand in mass production markets. Galbraith challenged the waste inherent in advertising, suggesting that the promotion of consumption itself may carry environmental costs, and that such promotion increases the costs of goods and services, contributes to inflation in prices, and carries other social or individual costs.

Marxist or other critical conceptions of the role of such marketing communication often begin from an analysis of the ownership and control structures of the so-called consciousness industry in capitalism. Such analysts look at the media and cultural sectors of the economy—especially advertising—and argue that promotional and entertainment images served to "train" citizens into lifestyles of consumerism. Or they may indicate, as did Dallas Smythe, that the volunteering of personal information is all a part of the "work of the consumer" in modern capitalism. Smythe argued that audiences, not programs, are the real product of media. Demographic information about audiences—types of employment, discretionary income, family size, lifestyle, and age—were sold to advertisers by media measuring services like Neilsen. Marketing communication has now extended this commodification of personal information to spheres of nonmedia transaction. In marketing and advertising, information is now as important as image.

Perhaps the most interesting arena of post-Marxist critical theory arises out of a history of the transformation of modern capitalism from *Fordist* to *post-Fordist production and consumption* (Harvey, 1991). Mass markets were forged by advanced mass production techniques, wide distribution of nationally advertised brand-name commodities, new mass media of communication, and a relatively stable economic and social culture. Together, these characteristics describe a period of capitalism that has been called *Fordism*—a term that stems from Henry Ford's crucial innovations in mass production and labour discipline, but one that also resonates with another key artifact of the age, the automobile. Social histories of advertising in this period of mass consumption are numerous (Leiss, Kline, and Jhally, 1990).

Starting in the late sixties, the central elements of mass consumption and mass production began to dissolve and reformulate—into what has been called *post-Fordism*. This term describes not only new modes of *flexible production and distribution*—such as just-in-time delivery systems—but also their relationship to changes in marketing and consumption. For example, innovations in inventory control, such as those pioneered by Wal-Mart, are made possible by the precise computer monitoring of sales information. Post-Fordism, then, also describes much wider changes in the social and cultural marketplace.

Changing demographics, changing family structures, entry of women into the workforce, and the arrival of immigrants from new countries of origin combine to fragment markets and diversify ethnocultural tastes. Lifestyle patterns change, involving new leisure, entertainment, and avenues of consumption. Social transformation occurs against a background of cyclical economic uncertainty, restructuring of the workforce, and declining real family incomes. Manufacturers, retailers, and advertising agencies, many with their own marketing departments, begin to reinterpret patterns of *flexible consumption* in the marketplace. *Market segmentation* becomes a central tool in designing a balanced "marketing mix" to communicate effectively to the right consumer group at the best time and place. Advertising is subsumed into the "marketing concept," or a vision of marketing communication as an integrated process in which research, design, promotion, and service are all carefully and precisely planned and tracked.

Targeting ad campaigns, finding new markets, or developing ways to reinforce the loyalty of customers require more and better organized information about consumers and continuous monitoring—in short, the development of marketing-communication management techniques that can continually provide a surveillance function. Critical social theories of the role of such scientific marketing-management techniques have developed various theses about the "surveillance society" or "dataveillance" enabled by new technologies (Flaherty, 1989; Lyon, 1994). Taken at its most simple or deterministic form, the surveillance society thesis argues that Orwell was right, a kind of 1984 is upon us. Corporate North America has become Big Brother. This implies a necessarily negative connotation for the individual, and uses liberal theory about the relationship between state and individual as a stepping-off point for pessimism about the boundaries of personal freedom. Other variations on the surveillance thesis explore the theories of Max Weber and his concept of rationalization in technocratic forms of management in society, or explore the theories of Ellul, Foucault, and Giddens about technology in society (Gandy, 1993). This model might be seen as the Brave New World: where the soma of consumerism has so pervaded capitalist society that it has lulled us all into an initially voluntary and then involuntary surrender of personal autonomy and privacy. From time to time, the rhetoric of Canada's own Privacy Commissioner slips into this metaphor, by pointing out how Canadians seem lulled into a "technological trance." Sceptics may question how absolute the engineering of the Brave New World can be, or how such a centralized surveillance system might work in an inherently decentralized, unplanned marketplace. More elegant models expand on metaphors where surveillance becomes comprehensive, automatic, routine, and invisible to the consumer or subject.[10] Other critics question how systematic, intregrated, and monolithic is the threat of such surveillance systems, and doubt the ability of any literary metaphors to capture the disparate and diffuse nature of actual surveillance practices (Lyon, 1992).

Thinking about Information and Social Control

What can be agreed is that in the contemporary marketplace, every point of exchange or contact between consumers and business is increasingly mediated by technologies of *information control*. The word "control" is understood as "increasing the probability of a desired outcome rather than its absolute determination" (Beniger, 1986). Fundamental to this definition is the avoidance of any crude Big Brother concept of social determinism or total, centralized control. Similarly, surveillance within the scope of this article can be understood not as a complete and constant monitoring of human subjects but rather as the routine collection and management of select types of data so as to reduce marketing uncertainty and increase the probability of buying. But systems of detailed personal records also develop under conditions of complex obligations and extended mutual dependency between organizations of all types and their publics (Rule et al., 1991).

Whatever their purpose and origin, surveillance technologies work to inscribe consumers within ghostly constellations of information control and management. These phantom numbers and categories that shadow our private and public activities may or may not be accurate. But they serve as decision tools for marketers and public policymakers, and may be said to guide many product or service designs, policy agendas, advertising, and marketing campaigns. As a consequence, these data shadows work as a type of managerial abstraction.

The empirical social science methods used to construct the data shadow of media consumers or product buyers have been critiqued in a number of studies of the "politics of knowledge." Students of communication may have already encountered the critiques of cultural commentators like Ien Ang, who argue against the totalizing process of abstraction that scientific "simulations" of the media audience or consumer marketplace try to achieve. Ang's work, *Desperately Seeking the Audience,* suggests that certain types of empirical behavioural science can never fully define the audience or market they seek because they are inevitably distorted and cannot deliver anything "unified and controllable." Yet, as Ang points out, such managerial surveillance has to be continuously pursued and constantly innovative, and seeks to use different and improved methods (Ang, 1991).

The challenge of surveillance and privacy issues, then, is to address changing social relationships within the contemporary marketplace. As marketplace activities are increasingly preceded by and shaped through information exchange and strategic implementation, the disclosure of personal information becomes an arena of control and negotiation. Those persons or firms with access to personal information can make inferences or decisions about the subject to whom the data pertains—whether discounts should be offered, loans or mortgages approved, insurance claims accepted. The data subject may not be aware of what, or if, information is being used, and consequently may be at a disadvantage in the marketplace relationship.

Thus the technologies of consumer surveillance have real material effects. Information can constrain and limit our access to the social world of credit ratings, entertainment, housing, jobs, and other economic and cultural opportunities. Controlling what information we disclose about ourselves helps us negotiate our way through our social environment. When the capacity of control over this information is lost, we slowly accede to decisions being made about us, based on inferences and assumptions made from our personal data, which we may or may not endorse. As the consumer marketplace becomes ever more mediated by information, it also changes the nature of relationships between markets and persons, and among persons *within* the social marketplace. As Kevin Robins and Frank Webster have written, "Information is not a thing, an entity; it is a social relation, and in contemporary capitalist societies it expresses the characteristic and prevailing relations of power" (Robins and Webster, 1988).

The most obvious form of power to be exercised in the marketplace is the ability to exclude someone from it. The use of new information technologies in selling allows exclusionary practices such as "redlining":

> telephone services which facilitate identification of the calling party will make it easier for firms to engage in "electronic redlining" where calls from low-income neighbourhoods identified by their telephone exchange can be routed to a busy signal, a long queue, or a recorded message suggesting that the desired information is not presently available (Novek et al., cited in Ruggles, 1993).

Callers may also be classified as unlikely sales prospects or bad credit risks, judgements which may be based solely on the data stream that precedes voice contact.

Who benefits from the use of database marketing or consumer surveillance technologies? Any answer can never be one-sided. It is evident that businesses require ever more detailed profiles of consumers so as to coordinate demand-management processes of consumption with those of flexible production. Value-added services afforded by new technologies enable them to form deeper relationships with consumers. In addition, the trade in consumer and market information provides a lucrative new source of revenue. Some consumers also derive benefits from a more specialized and targeted marketplace. They might be directed to new choices of goods and services of which they would otherwise be unaware. They may be eligible for discounts over time, or win a trip from a marketer. So there is little doubt that consumers often seem willing to divulge their personal information for the benefits they may receive, and may have indeed been conditioned to do so out of a growing reliance on credit for commercial transactions. Complicated tradeoffs are at the heart of the personal data boundaries, where the blurring of private, public, and voluntary sectors of activity is accelerating, but consumers may be at a disadvantage in negotiating or evaluating them.

The Public Policy Framework

Evidence suggests that Canadians are experiencing a growing unease about the impacts of such marketing-communication surveillance systems. In addition to the majority conviction that Canadians have "lost control" cited by Canada's Privacy Commissioner, the same survey found that 62 percent believe that present uses of computers are "an actual threat to personal privacy in this country."

The international framework for privacy and personal data protection has been developing since the early 1970s. These laws were based on international conventions setting out "fair information principles" (Kirby and Murray, 1993). The most complete set of guidelines on the protection of privacy and the transborder flows of information were put forward by the Organisation for Economic Co-operation and Development

(OECD) in 1981. They present a clear set of fair information practices, which involve the following:

- right of notice: the need to obtain informed consent before data is collected, to clearly notify of purpose for the data collected
- right of reply: the ability of an individual to access her records, challenge their accuracy, and obtain correction
- scope: limits on the amount and type of data collected for a specific purpose for a specific time
- third party use: limits on disclosure, loss, or unauthorized use, prohibitions on non-related or secondary use
- security: technical safeguards against unauthorized access.

The right to privacy was not entrenched in the Charter of Rights and Freedoms, although such a provision was proposed by a number of privacy advocates. However, Parliament enacted a Privacy Act in 1982 in conformance with these general precepts, and provincial Acts are in place in Quebec, Ontario, Saskatchewan, Alberta, and British Columbia.

In practical terms, Canada's privacy protection legislation covers many aspects of the data held by the public sector that citizens would consider most important—including medical, tax, welfare, immigration, and police records. What is not clear is the extent to which even this ground for privacy protection is under siege, given the pressures on social programs to find efficiencies, to red-flag offenders, and to cut costs (Bennett, 1993). With the exception of Quebec, such laws target only the use of personal information held by state agencies—and do not touch the sphere of commingled data matching from public and private sources or private-sector database trade in personal information.

Why is the "grey" economy of fused public and private information not currently regulated? Answers to such questions must return to the difficulty in advanced democratic states of intervening in markets where data protection laws can be construed as restraints on trade. Arguments can be made, for example, that prohibiting the development and exchange of sophisticated consumer information systems can slow innovation in the marketplace or effective matching of production with demand in the economy. Trade regimes differ in their views on these issues. The European Community, for example, is developing a new data protection code which may have serious effects on businesses trying to export to Europe.

In the North American trading area, most levels of government have tended to rely on indirect regulation of the traffic in personal data through existing legislation setting out the general framework for the operation of the marketplace. Policing unfair or deceptive marketing practices and misleading advertising would cover most direct mail, for example. Other areas covered under the Competition Act promulgated in June of 1986 include unsubstantiated performance and durability claims, misrepresentations on price, or promotional contests: essentially marketing communication that involves the baiting of the consumer transaction, but not the actual exchange of personal information at the point of transaction. Prosecutions must be made in Criminal Court, and, as a result, rarely involve individuals. The absence of a strong legal tradition of consumer class-action suits in Canada has made this section of the Act the preserve of large corporate players. Noncriminal matters covered by the Competition Act include exclusive dealing and tied selling;[11] the latter could conceivably affect direct marketing developments such as affinity marketing, but has not yet been tested. Noncriminal matters involve a hearing before the Director of the Competition Tribunal.

The sphere of much individual commercial transaction involves provincial jurisdiction. Provinces have played an important role in consumer protection in the retail industry. For example, the Ontario Consumer Protection Act, Business Practices Act, and Collection Agencies Act set out rules about the type of information that can be collected in a person's credit record, how it can be used, and avenues of consumer recourse if the information is false or inaccurate. Yet few Canadians even know that they have a right to call up their local credit bureau and look at their file, much less to monitor it over time or demand to have it corrected. On balance, the federal government and most provinces have elected to leave the arena of trade in personal information to self-regulation by the private sector, although they have often tried to exercise moral suasion to get the privacy codes improved by various sectors. As a result, the Canadian Bankers' Association, the Cable Television Association and the Canadian Direct Marketing Association in the past five years have all enacted privacy codes about personal consumer information. The code for the CDMA covers 1000 members, representing 80 percent of the direct marketing industry in Canada. It sets up the right for consumers to "opt out" by checking a box on the direct marketing ad material that will prohibit the transfer of personal data to third parties. It also allows consumers to see and correct information held by member companies. Like many codes, the CDMA's places the onus on the consumer to ask for the limitation or interruption of personal trading and guarantees only a period of three years, after which the consumer must say no again. In the absence of consumer action, personal information may be freely traded to third parties for profit.

Only in Quebec—which has an extensive history of more "dirigisme" in social and economic policy—is there any regulation covering the trade of personal information by the private sector.[12] Quebec's Act Respecting the Protection of Personal Information in the Private Sector (Bill 68), passed in 1993, requires the marketer collecting personal information to obtain informed consent, and expands upon the definition to include knowledge of the intent of such data collection, the use to which it will be put, the length of time it will be kept, and the right of the consumer to access and correct it. Businesses are compelled to ensure the information is up to date and accurate and may not release it to a third party without permission from the consumer. Fines for failure to comply with the Act begin at $10 000 for the first offence, and at $20 000 for the second. For many advocates, Quebec's Act is a model of privacy protection.

Inasmuch as trade in personal information uses the wires or airwaves of federally regulated carriers, the federal government can rely on special statutes. The Telecommunications Act passed in 1993 has two sections that directly pertain to privacy. Section 7i affirms that the Canadian telecommunications system has as one of its objectives to "contribute to the protection of the privacy of persons." This objective is the last of nine, and the section does not set out the hierarchy of competing objectives if protecting privacy conflicts with the need to "foster increased reliance on market forces" or encourage "innovation in the provision of services." A later section of the Telecommunications Act (Section 41) covers unsolicited telecommunications and sets out that:

> The Commission may, by order, prohibit or regulate the use of a Canadian carrier for the provision of unsolicited telecommunications to the extent that the Commission considers it necessary to prevent undue inconvenience or nuisance, giving due regard to the freedom of expression.

The obvious question is how binding this legislation is on the cable sector. Inasmuch as the revised Broadcasting Act makes no reference to privacy, it becomes a question of the extent to which cable companies are recognized as telecommunications undertakings. In Canada, only Rogers is now recognized as a telecommunications entity and therefore covered by both Acts. Most Canadians subscribe to cable companies that are not covered under the privacy provisions of the Telecommunications Act.

A second question explores the boundary of the telecommunications universe for new entities. Resellers of telephone services, for example—who do not own their own lines but buy in bulk from the telephone company and then resell them at a discount—are to greater or lesser degrees bound by the Telecommunications Act. In general, the trend to deregulation and the CRTC's power of forbearance, or the choice against the exercise of the power to regulate in certain sectors of the market, calls into question the varying degrees of accountability to the privacy provisions of the federal Act. Cellular companies in particular have treated their telephone messages as effective broadcasts since they use the public airwaves, unbeknownst to certain embarrassed customers. Recent results from a CRTC review of the regulatory framework have suggested that it may be in the public interest to permit competition for local service between service providers, but have offered no direction on whether reconciliation or merger of the Broadcasting Act and Telecommunications Act is necessary, or how privacy provisions should be amended.[13]

The most important test case adjudicated by the Commission in its interpretation of the privacy provisions, in fact, predated the Telecommunications Act, and involved the use of incoming call identification or call management services. This case has been widely identified by North American privacy advocates as important for determining the balance between individual rights to privacy, the need to aggregate markets for new technology, and the collision with corporate interests. Would consumers pay for the privilege of blocking the appearance of their number on an outgoing call?[14] After a three-year period, the Commission decided that Canadians would not have to pay for instituting a program of "universal call blocking," unlike the situation in other countries.[15]

On another issue—the right to retaliate on unwanted telemarketing or nuisance calls, which account for between 25-40 percent of the complaints reaching it—the Commission has proved more consistently pro-privacy from the outset. Under terms of the Telecommunications Act, automatic dialling devices must exclude unlisted numbers.

If a customer complains about receiving an annoying call from the same telemarketer more than twice within a 30-day period, Bell Canada, for example, may suspend the telemarketer's service for five days, and after three such infractions terminate service.

At the time the Telecommunications Act was passed, the annual report of the (federal) Office of the Privacy Commissioner called for "national privacy legislation to establish principles and framework" for both business and government, suggesting that in the Privacy Commissioner's mind, at least, ad hoc policy responses fragmented across a number of special statutes may not be enough.

As a consequence, attention is turning to other areas in voluntary self-regulation. The Canadian Standards Association (CSA) began in 1992, in conjunction with prominent Canadian privacy analysts such as Colin Bennett. Its purpose is to work on the development and promotion of a national standard on the handling of personal information by an institution and how this information is collected, retained, kept up to date, used, and disclosed. The model code will be used as the basis on which more detailed sector-specific codes can be developed. The CSA has a sterling record for multistakeholder consensus-building among data users, data subjects, public and private sector, and other interest groups such as the Civil Liberties Association or Coalition for Public Information groups, which are springing up from Library Associations. The draft CSA code was to be released in the fall of 1996.

Not until the inquiries by the Director of Competition into the allegations of abuse of dominant monopoly position by Interac, the monopoly on automated teller machines and other credit/debit information systems owned by a consortium of banks, were fundamental questions raised about the exchange of personal financial information on the emerging intelligent networks.

Public interest in the future of the information highway prompted the Minister of Industry, John Manley, to set up The Information Highway Advisory Council (IHAC). The council will assist the federal government in developing and implementing a strategy for Canada's information highway, and review and develop privacy initiatives. However, difficulties over jurisdiction will likely hamper any uniform privacy-protection rights across Canada.

As the highway unrolls, it is already possible to buy books and CD-Rom via the Internet by using your credit card. Security software to scramble your electronic identifier and locator, as well as messages, is now available on the market. But the current risk to personal privacy remains high. Some encryption experiments with "E-money"—electronic cash for use in anonymous on-line transactions—may offer some hope for technological solutions to protect data security, but these are still distant at time of writing.[16]

Problems Defining Privacy

The concept of privacy is a highly problematic and ambiguous one. It is a term wrapped up in other complex notions such as freedom, self-identity, family life, home, and property. The distinction between the public and private realms of social life is one of the most complex and enduring questions of social and political theory

(Lyon, 1994). Economic and technological developments in modern life continue to blur that distinction. Moreover, privacy expectations vary widely between and within cultures, as well as among individuals. Concerns about the value and importance of privacy change, depending upon what information is being disclosed or concealed.

Liberal-democratic conceptions of privacy fall into two fundamental schools. The first school sees privacy, or the restriction of personal information, as an end in itself, what James Rule has called an *aesthetic* notion of privacy. The other school sees the restriction of personal information as a means to some other end: fundamentally *strategic* in nature. In the first conception, privacy is usually defined as the right of persons to be left alone or to control and information about themselves. Outflows of information have been described as "none of your business" aspects of privacy, and inflows of information as "leave me alone" aspects (Samarajiva, 1994). Some privacy advocates, such as Alan Westin, insist that individuals can or want to determine how and when all personal information is communicated to others. This seems plainly unrealistic. How much control of information—think of everyday gossip—can any one person have?

Privacy might best be redefined in terms of an ongoing negotiation: "the capability to implicitly or explicitly negotiate boundary conditions of social relations" (Samarajiva, 1994). This looser conception of privacy follows from research in social and behavioural psychology (Petronio, 1991). It places the management of information at the centre of all types of relationships and insists that managing and co-ordinating private information "contributes to a sense of autonomy and independence." In this way, the "management of privacy...balances individual identity with social interaction" (Petronio, 1991).

The pervasiveness of database marketing and the emergence of the data shadow are shifting the balance of negotiating power within the marketplace and reducing individual autonomy. Personal information is increasingly collected and managed by outside agents to improve marketing efficiency. Consumer sovereignty is potentially *decreased*, and not increased. If a prospective consumer phones a mail order operator, would he or she realize that the price or service being offered may have been adjusted according to his or her presumed income or interest? How would a new homeowner know whether his or her mortgage rate is determined by the statistical risks attached to his or her postal code or telephone exchange? Can job applicants be assured that a prospective employer hasn't perused their personal databases, which may contain incorrect or incomplete information?

In a marketplace dominated by informational relationships and digital personas, unmediated market exchanges become increasingly rare. Buying, trading, and selling in the marketplace now take place in a three-way nexus: the physical person, the corporate entity, and vectors of information that bind them. Who has the right and the ability to control and shape that informational relationship?

Several privacy advocates in the United States, including James Rule and Lawrence Hunter, suggest that the ownership of personal information resides with the individual, who could lease its use under contractual agreement and should be eligible for royalties. While this intriguing suggestion has its merits, it may only solidify the market-driven commodification of information. It may also turn out to benefit the wealthy—who would either purchase privacy protection for a fee, or get larger royalty cheques because of the perceived value of their personal information.

Treating the trade in personal information in contractual terms does, however, raise some interesting questions. Corporations have the legal right to restrict the disclosure of information about their trade practices, capital goods, and expenditures. Should personal information be reconceptualized as a trade secret? (Branscomb, cited in Gandy, 1993).

Conclusion

Privacy issues in the age of the Information Highway raise a number of individual and collective concerns. Do the benefits of disclosure of personal information outweigh the costs to individual privacy? Do the goals of security, efficiency, and better overall management of society, through innovations in techniques of surveillance, exclude other longer term social values?

Each consumer potentially evaluates if benefits in price, convenience, or choice are sufficient to disclose personal information in a transaction. People often want and even demand easy, convenient credit, and other "fine-grained decision-making afforded by personal data systems" (Rule et al., 1991) They are often willing to yield personal data in specific instances where desired services are at stake. However, people often protest what they consider "unfair surveillance"—but concede discrimination based on detailed personal data can be made whenever the ends of such discrimination seem desirable—in, for example, criminal or tax record systems. A number of scholars like Rule identify no "natural limit" to the incorporation of personal information into data systems given this logic of the bureaucratic "efficiency criterion" guiding the extensions of application of information technology by governments and private corporations; the ambiguity at the heart of the liberal-democratic concept of privacy; and the enhanced innovation, flexibility, and precision in marketing to individual markets of one in contemporary capitalist economies.

Canadians need to debate whether privacy is outmoded or is still useful as a basic social value; whether apparent public indifference is rooted in a lack of awareness; whether consumers are entranced by technological conveniences; and whether apparent tradeoffs in disclosure of personal information are always negotiated fairly and really result in significant consumer and public benefits.

There can be little doubt that the personal information we have surrendered as consumers has significantly changed in degree and nature in this era of transition to the information economy. Tradeoffs in the surrender of personal information have become commonplace. Despite the vague concern expressed in polls about privacy, most Canadians don't appear to care enough about the issue to value it, or, by contrast, see only positive material and social benefits in disclosure. Only about one in ten Canadians pay to have an unpublished telephone number, for example, and most have a credit card, which puts them in the stream of exchange of personal information. Just 18 percent believe that they have experienced serious difficulties with invasion of personal privacy (EKOS Research Associates, 1993). Many may not feel there are any avenues to reduce privacy intrusions.

If such surrender is so widespread and voluntary, can it be considered a form of acquiescence to social control? Surveillance theory continues to find this ambiguous. Communication scholars need more study on the role of the active consumer, and the dynamics between negotiation and control in the market transactions. We know, for example, that many consumers take affinity cards precisely because they believe they capture "rents" from their personal information and from their "work" at consumption, in the form of bulk discounts, personalized promotions, or other benefits. However, they may not realize the cumulative impact of their transactions in the building of these data shadows, or the consequences of these shadows or profiles in limiting their choices in the marketplace.

The concept of privacy is rooted in liberal-democratic theory and laden with notions of possessive individualism, family life, and security. The concerns about privacy have led to restraints on state power over the individual, but they have ignored the interpenetration of state and private spheres in the area of data exchange and have not yet caught up to electronic commerce and the phenomenal rise of database marketing. We remain pessimistic about the prospects for a set of policy responses informed from the position of privacy fundamentalism, which would entrench the right to privacy in the Charter of Rights and Freedoms or rewrite the Quebec Act (Bill 68) for Canada. Not only is the climate for such initiatives chilly, but the root concept of privacy is too insubstantial to carry the weight of policy change. Instead, we need to develop distinctions between privacy, confidentiality, security, and data protection. This article shares the conviction of a number of privacy experts that new policies in the information age have to switch to technological standards for data protection in the design of new systems to ensure fair information practices by the collectors and managers of personal data. The array of statutory instruments setting out the rules of the market for fair commercial transaction need to be updated for the twenty-first century, and careful thought must be given to how consumer protection can be enhanced in Canadian law. The best defence of consumer data protection, however, is a good offence. Until Canadians become vigilant about private-sector surveillance practices, they will unwittingly drive into privacy potholes along the information highway.

Notes

1. Zellers' Club Z, a pioneer program of retail database marketing in Canada, has one of the highest "market penetration" rates in the world. In 1994, Club Z has 7.9 million members, a reach into 65 percent of Canadian homes. Seventy-five percent of all Zellers shoppers are members of Club Z. And yet, says Club Z director Douglas Ajram, "We're still in the horse and buggy era in terms of database marketing." See M. Simms, "Retailers Pin Hope on Marketing Skill," *The Globe and Mail,* February 15, 1994, p. B28.
2. Data matching—"the augmentation of records by high-speed electronic database comparison and merger," and transactional information—"information produced as a by-product of a transaction"—are two key terms in surveilllance and privacy literature. For their importance to the telecommunication sector, see especially, M. Ruggles, *Personal Information Flows and Boundaries in the Intelligent Network,* CIRCUIT (Australia) Policy Paper No. 28, 1992; and T. McManus, *Telephone Transaction-generated Information: Rights and Restrictions.* (Cambridge, MA: Harvard University Center for Information Policy Research, 1990).

3. Direct marketing is defined as nonretail sales from telemarketing, direct mail, and other sources such as catalogues or coupon promotion. Advertising estimates from Statistics Canada and Maclean Hunter typically size only mail and are expressed as gross or net sales. Canadian consumers spend an average of $307 per capita annually on goods and services through direct channels (*CDMA Annual Factbook*, October 1993). Direct mail alone accounts for 25 percent of the revenues of Canada Post, which in an average year delivers to 11 million businesses, homes and apartments.
4. Marina Strauss, "Ads to Embrace a New Sexy-ism," *The Globe and Mail*, January 3, 1995, pp. B1, B4.
5. Jonathan Berry et al., "Database Marketing," *Business Week*, September 5, 1994, pp. 56–62.
6. Marina Strauss, "War at the Checkout Counter," *The Globe and Mail,* November 1, 1994, pp. B1, B8. There is currently a federal competition tribunal dispute concerning the Neilsen company's monopoly on this market in Canada.
7. Joe Clark, "Privacy Issues Are Never Far from the Surface," *The Globe and Mail*, February 15, 1994, p. B29.
8. Beniger's *The Control Revolution: The Technological and Economic Origins of the Information Society* (Cambridge: Harvard University Press, 1986), is an excellent historical review of how information systems and technologies developed from the mid-eighteenth century onward.
9. For instance, in 1992, StatsCan had revenues of $26 million from the sale of information on Canadian citizens, and Ontario's Ministry of Transport sold $14.5 million worth of licence data. Both agencies exclude personal names. Warren Gerard, "The Coming End of Privacy," *The Toronto Star,* March 5, 1994, p. B1.
10. Many critical theorists, following from the work of Michel Foucault, rely on the metaphor of Jeremy Bentham's Panopticon to analyze surveillance systems. In this view, the Panopticon, a eighteenth-century design plan for prisons where subjects are routinely and unknowingly under continual surveillance, has been freed from its architectural restraints and has been extended by modern information networks. Foucault's work, especially *Discipline and Punish* (1980), is also important for emphasizing the role of institutional record-keeping in organizing, controlling, and disciplining populations. See also Robins and Webster, 1988.
11. Tied selling is the practice "whereby a supplier requires a customer to acquire a second product from him/her as a condition of being granted a supply of the first product or the supplier requires the customer to refrain from distributing, in conjunction with the tying product, another product not manufactured by that supplier" (Director of Investigation and Research, Consumer and Corporate Affairs Canada, "An Overview of Canada's Competition Act." Minister of Supply and Services Canada, 1993).
12. The Quebec Act, which protects all personal information held by both the public and private sectors, came into effect on January 1, 1994.
13. CRTC Telecom Decision 94–19, currently under various forms of appeal.
14. Initially, in Canada, free call blocking was conceded only to certain social classes of subscribers who could demonstrate personal jeopardy, such as rape or battered women centres, doctors, law enforcement officers. Others had to pay an additional fee of 75 cents per call in the period from 1989 to 1992—and subscribers to unlisted numbers had to pay twice for the right not to have their number released. In a recent decision (CRTC Telecom 94–687), the Commission instituted universal call blocking. Once again, the onus is on the caller to initiate a call to the operator to block the appearance of his or her number on the set of the receiving phone. But additionally, consumers may enter a false name on the service to save

the inconvenience of blocking each call. This is a textbook case of "negative option" marketing of privacy protection.

15. The telephone companies mounted the case that "publication" of the number electronically was an extension on publication already ceded in the phone book, and that publication by the majority of subscribers would enable the use of such call-management information technology in tracing obscene or nuisance phone calls. But the earliest arguments were based around the need to achieve high enough penetration or market size for the technology to recover its development costs. Such call-management services have been a boon to telemarketers and database developers.
16. Public key encryption systems allow the use of "blind digital signatures" to protect the privacy of users of electronic transactions and communications, such as e-mail. Any such proposals spark considerable debate between state security interests and civil libertarians, as was evident in the recent Clipper Chip proposals in the United States. See various issues of *WIRED* magazine, especially February, May, December, 1994.

References

Ang, I. (1991). *Desperately Seeking the Audience.* London, New York: Routledge.

Beniger, J. (1986). *The Control Revolution: The Technological and Economic Origins of the Information Society.* Cambridge: Harvard University Press.

Bennett, C. (1992). *Regulating Privacy: Data Protection and Public Policy in Europe and the United States.* Ithaca: Cornell University Press.

————. (1993). "The Regulation of Dataveillance in Comparative Perspective." Paper presented at a conference on New Technology, Surveillance and Social Control, Queen's University, May.

Blattberg, R., and J. Deighton. (1991). "Interactive Marketing." *Sloan Management Review* 33, 1: 5–14.

Branscomb, A.W. (1987). "Property Rights in Information." In *Mass Communications Review,* Vol. 6, edited by M. Gurevitch and M. Levy, 603–42. Newburg Park, CA: Sage.

Canada. (1993). *On Respecting Telecommunications* (Bill C-62). Third Session, Thirty-Fourth Parliament (Canada). 40-41-41 Elizabeth II.

Canadian Direct Marketing Association. (1993). *Annual Factbook*, 2nd ed., October. Toronto.

EKOS Research Associates. (1993). *Privacy Revealed: The Canadian Privacy Survey.* Ottawa: EKOS Research Associates, Inc.

Finlayson, A. and S. Martin. (1993). *CardTricks.* Toronto: Viking.

Flaherty, D. (1989). *Protecting Privacy in Surveillance Societies.* Chapel Hill: University of North Carolina Press.

————. (1992). *Telecommunications Privacy: A Report to the CRTC*, May 1.

Gandy, O.H., Jr. (1993). *The Panoptic Sort: A Political Economy of Personal Information.* Boulder, Oxford: Westview Press.

Harvey, D. (1991). *The Condition of Postmodernity.* Reprint. Cambridge, Oxford: Basil Blackwell.

Industry Canada. (1994). *Privacy and the Canadian Information Highway.* Supply and Services Canada, October, via World Wide Web at http:/debra.dgbt.doc.ca/ isc/isc.html.

Information and Privacy Commissioner/Ontario. (1994). *Privacy Alert: a Consumer's Guide to Privacy in the Marketplace*, May.

Kirby, M., and C. Murray. (1993). "Information Security: At Risk?" In *Global Networks,* edited by L. Harasim, 167–82. Boston: MIT Press.

Leiss, W., S. Kline, and S. Jhally. (1990). *Social Communication in Advertising*, 2nd ed. Scarborough: Nelson.

Louis Harris & Associates. (1992). *The Equifax Canada Report on Consumers and Privacy in the Information Age* .

Lyon, D. (1994). *The Electronic Eye: The Rise of Surveillance Society.* Minneapolis: University of Minnesota Press.

Novek, E., N. Sinha, and O. Gandy. (1990). "The Value of Your Name." *Media Culture and Society* 12: 205.

Organisation for Economic Co-operation and Development. (1981). "Guidelines Governing the Protection of Privacy and the Transborder Data Flows of Information."

Petronio, S. (1991). "Communication Boundary Management: A Theoretical Model of Managing Disclosure of Private Information Between Marital Couples." *Communication Theory* 1, 4:311–35.

Robins, K., and F. Webster. (1988). "Cybernetic Capitalism: Information, Technology, Everyday Life." In *The Political Economy of Information*, edited by V. Mosco and J. Wasko, 44–75. Madison: University of Wisconsin Press.

Ruggles, M. (1993). *Personal Information Flows and Boundaries in the Intelligent Network.* CIRCUIT (Australia) Policy Paper No. 28.

Rule, J.B. et al. (1991). "Preserving Individual Autonomy in an Information-Oriented Society." In *Computerization and Controversy*, edited by C. Dunlop and R. Kling, 469–88. San Diego: Academic Press Inc.

Samarajiva, R. (1994). "Privacy in Electronic Public Space: Emerging Issues." *Canadian Journal of Communication* 19, 1: 87–99.

Smythe, D. (1981). *Dependency Road: Communications, Capitalism, Consciousness and Canada.* Norwood, NJ: Ablex.

Wickens, B. (1993). "Preserving Individual Privacy." *Maclean's*, April 26, pp. 20–21.

PART III

POWER AND CHANGE IN THE CANADIAN MEDIA

THE GUTENBERG REVOLUTION OF TELEVISION: SPECULATION ON THE IMPACT OF NEW TECHNOLOGIES

Mark Starowicz

INTRODUCTION

In Lyons, France, the Lumière family owned a large film-plate manufacturing plant. In 1895, Louis and Auguste Lumière devised the world's first portable film camera. They called it the cinematograph.

Edison had invented moving pictures a couple of years earlier, but not a portable camera or a means to project an image. His camera was a huge room into which you stepped to be photographed. And his film could only be viewed by peering into a box.

The Lumière camera was half the size of a briefcase, and doubled as a projector by reversing the lens. But the Lumières weren't quite sure what to do with it. They shot some factory scenes and a sequence of a train arriving at Lyons station. Perhaps this instrument might have some application in medical photography, they speculated. Perhaps it might have industrial applications. They planned to manufacture 200 and to market this apparatus for its presumably limited applications.

On December 28, 1895, the two brothers went to Paris to hold a modest public screening at a small theatre they had rented off the Champs Elysees: The Salon Indien. It was the first public projection of moving pictures in the history of civilization. People were amused, but when the scene of the train arriving at Lyons station came on—a low angle of the locomotive coming toward the camera—spectators reacted in fright, because it seemed the train was coming at them.

Later in Lyons, the sons reported this to their father, Antoine Lumière, who instantly ordered all the cinematographs to be locked up. *None*, absolutely none were ever to be sold. Instead, factory workers were to be recruited to travel around Europe recording images. But they must guard their cinematographs with their lives, sleep with them, and never let anyone examine one.

The sons, perplexed at this order to shroud the camera in secrecy, protested: "Why?"

"Don't you see the point?" Lumière said. "The product is not the camera. It's the film."

That moment in Lyons, in 1885, less than 100 years ago, was the dawn of a medium that would shape our century.

Visual Factories and Monasteries

Although the camera invented 100 years ago was small, the industry that grew around it was cumbersome, and required large institutions to create the product. Massive newsreel companies arose. When television came, the institutions became even larger—networks, powerful television stations, and news agencies.

The visual equivalent of the book had been invented, but it was still being produced by modern monasteries. A newsreel or a television program was still terribly expensive. The crews were large. The editing, distribution, and transmission required millions of dollars of equipment.

So for most of the last hundred years we've had large monasteries, and also a priesthood of administrators, editors, and a select corps of journalists, with rules and codes and myths as intricate as the Old Testament. In fact, you became a journalist the way you became a priest; you started at the bottom, apprenticed, helped out at the altar, and eventually were admitted to the sacrament. (Can you imagine this in publishing? Do we tell Paul Theroux that before he can write a book he's got to work his way up from the mail room?)

Now, 100 years after the invention of the camera, many of the monasteries are about to fall, and much of the priesthood will disperse. We are at the threshold of the Gutenberg Revolution in Television and Film. The effect will profoundly transform politics, commerce, and art. The result will be both liberating and terrifying.

But before we consider the results, let's look at what is causing the revolution.

There are three stages to the television process—recording, processing, and transmission. All of them are extraordinarily expensive, so you couldn't play in this game without assembling enormous capital and infrastructure. Monasteries.

Visual Factories

Now three revolutions have sequentially fallen into place. The first and most profoundly revolutionary instrument made a very innocent appearance under our Christmas trees ten years ago. The Handycam. In those ten years it has developed in sophistication to the extent that an entire 24-hour all news channel in New York City functions with these. Make no mistake: this is the most profoundly subversive instrument of communication since the Lumière cinematograph. This, even more than satellites, destroys borders—who can stop someone from recording in China or in Iran? This places the power of recording within the hands of average people.

And I don't mean for tornadoes and "America's Funniest Home Videos." This camera, and most particularly its more expensive brother the three-chip Hi-8, is *broadcast quality*. You can buy it on your credit card. The monopoly of the priesthood is broken. A talented young producer or journalist has the means of production within his grasp.

But even if you can record very cheaply, and cross frontiers easily, there is still the next barrier. Editing and processing everything you've recorded used to require a $250 000 edit suite and an expensive editing infrastructure.

The next instrument of revolution, which destroys this barrier, has been on our desks for most of a decade too. The computer, which has already revolutionized every newspaper and magazine and publishing house on the planet, is taking us from desktop publishing, to desktop video. The instrument that replaces a half-million dollar edit suite at a TV network is a desktop computer. Enter your field tapes into the computer memory though a videocassette machine, the machine digitally stores all the moving images, and you then edit your entire story or documentary with a mouse. Right now you can buy a top-of-the-line system for $100 000, and do in your rec room virtually anything a television station can do. This means that thousands of small companies can proliferate, literally in rec rooms, editing and assembling productions.

A pair of talented people with a second mortgage on a house can enter the television game—you no longer have to be part of a visual factory, a monastery. This is a massive devolution of the power to create from large institutions, to cottage industries.

The final barrier is transmission. You had to negotiate with someone who had one of those scarce franchises: a spot on the dial or on the converter. These were the gatekeepers to the system.

Over the next five years, the gates will disappear. Through fibre-optic cable and direct broadcast satellite, the number of channels will double, triple, quadruple until they become virtually infinite.

In fact, the idea of a channel is really an old style of thinking. We will be summoning up whatever program we want at any time we want from the data storage systems in evolution today. We will come home and summon up the local news at our convenience—it may have gone out over the air at six, but if we get home at seven thirty we can simply summon it up from a central data bank. Television will become completely à la carte. I might want the local news, followed by tonight's "MacNeil/Lehrer," followed by "Dinosaurs," which I missed last night, followed by a video on sibling rivalry because my kids are fighting, followed by the series on The Civil War, which I never did get around to seeing two years ago, followed by tonight's "Late Night With David Letterman."

The television set is an appliance that accesses a gigantic magazine stand, which is being constantly replenished. A magazine stand that not only contains this week's releases, but remembers every magazine that ever appeared on that newsstand before. Another way of thinking of the TV set is as a terminal which accesses a gigantic central library. The programs are the books, periodicals, and newspapers in the library.

The Revolution

The conjunction of these three breakthroughs—recording, production, and distribution—is the Gutenberg Revolution of television, which I define as the moment at which the means of production becomes democratically accessible. The importance of this Revolution parallels the invention of the offset press and the computer for the liberation of information flow.

It's potent not only because it will cause thousands of new enterprises and voices to arise in an explosion of pluralism, but because it destroys the tyranny of linear time. Remember when college kids used to come to your door asking you to subscribe to the *Reader's Digest* or *Cosmopolitan*? What do you think the circulation of *Reader's Digest* would be if the terms of the contract were this: I will come to your door every

Thursday evening at 8 p.m., hand you a copy of the "Reader's Digest", and regardless of whether or not you're sick, or you're having a fight with your spouse, I will come back and collect it at 9? Yet I've just described the distribution of ABC's *20/20*. It's primitive, linear, and probably reaches 10 percent of the people who might otherwise have considered watching it.

The VCR has not solved this conundrum; surveys show 85 percent of VCR owners have no idea how to program them to time shift.

Just as the telephone answering machine is being replaced by voice-mail message banks, so the VCR will be replaced by the digital program bank. You will watch *20/20* at any time you choose, and if your tap is leaking, you'll request a video on basic plumbing.

We are witnessing one of the fundamental reorganizations of the world's distribution and storage of knowledge: the hybridization of the computer, the satellite, the visual archive, and broadcasting. Its scale parallels the great information revolutions of the millennium.

We can take many paths in examining the future. I want to take only two. One, the impact on our social and political lives. Two, how countries will become winners or losers in this fundamental shift of information distribution.

The "Atomization" of Television

First, let's begin to imagine the effect of this infinite channel universe.

We've already gone through the *fragmentation* of the television audience in the late eighties through the spread of cable and the birth of satellite services. Network shares have plunged to the 50–60 percent mark. This is nothing compared to the *atomization* of the audience which will be brought on by the advent of current technologies.

The 1000 channel universe, whether it comes through cable or satellite, will destroy regulation. The moral basis for regulating broadcasting throughout the twentieth century has been the limited spectrum: there were only so many channels possible on the radio or television dial. Not everyone could have a spot on the dial, so a mechanism of licensing these scarce spots was required. Therefore, the state appropriated it as a public space, and devised a system of allocation and a regulatory agency to administer it.

The moment one can have an *infinite* number of spaces, television becomes like newsprint—there is no apparent justification to regulate the allocation of this resource in a democracy. Regulation will collapse, and the unrestrained marketplace will shape television and radio.

The consequences of this collapse are extraordinary. We are embarking on an age which will parallel all the great newspaper wars of the 1920s—press barons, mergers and acquisitions, the emergence of new collectivities and interest groups, and considerable political impact will flow from this.

In this world, nothing restrains a community of interest, or taste, or political conviction, from establishing a channel or service, any more than they're restrained now from starting a magazine or a newspaper or publishing a book. There will be a national gay channel within a short space of time, several channels serving women's interests, regional interest services will spring up, there will be a second explosion of evangelical services, ethnic services...the list is infinite. (I use the word "channel" for convenience; I don't mean they would all be full 24-hour channels; they may be daily two-or-four-hour services, something between a channel and a program. The data storage systems of the future make the word "channel" somewhat antiquated.)

In fact, the future is visible in the present by staring at a large newsstand. Channels will parallel the magazine covers. Natural history channels, book channels, left-wing and right-wing channels, a variety of sex channels, a battery of sports channels, channels that address taste constituencies (in effect a *Rolling Stone* constituency channel, a *Vanity Fair* constituency channel, a home-repair channel, a spectrum of children's channels, and a vast array of shopping channels, which I'll return to later.)

If there are enough people to sustain a reasonable national circulation for a magazine today, these people will be serviced by a channel within a decade. A hundred thousand people will soon be a commercially viable community for a service. Just look at the largest periodical newsstand you can find, and you can see the future.

Social and religious constituencies, who already have organized followings, will flourish. Nothing restrains a Jehovah's Witness Channel, nothing restrains a channel by the Rev. Sung Myung Moon, any more than anything restrained his purchase of the *Washington Times*. The Televangelism phenomenon of the 1970s and 1980s will appear tame compared with the explosion that is imminent. Television is approaching accessibility to virtually any medium-sized cult. Elizabeth Prophet will recruit and maintain her flock through a specialty channel. It's wise to remind ourselves that at the dawn of radio, fundamentalist religion was almost the dominant force and entire stations arose around individual orators, with considerable political impact. Father Coughlin's violently anti-New Deal and anti-Semitic broadcasts out of Detroit were a considerable irritant for the Roosevelt administration.

That era also suggests to us that demagoguery will appear not only in evangelical but in political form. Senator Huey Long was a potent national force with his "Every-Man-A-King" movement, which had membership in the millions. Channels will emerge around political and social demagogues. Pat Robertson, and his translation of a religious following into a political one, is the smallest hint of the inevitably emerging television landscape. The political landscape will be more vulnerable to demagogic and charismatic leaders.

David Halberstam, in his book *The Powers That Be*, chronicled the fundamental change in twentieth-century politics as television created the single mass audience, helped destroy the party apparatus, and allowed the executive branch to communicate directly with the popular base without intervening local party bosses. The reverse trend is in the ascendancy now, as the majority fragments; and one can extrapolate the ascendancy of special interest groups.

These special interest groups, already powerful within our democracies, are effective users of the print form today, and will increasingly assemble their constituencies through the television form. A National Rifle Association Channel? Why not? What one sees now only at election time in commercial spots from political action committees will become constant services, with consequences we can only speculate on. The re-ordering of the televisual world will re-order the political world. Any revolution in communications has always changed the political power equations.

The Commercial Impact

The revolution will also radically change the commercial world. Once again, let's turn to the birth of radio. In the twenties and thirties, there were stations owned by commercial enterprises and entirely devoted towards distributing and advertising that enterprise's products.

The most extreme example was one station in New Orleans that was devoted entirely to selling a patent medicine based on extract from goats' glands. It did very well. Radio very quickly became a strange amalgam of patent medicine peddling and bible-thumping evangelism. There is a national horoscope infomercial I saw last month: a charismatic woman has a team of 20 numerologists, spiritual advisers, and fortune tellers who operate on 1-800 numbers. The informercial was repeated three times during the night, and it was clear that this woman had tapped a huge market where we can easily extrapolate entire horoscope channels that almost resemble the Home Shopping Channel.

The apparent conversion of late-night television into hours upon hours of infomercials is not just amusing, but very indicative of a commercial revolution. I don't know if you've viewed the latest generation of infomercials, some of which last an hour, but their growth is geometric, and it's not hard to extrapolate that what's an hour now will become an entire channel within a decade—a channel for each product line. The new television age will see a re-ordering of the marketplace, because the very nature of commercial distribution will change. What is a cosmetic franchise informercial today, repeated endlessly on late night, will become a much faster enterprise organized through a combination of television sales and IYS-pyramid distribution. Mary Kay Cosmetics is a distribution phenomenon of the 1950s, 1960s, and 1970s.

The new mass distribution enterprise of the year 2000 will be much larger, with wider product lines, plugged into a human sales force working from home, and which will dwarf the marketing phenomena of the past. That means the emergence of new corporations, and totally new methods of product distribution, which will have an unimagined restructuring effect on the consumer marketplace: an amalgam of the old franchise phenomenon, computer networking and television marketing, corporate franchise channels.

A fascinating article in a recent issue of *The New Yorker* chronicles Barry Diller's speculations into the future. After building the Fox Network for Rupert Murdoch, he struck out on his own and considered what to invest in, where the future lay. He passed on buying the NBC network, and finally shocked everyone by embracing the Home Shopping Network. The moment of epiphany is instructive. He was in the studio during one fashion clothing sales session:

> Diller made one more visit to QVC, at 9 a.m. on Saturday, November 7th, for Diane Von Furstenberg's first sale. Surrounded by her silk clothing, she sat beside the host on a small stage in a large brick cavern. Diller stood behind one of the eighty telephone operators there and watched the toll-free calls pour in. Diller was awed.... In less than two hours, the computer showed, Von Furstenberg had sold twenty nine thousand items to

> nineteen thousand customers, for a total of a *million* two hundred thousand dollars (*New Yorker* Magazine, February 22, 1993, p.60).

In another session, soap opera star Susan Lucci sold almost half-a-million dollar's worth of a hair care product carrying her name—in just one hour.

The QVC shopping channel made a net profit of nearly $20 million in 1991; in the first nine months of 1992, it already showed a profit of $36 million.

Liberty Cable Television in New York wants to create separate Bergdorf Goodman and F.A.O. Schwartz channels, and incidentally, is on the verge of announcing agreements with Lincoln Centre to offer a *live* concert, plays, and operas service.

Once again, we can see from this the possible scale of the change in the future marketplace. So far we've been conditioned to think that the future will make it possible for us to book a flight from our touch-tone keypad, or pay a telephone bill or check our bank balance by phone or computer. The temptation to buy cubic zirconia jewellery or Elvis busts on the Shopping Channel did not seem like the stuff of revolutions any more than the drive-in teller had been. This is pretty tepid stuff, and if that's the impact of the television and computer revolution, we can take the interactivity revolution in stride.

But what we haven't been seeing is the complete re-ordering of the consumer marketplace, the transformation of retailing and distribution as we know it, and the consequent emergence of entirely new retailing and marketing corporations dependent on the television—a sort of televisual mall. The television distribution revolution will transform the nature and structure of world retailing.

In fact, we may see a blend of general service and commercial interest. Take any industrial lobby that already produces a considerable amount of public propaganda—the nuclear industry, for example. It has an interest in advocacy advertising. It produces documentaries and magazines and educational material. Why would it not find common interest with other like-minded industrial interests and see merit in joint ownership of a technology/science/environment channel, which is not overt advocacy or advertising but which is a visually rich general interest channel that nevertheless commissions programs and works more fitting with its technological perspective—a sort of "technology is good" channel?

Now stand back from this televisual newsstand, stand back from the Technology channel owned by such a consortium of high-tech companies, imagine the Green channel funded by Greenpeace and the World Wildlife Fund, imagine the ten or twelve Shopping channels divided into high fashion, home repair, automotive, and cosmetics, stand back and see the horoscope, spiritual readers channel, the ultraconservative channel, the local and national gay service, the multiple women's channels, the Jehovah's Witness, the Moonie channel, the channels built around regional interests and a dozen different Ross Perots, the political-action committee channels and even political party channels, the Catholic Church channel, the channels built around literary interests, the vast array of music channels which will replace MTV, the health and medical channel, the personal fitness channels, the computer buff channel. The variety of all-news channels catering to specific interests… stand back, look at the news and magazine stand of today, and you see the future.

In it you see excitement in the multiplication of voices, pluralism, the acceleration of debate, and you also see the re-ordering of commerce.

But most of all you see the scale of the revolution.

And, you see a new information order, not all of it comforting.

The Disappearance of Public Space

The Israeli scholar Elihu Katz points out that a radio was once a force for national integration; then, with the advent of television, it become a medium of segmentation and individualization, with stations tailored to microtaste constituencies. Television became the medium of national integration. But now, television is becoming a medium of segmentation, but as Katz puts it "there's nothing there to replace television as a medium of integration."

This leads to what he and a number of scholars have called "the disappearance of Public space." As I alluded earlier, this appears to be the single greatest impact of this Gutenberg age of television—not the *emergence* of a majority, a body politic, a public arena that eventually followed the invention of the printing press, but ironically, the reverse—the *disappearance* of the majority, or at least its atomization into regional interests, commercial, cultural, and demographic clusters.

The so-called majority, which you could imagine watching the major newscasts and making informed civic judgements on the basis of such, was never that large, really. The combined evening viewing of the three U.S. network newscasts has hovered around 45 million, and CNN is consumed by a very small percentage of U.S. households, except in times of major events. In fact, as Les Brown observed, historically, U.S. newscasts have been scheduled where they will do the least possible damage to commercial revenue, not where they will reach the most people; it's always been interesting that the program which has been arguably the most influential forum of policy debate, ABC's "Nightline," has always had to be banished to the periphery of the schedule.

But even this fragile assembly of a civic prime-time majority seems to be doomed, and we learn from a recent article by Ken Auletta (*The New Yorker*, March 15, 1993) that NBC Nightly News might well disappear if GE sells off the profitable parts of NBC, and we also know that American TV News services are evacuating many of their world bureaux. Television News in general, it appears, is destined to be another segmented specialty service. There may be two or three national all-news services like CNN, just as there will undoubtedly be three or four cartoon channels and even more shopping channels. The atomization of TV News will accelerate the segmentation of the body politic.

Just as the large movie theatres fell to the Cineplex cubicle theatres, so the public television space is being "cineplexed."

Not only is public space being cineplexed, it is being segregated into economic layers. Much of what we get for "free" now, through commercial sponsorship, will have a value attached to it in the future. Just as we pay $5 per month for Time or 50¢ for a newspaper, so will we be spending money most of the times we access the central television databank or library. We have been accustomed to this in the electronic print form by toll charges to access a database. Television will surely go down the same road.

There will be rich neighbourhoods and poor neighbourhoods. There will be high value specialty services, where your child can access a rich televisual blend of programming and CD-ROM information on a subject. And off-air, or basic-cable commercial television will survive, but on a very low grade. The high-value product will have been stripped out, and off-air TV might, supported by commercials, become more of a poor man's medium.

Thus, not only is public space being segmented—"cineplexed"—but it is effectively being auctioned off into neighbourhoods, and televisual slums—which is the ultimate pernicious segmentation of public consciousness.

The gradual replacing of the collective experience by the individual or cluster experience extends far beyond news into comedy, drama, and all forms of televised entertainment. And if the 1000-channel universe combined with the production revolution accelerates this disappearance of the majority, we are witnessing a social and political sea change of fundamental proportions.

Elihu Katz, in an essay entitled "Individualization, Segmentation and Globalization," observes two simultaneous trends in the technology—segmentation and transnational globalization—and observes that these apparently contradictory trends have one common effect: neither addresses the nation-state. "If the medium is the message then media theory foresees that these new technologies mean the effective end of the nation state" (translated from the French text).
He writes:

> Why are governments contributing to this erosion of nation states and national cultures? Why don't they see that more leads to less—to insignificance... to endless distraction, to the atomization and evacuation of public space? Why don't they see that national identity and citizen participation are compromised? Why don't they realize that they're contributing directly to the erosion of the enormous potential which television has to enlighten and unite populations into the fold of national cultures? (Chapter 13 of *Le Défi des télévisions nationales à l'ère de la mondialisation. Les Presses de l'université de Montréal. 1992.*)

He speculates that governments of the past decade, particularly in Europe, have been more interested in economic than in social well-being, are happy to unload public broadcasting systems, and are more attracted by the potential economic benefits of globalization.

Whatever the motives, the trend is inescapable. Domestic space is being segmented. And transnational space is emerging, but in private hands, and outside the control of the nation-state.

The Transnational Megachannels

The 1000-channel universe is not only allowing microchannels but macrochannels. Again, as in the 1910s and 1920s, we are seeing the emergence of press empires, the new Hearsts and Pulitzers and Beaverbrooks. The difference this time is that the clusterings will be transnational.

We are seeing the emergence of transnational Media Barons in Murdoch, and Turner and Berlusconi; the empires are not as local and personal as they once were, and maybe because of that not so political, although that remains to be seen.

If we've underestimated the political and social effects of atomization, we should not underestimate the scale of globalization's effects.

Let's go back a few years to when Time-Life was contemplating its merger with Warner Communications. Time-Life, one of the ten largest communications conglomerates on the *planet*, stared at the future and decided that this communications giant was *too small a corporate unit to compete on a world scale*. Consequently, we see the reorganization of international communications into ever-larger vertically integrated corporations like Bertelsman and Hachette and Time Warner, at the same time that we are seeing services atomize.

For many years there's been a corporate vision of "global marketing," which has paralleled the financial community's vision of "global banking." The collapse of Communism has now opened up the Eastern European market; satellites have allowed such forces as Hong Kong's "Star" channel to have a satellite footprint that extends from Indonesia to Dubai, and which has tapped into India's burgeoning middle class in a way that has frightened the New Delhi government. China, which manufactures 60 million television sets a year, can't keep up with basic demand. The vision of global channels and global marketing to emerging middle classes hitherto inaccessible through terrestrial channels has been a communications and advertising Holy Grail, which has transfixed many of the world's communications giants.

This has raised many spectres—cultural homogenization, transnational media barons, the Coca-colonization of the planet—which are not for us to explore here, and which are, at any rate, quite familiar scenarios by now.

National Strategies in the Television Revolution

What I want to address now is some idea of strategies for survival in this televisual revolution, which is shattering into atoms on the one hand, and clustering into transnational conglomerates on the other. What are the policy consequences?

Policies of exclusion or controlled access to domestic markets have been suffering erosion throughout the world, though Katz is right that the principal reason so far has not been technological so much as the national government's enthusiasm allowing such services in.

Britain, which has most successfully limited the fragmentation of its own market, has proven to be farsighted. It has incubated and nurtured one of the two most powerful television industries in the world—the other being the United States'—and consequently is well poised to take the next step, enter the world arena with a sophisticated television production apparatus. The BBC, despite the degradations of the Thatcher era, survives now as the centrepiece of Britain's industry, and the most efficient exporter of televisual products in the world. The BBC Television World Service is growing throughout the planet.

The United States, as the largest single market in the English world, has never had to worry about protecting itself, and rather is more interested in world electronic barriers coming down.

However, the so-called "disappearance of public space" will probably have its most profound effect *in the United States*, where cost of fragmentation of the body politic will probably exact its greatest price. The price may not be cultural, because the United States is such a powerful generator of its own popular culture, but it may be political, in the sense that special interests and regional concerns will predominate at the expense of national consensus.

To the United States, I suspect, the key is the significant enlargement of public broadcasting, as the decline of networks diminishes public space. The American idea of public broadcasting has been unlike the British—for the British it was the main stage, for the Americans, public broadcasting was seen as a mechanism for minorities, classes, and interests disenfranchised by the commercial networks.

The impending segmentation of public space into premium neighbourhoods and commercial slums will, I think, create a moral imperative for the United States to assure that free basic television, television which serves the public agenda, is preserved and enlarged in the face of the electronic segregation of knowledge and information.

The United States will need the national stage, the arena for public policy, national news, national events, and needs public broadcasting in the national arena sense, the collective experience; and one hopes it will see fit to invest heavily in public television for the health of the democratic process. The home for national news, aside from CNN, may well become PBS. I suspect the public broadcasting era in the United States is just beginning.

For smaller markets, such as Canada and most European countries, the prospects are indeed difficult. The 1000-channel universe, once the satellite cracks the regulatory borders, will become a fierce challenge to the nation-state's capacity to define its agenda. Regulatory exclusion will at best retard the inevitable.

In the television revolution, a nation will be either an aggressive player or a cultural victim. Governments will eventually realize that television production is like steel or aeronautics. You're either in the game or you're not, you're just an importer. Unless you have a significant domestic television-production industry, you will not only increasingly lose control of your market, but you will not be able to participate in one of the emerging megaindustries of the twenty-first century.

The only formula for televisual survival in the global era is to *produce* television, not merely to *exclude*.

In a world where Time-Life feared that being the sixth largest in the world was too small to be a player in the field, the smart policy is not to dismember or fragment whatever television industries or corporations a country has. It is smarter to double their size and assure that you have global-class industrial units. Had the British fragmented the BBC, and flooded their own market (which they seemed tempted to do under Prime Minister Thatcher), it would have been the equivalent of dismembering an aircraft industry at the threshold of the jet travel era. Now they will reap the benefits of nurturing their public-sector investment.

Just as Japan targeted automobile production and the computer industry and focussed a national industrial strategy based on an assessment of the future, so national governments must develop an industrial strategy for the television age which is upon us. This means not only rebuilding the public sector, as an investment, but also developing a very strong private sector.

But governments have been slow to apprehend what is coming, and even slower to realize that television production is one of the most powerful growth industries on the planet. And the battle will not be over technology, but product.

The 1000-channel universe will create an unimagined market for programs. Distribution, in effect, is massively outstripping production. We have satellite footprints encompassing Indonesia to the Red Sea; we have the coming on stream of the East European markets; the addition of viewers in the millions annually from India and China—but where are the programs coming from? Right now, the most precious resource in the industry is not a satellite in the sky but a vault of films and series. But those vaults, which reside largely in Britain and the United States, will feed only a minuscule proportion of the appetite shaping in the global market.

Here, intermediate countries can find hope in a future that otherwise looks like an obliterating tidal wave. The playing field is relatively level. Except for the head start of Britain and the United States, the world television market does not inherently belong to anyone yet. Youth and children do not yet belong exclusively to Disney. Animation is not a Japanese monopoly yet. Britain does not have a monopoly on the classics.

Astute national governments will read current trends and see the equivalent of the automotive age or the computer age and will develop an industrial strategy to assure a significant national television industry. They will not only renew and refocus their public sector but assure the emergence of a globally competitive private sector. They will invest in craft training and development programs in their educational streams. They will also identify their niches in the global market as the British have capitalized on their news tradition.

The traditional idea of export will change too—not by sending a sales team to a program convention but by launching international satellite services. A country without two or three international satellite channels will be the technological equivalent of a Third World country in the emerging global competition. Unless you are home to a proportion of the channels in the 1000-channel universe, you will lose the coming competition. In the global village, you're going to need an address.

In the era of the televisual central library, an industrial strategy must assure that you put your cultural and information product on the shelf.

An exhilarating and terrifying re-ordering of the world information order is under way. It presents colossal opportunities for countries able to lead the way in the production of the visual form, and cultural perils for those countries that misread the awesome scale of the world industry that is dawning.

So far, most governments have been obsessed by the technology—the fibre-optics, the satellites, high definition, the computer networks. The revolution is *occasioned* by technology. But the most dramatic competition, and the greatest rewards, will not be in the technology. They will be in the *software*, the programs and the services.

Remember what Antoine Lumière said when his sons reported the impact of their first public film exhibition at the Salon Indien in Paris. He held his invention, the cinematograph, in his hands and said: "Don't you see the point? The product is not the camera. It's the film!"

EXTINCTION REVISITED: CULTURE AND CLASS IN CANADA

John Meisel

On first blush, an oxymoron seems to be lurking in the two principal terms comprising our title. If extinction is anything, it is final. How can it be revisited? In this instance, it may, like the news of Mark Twain's demise, be premature or exaggerated. Still, the heading does make sense, as we shall see.

Some years ago I gave a lecture entitled "Escaping Extinction: Cultural Defence of an Undefended Border,"[1] in which I argued that the overwhelming presence on Canadian television screens of American programs, particularly in the entertainment category, led to the attenuation of a sense of Canadian identity. The crushing "invasion" of Canadian cultural space, I feared, diminished our shared national experience and filled Canadian minds with foreign reference points. Under these circumstances, distinctive Canadian modes of thought and behaviour were in danger of dissipating, and our culture was at risk of ultimately merging with that of our southern neighbour into a North American pattern bereft of an identifiably Canadian character. This, I concluded, was for several reasons a most undesirable prospect. A policy of cultural nationalism was, therefore, necessary if we were to escape extinction.

The original argument was much more nuanced than the skeletal summary presented here, of course. Although it evoked a good deal of positive resonance, it also elicited criticism from some observers. I have, for this and other reasons, decided to revisit the case. Overall, I believe that the original assessment still holds. But it requires refinement and extension. One phenomenon, in particular, has troubled me from the very beginning and has claimed additional thought and analysis. For, although the far-reaching consequences of foreign cultural domination for Canadian identity cannot effectively be challenged, another feature of our national landscape was (and is) also undeniable: Canadian high culture has experienced luxuriant growth and success at the very same time as our eyes and ears were being surfeited with American entertainment, most notably via television.

Although the data are less than perfect—perforce often calling for highly subjective evaluations—there is no doubt that the 1960s, 1970s, and 1980s witnessed the growth of Canadian cultural activity on a very wide front. A record number of Canadian periodicals and books were published; Canadian belles lettres flourished, increasingly receiving international acclaim; Canadian plays and theatres attracted even larger audiences; Canadian creators and performers of music found new audiences not only in the metropolitan areas but in smaller places as well; this art scene continued to hold and extend its clientele; our filmmakers—even beyond the well-established works of the National Film Board—attracted international acclaim. Almost all other artistic activities enjoyed similar successes.

On another level, arts organizations, and most notably their strongest voice—the Canadian Conference of the Arts—were gaining recognition as important players in cultural policy-making. They made of the cultural community a legitimate player on the national scene. It is no exaggeration to say that Canada's cultural life—as expressed in literature and the arts—was never healthier, at the very same time as the average Canadian was watching over 30 hours a week of television, most of which (particularly the drama) was largely American.

The Two Worlds of Cultural Experience

How can we reconcile the co-existence of two seemingly incompatible patterns: deep enduring immersion in U.S. television and the creative explosion of Canadian arts?

One possibility is that the original contention was mistaken, that the heavily American content and viewing of television are not incompatible with Canadian mindsets and Canadian artistic productions. It is, in other words, possible to continue absorbing heavy doses of U.S. television programs while at the same time creating or consuming indigenous works of art. Such cases of "segregation" exist, but it is doubtful whether there are many of them. While the creators of Canadian culture likely comprise part of the television audience, they are almost certainly, for the most part, "light," or only occasional TV viewers.

This probability leads to a different explanation of our paradox: that the co-existence of two seemingly discreet, or only very tenuously linked, groups of Canadians explains the dilemma. Although simple, it is richly suggestive and calls for full development. It assumes that the architects and builders of our recent cultural growth are not part of the mainstream of the television audiences, and that because of this they have remained largely aloof from the Americanizing impact of television. There are, in short, two separate identifiable groups of Canadians: habitual television viewers and the creators of our literature and live arts. These two groups have very little to do with each other. I almost said that the twain shall never meet, but that would be going a little too far.

For the purposes of the present discussion, we can therefore postulate that the Canadian population can be divided into two parts. Let us call them viewers (Group V) and the cultural community (Group C). These categories constitute Weberian ideal types. No such "pure" groups exist in the real world—but a great many Canadians approximate one pole, or set of characteristics, more than the other. Group V is much more susceptible to the influence of American television than Group C and its members are consequently likely to think of the world and themselves less in Canadian terms than Group C. They are more knowledgeable about and involved in matters American and are less aware of and affected by Canadian experience. One might hypothesize that in an opinion survey a larger proportion of them would support the annexation of Canada or their province to the United States than would members of the other group.

This analysis is not very startling and is quite plausible. But, alas, it is all too simple. There are many Canadians who do not fall into our V group who are not culture vultures. There are often interests, contexts, professions which offset the de-nationalizing forces of heavy doses of non-Canadian viewing.

The political class, for instance, comprises another grouping which is not particularly susceptible to the Americanizing impact of foreign programming. By political class we here refer primarily to those who are full-time or nearly full-time politicians, public servants involved in the formulation or execution of public policy in Canada, the press corps and academics, who never tire of following and analyzing Canadian public life. Some of the political junkies may also avidly follow U.S. public life, but the chances are that government and political games in Canada are much closer to their hearts.

An intriguing aspect of their viewing behaviour is that they may well be quite heavy television viewers, particularly of electoral content, or political crises, because television is for many people the principal means of "following" politics. They are, therefore, frequently to be found watching public-affairs programming of which Canadian networks provide a massive supply. Their exposure to the U.S.-dominated entertainment/drama fare is therefore probably light.

It should, however, be noted that some Canadians are fascinated, if not mesmerized, by American politics. This group is more likely to fall under the Americanizing spell of television, because of their involvement with U.S. news broadcasts and analyses, which are less well covered on the Canadian airwaves.

Another group equipped with resistors to the de-nationalizing effects of Canadian television is made up of people who have a keen interest in voluntary and professional associations, when these are strongly rooted in Canada. Their focus of attention is likely to be "local," and this immunizes them against being swallowed up in the visual and verbal universe of most of Canada's entertainment programming.

It is also likely the case that individuals whose work, profession, or business are strongly influenced by their Canadians contexts will control or filter their viewing in a manner diminishing American influences. They comprise yet another group of viewers who should not be placed in our V category.

A very special audience—and one which deserves careful empirical study—is made up of Canadian nationalists who seek out Canadian programming. They go out of their way to consume shows relevant to Canada and to Canadian experiences and are probably as strongly fortified against being Americanized by television as anyone, although even they cannot be totally immune.

Two smallish but extremely interesting groups in the present context are the devotees of the CBC. They no doubt fall into the category of Canadian nationalists, noted earlier, but they constitute informed subgroups: the first is interested in the kind of television programming provided by the federal public broadcaster because of its character but also because of its provenance; they have an emotional attachment to the so-called "mother corporation." And then there are the radio buffs. Because of the unique qualities of CBC radio programming, which is *hors de concours*, they have a strong attachment to the CBC. To the extent that they watch television at all, it is likely that they prefer programs that most resemble in subject and treatment the conventions of CBC radio—and are very often to be found only on CBC television, on the provincial education networks, or on PBS. Because of their educational background, occupation, interest in public affairs, and often a strong emotional and even moral commitment to public broadcasting, these two groups exert influence by far exceeding their numerical strength. This is an important factor in the present analysis, to which we shall return.

The foregoing thoughts not only reconcile the seemingly baffling inconsistency between very high viewing of U.S. programs on television and the simultaneously vigorous and growing extension of Canadian culture, they also point to possible policy options and areas of private initiative through which the potentially harmful effects of American cultural domination can be mitigated and even perhaps harnessed towards the enrichment of Canadian life. A clue toward the means through which these tasks might be accomplished is provided by a quintessentially Canadian experience shared by Canadians of widely divergent backgrounds: "Hockey Night in Canada." This popular CBC program cannot, of course, be seen as a cultural spectacle in the same category as opera or ballet. But despite its predominantly competitive, pugilistic, and violent aspects, it does also possess distinct aesthetic qualities. In its appeal, it reaches both highbrow and lowbrow audiences. Like all mass sports events, it is basically a ruthless commercial enterprise exploiting a host of public tastes and loyalties.

In packaging this entertainment, the CBC and its advertisers try to bring together diverse elements so as to maximize viewership. Since the CBC, as compared with its private competitors in both Canada and the United States, caters somewhat more to people with high or middlebrow tastes, "Hockey Night in Canada" is used to broaden the audience patronizing its services. Not only is sport an effective mediator of at least some class divisions, but the manner in which the CBC covers the closest we have to a national sport is calculated to appeal to audiences that normally eschew highbrow or middlebrow shows. The already wide appeal of hockey is enhanced by the inclusion in the whole package of Coach's Corner—the vehicle in which Don Cherry glorifies the macho, physical, aggressive elements of commercial hockey, and in which he appeals to tastes which are normally avoided by the public broadcaster—including thinly veiled xenophobia. His robust style, it appears, is extremely popular, particularly in sports bars and similar watering holes frequented predominantly by blue-collar hockey fans. Whatever one may think of Cherry and the CBC's use of him, the presence of Coach's Corner has somewhat broadened the audience appeal of the national broadcaster in class terms.[2]

This mediating role is admittedly exceedingly modest and cannot be considered anything more than a minor example of the capacity of certain kinds of programming to extend its appeal across class lines. It is nevertheless instructive and, as we shall see, relevant to our analysis.

Having noted it, we can now return to the paradoxical incongruence between the profile of general television viewing and the simultaneous health of cultural life. We saw that to some extent this phenomenon can be explained in terms of there being two distinct constituencies, so to speak: heavy television viewers and the cultural community. But this dichotomy was seen as presenting all too simple an explanation. It needed to be modified by the recognition of the fact that the effects of television programs depend on certain unrelated characteristics of the audience. Not only the cultural community but also the political class, people deeply involved in the voluntary sector, individuals with strong involvement in local Canadian life among others, manage to escape, or minimize, the de-nationalizing effects of overexposure to foreign programming. Some Canadians "consume" fewer American cultural products than others, or, the effects of these products on them are diminished or outweighed by powerful Canadian experiences arising from their daily lives. At the same time, of course, Canadians lacking such experience are much more vulnerable to the consequences of the frequent exposure to foreign cultural products. They risk becoming absorbed into a non-Canadian world. This process diminishes Canadian distinctiveness and so impoverishes our national life.

Although the evidence is rather impressionistic and fragmentary, it suggests strongly that there are important differences between our V group—the Viewers—and the rest, whom we shall henceforth call "Others." Its members tend to be less well-educated, less articulate, less politicized—and consequently they are less effective in influencing policy-making. They are disposed to be followers rather than leaders, although their numerical weight endows them with importance in the political process. To some extent, all political parties try to enlist their support, since without it, electoral success may be elusive.

Bridging the Chasm

It is reasonable to assume that the quality of political life—the values pursued by Canadians, the nature of policy-making, the successful defence of Canadian national awareness, and the protection of Canadian culture—would be enhanced if the chasm separating the lifestyles and preferences of Viewers and others were to narrow. Each group's well-being, and that of the country as a whole, would be enhanced if they were to benefit from their effective interaction and mutual enrichment. The realistic appreciation of the Viewers' background and general concerns would enable cultural elites (including our C group) to gain a fuller sense of the national experience; an ongoing exposure to Canada's high culture would give Viewers a heightened awareness of aesthetic pleasure and of Canadian distinctiveness.

It is somewhat easier for the Others to acquire familiarity with the world of the Viewers—in part because many of them share *some* of the television viewing experience of the larger group. The introduction of more eclectic television programming would, nevertheless, expand the knowledge of Canadians of one another's worlds. It is, for instance, the case that North American consumers of television drama have access to a fairly restricted range of settings, since situation comedy and drama in North America tend to depict a narrow range of types of family and work sites. Once a program format, including its type of ambience—hospitals, for instance—acquires a following, it is widely copied to the point where the airwaves become inundated by one particular milieu. Alternate situations are neglected. It is, for instance, instructive of the context of comparative television cultures that there is no equivalent in North America to the phenomenally successful—and universally valued—British series like "East Enders" or "Coronation Street," which portray working-class cultures. This aspect of North American life receives only sporadic treatment on the American or Canadian commercial networks, or the CBC.

A number of policy, behavioural, and programming changes could narrow the gap separating the worlds of the intensive and more casual television viewers in Canada. Some of these changes are rather remote from viewers, and their consequences would not be felt for quite a long time. Others are more proximate and immediate.

Among the former, educational reforms are particularly compelling. Improved ways of imparting television literacy and the capacity of children to become more critical viewers are obviously important. Equally relevant is to develop the tastes in children for the enjoyment of the arts, as well as an appreciation of the rich fabric of Canadian society in class, ethnic, regional, and other terms.

Cultural policies—among which none is more important in the present context than the stance taken by the CRTC and various federal and provincial cultural agencies and granting councils—are required to ensure that a large number of Canadians partake in a creative Canadian cultural life, and that television programming in Canada is encouraged to escape the formula driven, narrow format of its present programming. A high level awareness of Canada's multicultural realities, including the issues raised with respect to maintaining some sort of Canadian homogeneity, is required and must be imparted by the electronic and other media. Indeed, a more alert and responsive media treatment of Canada's varied texture and of its cultural life is a necessary precondition of the resolution of the paradox we have identified above.

At the most general level, measures designed to diminish social and economic differences of Canadians will, in the long run, bring about the narrowing of the gap between Viewers and Others.

More directly and immediately, cultural elites could usefully familiarize themselves with the experiences and concerns of Canadians whose major interests are not cultural, by means of heightening their awareness of the manner in which they live and of their preoccupations. The popular arts and notably television are one useful avenue, but there are many others. The most important tactic is to *acquire an interest* in the lives of one's fellow citizens who subscribe to different values and who have different concerns from oneself. The sometimes unfamiliar and aloof perspective of the cultural community would be enriched and set in a realistic context if it were to include knowledge of the world experience by those whose aesthetic preoccupations are either absent or modest. Such widening of the horizons of the creative artists would, in some instances, make their work more meaningful and accessible than would otherwise be the case. As already suggested, sports activities often appeal to a wide spectrum of social classes and can mediate between quite incongruous social traditions. Coach's Corner—whatever one may think of the views of its star—broadens the appeal of the sometimes elitist image of the CBC.

In this instance, the relevance of an institution with some modest cultural pretensions is extended toward a wider audience. An inverse process occurs predominantly when sports events become associated with cultural programs. A notable example is the recent phenomenon of the Olympic games reverting to an earlier Greek practice of accompanying tests of physical prowess with artistic programs. Here, as during the Calgary Winter Games, for instance, audiences attracted mainly by sports competition also enjoyed a variety of excellent cultural programs.

The thesis I am developing here puts a good deal of weight on government initiatives in mediating class differences and associated cultural differences which affect a sense of Canadianness and Canadian identity. But as we approach the twenty-first century, it is becoming obvious that, in at least the immediate future the role of the state is likely to diminish and that other players will increasingly affect everyone's lives: we are not witnessing the end of state influence but a redefinition of its role and revision of its interactions with the private sector.

In the context of the rapprochement of elite culture with popular and mass culture, new partnerships are evolving—and need to be strengthened and multiplied—between public and private initiatives. The latter are likely to involve not only commercial enterprises but also private donors and the voluntary sector: voluntary support agencies and personal contributions of interested individuals. It is likely that senior citizens will play a particularly critical role here.

The critical factor is that the goal of removing obstacles standing in the way of a more effective interaction and mutual enrichment of popular and elite culture will only be attained if the task is undertaken on a broad front: governments, firms, associations, and volunteers are all required to play an active and sustained part. This is necessary not only with respect to the divergences arising in relation to culture but also because, as I have argued, the problem goes deeper and extends more widely; the whole class structure is involved.

This is, of course, a very tall order indeed. But perhaps not quite as tall as might seem at first. Because of innumerable factors widely noted and discussed at the present time, the world—and Canada—are undergoing truly radical change. Everything is in a state of flux. Under such conditions, profound metamorphoses are inevitable. Their nature will depend on a complex network of interacting factors, factors not randomly caused and linked but susceptible to human volition. The character of the emerging human and social relations can therefore be shaped, at least in part, by the preferences and priorities of individuals and collectivities; the political effectiveness of a relatively small group deeply loyal to the CBC, mentioned above, is instructive. Its voice, Friends of Canadian Broadcasting, has been an important player in shaping policy.

Although the spectre of "extinction" feared in my earlier paper may have been exaggerated, it was by no means unfounded. Threats to Canada's cultural sovereignty abounded then and they continue to be in evidence today. If anything, they are more menacing than ever. The Free Trade Agreement and the North American Free Trade Agreement have enhanced Canada's ties and contacts with the United States and have left uncertain the extent to which cultural industries may in the long run be affected by the American insistence that cultural matters are merely an aspect of international trade, as compared with the Canadian view that they are relevant to Canada's survival as an autonomous state. Quite apart from broadcasting in the age of the Death Star satellites, increasing takeovers by U.S. companies of Canadian publishers, and the impotence of successive Canadian federal and provincial governments in the face of the virtually complete domination by the American motion picture industry of film distribution in Canada, remind us that Canadian culture is seriously threatened. Drastic cuts in government spending, evident at all levels, also put our cultural life at risk. Under these circumstances it is essential that Canadians, in seeking to confront the far-reaching changes engulfing them at the end of the century, address the issue of cultural sovereignty head on.

As we have seen, this can best be done in a context of overall societal change, and one in which a serious effort is made to narrow the chasm now separating those we have only in part described metaphorically as Viewers and the Others—followers of mass and popular culture and aficionados of elite culture. The character and strength of a shared sense of Canadian consciousness will depend on the success of this "bridging" exercise.

Notes

1. John Meisel, "Escaping Extinction: Cultural Defence of an Undefended Border." In *Southern Exposure: Canadian Perspectives on the United States*, edited by D.H. Flaherty and W.R. McKercher (Toronto: McGraw-Hill Ryerson Ltd., 1986), pp. 152–68.
2. I am indebted for some of the ideas on "Hockey Night in Canada" to Mike McWhinney, a recent M.A. student at Queen's. See also James Gillet, Philip White, and Kevin Young, "The Prime Minister of Saturday Night: Don Cherry, the CBC, and the Cultural Production of Intolerance," in this volume.

NEWS FOR WHOM? HEGEMONY AND MONOPOLY VERSUS DEMOCRACY IN CANADIAN MEDIA

Robert Hackett, Richard Pinet, and Myles Ruggles

Canadians live in a world of second-hand experience. Our understanding of social reality derives not just from personal involvement or from speaking to other people, but from images, stories and reports transmitted by radio, television, and the daily press. Canadians spend about seven hours a day with such mass communications media—more than with any other activity except work and sleep. The mass media form a key institution through which our understandings and judgements about social life are reinforced and challenged. That is particularly true of the news media, which claim to offer factual and accurate representations of the social and political worlds, and which consequently enjoy considerable credibility as well as access to mass audiences. By directing attention toward some events and issues and away from others, and indeed by defining reality for their audiences, media help to set the agenda for both publics and government policy-makers.

On the media's power, few would disagree. But other central questions about the media's role in democratic political life are more controversial.[1] What forces shape the contours of news reportage? What cultural values, institutional needs, political interests, or ideological assumptions underlie news patterns? How are journalism and news organizations related to other institutions and to society's overall power structure? In a self-proclaimed democracy like Canada, how (and by whom) should the media be financed, structured, and controlled?

Most answers to these questions imply one of two very general perspectives, not only on the media as a political institution, but more broadly on power in Canadian society. In the dominant view, often labelled liberal-pluralism, power (conceived as something observable in decision-making situations) is diffused, shared among contending and overlapping interests. The power structure is fluid, flexible, and open; no one group or interest is consistently dominant across a range of issues. To be sure, some people (such as political or corporate leaders) have much more power than do others. Nevertheless, excessive concentration of power is avoided, both because power-holding groups compete against one another to influence government policies, and because there are mechanisms (such as elections and the marketplace) that keep power-holders accountable to a much broader public.

In the pluralist view, competition between interests is bounded and kept manageable by an overriding consensus around basic social values—individual liberty, free enterprise, the rights of property owners, patriotism, representative government, the competitive pursuit of individual self-fulfilment. To be sure, this commitment to such liberal values is tempered in the Canadian (but not American) case by such tory and socialist "fragments" as deference to authority, caring for the underprivileged, and "peace, order and good government" for the whole society (Horowitz, 1979). There are also significant (and apparently growing) undercurrents of nonliberal authoritarian attitudes (racism, religious fundamentalism) throughout North America. Still, in the pluralist view, an overwhelming majority of the population is well served by the existing social and political structure; so social consensus is the normal state of affairs in industrialized liberal democracies.

With regard to the mass media, pluralists see news organizations as generally autonomous from other power centres in society, and as able to pursue the role of independent watchdog on possible abuses of power by other institutions, especially government. Indeed, some conservative-minded pluralists see the media as too independent from mainstream opinion, and as excessively cynical or hostile toward rival institutions, notably business, government, and political leadership. On the whole, though, pluralists see the media as substantially accountable and responsible to their audiences and to the social system as a whole, through the mechanisms of consumer choice, the legal framework (such as defamation laws) established by elected governments, and journalists' own sense of professional responsibility. Likewise, journalism is held to be open to the expression of diverse viewpoints and interests.

In the 1960s, however, the entire pluralist paradigm in North American social science began to fracture from within. The concept of social consensus came increasingly to be seen as a problem to be explained, rather than something to be taken for granted and celebrated: the mass media (and other social institutions) do not merely reinforce, but actively produce, consent to the existing social order. In that work of producing consent, media-circulated "definitions of the situation" (and indeed the broader social use of language in general) were key aspects, helping actively to define rather than merely to reflect reality (Hall, 1982, 62–65). Bloody political conflicts, notably the black freedom struggle and the war in Vietnam, further called into question the degree of fairness and consensus in the American social order.

In that context, it became increasingly apparent that pluralist media research had significant blind spots. It focussed too narrowly on electoral politics and persuasive campaigns. Pluralism had no way to theorize the influence of social and political power structures on popular consciousness, and no conception of fundamental stresses or conflict within the capitalist social system. Such concepts were central to the alternative critical paradigm that emerged during and after the 1960s.

In the critical view, Canada is a stratified society; power is excessively concentrated in the hands of a ruling group that has interests distinct from, and in opposition to, the underlying majority of the population. Ordinary people are denied not only a fair share of society's wealth, but also effective political participation in shaping the State's basic policies. Consequently, what requires explaining is social stability. Why do the majority of people put up with a society that empowers and rewards the few rather than the many?

To answer this question, many critical media researchers have turned to the concept of hegemony, developed decades ago by the Italian writer and activist Antonio Gramsci. Gramsci realized that no ruling group or class could establish stable long-term dominance over the rest of the population through physical coercion alone. Especially in ostensibly democratic countries like Canada, where most of the adult population enjoys literacy and the right to vote, the ruling group needs to win allies and to maintain substantial popular consent to its social system. That consent is won, in part, by getting people to understand and interpret the real conditions in which they live their daily lives in ways which support, or at least do not radically challenge, existing social relations.

Hegemony combines persuasion from above with consent from below. The major social institutions that generate ways of understanding the world generally (although not necessarily deliberately or without opposition) reproduce a whole system of values, attitudes, and beliefs—ideology—that in one way or another supports the established order and the social interests that dominate it. Those institutions of ideological production include the mass media, which exercise significant power given their distinctive characteristics: their continuous availability and lifelong flow, their simultaneous access to mass audiences, their constant provision of categories for defining reality, their ideological similarity concealed beneath a diversity of forms, their appropriation of leisure time and pseudo-resolution of people's needs in fantasy and entertainment, and their meshing with other hegemonic institutions such as the family and political parties (Downing, 1980, 160–72).

Hegemony is never completely and finally achieved; it is always contested or resisted, as alternative and oppositional meaning systems (such as environmentalism and feminism) struggle for political and cultural change. But when hegemony is more or less successful, ordinary people themselves accept hegemonic ideology: it becomes enmeshed with the "common sense" through which people make their lives and their world intelligible, to the exclusion of possible alternatives. If news is indeed a hegemonic institution, then it typically helps to produce and reproduce the dominant values and meanings that most people learn to accept as "common sense," part of what "everybody knows."

We must therefore emphasize a paradox. The dominant news media inhibit popular democracy in Canada not by those shortcomings and blunders that critics usually identify, but by their very successes and routines. The problem is not that the media are "biased," but that their very standards of "objectivity" reinforce dominant definitions of social reality; not that the media impose an alien ideology or manipulate audiences, but that they are able to win the consent and participation of audiences.

We can begin to understand how news media circulate and reinforce dominant values and meanings by examining ownership of the Canadian media, their dependence on advertising revenue and its implications, and some typical patterns of news presentation. We then conclude this essay by considering the possibilities for more democratic relations of communication.

Canada's Dominant News Media: Ownership and Its Implications

Media critics (including blue-ribbon bodies such as the 1970 Special Senate Committee on Mass Media, and the 1980–81 Royal Commission on Newspapers) have repeatedly expressed concern about the way the media are owned and organized in Canada. Perhaps the most obvious point is that the dominant news media (except for the Canadian Broadcasting Corporation) are privately owned, profit-oriented corporations. This means (amongst other things) that the editorial content provided by these media is regarded by their management not as a public service, but as a business cost to be met as inexpensively as possible.

For example, it is cheaper to purchase syndicated columns that recover their costs over a national or continental market than it is to pay local writers. This is why so much coverage of international events in Canadian media is still supplied by large American-based news agencies: it is more economical to print or modify their copy or to televise their images than it is to send Canadian reporters overseas. Similarly, it is relatively cheap for a broadcaster to buy the exhibition rights to expensively made U.S. programs, which can recover their costs in the huge American market, and which have sophisticated production values and audience appeal. The average Canadian TV show costs much less to *produce* than its American counterpart, but it is more expensive for the broadcaster to *purchase*, since it is often difficult to market beyond Canada. Moreover, its necessarily lower budget gives the program less appeal to audiences and advertisers than American programs of the same type. It is therefore little wonder that as presently organized, commercial television does very little to enable Canadians to express their own cultural values or to engage in communication with each other.

Another implication of corporate ownership is the hierarchy of decision-making within media organizations, with ownership ultimately determining the key hiring and resource allocation decisions, and with management accountable primarily to the dominant shareholders rather than to the audience or to those who work in cultural activities. It also suggests that media owners are likely to be tied to the business community through shared social interest, background, and interaction, as well as through interlocking directorships. Through the latter, the newspaper giant Southam, for example, is tied to many other big companies in energy and resources, finance, and other media (Winter, 1988). There is no reason to revise the conclusion sociologist Wallace Clement reached twenty years ago—the "media elite", the directors and senior managers of Canada's largest media companies, are really part of a broader "corporate elite" (Clement, 1975). Consequently, Clement and other critics have argued that corporate news media are likely to have a "basic commitment to the business community's views on public issues rather than to a wider range of interests" (Audley, 1983, 27).

Ownership is not only private, it is also highly concentrated. At the national level, ten companies accounted for 86 percent of total TV revenues by 1991 (up from 57 percent in 1983); five corporations reached 62 percent of TV viewers in 1993. In radio, with 479 stations, just ten companies account for 55 percent of the revenue share, while in the magazine industry, the twelve largest publishers control 52 percent of circulation (Winter and Hassanpour, 1994).

It is the daily newspaper industry, however, that has a particular responsibility for disseminating the news that Canadians receive. While North Americans rely more heavily on television than newspapers as a news source, prestigious dailies (such as *The Globe and Mail*) and print-based news services (notably Canadian Press) still tend to set the news agenda for the broadcasting media. With only a few exceptions (CBC, CNN), broadcasters do not try to compete with the press in providing in-depth information.

It is especially significant, then, that ownership of Canada's daily press is amongst the most highly concentrated in the Western world; most of Canada's dailies are owned by a handful of very large media conglomerates (companies with a range of holdings in different industries). The four largest chains (companies that own two or more dailies) accounted for 68 percent of daily circulation by 1993, up from 53 percent in 1970. Just two chains (Southam and Thomson) controlled nearly half of national circulation. With 17 dailies from Montreal to Vancouver, 27.5 percent of national daily circulation, and over $1 billion in revenue in 1992, Southam is Canada's biggest newspaper chain and one of the five largest media companies. While its own holdings are confined to the communications industries, Southam has significant ownership links with two other huge corporations. Since 1992, one of Southam's dominant shareholders has been Conrad Black. Known for his decidedly right-wing views, his affinity for powerful politicians, and his cost-cutting approach to journalism, Black's Hollinger Inc. includes 13 Canadian dailies (mostly in Quebec and B.C., accounting for 3.7 percent of national circulation), as well as two dozen weeklies and the prestigious *Saturday Night* magazine. The Hollinger media empire extends well beyond Canada, to include about 55 dailies as well as weeklies in the United States, the *Jerusalem Post*, London's *Daily Telegraph*, and one-fifth of Australia's Fairfax newspaper chain (Romanow and Soderlund, 1992, 289–91).

Southam's other dominant shareholder is Paul Desmarais of Power Corp., a true conglomerate. The four Quebec dailies of its Gesca chain (5.9 percent of national circulation) are only a small part of Power's empire, which also comprises 40 weeklies in Quebec, eighteen radio and three TV stations, and large financial companies. The conglomerate's 1992 revenues of $12.5 billion (U.S.) exceeded the Royal Bank of Canada and placed it third amongst all Canadian companies. Desmarais's connections illustrate the close links between economic, political, and media power in Canada. Power's board of directors includes former Ontario premier Bill Davis and other political notables, while Desmarais himself is the father-in-law of Prime Minister Jean Chrétien's daughter, former employer of finance minister Paul Martin Jr., and current employer of former prime minister Brian Mulroney (Winter and Hassanpour, 1994, 13).

With 1992 revenues of about $6 billion, the Thomson Corporation is Canada's largest media-based conglomerate, and the fourth biggest in the world. Tracing its roots to Roy Thomson's acquisition of a North Bay radio station and Timmins newspaper in the 1930s, the Thomson empire included 156 dailies and 36 weeklies in Canada and the United States by 1989 (Romanow and Soderlund, 1992, 293). Its 40 Canadian dailies accounted for 20.5 percent of national circulation, making it second only to Southam amongst Canadian chains. Renowned for their journalistic blandness and penny-pinching, most of these dailies operate as monopolies in small and medium-sized cities. But Thomson also owns the prestigious *Globe and Mail*, Canada's self-proclaimed national newspaper, which is managed separately from the rest of the chain. Large conglomerates, like Thomson, may well regard ownership of prestigious dailies, even if they are costly to buy or maintain, as an investment in their own public image and political influence (Dunnett, 1988, 50).

Quebecor is another of Canada's newspaper giants. Owned by Pierre Peladeau, its 1992 revenues of about $4 billion and its 9 percent of national daily circulation (including two Quebec tabloids and the *Winnipeg Sun*), made it the country's second-largest media corporation. The third-largest is Rogers Communications Inc., which took over Maclean Hunter in 1994, giving the combined companies $3.1 billion in 1992 revenues. Rogers now controls cable access to 43 percent of English-language households, 41 radio, and two TV stations, the YTV youth-oriented television network, a 32 percent stake in the Unitel long-distance phone company, a cellular phone, paging, and other communications services, fifteen printing plants—and that's not to mention print media. Through its acquisition of Maclean Hunter, which itself had owned the Toronto Sun Publishing Corporation since 1982, Rogers takes over publication of four tabloid dailies in Toronto, Edmonton, Ottawa, and Calgary, the business daily *Financial Post*, and 191 periodicals, including the newsstand staples *Maclean's* and *Chatelaine* (Dalglish, 1994; Morrison, 1994).

If concentration of ownership is considerable at the national level, it is magnified within regions or provinces, where much of Canada's political life takes place. The appearance of media diversity is deceptive. British Columbia, for instance, has about 100 radio stations, ten TV stations, and seventeen daily papers. But only five companies dominate the province's news agenda overall. Few broadcasters are serious originators of news programming, apart from CBC and a handful of private stations, such as Vancouver's largest radio (CKNW) and television (BCTV) outlets, both of which are owned by WIC (Western International Communications Ltd.). In the print media, three chains own all of B.C.'s dailies. Out of every 100 copies of daily papers published and sold in B.C., the four dailies owned by Southam (including both Vancouver papers) account for 73 (Hackett, 1993).

What are the implications of such concentrated ownership? Whatever the economic efficiencies of media chains, critics fear the danger of homogenized content, a loss of diversity in the media system. Newspapers rely increasingly on group or chain news services rather than their own writers to cover federal and provincial legislatures. The chain tends to impose a common stylistic mode on its various "links," and there is always the threat (however improbable under normal circumstances) of centralized control of editorial policy.

Diversity of public expression may be further threatened by the tendency to monopoly in newspaper markets. Most Canadian cities have a single daily; in the several Canadian cities that still publish two or more dailies, one is typically a Southam broadsheet, an "omnibus" paper trying to reach the broadest possible market, while the other is a splashy tabloid (typically in the Toronto Sun chain) oriented toward working-class readers and toward a generation of media consumers more accustomed to television than newspapers. While newspapers do compete with other media for advertising dollars, there is much less direct competition for readers or editorial content within the newspaper industry than there was during the early decades of this century. Monopoly papers are particularly given to trimming editorial spending, even though they are generally quite profitable, because there is little economic incentive to do otherwise. Why spend money on more reporters or better researched stories if you already reach the whole market? One-newspaper towns are dependent on the extent to which the local paper's owners take their journalistic responsibilities seriously. The problem is that owners who spend more than the necessary minimum are vulnerable to takeover bids by less generous and more profit-oriented rivals.

Other structural aspects of ownership likewise potentially threaten diversity of access and expression in Canada's media. Some corporations own different types of media, and such cross-media ownership is especially worrisome when it occurs within a single community (or "market"). For instance, in metropolitan Vancouver, Southam controls not only both dailies, but also fourteen community papers and a string of real estate weeklies, while WIC owns the first- and fifth-largest radio stations, and the first and fourth most-watched TV stations (Hackett, 1993). Cross-media ownership may have economic benefits through cross-subsidies and the sharing of resources and management skills between two or more media outlets, but some studies show a significant loss of quality and diversity in the news product in cross-media monopolies. Further dangers include the excessive concentration of power within the community, and the especially chilling impact on independent journalism if newsworkers have few alternative employers within a region.

These tendencies are made even more problematic by the trend toward ownership of the media by conglomerates with extensive nonmedia holdings. The archetype is the Thomson family's corporate empire, which includes interests in wholesaling, retailing, real estate, oil and gas, insurance, and financial and management services. This situation increases the risk of the abuse of power in that media outlets may be used to support, or at least to avoid embarrassing, other parts of the corporate empire.

What are probable future trends in media ownership? In the past, analysts like the Kent Commission worried about the ongoing takeover of independently owned news outlets by media chains and conglomerates. This is now less likely in the future, simply because there are few major profitable independents left. In the daily newspaper industry, for instance, chains control 82.9 percent of national circulation. A further 10.5 percent is accounted for by *The Toronto Star*, an independent daily which is itself the centre of a media conglomerate, and which has significant ties with the Southam chain through a shared news service, joint ownership of the Infomart electronic publishing service, and (until recently) reciprocal ownership of shares.

The most likely kind of ownership trend in the future, in the absence of effective public policy to prevent it, involves mergers and takeovers of entire media companies—big fish being swallowed by even bigger fish. The Thomson takeover of FP Publications in 1980, and Southam's growing corporate ties over the next decade with first Torstar, and then Hollinger and Gesca, were mere harbingers of developments to come. In 1994, as noted, the cable TV giant Rogers Communications moved to take over Maclean Hunter. As Canada enters the era of the far too glibly named "information highway," the implications of this takeover are serious indeed. For public interest advocates like the Friends of Canadian Broadcasting, the takeover could unduly increase Rogers' control over both the rates charged, and the selection of channels delivered, to Canadian cable households (Morrison, 1994). Potential competitors in the electronic publishing business (such as Southam and Torstar) worry that Rogers could use its cable monopolies to give its newly acquired publications an unfair advantage in the electronic delivery of text (Austen, 1994).

The above ownership characteristics all constitute blockages to democratic communication, to the extent that they limit the quality of information, the diversity of viewpoints, and the equality of access available in the media system. But they are not the result of malevolence or conspiracy. Rather, they are the product of rational, profit-maximizing business decisions. Newspaper monopolies, for example, are largely attributable to the economic realities of mass advertising and economies of scale in the newspaper industry; and the growth of chains derives in part from the rational deployment of high profits from monopoly papers. Indeed, the market puts limits on what owners can do with their media, for the media can only make a profit by appealing to a salable audience. The era of the swashbuckling press barons using newspapers as vehicles for their own views is largely over. The commercial mass media are there to make money more than to promote particular ideas. Perhaps even more significant than private, concentrated, and conglomerate ownership are the implications of the commercial imperatives of these media.

ADVERTISING AND AUDIENCES

Whereas Canadian daily newspapers collect over $800 million annually from their readers, they earned over $1.9 billion from advertisers in 1992. In other words, at least 70 percent of daily newspaper revenues derive from advertising. In Canadian periodical publishing, 63.9 percent of revenues for 1991–92 came from advertising, which is still the major source of revenue for the broadcasting industry, notwithstanding the importance of cable-TV subscription fees.

Even the CBC, with a mandate to provide a "public service" alternative to commercial broadcasting, depends on advertising for about one-fifth of its operating revenue and relies in part on private/commercial affiliates to broadcast its programming across the country. In addition, CBC TV feels compelled to compete for audiences with the commercial stations that fill the airwaves with popular American entertainment shows.

The standard argument in defence of market relations, advertising, and the commercial media is that all firms simply respond to the demands of consumers. But if this is so, why are such vast sums spent on advertising? It is clear that advertising is effective and that it is intended to manage consumer (and political) demand. (See, for example, Ewen, 1976; Smythe, 1981.)

The main product of the commercial mass media—what they sell in the marketplace in order to make money—is not the programming or editorial content. After all, when we buy a copy of a newspaper, we are paying only a fraction of its total production costs. And, aside from cable subscription fees, the programming on commercial TV appears to be free of charge. Yet we know that media outlets are not charitable institutions. The main product of the media is the audience, whose willingness to pay attention is sold to advertisers, who pay on the basis of audience size and demographics.

Those who defend advertising as the basis of the media argue that commercialism ensures responsiveness to audience tastes, because advertising rates are related to the size of the audience. They also claim that it ensures financial independence from the government and hence makes possible "freedom of the press." That freedom from governmental coercion (except where untrammelled expression would infringe on other rights, such as an accused's right to a fair trial) is of course important. But what is less widely recognized is that market relations, just as easily as the State, can inhibit popular democratic communication.

In fact, the systematic pressure to produce profitable audiences has acted historically as a powerful form of political censorship. As the market for mass-produced consumer goods emerged, the financial basis of the press shifted from readership sales and political subsidies to advertising by the producers of brand-name products. Advertisers were interested in two kinds of audiences: the affluent, who had sufficient disposable income to purchase luxury products; and the mass audience, whose lack of purchasing power as individuals was offset by its huge size. Because advertisers were prepared to pay more for each affluent reader than for each mass reader, the former had a disproportionate say in determining which media survived. As the media and advertisers sought a wealthier audience, content changed to reflect the interests and concerns of the affluent. (See, for example, Bagdikian, 1992, Ch. 11; Curran, 1979.) As the Kent Commission admitted, "It was left-wing viewpoints that tended to be under-represented as commercialism increased its hold" (Canada, Royal Commission on Newspapers, 1981, 15). Such market-imposed structural censorship is consistent with, but not dependent upon, the intentions and manipulations of owners.

Similar problems are introduced by the way information and entertainment programming—which we are accustomed to regard as media content—works as a "free lunch" to entice an audience for the most important content—the commercials. Sometimes the match between program and ad content can be so close that the line blurs between the two. Both offer images of the "lifestyle" of the desired audience and promote the forms of consumption appropriate to it. The commercials are often more interesting than the programs—which is not surprising, since they are so much more expensively produced.

In short, commercial media do not simply "give people what they want." They give some of the people part of what they think they want—programming that media corporations find economical and convenient to offer, that is generally compatible with a consumerist stance, and that affluent and/or mass consumers (who lack ready access to the full range of potential alternatives) are prepared to accept as a reward for joining the audience. The media satisfy primarily those needs that are compatible with the marketing of commodities. Needs that no one can make money from or that threaten our consumer culture are left unattended. These include the need for democratic communication.

The Light of the Sun

The way commercialism affects the media becomes clearer if we take a brief look through a copy—any copy—of British Columbia's most read newspaper, the Vancouver *Sun* (average weekly circulation, about 185 000). The patterns do not differ substantially from day to day. Several features are apparent.[2]

First, in what is still described as a *news*paper, more than half is devoted to advertising. In the New Homes, Travel, Sports, and Entertainment sections of the *Sun*, everything—both news and advertising—is targeted at the consumer of airline, cruise ship, and hotel services, of spectator team sports, suburban homes, and gardens, furniture, films, and fitness. The ads corroborate, fill in the picture, urge the reader to fulfil the curiosity whetted by the surrounding articles.

What about the *real* news in the *Sun*'s bastion of integrity, Section A? News editors pride themselves on their autonomy from the marketing and advertising departments. In the sense that advertisers do not directly influence editorial copy at a large metropolitan daily, this autonomy is real. But there are more subtle constraints. Consider the narrative form of the typical "hard news" story. It is an "inverted pyramid," with the "facts" of the story presented in descending order of (perceived) importance. The story has no particular conclusion; should more advertising space be required, the article can be reduced by deleting as many sentences as necessary from the bottom up. The news and commentary also are shaped by a consumerist orientation. Oil price increases are interpreted in terms of what they will cost the driver "at the pump." Labour/management conflict is interpreted in terms of the disruption of services to the consumer. We, as readers, are asked to take the standpoint of the abstract "average" consumer.[3]

Although consumerism may have progressive aspects (for example, it may promote consumer protection legislation), it is also a barrier to change. For one thing, it neglects the sphere of production and our varying relations with it. It overrides the identity of the huge majority (about 77 percent) of Canadian income earners as employees. The interests that employees or workers have in common—improved wages, safer working conditions, more control over the workplace—are fragmented and disguised in media accounts of the industrial world. Particular groups of workers struggling for better conditions are pitted against "the public" or "consumers" in these accounts. The more militant the workers are, the more they are cast as deviants: witness the media barrage directed against striking postal workers. Consumerism also encourages an acceptance of meaningless, routinized, or unsatisfying work in exchange for the pleasures of commodity consumption. To the extent that we accept our positioning as consumers and opt into privatized lifestyles, the sphere of public discourse is diminished. Our collective ability to take charge of the conditions of our lives is reduced (Keane, 1984).

The targeting of news narrative toward consumer audiences also serves to obstruct inequalities of income. These inequalities involve contrasts of lifestyle, expectation, and consumption patterns so great that those at the upper and lower ends of the income scale can hardly be termed consumers in the same sense. To address the various users of mass media as "consumers" both mystifies social relations and obstructs the emergence of the social consciousness needed to change those relations. Yet such a form of address is imperative for commercial media, which must attract both advertisers and audiences—audiences prepared to purchase advertisers' commodities.

A number of other ways in which the *Sun* addresses its readers have profound political implications. A definition of politics is suggested by the very layout of the paper. Politics is confined to the public world reported in Section A and is thus separated from the personal and private world of home, lifestyles, and travel, as well as from the bottom-line world of business. That all forms of social and economic power, including corporate control of economic resources, are political, and that personal life and extra-parliamentary movements are important sites of political activity, are denied by the very way in which the paper is organized.

The Business section is useful mainly for the small minority of Canadians who own stock or who regularly employ (and lay off) workers. It is not helpful for those who would subject business to more effective social control. We do not even *expect* to find a Worker section in a Canadian daily. The comics and light features amuse the young and work weary. The amusements go with the styles and forms of consumption the advertisements encourage.

The political news is aimed at those who enjoy or feel obliged to watch the spectacle without becoming politically active. The columns of political commentary presented in Section A give outsiders an "insider's" look into the rituals, strategies, and personalities of the powerful—but very little information that would help citizens themselves intervene in the political process. Politics is covered as a spectator sport in which we can cheer or jeer the active participants and every few years help decide the winners and losers. Much political coverage focusses not on the players, their interests, the issues, or what is at stake, but on the "horse race." This is exemplified by the media obsession with polls on voting preferences. The exercise of power outside the electoral and parliamentary area (in corporate boardrooms or bureaucrats' offices, for example) largely escapes the media spotlight. For different reasons, extraparliamentary organizing of grass-roots movements for social change is also ignored—unless the organizations stage photogenic or disruptive protests. And although it sells papers (and advertising), protest that goes beyond what the media present as responsible, serious, and legitimate politics is almost automatically discredited.

The news in general is presented as a mixture of the conflictual, the whimsical, the curious, and the inspiring. It is about the actions and statements of the powerful, and about threats to, or disruptions of, "normal" daily life, dominant social values, and established institutions. The *Sun* does *not* scan the world in terms of how established institutions and their ruling elites may systematically jeopardize the well-being of the less powerful. On the contrary, one of the key principles of news selection and construction is the assumption that society is characterized by a basic harmony of interests and consensus of values (allowing us to get on with the really important business of consumption). The *Sun* presents conflict in ways that take for granted the permanence and legitimacy of existing institutions, power structures, and official information sources.

The paper depends for information on the elites who benefit most from the appearance of consensus: leaders of the major electoral political parties (especially cabinet ministers), and the official spokespersons of established institutions—the police, business, organized interest groups, government departments. The journalistic reliance on official and bureaucratic sources extends beyond quoting their opinions and statements. It can extend to the incorporation into news reports, sometimes without attribution, of official definitions of reality. A good example is the unemployment rate calculated by Statistics Canada, which, some observers charge, excludes many people who would like full-time work. Similarly, crime reporting is based on how the "phases" of each case are structured by the police and judicial bureaucracies: arrest, arraignment, preliminary hearing, trial, sentencing, and so on (Fishman, 1980). These institutionally structured events also structure the media's reporting. Possible alternative perspectives, such as treatment of the prisoner or the patterns of social violence associated with crime, are generally hidden from public view.

The problem of access is particularly important in the coverage of overseas stories. Coverage of non-Western societies is sparse and dominated by accounts of disasters, coups, atrocities with political implications, and the misfortunes that befall whites. If the press simplifies the richness and complexity of economic and political life in the West, it virtually ignores the Third World. The problem arises partly from the domination of the flow of news by several Western-based international news agencies. For the most part, by presenting the outside world as a place of danger and disruption, these agencies help to reinforce our attachment to the system in which we live.

It would be unfair to suggest that the patterns of news coverage we have noted here are unique to the *Sun*. On the contrary, they are typical of the commercial mass media. What we have said here would apply, with little alteration, to private television stations or the commercial radio stations. This is the reason for our concern: we are dealing not with the failings of a particular paper, but with the *successes* of the commercial media in shaping our understandings of the world.

Mass Media and Democratic Politics

The common-sense notions of "bias" and "objectivity" are inadequate for understanding the ideological role of media, or for organizing to change it, for the following reasons. First, "objectivity" implies the possibility of value neutrality in reports of social reality. Not only is this possibility philosophically dubious, but we have already seen that the values of consumerism—free choice in the marketplace, etc.—are firmly embedded in the routines of "objective" news production. Second, "bias" implies that the main problem with news is that it is deliberately manipulated. Our discussion of the structure of the Canadian media suggests that they are shaped by impersonal market forces, particularly the imperative of selling audiences to advertisers, more than by the partisan prejudices of some elite of media owners or news managers. Therefore, adherence to the norms of objectivity is precisely the means by which the media retain the consent of audiences. Indeed, charges of bias against particular media reports are given a hearing, and are even encouraged, through such manageable avenues as letters to the editor and complaints to the Press Council. This is because the example of the media's own occasional departures from the norms of objectivity highlights and legitimizes the "objectivity" of the majority of their reports.

Thus the hegemonic function of the media is achieved through the active participation of the audience. Readers and viewers may challenge particular media accounts. But such challenges underline audiences' acceptance of both the routines of conventional journalism, and the media's right to monopolize the representation of public life—so long as the media do so "objectively." It is less a matter of an elite telling us what to think than a set of structures that established the conditions under which dissent can be voiced.

The attempt to develop more popular, democratic media must involve more than a struggle to change the explicit political content of the media or to put popular representatives on media boards of directors. We have to change the way we experience mass communications, create a new relationship to the media, become *speakers* as well as listeners and readers. Mass communication must express the popular initiatives that transform our roles as citizens.

The fate of the CBC indicates what happens when the state creates institutions that leave intact our way of relating to institutional authority. The CBC is the closest approximation of a noncommercial mass medium in Canada at large. It is publicly owned. Its radio services and part of its television service are noncommercial. Unfortunately, the CBC has to fit into a pattern of mass communications and audience relations established by the commercial media. The government expects it to operate a commercial television service to offset the costs of public service broadcasting. If it fails to attract large audiences, the CBC is vigorously criticized in the commercial media and in Parliament. Adherents of the commercial media resent paying for a service they do not use. As a result, the CBC tries to make itself more popular, and this means imitating the commercial media. The gap between commercial and public broadcasting is narrowed, and the alternative offered by the CBC becomes more apparent than real.

Obviously, public ownership is not the whole solution to the problem of the commercialized media, valuable as the CBC and its provincial counterparts may be. In a sense, we get the media we deserve. The commercialism of our society—the dominance of the market and the big corporations, the emphasis on getting and spending, the neglect of public life—is reflected in the nature of the media, both private and public. The government-owned media reproduce the conventional relationship between the state and its citizens: the CBC speaks from on high to a passive audience. The ethos of journalism, the understanding of politics as a spectator sport, the perspective of the consumer carry over from the private to the public media. Breaking through this web of relationships means establishing outselves as the agents of democratic communication and refusing to be sold as a passive audience to private corporations or government leaders. The question is how.

New Media Relations

Things can be done to maximize the democratic potential of the existing media. Movements for social change should continue to use the opportunities presented by the contradictions and "leaks" within the media in order to influence its content. Journalists, technicians, and printers can attempt reform from within. Critics can continue to expose the more blatant biases, reveal the limitations of journalistic norms of objectivity and balance, and increase a popular receptivity to alternative journalism. It might be possible to institutionalize a pressure group to sponsor public debates on questions of media structure and orientation, conduct studies, undertake public education, and lobby for progressive legislation on the media industry. Ordinary readers, listeners, and viewers can become involved in criticizing the media and enforcing their demands by boycotts or other forms of protest.

All this involves a politics of audience resistance and transformation. The danger is that such a politics may be simply negative. People need positive outlets for their energy. This means creating new, authentically democratic media. Without such media, it is impossible to establish new relations within the audience or to develop the popular capacity for collective action.

These media should be alternative in a number of senses. Their internal operations should be co-operative and democratic rather than organized into a rigid and hierarchical division of labour. The political news they report should not be confined to elections and governments' actions. The statements of official spokespersons and leaders of the dominant electoral parties should be treated with less prominence and greater scepticism. Conversely, more attention should be given to the response of the ordinary people affected by governmental and corporate policies. Readers, listeners, or viewers should be regarded as participants in a community rather than as commodities whose attention can be bought and sold. The information supplied to (and by) audiences should help them build an alternative political culture and take collective control of their lives, rather than encourage consumption. While the conventional media focus on events that threaten or disrupt established institutions and values, the alternative media should reveal how these institutions and values themselves affect the well-being and rights of ordinary people. Alternative media should be willing to report on ongoing social and political *processes* without being restricted by a dependence on "hard news" *events*.

Some observers see the Internet as a vital forum for democratic exchange. It has the capacity to be the "new town hall" except that it has the advantage of linking people in conversations that span the globe. Communication can be virtually instant and its many webs are continually growing. But others argue that it lacks the resonance and power of the conventional media and is subdivided into narrow audiences based on highly specialized interests, connections, and hobbies. It is also limited to people with the resources and time needed to "surf the net." It is too early to tell whether this form of communication will be able to influence public debate in a meaningful way.

An instructive example of an unambiguously alternative medium in British Columbia is Vancouver Co-operative Radio (CFRO, 102.7; 104.9 on most cable systems). Like all Canadian radio stations, Co-op Radio must be 75 percent-owned by Canadian citizens. But any member of the audience may, subject to this rule, buy shares and annual memberships, which are the core of the station's financing. Members in good standing have one vote each, regardless of the size of their shareholding, in the

Annual General Meeting that elects directors. Co-op Radio is thus controlled through an open and democratic process that vests ultimate power in the public as subscriber-members of the audience.

All programming is produced by shareholder-volunteers. Program applications are considered by a programming committee and by the Board. Volunteers organize themselves into program collectives, dividing up the roles of studio operator, producer, host, reporter, and so on. The material they produce ranges from local music, drama, and poetry to coverage of city hall, labour issues, provincial, national, and international news and analysis, and programs of interest to a wide range of minority groups. All of this material is originated and produced by the audience itself to meet its own cultural and political needs. Listeners become speakers.

Co-op Radio is by no means perfect, but it is an example of an authentically democratic medium of communications. It is not dependent on advertisers (like the commercial media), or on the state (like the CBC), or even on the unions (like the now defunct *Solidarity Times*). It is an organization of its own listeners. Only as such can a medium of communications be empowering, enabling people to change the commercial society they confront. As CFRO demonstrates, democratic change in the media of communications need not wait on the election of a progressive government. On the contrary, establishment of alternative media is essential to building popular democratic movements, without which the hope of progressive social transformation is in vain.

Notes

1. The following section draws heavily from Robert A. Hackett, *News and Dissent: The Press and the Politics of Peace in Canada* (Norwood, NJ: Ablex, 1991), pp. 51–59.
2. Since this section was written, the *Sun* has experimented several times with its format, and has adopted a new name (the *Vancouver Sun*). Our general argument is unaffected by these changes, which are largely cosmetic.
3. Graham Knight, "Strike Talk: A Case Study of News," *Canadian Journal of Communication* 8, 3 (1982): 61–79; Robert A. Hackett, The Depiction of Labour and Business on National Television News." *Canadian Journal of Communication* 10, 1 (1983): 23–29; Todd Gitlin, *The Whole World is Watching* (Berkeley: University of California Press, 1980) p. 282.

References

Audley, P. (1983). *Canada's Cultural Industries*. Toronto: James Lorimer/CIEP.

Austen, I. (1994). "Roger Merger Silence 'Alarming'." *Vancouver Sun*, March 18.

Bagdikian, Ben. (1992). *The Media Monopoly*, 4th ed. Boston: Beacon Press.

Canada, Royal Commission on Newspapers (Kent Commission). (1981). *Report*. Ottawa.

Clement, W. (1975). *The Canadian Corporate Elite*. Toronto: McClelland and Stewart.

Curran, J. (1979). "Capitalism and Control of the Press, 1800–1975." In *Mass Communication and Society*, edited by J. Curran, M. Gurevitch, and J. Woollacott, 195–230. Beverly Hills: Sage.

Dalglish, B. (1994). "King of the Road." *Maclean's*, March 21, pp. 36–40.

Downing, J. (1980). *The Media Machine*. London: Pluto Press.

Dunnett, P. (1988). *The World Newspaper Industry*. London: Croom Helm.

Ewen, S. (1976). *Captains of Consciousness: Advertising and the Social Roots of the Consumer Culture*. New York: McGraw-Hill.

Fishman, M. (1980). *Manufacturing the News*. Austin: University of Texas Press.

Hackett, B. (1993). "Is There Censorship in Democratic Canada?" *New Directions* (October): 28–34.

Hall, S. (1982). "The Rediscovery of 'Ideology': Return of the Repressed in Media Studies." In *Culture, Society and the Media*, edited by M. Gurevitch, T. Bennett, J. Curran, and J. Woollacott, 56–90. London and New York: Methuen.

Horowitz, G. (1979). "Conservatism, Liberalism and Socialism in Canada: An Interpretation." In *Party Politics in Canada*, 4th ed., edited by H.G. Thorburn, 52–72. Scarborough: Prentice Hall.

Keane, J. (1984). *Public Life in Late Capitalism: Towards a Socialist Theory of Democracy*. Cambridge: Cambridge University Press.

Morrison, I. (1994). "Just What We Don't Need: A Bigger Cable Monopoly." *The Globe and Mail*, February 15.

Romanow, W. and W. Soderlund. (1992). *Media Canada: An Introductory Analysis*. Mississauga: Copp Clark Pitman.

Smythe, D. (1981). *Dependency Road: Communications, Capitalism and Consciousness in Canada*. Norwood, NJ: Ablex.

Winter, J. (1988). "Interlocking Directorships and Economic Power." In *Press Concentration and Monopoly: New Perspectives on Newspaper Ownership and Operation*, edited by R. Picard, J. Winter, M. McCombs, and S. Lacy, 105–15. Norwood, N.J.: Ablex.

Winter, J., and A. Hassanpour. (1994). "Building Babel." *Canadian Forum* (January/February): 10–17.

THE DECLINE OF THE DAILY NEWSPAPER

Gillian Steward

THE LAST WAVE

When I was a young, and eager, reporter for the *Calgary Herald* in the 1970s, I had no inkling that within twenty years the daily newspaper as I knew it would be a thing of the past. I didn't know that I was part of a wave that was about to crash, leaving disappointed journalists, confused publishers, and indifferent readers in its wake. In those days journalism was nothing if not fun: women reporters were no longer relegated to the "women's pages"; the work was always interesting, one day a lurid court case, the next day a chance to rub elbows with Prince Charles as he toured Indian reserves in Southern Alberta; the pay was decent; and there was lots of time for shop talk with colleagues in the tavern of the nearby Empress Hotel. Drinking and partying were integral to the job, so much so that reporters straggling into the newsroom late in the afternoon, looking for advice on how to put together a story from the press conference or city council meeting they had just attended, often had to troop down to the beer parlour to consult an editor.

At the time it seemed normal, the way things were done in the newspaper business. Now I look back on that period with amazement. For in 1972, when I was hired at the *Herald*, it was the only game in town, for both advertisers, and Calgarians interested in the daily ebb and flow of international, national, and local news. There was a second daily—*The Albertan*—but it was firmly ensconced as the underdog paper. Television was still mainly an entertainment medium. The *Herald*'s position was so secure that the advertising department didn't really sell advertising space, it simply set rates and took orders. So what did it matter if senior editors were too pie-eyed to understand the ramifications of city council's latest decision? *Herald* management was confident Calgarians would buy and read the paper anyway. The proprietor, Toronto-based Southam Inc., looked to the *Herald* and *The Edmonton Journal*, which had no competition at all, for a significant portion of their annual profits. The future looked rosy and rich; they had little reason to be concerned about lazy managers or sluggish newsrooms.

In those days, a mere twenty years ago, the daily newspaper was an institution of authority and credibility. Readers looked to it to tell them what was important in the world, and for the most part, they accepted the agenda decided upon by editors and publishers. They also accepted reams of dark, murky type, and writing, about the machinations and decisions of the federal government, the provincial government, the school board, any organization that had the smell of authority or establishment about it. Natural disasters, crime (usually from the police point of view), local celebrations like the Stampede or the C.N.E., and certain wars were also important. Front-page headlines bounced from the latest utterings of the premier to the latest skirmish in Northern Ireland. In those days, it all made sense somehow—to the reporters and editors, and the people who read the newspaper.

The newspaper played another role too: it was a reflection of the community. Readers looked at it, read it, and saw it as an integral part of their lives. A mirror of sorts that reflected back to the reader a picture of the community that he or she lived in. If readers didn't see themselves in that picture, at least it gave them some clues as to how to best fit into the community, how to make the most of life. One could see from reading the newspaper the common assumptions of most people in the community. There was faith in the political system, and the people who had either been elected or appointed to run it. There was admiration for the acumen and power of business leaders, especially those who ran large corporations. Only men were qualified to take on important positions in the community. Education at all levels was really important. Crime was bad, but criminals, if given a chance, could be rehabilitated. Poverty would eventually be eliminated with the combination of an expanding economy and tax-supported social programs. Christianity was the common religion, although people weren't going to church as much as they used to.

In the early 1970s, these were the assumptions of the time, and for the most part newspapers across Canada upheld them, some with vigour, others through inertia. *The Toronto Star* was more of a crusader for the ordinary man than most large daily newspapers. The Vancouver *Sun* was feisty and brash. The *Winnipeg Free Press* was the prestigious voice of the West. There were no morning tabloids like the Calgary, Edmonton, Toronto, and Ottawa *Suns*. It's hard to imagine now, but television was seen as a threat to radio and the movies, not to newspapers, because the networks still devoted most of their air time and energy to entertainment. But throughout the 1960s, television had been expanding its news coverage. And in the early 1970s it significantly expanded local news coverage.

Nevertheless, newspaper circulation, in Canada and the United States, continued to zoom upward. More people than ever were finishing high school and going on to post-secondary education. The expanding economy meant more people had money to spend, and businesses were only too happy to fill newspapers with ads encouraging them to spend. Most women weren't employed outside the home. They had time to read the newspaper. The man of the house often read it while his wife was preparing supper. In those days, newspaper subscribers picked up the broadsheet from the front steps in the late afternoon and sat down in an easy chair for a leisurely read. Most Canadian newspapers were run off the presses just after lunch so readers could expect to learn what had happened just that morning. They also read about what happened the day before, or the day before that. Twenty-four-hour TV news channels hadn't been invented yet. Most people didn't expect up-to-the-minute news. That is a relatively new idea, made possible by the combination of advances in television and communications technology.

And they didn't expect the kind of specialized coverage that is now available through everything from computer magazines to science and popular-music channels on TV. But perhaps the most singular difference between newspapers then and now is the way readers perceive them. For the reader in the early 1970s, newspapers had authority and credibility. The old cliché that if you read it in the newspaper it must be true was not a cliché then, it was the way things were. The printed word had a finality about it that few wanted to dispute. The judgement of editors and reporters was thought of as superior to that of most readers. The point of view, the objectivity, of the story, was accepted as being fair and neutral. If a person went to a meeting and came home with a certain understanding of what had happened, he or she would often abandon that understanding if the reporter at the meeting saw it differently, which of course was the case.

This acceptance of authority wasn't based on superior education. For in those days, reporters and editors didn't have to have university degrees or journalism courses; they could start as typesetters or copy runners. Experience and knowledge were gained on the job, or in the press club. I often wondered if readers would have been so quick to accept the authority of the newspaper if they could have actually spent a morning watching hung-over reporters and editors put it together and then run for the tavern the minute the presses started rolling. Daily newspapers may not have had a monopoly on education (or sobriety), but they did have a monopoly on information in those days. They had control of the news services such as Associated Press and Canadian Press that would gather news stories from across the country and around the world. Newspapers could afford to hire numerous reporters to find out what was going on in the community, and further afield, daily newspapers had the money and resources to put all this together and deliver it to however many households wanted it. Where else would a person go other than to his or her daily newspaper for information about current events around the world and around the block? The daily newspaper was the bulletin board, and the conscience, of the community.

In the 1970s, this combination of a deferential public and the massed authority, information, and resources of the daily newspapers looked formidable. But the signs of deterioration were already showing, for while the number of subscribers was increasing, particularly in the large, expanding metropolitan centres, there was evidence that more and more people weren't reading the newspapers they were buying. Surveys in the United States showed that although most people had seen their leisure time increase between 1965 and 1975, they were spending less time reading the newspaper. The National Opinion Research Centre at the University of Chicago reported a 9 percent decline in the public's reported daily use of a newspaper between 1975 and 1978, and the younger the readers, the less time they spent with the newspaper.

Most of us who worked in newsrooms at the time were blissfully unaware of these trends. When the *Ottawa Journal*, the *Winnipeg Tribune* and the *Montreal Star* were shut down, we accused management of being too greedy and fought even harder for better wages and working conditions. Southam Newspaper publishers and executives didn't seem too concerned about the emerging trends either. They simply cashed in on rising circulation in their monopoly markets by boosting advertising rates. As the 1970s drew to a close, the *Calgary Herald* benefited from the oil boom as well. Circulation climbed, advertising flowed in. On weekends the paper was so heavy a small child could barely lift it. Confident that Calgary's economy, and the newspaper, would continue to grow at this astounding rate, *Herald* management made plans to build a huge new plant, away from the heart of the city and the late-afternoon traffic snarls that made it difficult to get the paper to the new suburbs on time. It all seemed to make sense then. But now the red brick building looks like a monument to myopia: the ultimate symbol of the arrogance and shortsightedness so pervasive in the newspaper industry until the early 1980s.

Head Office Hastens the Demise

I now have the luxury of hindsight as I look back on a journalism career that has spanned 25 years. And since I have worked as a reporter/writer, and as a manager/editor for the *Calgary Herald*, I have had the opportunity to appraise the newspaper industry and its relationship with readers from many points of view. Between 1985 and 1990, as assistant managing editor, then as managing editor responsible for newsroom operation of almost 200 employees, I had a front row seat during the tumultuous soul-searching and restructuring that went on in Southam Inc. I left the *Herald* in 1990, thoroughly disenchanted with a business I had once loved. Now that I have had more than four years to reflect, and a chance to see the newspaper as just another reader, someone outside the daily hubbub of gathering and disseminating news, I believe I can see where daily newspapers went wrong in the 1980s and why they are unlikely to recover their status as community bulletin board and conscience, even though most of them have remained profitable. I don't mean to imply that the demise of the daily newspaper is entirely the fault of those producing them; there are many factors that lead me to believe that no matter what daily newspapers do, most of them will eventually be reduced to a mere shadow of their former selves. But I do believe that those responsible for newspapers may have hastened their demise, sometimes out of greed, other times out of well-intentioned, but shortsighted thinking.

The daily newspapers that have suffered the most are outside the Ottawa-Toronto-Montreal triangle. Ottawa will always be a good place to sell newspapers simply because it is full of politicians and bureaucrats who thrive on political intrigue, policy pronouncements, and leaked memos. Toronto is a newspaper market like no other in North America. Readers there have a choice of three strong dailies, *The Toronto Star*, the *Sun* and *The Globe and Mail*. Consequently, Torontonians get a much more thorough airing of local issues and concerns than people in other parts of the country. The French press in Quebec is also lively and competitive and has the luxury of a constituency of readers that really needs it.

And then there is the rest of Canada. Southam Newspapers represent 27 percent of total daily newspaper circulation; Thomson Newspapers, 21 percent; Toronto Sun Publishing, 11 percent; Hollinger Inc; 6 percent; and Irving Group (the Maritimes), 3 percent. At many of these newspapers, executives and staff are in a continuous state of angst. Instead of watching circulation numbers go up with the increase in population, circulation managers are watching a steady erosion. No matter what they do, no matter how many subscription contests and campaigns they undertake, circulation slips, or at best remains stagnant. Between 1986 and 1994, the *Calgary Herald*'s Friday circulation (the biggest circulation day of the week because the newspaper contains the *TV Times*) fell from 183 000 copies to 158 000 (13 percent) even though the city's population increased 15 percent during the same period. Between 1986 and 1994, the weekly circulation of Southam's Vancouver *Sun* dropped by almost 220 000 copies, even though the population on the lower mainland exploded. The *Winnipeg Free Press*, a Thomson newspaper, has seen Saturday circulation dip by 25 000 copies, or close to 10 percent, in the last eight years. The erosion continues, despite millions spent in the last decade on readership and marketing surveys, internal reorganization, newspaper redesign, and promotion. Further millions were spent converting afternoon newspapers to morning newspapers. Whereas all the major dailies in Canada were afternoon newspapers when I started in the business in 1972, they are all now morning papers. In some cities, the broadsheet dailies couldn't compete with the brash, sports-oriented Sun tabloids. But even where there were no tabloids, readers found they didn't have time to read an afternoon paper when they got home from work; besides the news was stale already, so they caught up on the day's events by tuning into the supper hour television news. Daily newspapers switched to morning delivery, splashed more colour on the front pages, and hoped for the best. Many newspapers also added Sunday editions in hopes that people would spend more of their leisure time reading them.

Readers could easily see that daily newspapers were changing. What they didn't see were the changes going on inside Southam Inc., Canada's largest newspaper chain. During the 1980s Southam was corporatized and centralized, and while the people who ran the company considered it simply an internal matter, the reverberations would be felt in newsrooms, living rooms, and communities across Canada.

William Southam started the chain when he and a partner bought the Hamilton *Spectator* in 1877. He and his six sons eventually assumed full control of the company. Even when Southam Inc. was listed on the Toronto Stock Exchange in 1945, Southam descendants and assorted in-laws maintained a firm grasp on most of the shares, and executive power. They were fairly benign rulers who had a sense of the importance of the daily newspaper to the local community, and the country as a whole. They believed that "newspapers are essentially community services that must be published and administered in their own regions." They didn't interfere with local editorial boards; there were no pronouncements from head office about what stands to take on the issues of the day. Each newspaper was a little kingdom unto itself with the publisher serving as the local baron. He (they were all men until the late 1980s) protected the franchise, and made sure enough money flowed into the treasury in Toronto. But by the 1980s, the Southam family was running out of heirs who knew enough about newspapers to control the family business with the same old-fashioned sense of service to the community. When John Fisher took over as president in 1986, he would be the last Southam descendant at the helm. Unfortunately, he had little expertise in the newspaper industry, because he had spent most of his working life in the pulp and paper industry. To make up for this lack of knowledge and experience, Fisher turned to the high priests of

Canadian business—Bay Street financial consultants and stock traders who looked at businesses as cash flow, return on revenue, profit, share value, and takeover targets.

I can remember countless presentations by Fisher himself, and other head office types, as they preached the gospel of the bottom line. They set targets for improved return on revenue—another word for profit. At that time, Southam Newspapers, as a group, had about a 12 percent return on revenue—although the figure varied from newspaper to newspaper; some were lower, others were much higher. But now every newspaper would have to make more money, and head office would tell them exactly how much more. Their budgets would have to be approved in Toronto at the beginning of each fiscal year, as would any significant expansion of staff. This centralizing of financial control was new for Southam Inc. In the past, Southam had let each publisher decide how best to make a profit. Publishers turned in financial statements at the end of the year, and as long as their newspaper was in the black, nobody at head office asked too many questions.

That wasn't the only change. The Southam Newspaper Group had long been responsible for most of Southam Inc.'s profits and was also the most prestigious of Southam's holdings. But Southam also owned a large printing division, Coles Book Stores, and dozens of trade and specialty magazines, none of which were as profitable as the newspapers.

When John Fisher took over as president, he insisted on treating all the divisions of Southam as equal members of one happy family. We were all to consider ourselves as employees of Southam Inc. Our goal was to make Southam Inc. as profitable and successful as possible. "The employees are the engines that drive this company. When our people succeed, so does the company. And so do the shareholders," Fisher declared on the cover of Southam Inc.'s 1987 *Annual Report*. The idea of newspapers as a community service seemed to have slipped his mind.

But most employees in the newspaper group didn't think of themselves as working for Southam Inc. They identified with the newspapers they worked for, not with head office. They worked for the Vancouver *Sun* or *The Edmonton Journal*. They saw themselves as part of a daily newspaper that was integral to their community. But Fisher persisted with his new vision of the company. Soon after being named president, he began crisscrossing the country so he could personally speak to employees. Once when he came to Calgary he invited representatives from all Southam divisions in Southern Alberta to a reception at a large downtown Calgary hotel. As was his usual practice at these affairs, he led off his presentation with a discussion of Southam's financial position: how much money it had made in the past year and what it hoped to make in the year to come. He talked about everyone putting on their Southam hats and doing all they could to make sure the company improved its return on revenue. He didn't seem to understand that journalists from the *Herald* newsroom had very little in common with people in the printing division who sold business forms, or the people who ran Coles Book Stores. And he seemed completely oblivious to the notion of loyalty to a newspaper and a community.

Fisher's vision also included a deep set fear of a hostile takeover. He was convinced (likely by his Bay Street advisors) that Southam was a vulnerable target. Shares were widely dispersed, and many of the newspapers could have been made much more profitable if turned over to determined money managers. The prime suspect was the well-known Canadian business magnate, Conrad Black, who already owned Sterling Newspapers as well as newspapers in England and Israel. Number two suspect was Torstar Corporation, which owned *The Toronto Star*. Fisher reasoned that if we pushed up return on revenue, Southam share prices would rise too. Then a takeover would simply become too expensive. Some of us suspected that he was also haunted by the possibility that he would be remembered as the Southam descendant who let the company slip into someone else's hands.

The Trivialization of the News

The easiest way to inflate profits at a newspaper is to increase revenues from advertising and circulation, and cut expenses. Since the news gathering operation is the most expensive part of the newspaper—it produces no money like advertising or circulation, it simply costs money—newsroom managers were directed to cut back on travel expenses, training, and staff. I have never been opposed to business making reasonable profits, or using resources in an efficient manner. But what I found most disappointing was that whenever I, as a new manager, had a chance to attend meetings with executives and other managers in the chain, all they ever talked about was the bottom line, the newspaper as a cash cow whose only value was the milk that could be squeezed out of her. I was still somewhat idealistic then, some would say naive, but I was truly disappointed that none of these people saw the newspaper as a service to the community. In fact, they appeared not to see the newspaper at all; they saw only the balance sheets that told them how much money it was making, or losing. The fact that the newspaper was something people bought because it was important to them seemed entirely irrelevant to these money managers. The newspaper had been reduced to return on revenue. And not only did the head office types look at it that way, they now expected editors, newsroom managers, reporters, and photographers to regard it that way too. Everyone was expected to do their part to push up the stock price.

Traditionally the news, or editorial, department of a newspaper had much more independence than the production or advertising departments. The editor was second-in-command to the publisher and could overrule decisions made in other departments if they adversely affected editorial. But in the new business environment, the editorial department would have less privilege and independence. If the advertising department wanted to run ads about new homes that looked like articles written by reporters, the editor could do little about it. If the production department wanted to impose earlier deadlines so as to avoid overtime for pressmen, reporters would have to resign themselves to getting their stories in by 5 p.m. Only the most urgent evening events would get full coverage. The bottom line was the most important consideration. Everything else, including service to the community, was secondary.

The jargon of business even started to creep into newsroom conversations and coffee klatches. The sense of the newsroom as independent from the financial considerations of the newspaper was being eroded. Where once reporters and editors used their own judgement to determine if information or events were newsworthy, or of interest to the public at large, they now had to consider how much the story cost, whether it would offend or impress a major advertiser or segment of the business community, whether it would attract a meddlesome, but expensive, lawsuit. There were no overt rules and regulations about these matters, but amid talk of cost cutting and takeover threats, it became more difficult for journalists and editors to pursue stories and investigations that required a lot of time or money. Articles that might offend the rich and powerful were also discouraged, because the rich and powerful could afford to hire lawyers to defend their name and reputation. Even if the newspaper is confident that it will eventually be proven right, the costs of going to court can run into the hundreds of thousands of dollars. Under the new regime, this was seen as a waste of money.

Canada's other large newspaper chain—Thomson Newspapers—had been operating like this for decades. Head office called the shots, set high profit margins (25 to 30 percent return on revenue), and demanded that newspapers in cities and towns across the country meet those targets any way they could. The newspaper as community bulletin board and conscience had never been a priority at Thomson. Now Southam was headed in the same direction. The people who ran the company had little interest in the local communities their newspapers served. They were only interested in the bottom line and the approval of Bay Street. Many of the Southam publishers were unhappy about this departure from the old way of doing things. But most of them simply grumbled in private and went along with head office. One exception was *Herald* publisher J.P. O'Callaghan. He fought the changes loudly and adamantly, and pushed hard to maintain local control of the newspapers. But he was outnumbered, and when presented with a take-it-or-leave-it retirement package at the end of 1988, a year before he was due to retire, he took it.

Marketing Ourselves to Death

It would have been much easier to improve profit and share value if newspaper circulation was on the upswing, but it wasn't. In every part of the country, the number of subscribers to Southam newspapers was slipping. Advertisers needed more and more convincing that higher rates for ads were worth the money, especially in areas like Calgary where economic recession had set in in the mid-1980s. Enter the marketing consultants, a new breed of newspaper expert who would find out why circulation was eroding and what each newspaper could do about it.

When the marketing consultants, most of them from the United States, were added to the churn, daily newspapers went through another transformation. They became "products" and readers became markets. Managers like me attended conferences and seminars so we could learn from the mistakes and successes of other newspapers. Consultants spewed demographics and data from hundreds of readers interviewed about their preferences and priorities. Some of us knew that if we had to use professional survey companies to find out why our readers were losing interest, we were in deep trouble: we had already lost an essential connection with those readers.

Nevertheless, we succumbed to the business gospel of the day and enthusiastically adopted the marketing survey as a modern tool that would help us preserve the daily newspaper as an integral part of the community and the democratic process.

Each newspaper undertook its own surveys, tailored to the particular problems of that newspaper, and the particular demands of the community it served. But in cities across Canada, readers sent back the same message. Newspapers are boring and stale. Newspapers don't tell me enough about what I want to know. Newspapers are full of articles about boards and councils and officials and spokesmen, but they have little to do with real people and their problems, their hopes and dreams. I don't have time to read a newspaper—I'm too busy.

Many people at newspapers took all this to heart. They redesigned the newspaper so it had more colour, more white space, more of a compelling layout, changes designed to make newspapers quicker and easier to read. They embraced the notion of more "people" stories. Reporters were as bored covering all those city council and school board meetings as people were reading them. As a result, many newspapers began to feature the "aggrieved" individual: the person who had been ignored by the bureaucracy, trampled on by the justice system, or denied assistance by social services. The success story came into vogue too: the volunteer who had made a difference, the entrepreneur who had beat the odds and made a million, the woman who had risen to prominence. But whether the articles dealt with an aggrieved or successful person, there were more and more articles about individuals.

Newspapers became more like television. They focussed on giving people easy-to-digest, uncomplicated information. And like television they began to focus on personalities. Political parties were reduced to political leaders. Government was reduced to the prime minister and a few key cabinet ministers. Since television in North America is primarily an advertising vehicle, the people who run networks want programming that will "hook" as many viewers as possible. Fast-paced entertainment served that purpose. And so did fast-paced, emotional news and current affairs. And the best, and cheapest way to inject emotion was to have two well-known people in conflict. That became the story. The issues they disagreed about were secondary. Since television was by now the most important mass medium, not newspapers, many readers wanted the same jolts out of their daily broadsheet, or tabloid. Many people also expected to have their individual needs and preferences met by the newspaper, just as they did when they went shopping for clothes or cars. Time was another important factor. Parents were holding down full-time jobs, as well as looking after children. There was barely enough time to get the kids breakfast, let alone read the newspaper. And as people became more environmentally conscious, they felt guilty about all the unread newspapers they piled up and then threw in the garbage.

Since these trends appeared to be unstoppable, it seemed prudent to adapt rather than ignore them. Besides, newspapers needed to change. They had grown used to monopoly markets and giving readers what they thought was good for them rather than what they wanted. The idea of more "people" stories appealed to many journalists. Many of us felt that there was too much emphasis on official organizations and boards and not enough on "real" people and their views and activities. Often the political disputes of aldermen or school trustees didn't reflect the larger concerns of the community. After all, education wasn't just a matter of school board meetings. Education was about children, parents, teachers classrooms, curriculum, and taxes.

A lot of energy went into changing the format and the content of papers like the *Calgary Herald*. But the snazzy new layouts, the new features designed to attract everyone from wine buffs to square dancers, and the emphasis on "people" stories didn't improve circulation. It kept slipping. So more marketing surveys were intitiated to find out what we were doing wrong. I can still clearly remember a meeting at the *Herald* in the late 1980s. A group of us were examining the latest data from a reader survey. One of the questions had asked people to rate the kind of news they most wanted to see in the paper. They could choose categories such as local, international, sports, and community. The response to the community category was so high it almost went off the scale. We all looked at each other in amazement. What did people mean by that? Isn't that what we were already doing?

That we didn't know what readers meant by more community news was an indictment of our "professional" attitude. As journalists and managers we had become used to the idea that we knew what was newsworthy and what was not. Add to that the fact that journalistic principles did not allow us to be part of the community; we couldn't belong to any groups or organizations lest we be seen as biased in their favour. Professionalism dictated that a journalist couldn't be objective if he or she were too involved in a cause or organization, other than a church or a gardening club. Consequently, we were really cut off from what people were discussing and arguing about in community groups and organizations. We always knew the official line as it was handed out through press conferences and press releases, but we weren't grounded in the reality of everyday life as most people live it. We didn't have a sense of people trying to figure things out and organize themselves to deal with the problems they faced.

In our quest to adapt to the results of the marketing surveys, we had missed an important undercurrent in the minds and hearts of the people surveyed. Amidst all the fragmentation and individualism there was a desire for more community—common goals, common assumptions, and a common understanding of what was important and what wasn't. Of course, marketing surveys aren't designed to speak to people as members of a community. They are designed to find out what people want to buy and why and how much they are willing to pay for it. So it's not surprising that the answers that came back reflected consumer attitudes and desires. But a good newspaper had always been an integral part of the community, not just a product to be sold to as many people as possible. Even the Southams recognized that in the early days of the chain when they described the newspaper as a "community service." Nevertheless, the underpinnings of the community that had been so evident in the newspaper as late as the 1970s had almost disappeared by the 1980s.

The Beached Whale

I don't mean to imply, of course, that all the problems that are part of life in the 1990s are the fault of daily newspapers. Far from it. They are the result of many converging factors. And it could be argued that print journalists and daily newspapers are simply victims of changing times, that no matter what they do, the world has changed and they must change with it or wither. I can't help but think of the last blacksmith. As people gave up horses in favour of cars, would it have really mattered what kind of horseshoe the blacksmith forged? Or how friendly he was? Or that he provided better service than the blacksmith down the street?

But even if the daily newspaper can't be compared to the last blacksmith, a strong argument can be made that daily newspapers in Canada in the 1980s contributed to the fragmentation of our community life, and in doing so hastened their own demise. They had lots of help, of course. The recession gutted advertising revenues; readers were seduced by 24-hour news channels, computerized information banks, and specialty publications. And the increased busyness of most people's day-to-day lives meant they simply didn't have time to sit down and read a newspaper.

But what about those marketing surveys? Was it really a productive idea to reduce readers to consumers of news and classified advertising? Is that what people were doing—consuming—in the 1950s, and 1960s, and 1970s when the daily newspaper was an integral part of their lives? The marketing survey itself is a mechanism that approaches people not only as consumers of products but as individual consumers, people unrelated to their neighbours, friends, and community at large. The marketing survey asks people what they want as individuals, about their personal likes and dislikes. It prompts quick, superficial, anonymous answers. There is no time for discussion or debate, no time to listen to someone else's idea of a good newspaper. No time to talk about the reader as citizen, a person who has interests beyond satisfying his or her personal desires, a person who has some notions about the good of the community at large. For Southam newspapers the headlong charge to turn daily newspapers into just another product to be packaged and sold like wieners or toothpaste was led by the people at head office. Their insistence that the newspapers were simply part of a huge corporate empire, that above all else must keep the share price high, was arrogant and completely self-serving: the people at head office would have been the first to lose their jobs if Conrad Black or Torstar had taken over the company. They also owned a lot of Southam shares.

Newspapers across the country were forced to reduce their staff and coverage of local and national affairs in order to satisfy the financial priorities of the people at head office. The idea of service to the community was turned upside down. But the strategy failed. Conrad Black eventually bought enough shares that he was named to the Southam Board of Directors, where he had a great deal of influence. John Fisher has retired, and for the first time in its history, Southam has a president who is not part of the family.

Daily newspapers also could have done something completely different, and worthwhile, than what television was doing. But with money managers anxious to cut costs and increase profits by the next quarter, there was no such thing as long-range planning, or long-term investment. Daily newspapers actually had the resources, and brain power, to root themselves deep into the community, to find out what was really going on, and to express that in a coherent, interesting, and useful way. Television simply could not compete. Television newscasts are not suited to reporting on the messy, complicated ways that people organize themselves, express themselves and take small, but significant actions. That's grass-roots democracy, networks of local organizations and groups that take responsibility for improving life in the community at large. They are the glue that makes democracy, and community on a larger scale, possible.

The relatively sudden death of the daily newspaper as a force in the community hasn't been pleasant to watch. Many journalists and other newspaper employees have lost their jobs, others have lost the pride they once had in simply being associated with the newspaper industry. I rarely hear people in Calgary commend the newspaper any more. If they mention it, it is usually to criticize, or to remark on how they don't read it and they don't miss it. I don't yearn for the old attitudes of newspapers, and the people who worked at them, so cocky that readers were of little concern to them. But I do long for the days when newsrooms were full of extraordinary people, many of them eccentric to be sure, but so much more sceptical and rebellious than the university-educated, professionalized, middle-class journalists that fill today's newsrooms. I believe that education, that familiarity with orthodoxy, made it easier for the executives at head office to implement the changes they imposed from the top in the name of a better bottom line and return on revenue. Many journalists of the 1980s easily digested all the marketing jargon, too, because it was developed at business schools and universities just like the ones they had attended.

In any event, the daily newspaper became a business, just like any other business—except it isn't. Most businesses don't have the same responsibility to the community as a newspaper. Most businesses are not an integral part of the democratic process as a good newspaper is. I don't think the passing of the daily newspaper as an important community forum is necessarily bad, as long as something emerges to take its place. But so far, nothing has.

THE MANDATE, STRUCTURE, AND FINANCING OF THE CBC

Colin Hoskins and Stuart McFadyen

National public broadcasters worldwide are under attack. Even in Europe, where public service broadcasting "...in the past was positively wanted by national governments, now it is only being tolerated...There is enormous political pressure to privatize" (Burgelman, 1986, 173). Burgelman gives as reasons the declining confidence in government institutions and the effect of new distribution technologies, notably satellite and cable, in eliminating scarcity of broadcast frequencies. As audiences for public broadcasters decline, people question whether they are getting their money's worth. In Canada, largely due to increased competition from specialty and pay services delivered by satellite to cable, CBC English Television's audience share declined from 21.8 percent in 1984–85 to 15.0 percent in 1990–91 (Ellis, 1991, 22), to 13.5 percent in 1992–93. In addition, survey results reveal that there was an eight percentage point decrease, from 39 percent in 1985 to 31 percent in 1991, in people responding that CBC does a "great deal" in "maintaining distinctive Canadian culture" (Report of the Standing Committee on Communications and Culture, 1992). There has been a growing gap between the resources the government is willing to provide the CBC and the mandate it is expected to carry out. This culminated in the CBC decision in December 1991 to close three of its owned-and-operated stations and reduce eight others to news bureau status.

The appropriate mandate, structure, and financing of the CBC are a function of the rationale (if any) for retaining a national public broadcaster. Prior to considering these, we provide background by examining the current status of the CBC. Controversy about the CBC invariably centres around its English-language and French-language television services and the paper concentrates on these.

THE CURRENT STATUS OF THE CBC

The Mandate

Sections 3(1)(l) and (m) of the Broadcasting Act (1991), read:

> (l) the Canadian Broadcasting Corporation, as the national public broadcaster, should provide radio and television services incorporating a wide range of programming that informs, enlightens and entertains;

> (m) the programming provided by the Corporation should
>
> i) be predominantly and distinctively Canadian,
>
> ii) reflect Canada and its regions to national and regional audiences, while serving the special needs of those regions,
>
> iii) actively contribute to the flow and exchange of cultural expression,
>
> iv) be in English and in French, reflecting the different needs and circumstances of each official language community, including the particular needs and circumstances of English and French linguistic minorities,
>
> v) strive to be of equivalent quality in English and French,
>
> vi) contribute to shared national consciousness and identity,
>
> vii) be made available throughout Canada by the most appropriate and efficient means and as resources become available for the purpose, and
>
> viii) reflect the multicultural and multiracial nature of Canada.

This mandate is essentially similar to that under the Broadcasting Act (1968), which it supersedes. The controversial clause in the 1968 Act about "contributing to the development of national unity" has been omitted. Additions include a "cultural" mission, a concern for "the particular needs and circumstances of English and French linguistic minorities," the need to strive for "equivalent quality in English and in French," the need to "reflect the multicultural nature of Canada," while the programming should be distributed throughout the country by the "most appropriate and efficient means." The 1991 Act stipulates that programming responsibilities at CBC are to be split between French and English service committees.

The Current Structure

CBC's primary television services are its English-language network (based in Toronto), French-language network (based in Montreal), and regional and local programming operations. Nineteen (11 English, 8 French) owned-and-operated TV stations provide the regional programming, contribute items to the network, and distribute the network signal locally. Local distribution is supplemented by 27 (22 English, 5 French) private affiliates and more than 600 rebroadcasters. Distribution of the network signals from Toronto and Montreal to the over-the-air regional distribution centres is by Anik E2 satellite, with use of delays to feed across five time zones. The distribution system makes the English-language service available to 99 percent of anglophones and the French-language service available to 99 percent of francophones.

The Financial Situation

In 1989–90, parliamentary appropriations for the CBC accounted for 45 percent of all federal government expenditures on culture (see Report of the Standing Committee on Communications and Culture, 1992, 33).

A difficulty in assessing CBC's finances is the unavailability of detailed financial and operating data; this is regarded as confidential commercial information.[1] Information that can be derived from the *CBC Annual Report* regarding the source and disposition of CBC's budget for the fiscal year 1991–92 is shown in Table 1 Program activity expenditures were $494.5 million for English-language television and $304.9 million for French-language television, a total of $799.4 million, of which $606.5 million was spent by the networks and $192.9 million by the regions. Distribution of the television signals cost $73.9 million for the networks, $21.7 million for stations, and a $18.6 million payment to private affiliates for a total of $114.2 million.

Recent trends (1981–82 to 1992–93) in real funding (constant 1988 dollars) of CBC can be inferred from Table 2 Total parliamentary appropriations (PA) in constant dollars rose from $933.6 million to $972.0 million but were virtually unchanged if the one-time assistance in the 1992–93 year is excluded. However, PA peaked in 1984–85 at $1,036.9 million and fell 12 percent to $915.3 million in 1988–89 before a partial recovery. The capital appropriation, presumably because of the building of the new broadcasting centre in Toronto, fared much better than the parliamentary operating appropriation (POA). The POA decreased 5 percent from $864.6 million in 1981–82 to $818.3 in 1992–93, or 10 percent if the one-time assistance is ignored. Again, however, the treatment was generous up to 1984–85 when POA peaked at $943.3 million before declining. Not surprisingly, CBC usually takes 1984–85 as the base year when discussing its financial situation. The figures support the contention that CBC suffered a decline in real POA and PA under the Conservative government, although this was in a context of general constraint.

The CBC has been successful in offsetting the decline in POA by increasing advertising revenue and miscellaneous revenue (from program sales, sales of compact discs etc.). Real advertising revenue increased 83 percent from $188.0 million in 1981–82 to $344.2 million in 1990–91 (as a share of total noncapital funding from less than 18 percent to more than 28 percent). This translated into a POA decline of from over 80 percent to less than 69 percent. However, because of the recession, advertising revenue fell after 1990–91 to $258.7 million in 1992–93. Constant dollar noncapital funding rose 6 percent from 1981–82 to 1992–93. However, there is evidence that the inflation rate applicable to some of CBC's expenditures has been considerably in excess of that implied by the GDP deflator. For example, the cost to Canadian broadcasters of acquiring foreign, mainly U.S., programs increased at an annual rate of 12.9 percent between 1985 and 1989 (Girard and Peters, 1991, 37).

The CBC's television program budgets are shown in current and constant (1981–82) dollars in Table 3. In constant dollars, total television program budgets rose 1 percent from 1981–82 to 1988–89; however, since 1984–85 the budget was cut from $460.7 million to $404.5 million, a 12 percent reduction (surprisingly this is greater than the 2 percent reduction in total noncapital funding during the same period).

TABLE 1

CBC Operating Activities 1991–1992 (in millions of dollars)

Sources of Funds:		
Net advertising revenue		320.1
Miscellaneous revenue		56.6
Parliamentary operating appropriation		900.6
Previous year's carry forward		8.3
	Total	1,285.6
Application of Funds:		
PROGRAM ACTIVITIES		
Television—English language		
Network		362.5
Regional contributions to network		45.4
Regional		86.6
		494.5
Television—French language		
Network		244.0
Regional contributions to network		23.1
Regional		37.8
		304.9
Radio—English and French language		250.2
		1,049.6
DISTRIBUTION ACTIVITIES		
Television		
Network/Station distribution		95.6
Payments to private stations		18.6
Radio		43.2
		157.4
OTHER ACTIVITIES		
Specialty services less government assistance		32.1
Corporate engineering services		9.2
Corporate management and services		43.6
Selling and merchandising		45.8
Expense reductions and restructuring		16.3
		152.0
Plus income taxes		1.7
Less items not requiring current operating funds (mainly amortization)		73.9
	Total	1,286.7
(Deficit) Surplus to be Carried Forward		(1.1)

Source: CBC *Annual Report,* 1991–92, pp. 24–27.

TABLE 2

Funds and Revenues of the CBC, by Source, 1981–82 to 1992–93, in 1988 Dollars (millions)*

	Parliamentary appropriations			Other							Percentage of Total Noncapital Funds		
Fiscal Year[a]	Operating (POA)[b]	Capital	Total (PA)	Ads	Misc.	Total Noncapital	Total	POA, $ per capita	PA, $ per capita	POA	Ads	Misc.
1981–82	864.6	69.0	933.6	188.0	17.5	1070.1	1139.1	35.6	38.4	80.8	17.6	1.6
1982–83	871.6	68.2	939.8	197.4	16.0	1085.0	1153.2	35.4	38.2	80.3	18.2	1.5
1983–84	912.5	75.0	987.5	238.5	16.1	1167.1	1242.1	36.8	39.8	78.2	20.4	1.4
1984–85	943.3	93.6	1036.9	246.3	18.8	1208.4	1302.0	37.8	41.5	78.1	20.4	1.6
1985–86	879.2	65.2	944.4	242.4	25.6	1147.2	1212.4	34.9	37.5	76.6	21.1	2.2
1986–87	849.6	68.4	918.0	257.8	29.8	1137.2	1205.6	33.4	36.1	74.7	22.7	2.6
1987–88	828.2	91.7	919.9	307.3	31.1	1166.6	1258.3	32.3	35.9	71.0	26.3	2.7
1988–89	814.4	100.9	915.3	330.0	33.1	1177.5	1278.4	31.4	35.3	69.2	28.0	2.8
1989–90	812.5	113.9	926.4	339.2	35.3	1187.0	1300.9	31.1	35.4	68.4	28.6	3.0
1990–91	831.0	112.9	943.9	344.2	35.3	1210.5	1323.4	31.3	35.6	68.6	28.4	2.9
1991–22	796.1	128.4	924.5	281.7	51.0	1128.8	1257.2	28.2	32.8	70.5	25.0	4.5
1992–93	818.3[c]	153.7	972.0	258.7	57.2	1134.2	1287.9	28.8	34.3	72.1	22.8	5.0

[a] April 1 to March 31.
[b] Includes working capital appropriations.
[c] Includes one-time assistance of $40.6 (million) to fund the CBC's shortfall.

Note: the data were adjusted as follows: operations, advertising, and miscellaneous revenues were adjusted using the government current expenditure on goods and services implicit price index, and capital revenues were adjusted using the government investment in fixed capital implicit price index, as developed by Statistics Canada (1990b and 1993). The price indices used are for December 31 of each fiscal year.

*This table is based on Groves (1991, Table 3, 462), and updated two years

Sources: Adapted from John C. Groves, "Federal Expenditures on Public Broadcasting in Canada," Fiscal Figures Feature (1991), *Canadian Tax Journal* 38, 2, pp. 457–73.

TABLE 3

CBC Television Program Budgets, 1981–82 to 1988–89 (in millions of dollars)

	Network			Regional			Total	
	Current $	Constant $[1]	%	Current $	Constant $	%	Current $	Constant $
1981–82	262.8	262.8	65.8	136.5	136.5	34.2	399.3	399.2
1982–83	304.4	274.8	67.0	150.0	135.4	33.0	454.4	410.2
1983–84	335.1	285.9	66.4	169.4	144.5	33.6	504.5	430.4
1984–85	384.0	314.0	68.2	179.4	146.7	31.8	563.4	460.7
1985–86		not available						
1986–87	413.4	312.2	76.0	130.5	98.5	24.0	543.9	410.7
1987–88	432.5	313.0	75.8	137.7	99.7	24.2	570.2	412.7
1988–89	438.8	305.1	75.5	142.8	99.3	24.5	581.6	404.5

[1] Deflated using the CPI—with 1981–82 as base year.

Source: Adapted from John Gormley (chairman), *A Broadcasting Policy for Canada: A Report of the Standing Committee on Communications and Culture* (June 1988), p. 111. Reprinted by permission of the House of Commons, Ottawa, Canada.

The cuts between 1984–85 and 1987–88 were borne entirely by regional programming. Even though network programming bore the brunt in 1988–89, by then expenditures on network programming accounted for three-quarters of the total programming budget, up from around two-thirds earlier in the decade. In 1992–93, the situation was unchanged with network program activities accounting for 75.9 percent of total program expenditures (CBC *Annual Report*, 1992–93).

CBC Programming

With the increased importance of advertising as a source of funds, it is not surprising that CBC has been criticized for becoming too commercial. For example, Adrien Pouilet, owner of Television Quatre Saisons Network, is reported to have complained that CBC French-language programming has become virtually indistinguishable from that of private broadcasters in Quebec (Partridge, 1992, B2). CBC conducts an *Annual Media Survey*, which includes questions comparing viewer perceptions of the CBC English-language service and CTV; Ellis (1991, 163) reports that in the 1990 survey "the striking thing is that on more than half of those measures…the differences in the scores (of CBC and CTV) are relatively small".

Nevertheless, the CBC English-language service does differ from the private sector by offering more Canadian programming, and this programming is responsible for a more than proportionate level of viewing. As Table 4 reveals, the overall viewing/availability ratio for Canadian programming is 1.05 for CBC compared with 0.82 for CTV and 0.64 for Global. CBC's ratio is particularly impressive relative to CTV and Global for news (1.80 compared with 1.64 and .79 respectively), current affairs (1.60 compared with 0.89 and 1.00 respectively), and drama (0.67 compared with 0.43 and 0.20 respectively). It should also be noted these are program categories where CBC exhibits more programming than CTV or Global. The dearth of Canadian drama exhibited by private English-language broadcasters is not surprising. In their 1991 submission to the CRTC, CTV reported that while a typical hour of Canadian drama costs the broadcaster $112 500, it attracts net revenue of only $69 600 (Ellis, 1991,140). Documentaries are not explicitly identified in Table 4. Data for 1984 indicate that CBC was the only network exhibiting Canadian documentaries (in addition to regular current affairs series).[2]

Rationale for a Public Broadcaster

Many reasons for subsidy support for Canadian culture have been put forward.[3] Here we will examine the arguments put forward by the Peacock Committee Report (1986) in the U.K., and present our own views.

One argument put forward by the Peacock Committee (1986, 133) is that "so long as the number of television channels is limited, and there is no direct consumer payment, collective provision and regulation of programmes does provide a better simulation of a market designed to reflect consumer preferences than a policy of laissez-faire." This is based on the Steiner (1952) spatial competition prediction that an oligopoly of private,

TABLE 4

Canadian Programs: Availability[a] compared to Viewing[b] by Program Type and Network (6 a.m.–midnight), 1988–89

	News	Current Affairs	Sports	Drama	Variety	Other	Canadian Total
CTV[c]							
Availability	14%	9%	1%	7%	18%	2%	51%
Viewing	23%	8%	5%	3%	3%	1%	42%
V/A Ratio	1.64	.89	5.00	.43	.17	.50	.82
CBC[d]							
Availability	10%	10%	4%	9%	29%	2%	64%
Viewing	18%	16%	16%	6%	7%	4%	67%
V/A Ratio	1.80	1.60	4.00	.67	.26	2.00	1.05
Global[e]							
Availability	19%	1%	1%	5%	21%	5%	52%
Viewing	15%	1%	8%	1%	7%	1%	33%
V/A Ratio	.79	1.00	8.00	.20	.33	.20	.64

[a] Availability based on 14-week sample.
[b] Viewing data from CBC Research (A.C. Nielsen).
[c] CTV data based on CFTO TV (total program hours = 250).
[d] CBC data based on CBLT TV (total program hours = 221).
[e] Global total program hours = 253

Source: Adapted from D. Ellis and Gerald Grant Associates, *Networking*, a report prepared for the Friends of Canadian Broadcasting (October 1991), Table 7, p. 63.

advertising-financed broadcasters will offer few distinctive program options (as each gets a larger audience from showing similar light entertainment, and sharing that vast audience, than from gaining all the audience for a minority interest program). This question has been addressed in the Canadian context by Hoskins and McFadyen (1982, 1984) and Boardman and Vining (1984). The argument is becoming less persuasive as viewer choices increase. Pay-per-view TV, which most directly permits matching programs to consumer preferences, is already available.

The Peacock Committee also argues that even those who believe viewers and listeners are in the last analysis the best judges of their own interest will support public subsidization of programs concerned with knowledge, culture, criticism, and experiment, because:

> (i) Some people may come to enjoy what they do not do already as a result of new opportunities being presented.
>
> (ii) Some people will accept guidance or stimulus from others on matters where they perceive that their knowledge or taste is limited.
>
> (iii) Many people would like high quality material to be available even though they would not willingly watch or listen to it themselves in large enough numbers for it to be paid for directly. (1986, 127–28)

With respect to the first argument, while it is undoubtedly true that devoting time to viewing some types of programs, for example classical music, leads to increased knowledge and appreciation of further programs, it is not apparent in the Canadian broadcasting environment of multiple program choices that many people will partake of such opportunities. The second point assumes individuals lack the information to enable them to make rational decisions consistent with their preferences. It has paternalistic, "merit good" overtones and effectively amounts to giving the national public broadcaster licence to impose the broadcaster's own perception of correct taste. The final point is a variant of the "option demand" argument where the availability of certain kinds of programs gives the individual satisfaction irrespective of whether the individual chooses to view. There may be some validity to this, for example, a person may pledge to TV Ontario although he or she rarely watches.

We believe that a more convincing argument, strangely one not suggested by the Peacock Committee, is that there are benefits to society as a whole (as opposed to direct benefits to the viewer herself/himself) resulting from citizens being exposed to (some types of) indigenous programming. If this is the case, then there is market failure in this area because program producers and exhibitors, whether advertising financed or pay channels, do not receive revenue for the provision of such consumption-external benefits. Hence, the private sector, in the absence of a subsidy, will produce less than an optimal quantity of such programming.

It would seem that some types of programs are more likely to provide external benefits than others. Current affairs, documentary, and news programming are likely to promote a population more informed on Canadian events and issues, and a Canadian perspective on foreign affairs. Drama programming may provide external benefits in the form of an increased sense of Canadian identity or awareness of Canadian themes and values. The externality argument for Canadian television drama is essentially that made by André Guérin (president of Quebec's Régie du Cinéma et de la Vidéo), in the context of feature films: "A given population should from time to time be able to see itself on the screen. That just seems fundamental and not even for nationalistic reasons but because of questions of identity. Having constantly to deal with foreign models, you end up rather deeply damaged by the never-ending exposure to foreign dramatic situations."[4] If this premise is accepted, it should obviously be of concern that Canadians watch, in prime time, fifteen times more U.S. television drama than Canadian (Ellis, 1991, 31). Obviously, consumption externalities accrue from programming that is distinctively Canadian (defined in terms of output rather than input). This rationale seems consistent with the CBC's mandate to "contribute to (a) shared national consciousness and identity" (The Broadcasting Act, 1991). However, like Collins (1991), we are dubious of some of the nation-building claims made for television programming, particularly drama. The CBC's contention that "there can be no political sovereignty without cultural sovereignty" (1985:9) is disputed by Collins who argues that, to the contrary, "Canada better represents a weak rather than a strong connection between television consumption and political identity and citizenship" (1991, 234).

Even if the market failure argument is accepted, a government subsidy is justified only to the extent that the external benefit generated by viewing of the marginal program induced is greater than the subsidy necessary to induce it. The problem is that no one has managed to measure the external benefit. Thus, no rigorous cost-benefit analysis has been done, and everyone resorts to their gut feelings on the issue (of course, in the case of the cultural community, gut feelings may on occasion be influenced by pecuniary interests). Also relevant is the fact that Telefilm Canada, through its investment in independent television productions, already provides a subsidy to some types of television programs including drama and documentaries (see Hoskins and McFadyen, 1986).

In a broader cultural context, Globerman (1983, 61) concludes, "it would appear that the burden of proof for cultural intervention rests with the cultural nationalists." However, given the long history of public support for the CBC, if history matters it may be appropriate to reverse the burden of proof in this instance. In any case the implications for the role and the size of the CBC merit further examination.

WHAT MANDATE FOR THE CBC?

If one accepts the market failure argument previously discussed, the CBC's primary mandate should be the provision of distinctive (culture-specific) information, drama, children's, and variety programming. In addition, modest support of programming appealing to a small number of viewers can be justified by option demand and diversity arguments. In an increasingly multichanneled environment, the current mandate to provide "a wide range of programming that informs, enlightens and entertains" (The Broadcasting Act, 1991) is too broad.

CBC programming should be "distinctive" rather than duplicate programming that is plentifully supplied by the private sector. The provision of U.S. light entertainment by the CBC used to be rationalized on the basis that the CBC signal was the only one received in remote areas, and viewers in these areas should not be deprived of such programming. With CANCOM serving remote areas, this argument is no longer valid.

The case of sports is similar. There is a substantial amount of sports programming offered by the private sector, and CBC's withdrawal from this field would result in most of the events currently covered being picked up by a commercial network or The Sports Network. One effect of CBC's competition is to raise the price paid for coverage of events like the Olympic Games. This no doubt was a consideration in CTV's decision to commission and publicize a report (CTV, 1994) that claims CBC loses money on its sports coverage. Irrespective of whether it makes or loses money, coverage of sports is inconsistent with provision of distinctive programming.

An important issue is whether the national public broadcaster should provide local and regional programming. The local programming provided is mainly news/sports/weather. In most markets, this is an area already well served by private television broadcasters. Even without CBC offering this service, Canadians would enjoy considerably better local television coverage than is common in Europe. CBC's own *Annual Media Surveys* reveal that a majority of viewers consider CTV to be more locally oriented than CBC (see Ellis, 1991, 162), while there is evidence that the private sector provides such programming more efficiently (Liebowitz, 1985).[5] In addition, there are non-television substitutes for local/regional news/sports/weather programming that often include CBC radio, private radio, and newspapers. We conclude that local/regional programming for a local/regional audience should not be included in the CBC's mandate. However, the CBC must continue to exhibit news and current affairs of national significance from all parts of Canada. Drama production should also include regional representation for a national audience.

In programming, quantity often mitigates against quality. There is no need for CBC to continue to broadcast about nineteen hours per day. Something like seven hours (6 P.M. to midnight, with one day-time hour aimed at younger children) would be more appropriate for our vision of a scaled-down, distinctive CBC. The channel could be made available to another service for the remainder of the day.

For several years, CBC programming and scheduling had been growing more distinctive and complementary to the private sector. U.S. light entertainment had shrunk, CBC moved away from competing directly in local news, and the program schedule was revamped in 1992–93 to show "Prime Time News" at 9 P.M., preceded by two hours of family and general audience programs and succeeded by two hours of specialized and adult programs (such as the "Cinema Canada" anthology). However, there have been some disturbing reversals in the 1994–95 schedule. "Prime Time News" is back to 10 P.M., and regional news has returned to 11 P.M. Meanwhile, expenditures on sports programming by the English-language network are considerably greater than on news and current affairs (Skene, 1993, 162), and are increasing; the 1994–95 schedule marks the introduction of "double headers" to "Hockey Night In Canada."

Alternative Structures for the CBC

Program Production versus Purchase

Whether the CBC should produce programming in house or buy it from Canadian independent producers is an important issue. CBC has developed a reputation for news and current affairs and continued in-house production appears justified. However, local or regional production centres (stations) are unnecessary as CBC could employ bureaux throughout the country. Use of ENG (light cameras recording on tape in electronic news gathering), and up-linking to a satellite to send back video reports, make satellite news gathering (SNG) of regional and local stories of national significance straightforward, without the need for a substantial local station infrastructure.

Channel 4 in the UK, which buys all its programming externally, has achieved widespread critical acclaim. Except for news/current affairs and sport, the CBC already procures approximately half of its programming from independent producers. We recommend all such programming should be purchased from independents. Such a policy would provide additional stimulus to the development of a competitive independent production industry and, we suspect, lead to lower production costs. Regional goals would be more achievable as there could be a policy to spread purchases geographically.

The Relationship between English-Language and French-Language Services

The single policy that would do the most to "contribute to (a) shared national consciousness and identity" (The Broadcasting Act, 1991), and provide externalities on this basis, would be to encourage more co-operation between CBC's English-language and French-language network services. The exchange of programs should be actively pursued and some programs should be jointly produced or procured. Such a policy would require voice-over translation or subtitling of informational programs and double-shooting, dubbing, or subtitling for drama (which might also have the benefit of increasing second-language export possibilities). With the increase in the number of television sets able to receive secondary audio signals, having two soundtracks for programs becomes a possibility. Despite the cost, this should result in net savings because it permits the same program to be shown on both networks. The CBC appears to be moving in this direction. There was the "The Journal"/"Le Point" joint debate on Meech Lake in 1990, while "Emilie", a dubbed version of "Les Filles de Caleb," appeared on the English-language network in Fall 1992, and a dubbed version of "Avonlea" has appeared on the French-language network.

An objection to increased program exchange might be the anticipated effect on overall audience size. Some loss of audience would be more than compensated for if such a policy helped break down the barriers separating the two solitudes. Even the objectivity of news and informational programming might improve if reporters realized they were not catering to one linguistic group.[6]

Signal Delivery Options [7]

With no local/regional production, the broadcasting facilities of CBC's owned-and-operated stations could be sold. Even if not used for broadcasting purposes, the real estate would in many cases be of substantial value, and CBC operating costs would fall. Maximizing sale proceeds in some markets would entail sale as a going concern, complete with broadcasting licence and transmitter.

Elimination of the CBC's existing terrestrial distribution system for its mainline television services would greatly reduce the cost of signal transmission. Cable delivery would be costless to the CBC. Statistics Canada data indicates that in May 1993 about 9.8 million of the 10.3 million households in Canada were in areas wired by cable. About 7.7 million households actually subscribed. Some of the 2.1 million who choose not to subscribe would no doubt change their mind if CBC was not available off air. However, to reach these people, we advocate that the CRTC require cable companies to carry a free first tier comprised only of the CBC mainline network signals. In areas not served by cable, CANCOM's current low-powered direct-to-home satellite service, which includes CBC, has 31 000 subscribers, although it is estimated there are some 300 000 to 500 000 large dishes in existence. To reach households in noncabled areas, we advocate CBC phase in high-power DBS satellite transmission that can be received on a 60-cm dish. John Godfrey, Chairman of the Standing Committee on Canadian Heritage, states that "it is technically possible, and may even be commercially desirable" to give any noncabled area household that wishes a free dish and black box programmed to receive CBC only.[8] The benefits-costs of this are worth examining. In the not too distant future, the telecoms may provide an attractive delivery option. Termination of off-air delivery would entail phasing out CBC affiliation agreements, and some compensation might be necessary.

Alternative Methods of Financing the CBC

The CBC has traditionally obtained 80 percent or more of its operating income from the parliamentary operating appropriation, and 20 percent or less from advertising; however, as we saw earlier, from the mid-1980s this has changed, with advertising increasing (although being sensitive to the state of the economy) and the parliamentary operating appropriation falling. Both of these sources of finance have their drawbacks.

A difficulty with an annual parliamentary appropriation is the uncertainty caused by its short-term nature and the problem this causes for long-term planning in an industry where the product, the program, can have a gestation period of several years. Related to this is the vulnerability of such funding to political pressures. In the words of the Peacock Committee (1986, 138), in the context of a television licence fee rather than a parliamentary appropriation, "it would indeed be astonishing if he who paid the piper did not occasionally hint at the tune; and it would be equally astonishing if the piper did not occasionally anticipate his paymaster's call." The Caplan/Sauvageau Task

Force on Broadcasting Policy, (1986, 138) recommended that the CBC receive a five-year parliamentary appropriation, while the Peacock Committee (1986, 138) recommended that the BBC licence fee be indexed to inflation although "the Government would be able to propose suspending the licence fee in an economic emergency."

An annual licence fee paid by viewers, usually a given amount per television set owned, is sometimes supported over a parliamentary appropriation on the grounds that it is an independent source of income; however, as it is the government that enforces the licence fee and determines the level permitted, we are not persuaded that there are significant advantages in this respect. In addition, a licence fee is more costly to administer and collect and less progressive as a form of tax.

With respect to the effect of advertising on the CBC, the Task Force on Broadcasting Policy (Caplan/Sauvageau, 1986, 312) concluded that it "militates against its being distinctive in a sea of look-alike commercial networks." Acheson and Maule (1990, 290) expressed similar concerns. Advertising was removed from CBC radio networks in 1975, and it may be no coincidence that CBC network radio seems to have established a distinctive and widely valued role. During a period of cutbacks in the parliamentary appropriation, the CBC has aggressively sought advertising revenue and it strains credulity to believe that commercial considerations do not have a profound effect on programming decisions. An example is provided by the blanket CBC coverage of the NHL play-off games with consequent frequent and unpredictable rescheduling of "The National" and "The Journal" and their successor "Prime Time News." Indeed this situation sparked a debate within the CBC with Mark Starowicz, executive producer of "The Journal," openly upset. Advertising should be eliminated on CBC. Distinctive programming is unlikely to be forthcoming if CBC continues to be subject to commercial pressures.

It is reported that the Canadian Heritage Department is weighing various new sources of funding for the CBC and Canadian programming (Bronskill, 1994). These include taxes on cable subscriptions, movie tickets, videocassette rentals, radios, TV sets, and satellite dishes. A CBC shutdown of local production with sale of studio facilities and some transmitters would permit another way of generating funds from within the broadcasting system; the receipts from such sales could be placed within a CBC endowment fund. However, while generating funds for the CBC within the broadcasting system has appeal, there are drawbacks: for example, a cable levy is regressive and an endowment fund involves earmarking, and, hence, inflexibility in the use of government revenues.

Weighing the alternatives, a parliamentary appropriation appears the most satisfactory method of financing CBC. To eliminate the annual uncertainty with respect to its level, and the ensuing difficulties this causes for long-term planning, the level of appropriation should be determined every three years with inflationary adjustments within this period. A Peacock Committee-type clause allowing reconsideration in the event of an "economic emergency" should be included.

Conclusion

We recommend that the CBC restrict its primary television operations to commercial-free national network schedules, concentrated in prime time. The CBC would provide a superior service (in terms of distinctive programming consistent with the externalities rationale for having a national public broadcaster) at a lower operating cost. Capital savings would come from the sale of the owned-and-operated stations and transmitters.

With respect to programming, we recommend that CBC no longer exhibit local programming for a local audience, foreign programming, and sports. Except for news and current affairs, programs should be bought from independent producers with purchases spread geographically. Program exchanges between the English-language and French-language networks should be increased.

In an era of technological change, alternative delivery possibilities should be regularly assessed to determine the most cost-effective method or mix consistent with near universal coverage.

POSTSCRIPT [9]

Restructuring the CBC has become a top priority following the Budget of February 27, 1995. The Budget announced that there would be a fundamental review of the CBC's mandate and that the CBC's parliamentary appropriation for 1995–96 would be reduced by $44 million. Furthermore, Mr. Manera, who subsequently announced his resignation as CBC President, was led to believe there would be similar cuts the following two years. When added to previously announced cuts, this would amount to elimination of $350 million and reduce the parliamentary appropriations to $839 million by 1998–99.

In another study (Hoskins and McFadyen, 1995), we have attempted to quantify the extent of the cost savings that would likely occur from the restructuring of the CBC proposed here. Our estimates of the cost savings are:

Quantified Annual Cost Savings:

- Elimination of regional /local production for a regional/local audience: $127 million
- Buying all programming, except for news/current affairs, from independent producers: $72 million
- Economies from program exchange and co-production between CBC networks: $3 million
- Eliminating sports programming: $74 million
- Eliminating foreign programming: $76 million
- Savings from additional reductions in broadcasting hours: $108 million
- Annual cost saving on capital items from privatizing CBC owned-and-operated stations: $64 million
- Elimination of operating expenses associated with over-the-air transmission: $100 million

- Less net advertising revenue forgone: ($270 million)

TOTAL Annual Cost Savings are $354 million. One-time proceeds from privatizing CBC- owned and-operated stations: $500 million.

NONQUANTIFIED ITEMS IMPACTING ANNUAL COST SAVINGS:

- Items that will add to cost savings: reduction in Toronto and Montreal production centres and head office operating expenses; lease or sale of surplus capacity at Toronto and Montreal production centres and perhaps head offices; savings in transponder costs from reduced broadcasting schedule.
- Items that will subtract from cost savings: establishing and operating regional news bureaux; DBS signal distribution and any other costs incurred extending coverage; any compensation necessary for ending affiliation agreements.
- Net effect of nonquantified items: obviously uncertain, but we consider it likely these items will result in a net addition to cost savings.

The annual cost savings associated with the restructuring we are proposing would thus permit CBC to operate a quality enhanced service at a level of subsidy reduced by $350 million. The $500 million or so from sale of CBC owned-and-operated stations and transmitters could be applied to deficit reduction.

NOTES

1. We made a request, under the Access to Information Act, to obtain a document containing economic and financial information and analysis submitted by CBC in support of a CBC television network licence-renewal application; our request was denied.
2. In 1984, the CBC English-language network exhibited 73 hours of Canadian documentaries (excluding regular current-affairs series); the CBC French-language network exhibited 22.5 hours; Global 3 hours; and CTV and TVA zero hours (Task Force on Broadcasting Policy, 1986, 118–19).
3. For an excellent review and critical assessment see Globerman (1983).
4. From an interview by M. Dorland in *Cinema Canada*, March, 1985, pp. 6–10. As quoted by Collins (1990, 250).
5. Using admittedly somewhat dated 1978 data, Liebowitz found the average CBC-owned station in that year lost $1.4 million while affiliates made profits of $1.1 million. Costs for CBC-owned stations were 233 percent higher than for the affiliates.
6. Would the great difference in prominence and tone of coverage that the two CBC network services gave to the 1990 Quebec flag-stomping incident in Ontario have occurred if the reporters had known that their stories would also be carried on the "other" network?
7. This section is drawn from Hoskins and McFadyen (1995).

8. Minutes of Proceedings and Evidence of the Standing Committee on Canadian Heritage, November 17, 1994, p.24.
9. This section is drawn from Hoskins and McFadyen (1995). See this paper for details on the bases used for the estimates and for the data sources employed.

References

Acheson, K., and C. Maule. (1990). "Canadian Content Rules: A Time for Reconsideration." *Canadian Public Policy* 16, 3:284–97.

Anderson, C.L. (1992). "Canadian Content Laws and Programming Diversity." *Canadian Public Policy* 18, 2:166–75.

Boardman, A., and A. Vining. (1984). "Canadian and British TV Markets: Why the CBC Should Not Be Like the BBC." *Canadian Public Policy* 10, 3:347–52.

Bronskill, J. (1994). "CBC May Raid Canadian Wallets for Extra Cash." *Edmonton Journal*, July 28, p. A3.

Burgelman, J.C. (1986). "The Future of Public Service Broadcasting: A Case Study for a 'New' Communications Policy." *European Journal of Communication* 1:123–201.

Canada, Department of Communications. (1988). *Canadian Voices: Canadian Choices.*

Canadian Broadcasting Corporation. (1985). *Let's Do It! A Vision of Canadian Broadcasting.*

Collins, R. (1990). *Culture, Communication and National Identity.* Toronto: University of Toronto Press.

———. (1991), "National Culture: A Contradiction in Terms?" *Canadian Journal of Communication* 16, 2:225–38.

CTV. (1994). *A Perspective on the CBC.* Report prepared for the CTV.

Ellis, D., in collaboration with Gerald Grant Associates (1991, October). *Networking.* A report prepared for the Friends of Canadian Broadcasting.

Girard J., and J.R. Peters. (1991). *The Economic Status of Canadian Television: Report of the Task Force.* Ottawa: Minister of Supply and Services.

Globerman, S. (1983). *Cultural Regulation in Canada.* Montreal: Institute for Research on Public Policy.

Groves, J. (1991). "Federal Expenditures on Public Broadcasting in Canada." *Canadian Tax Journal*: 457–73.

Hoskins C., and S. McFadyen. (1982). "Market Structure and Television Programming Performance in Canada and the UK: A Comparative Study." *Canadian Public Policy* 3:347–57.

———. (1984). "The Role of the CBC in the Canadian Broadcasting System: Revisited." *Canadian Public Policy* 10, 3:352–58.

———. (1986). "The Canadian Broadcast Program Development Fund: An Evaluation and Some Recommendations." *Canadian Public Policy* 12, 1:352–58.

———. "Cost Saving through Restructuring the CBC." March, Winning entry, federal government strand, in the 1995 Fraser Institute Economy in Government Competition.

Liebowitz, S.J. (1985). *On The Canadian Broadcasting Corporation's Costs of Operations.* Vancouver: Fraser Institute.

Nunes, J. (1990). "News Producers Cry Foul as Hockey 'Takes Over' Prime-Time." *The Globe and Mail*, April 14, p. C3.

Partridge, J. (1992). "Ottawa Freezes Funding for New TV Series." *The Globe and Mail*, December 10, B2.

Peacock Committee. (1986). *Report of the Committee on Financing the BBC.* London: HMSO.

Standing Committee on Communications and Culture. (1988). Report. *A Broadcasting Policy for Canada*. Ottawa: House of Commons.

————. (1992). Report. *Culture and Communications: The Ties that Bind*. Ottawa: House of Commons.

Skene, W. (1993). *Fade to Black: A Requiem For The CBC*. Vancouver: Douglas & McIntyre.

Statistics Canada. (1987). *Canadian Economic Observer*. Historical Statistical Supplement, Catalogue No. 11-210.

————. (1990a) *Canadian Economic Observer*. April, Catalogue No. 11-010.

————. (1990b). *National Income and Expenditure Accounts*, August, Catalogue No. 13-001.

————. (1993). *National Income and Expenditure Accounts*, Catalogue No. 13-001, Third Quarter.

————. (1994). *Canadian Economic Observer*. January, Catalogue No. 11-010.

Steiner, P. (1952). "Program Patterns and Preferences and the Workability of Competition in Radio Broadcasting." *Quarterly Journal of Economics* (May): 194–223.

Task Force on Broadcasting Policy (Caplan/Savageau). (1986). *Report*. Ottawa: Minister of Supply and Services.

PRIVATE TELEVISION: THE VILLAIN OF THE PIECE SEEN IN A NEW LIGHT

Peter Desbarats

Since the beginning of Canadian television in the 1950s, competition between public and private television[1] systems has been portrayed as a medieval morality play with private television cast as the villain. In recent years, however, the history of private broadcasting in Canada has been revised to provide a more complex picture of the relationship between the two systems. At the same time, after years of awkward and disappointing attempts to "Canadianize" the industry by regulation, technological and market developments are forcing private television to play a larger role as a producer and distributor of Canadian programs. This seems destined to continue, supported by public subsidies for independent television production.

Coincidentally, an international trend to increase the role of private broadcasters in countries previously dominated by public radio and television systems, reflected in Canada by reductions in funding and activities of the Canadian Broadcasting Corporation (CBC), has further blurred old black-and-white distinctions between public and private television systems.

By the mid-1990s, an explosion of new information technologies was shaking the foundations of broadcast industry regulation. The curtain was coming down rapidly on the old morality play, before it had properly concluded, while in the "virtual theatre" of the new digital media, old and new players were jostling for position.[2]

The Traditional Villain of the Piece

Private television in Canada was less than a decade old when the Special Senate Committee on Mass Media began its inquiry and set the tone for public discussion of the industry's shortcomings. The Committee decided that private television broadcasters collectively had achieved a level of performance "perhaps best described as neanderthal" (Special Senate Committee, 1970, 240).

Formulating a critique that would be repeated over and over again in the decades ahead, the Committee stated in its report that "the vast majority of private broadcasters have done the minimum required of them by law, and no more...They have been content to let the networks fill the prime-time hours with imported programmes; they have been happy to take whatever the networks would supply free; they have filled the rest of their hours with as much syndicated material as possible, producing themselves as little as possible." This lacklustre performance had been exhibited even by "immensely profitable" private television stations. In sum, the Committee confessed that it could not find "any reason at all why some of the healthy profits of private broadcasting might not be turned into something more than the legal minimum of Canadian programmes" (Special Senate Committee, 1970, 206).

This critique, with minor variations, has remained the orthodox view of private television among most academics, journalists, and other critics of popular Canadian culture for the past 25 years. Robert Fulford, for example, showed how potentially vitriolic criticism of private television still was in 1987 when he thundered from the editor's chair at *Saturday Night* that "private TV simply doesn't do what TV is supposed to do. It never has, and long experience suggests that it never will" (Fulford, 1987, 6). Targeting the dominant group of Bassett-owned stations within the CTV network, Fulford claimed that they had never made "more than the most meagre and pitiful contribution to the entertainment business of which they are ostensibly a part....Their record, over a whole generation, amounts to the most appalling regulatory failure in modern Canadian history," he continued, "and calls into question not only the role of the federal regulators in broadcasting but the very idea of private television in Canada" (p. 5).

But Fulford's tirade, while illustrating the undimmed fury and frustration of private television's critics almost 25 years after the Special Senate Committee's report, also indicated an important shift of focus from broadcaster to regulator. By the end of the 1980s, the critics hardly seemed to know where to place primary responsibility for what they regarded as an unmitigated fiasco—whether to blame the private broadcasters for ignoring regulations enacted to improve their performance, or the federal regulatory authority, the Canadian Radio-television and Telecommunications Commission (CRTC), for failing to enforce its own regulations.

One of the most detailed criticisms of private television published in the past decade, Herschel Hardin's *Closed Circuits—The Sellout of Canadian Television*, was essentially an attack on the record of the CRTC. Hardin said that the federal regulators, "by handing out licences on the basis of certain promises and then backing off denying renewal when the promises were not fulfilled...created an Americanized broadcasting structure that was never intended and never envisaged in the legislation that the agencies were created to implement" (1985, 167).

Criticizing the regulatory agency, however, proved to be a more complex task than launching diatribes against the allegedly greedy capitalists who owned private television stations. Anyone could understand the proposition that profit had replaced public service as a corporate objective in the boardrooms of the private stations. Quoting the famous dictum of the 1965 Fowler Report that "the only thing that really matters in broadcasting is program content; all the rest is housekeeping," one analyst in 1987 insisted that "actually, the only thing that *really* matters in *private* broadcasting is the bottom line; all the rest is window dressing" (Mill, 1987, 2). It didn't require a Ph.D. to grasp this message, particularly if the criticism was accompanied by statistics, as it was in this case, showing that CTV's profit as a percentage of revenue in 1986 was 22.9 percent compared with a general industry average of less than 6 percent (Mill, 1987, 3).

Focussing on the regulator required more complex analysis and tended to produce a lower degree of invective. Compare the tone of the Special Senate Committee's Report, for instance, with the assessment sixteen years later by the Federal Task Force on Broadcasting Policy. While the Committee suggested that Canadian broadcasters should develop a "concept of broadcasting as something other than a form of strip-mining" (Special Senate Committee, 1970, 204), the Task Force in 1986 found "encouraging signs" in the industry's performance. "We believe it is fair to ask them to do more," it gently suggested, "and to do more in a continuing and systematic way" (Caplan-Sauvageau Task Force, 1986, 418). The change of tone was the result of a realization that remedying the shortcomings of private television would require more than Dickensian repentance by the Scrooges of the industry.

In the 1980s, critics of private television had to face the fact that several decades of regulatory pressure designed to increase private stations' Canadian programming had produced disappointingly little in the way of results. Why was this? The simplest and most common reason given was that private broadcasters, possessing a great deal of economic and political clout, had simply thumbed their collective nose at the CRTC and had been able to get away with it. While this was true to some extent, groups such as the Task Force, with the resources to do research in depth, discovered other and more substantial reasons for the apparent timidity of the CRTC. They had to do with such concrete factors as the size of the Canadian population, the lack of television production experience and resources in the Canadian private sector, and above all, the availability of relatively cheap American productions. Attempting to overcome these barriers to the creation of a truly Canadian private television production industry, or even trying to imagine how to do it, was a far tougher task than fulminating against the owners of television stations.

The traditional criticism of private television had been based on the assumption that a few million dollars, taken from the pockets of the owners and given to Canadian television producers, would solve the problem. No one ever demonstrated that this was true. On the contrary, the experience of the late Al Bruner, who drove Ontario's Global TV into bankruptcy in its first season in 1973–74 on a rich diet of new and imaginative Canadian programming, seemed to indicate that many complex factors were involved in the "failure" of private television.[3]

There was no doubt that profits at some private stations were grotesquely out of proportion when compared with the economy-model local television shows produced by these same stations. But there was also no guarantee that simply throwing the owners' money at the problem would resolve it.

Coercion to spend more on Canadian production was the principle behind content regulations enacted and re-enacted over the years by the CRTC. No matter how the formulas were juggled to force private broadcasters to air more Canadian productions, particularly during prime evening time, the results were always disappointing.

Licensing new stations to provide more competition and more outlets for Canadian programming proved to be even more unproductive. Experience showed that the new

Canadian-owned stations became additional conduits for U.S. programming; as the number of Canadian stations in a community increased, so did viewing levels of American programming (Starowicz, 1989). The new private stations were described by one observer on the public broadcasting side, Mark Starowicz, executive producer of CBC's "The Journal," as "pocket video slums, unable to climb out of an economic niche equivalent to a small U.S. station surviving on syndicated re-runs." Their biggest problem, as Starowicz defined it, was not a lack of entrepreneurial leadership or excessive greed but the fact that they "did not generate enough critical mass to allow investment in quality drama" and other types of Canadian production (Starowicz, 1989). Their inability to act as channels of Canadian culture was related to the size of the market and the structure of the industry, complicated by the proximity, across the Canadian border, of the world's most productive television entertainment industry.

The experience of the owners of Quebec's francophone private television stations provided additional evidence that their counterparts in English-speaking Canada might have behaved differently under other conditions. In the 1984–85 season, for instance, English-language broadcasters, both public and private, spent 21 percent of their programming budgets on foreign programs, while French-language broadcasters spent only 6 percent on such (Caplan-Sauvageau Task Force, 1986, 429). Francophone broadcasters, located in a strong market for domestic product and deprived of ready access to suitable foreign programming, traditionally have spent relatively heavily on Canadian production. Although their motive was primarily commercial, it contributed to the cultural development of their own community. The same commercial motive produced different results in English-speaking Canada, where private broadcasters in 1984–85 paid $133 million for imported television shows that cost up to $5 billion to produce in the United States and that were eagerly watched by Canadian viewers. "It is not surprising that private broadcasters find this an attractive proposition," noted the 1986 Task Force, "particularly when these shows come with the backing of extensive publicity and advertising that spill into the Canadian market" (Caplan-Sauvageau Task Force, 1986, 433).

Moving into the 1990s, the CanWest Global System of private television stations, the reconstituted successor to Al Bruner's Global TV, indicated a new pattern of development by remaining a loose alliance of stations rather than a traditional network, becoming the most profitable television broadcasting entity in Canada and using these resources to expand into international program production and foreign ownership. One commentator speculated that Global's success "might set a trend for Canadian broadcasters in a global, post-network, deregulated environment."[4]

History Revisited and Revised

Other factors in the 1980s contributed to a blurring of the distinctions between private and public television broadcasters that had given such zest to the old morality play. As state ownership of various types of enterprises fell into disfavour, first in the United States and Western Europe and then with a cataclysmic rush in the Soviet bloc, public broadcasters found themselves working against the current of public opinion and political fashion. In Western Europe, one country after another "Canadianized" its broadcasting system by eliminating state monopolies and permitting competition by commercial broadcasters; this orderly process became, in the Soviet bloc, a confused dismantling of previously dominant and protected state publishing and broadcasting enterprises and their replacement by almost unregulated private-sector activity, at least in the short term.

In Canada, public broadcasting had to contend not only with this hostile international tendency but with the beginnings of a revisionist school of broadcasting history that threatened its philosophical underpinnings.

Until very recently, histories of Canadian broadcasting have usually been produced by authors closely connected to and in sympathy with the Canadian Broadcasting Corporation.[5] These histories tended to downplay the importance of private broadcasting, particularly in the critical early years of radio; they typically portrayed the beginnings of public broadcasting in Canada as a kind of virgin birth inspired by the purest national cultural motives. In the 1980s, more extensive research by historians with different backgrounds and approaches to the subject began to produce a more complicated version of the nativity of the CBC.

At the University of Western Ontario, Dr. Michael Nolan, an historian with experience as a journalist in private broadcasting, produced in 1986 a biography of Alan Plaunt, a major figure in the development of Canadian radio, that contained the outline of a revisionist history of Canadian broadcasting. It called for "a clearer understanding...of the cultural myth surrounding the broadcasting industry and a fuller grasp of the commendable role played by the private sector, especially in the early days."[6]

In this and other writings, Professor Nolan began the task of rescuing from official neglect the accomplishments of private radio broadcasters in Canada during the industry's initial years. He demonstrated, for instance, that the support by many Canadian newspapers of a highly effective lobby in the 1920s to promote public broadcasting was based in large part on the newspapers' fear that commercial radio would develop into a significant competitor for advertising. For the newspapers, arguments in favour of cultural nationalism were convenient instruments of commercial advantage

"That private broadcasters operated stations with a crude radio technology...during this pioneer period to provide programs that had sizable Canadian audiences is an historical development that officialdom today sometimes seems reluctant to acknowledge." wrote Professor Nolan in 1984. "These stations were in existence a full fourteen years before the formulation of a comprehensive federal policy which had, at its core, the notion that radio should serve as an electronic instrument for cultural uplift" (Nolan, 1984, 34).

Revisionist history was reinforced by more careful study of the cultural effects of television on Canadians' sense of national identity, particularly in English-speaking Canada. (In Quebec, of course, television has long been credited as being instrumental in promoting the social, religious, and political changes that contributed to the "Quiet Revolution" of the 1960s.) Private television traditionally had been criticized for carrying imported programs that would "Americanize" Canada; one of the main arguments for public television was that it would prevent this cultural subversion. But by the end of the 1980s, after three decades of private television, cultural activity in English-speaking Canada showed no sign of withering away. On the contrary, according to

Canada's foremost media historian, the Canadian experience showed that fear of television as "the instrument of assault on particular cultures...can easily be exaggerated by anxious nationalists" (Rutherford, 1990, 491).

In his 1990 history of the first fifteen years of Canadian television, Paul Rutherford concluded that "the fears of...the highbrows back in the early 1950s, that the Americanization of the airwaves would somehow undo Canada, weren't realized.

"True enough, the accessibility plus the popularity of Hollywood entertainment made virtually impossible the survival of an indigenous and vigorous PopCult in English Canada," he wrote. "But this so-called colonization of the imagination didn't prevent the flowering of the arts and letters that has been so notable a feature on the cultural landscape of English Canada over the past three decades" (1990, 50).

The Rocky Road to Damascus for Private Television

One can argue that the morality-play approach to private television served Canada reasonably well in the first few decades of the industry. It provided a philosophical basis for maintaining a strong public television system and for closely regulating its private competitors, even if rules setting quotas for Canadian content didn't always achieve the desired results. During the 1980s, however, as the historical and nationalist themes of the morality play came into question, technological and commercial developments forced private television into new patterns of behaviour.

In the early decades of Canadian television, public and private broadcasters operated in markets with limited numbers of competitors. Most communities were served by only two Canadian stations, the CBC and a private broadcaster, with the CBC providing only restricted competition for advertisers. In many markets, the demand for television advertising surpassed the available supply. Under these conditions, the temptation to "strip mine" the territory was overwhelming.

Even competition from U.S. stations, unregulated in the days when Canadian viewers near the border used antennas to pick up American channels, came under CRTC control as cable systems brought both Canadian and U.S. channels to more and more homes. Legislation introduced in the mid-1970s required cable systems to replace a foreign signal with a local one if the same program was being shown simultaneously, thus protecting the audience and the advertising revenue of local broadcasters. At the same time, Bill C-58 used tax regulations to discourage Canadian companies from advertising on U.S. stations close to the border. This uncomfortable market provided Canadian stations with little incentive to invest in Canadian programming apart from news, current affairs, and sports, which had always attracted large Canadian audiences. In those areas, there was vigorous competition between public and private Canadian stations, and standards of production were high. In the entertainment programming that makes up most of the television schedule, American programs continued to dominate the Canadian market. Even the publicly owned Canadian Broadcasting Corporation competed with private stations for the rights to popular U.S. shows.

In the past decade, Canadian broadcasters have felt the cold winds of competition blowing through this cosy world. The licensing of new private Canadian stations and specialty channels has fragmented a television audience already diminishing because of growing numbers of VCRs in homes and changing lifestyles.

These developments have not been exclusive to Canada. In the 1980s, network audiences in the United States started to shrink for the first time in the history of the industry. "The really serious thing is the loss of one or two percent of the audience every year," according to Bill Munro, editor of the *Washington Journalism Review* and a former producer for NBC News. "And there is no horizon for that stopping" (TV Network, 1988).

The fragmentation of the television audience and its movement away from conventional television programming toward other types of on-screen entertainment—or, in some cases, abandoning the couch-potato lifestyle entirely for more active pursuits—has forced all broadcasters to review and revise programming.

On the public side, CBC television was influenced by the success that CBC radio had achieved in meeting competition from television in the 1960s and 1970s. Faced with the loss of its mass audience for sports, drama, and other types of entertainment programming, CBC radio had discovered a new sense of national mission by focussing on news and information programming. In the 1980s, CBC television followed this example by concentrating much of its dwindling resources on news and current affairs (Desbarats, 1990, 40–49).

Private broadcasters and the Canadian Radio-television and Telecommunications Commission, locked in a cosy embrace that threatened to turn into a dance of death under the new market conditions, were slower to respond. The CRTC continued to tinker with Canadian content rules by tying them to station profitability and more specific content requirements. This enabled the industry to focus on fewer productions of higher quality rather than trying to spread low-cost Canadian productions across the schedule. Starting in 1983, higher subsidies were provided to independent producers through the Broadcast Program Development Fund of Telefilm Canada, although about half of these private-sector productions ended up on the CBC rather than on private stations (Vipond, 1989, 156–57). After a private broadcaster, Andre Bureau, began a five-year appointment as chairman of the CRTC in 1983, the regulatory agency relaxed restrictions on cross-ownership (simultaneous ownership of properties in various media, both print and electronic) and on concentration of ownership in radio and television. "The nub of Mr. Bureau's big-is-dutiful approach," according to a 1989 report of the Consumers' Association of Canada, "was to encourage the development of enterprises financially strong enough to tackle the Canadianization of peak-hour drama and entertainment programming, then to impose more demanding Canadian programming requirements in their conditions of licence" (Creery, 1989). None of these changes, at the time, seemed to represent the breakthrough needed to reform private television, but collectively they now can be seen as the beginning of an important new phase.

The Light at the End of the Tunnel

It was significant that, by 1989, even organizations such as the Consumers' Association, long critical of concentrated media ownership, had come to the conclusion that regulation of private television had failed to produce the desired results and now threatened to become even less productive in a competitive world of proliferating video technologies.

"The licensing of supervised concentration in the electronic media is one of many ways in which Canada's paternalistic broadcasting regime is limiting freedom of expression and enterprise to the detriment of the public," the Association stated in the 1989 Creery report. "Consumers would benefit from a new policy to dismantle program control, leave competition and content questions to general laws, and retain only those controls needed to regulate technical matters and assure non-discriminatory service at reasonable rates from common carriers and monopolies."

Other students of the broadcasting system have tended to agree that the old structure of content restrictions is now often counterproductive and should continue to be replaced by incentives. A 1986 survey of research literature on the economics of Canadian broadcasting showed an apparent trend among experts toward the opinion that "attempts to force private broadcasters to act against their own self-interest can never be effective" (Hoskins and McFadyen, 1986, 36). However, "there is no evidence, even where protective measures are successful in boosting broadcasters' profits, that these additional profits lead to additional expenditures on Canadian programming." Larger subsidies for Canadian productions would appear to be a more effective method, particularly if the subsidies can be justified on cultural and economic grounds (Hoskins & McFadyen, 1986, 37). In her 1989 study of the mass media in Canada, Mary Vipond concluded that "better ways must be found to ensure that Canadian alternatives to the products of the U.S. media also exist. The banning of imported products is unacceptable, but stimulation of the creation of local works, by quotas or other devices, is quite legitimate" (Vipond, 1989, 183).

Worried by continuing declines in audience numbers and the prospect of reduced levels of profit in the decade that opened with the recession of 1990, private broadcasters also have been re-examining old assumptions. If North American television viewers are switching off because they find much of the American entertainment on the small screen boringly predictable and cluttered with commercials, that is particularly grim news for the private Canadian stations that have prospered for decades on imported U.S. programs. Once this programming base starts to erode, and if the CBC continues to dominate network television news and to compete strongly in local news markets, private Canadian television will experience decreases in profitability, ratings, and political clout. The only apparent alternative to this dismal prospect is more and better Canadian programming on private stations to provide viewers with a reason for watching Canadian rather than American television, or not watching television at all.[7]

This option is now more appealing than it was in the past because of the rising cost of imported American programming in a world of increasing competition for programming of any kind, in Canada and internationally, and because of higher prices paid overseas for quality Canadian television programs.

Private television already has started to move in this direction. By 1987, more than two-thirds of the programming budgets of private broadcasters was spent on Canadian programming (Canadian Association of Broadcasters, 1989, 2). In 1990, one of the first major decisions by CTV's new president, John Cassaday, was to upgrade the network's news and current affairs programming. In its strategic plan for the 1990s, the Canadian Association of Broadcasters (CAB) recognized that "government policy, the need to be both distinctive in the marketplace and locally relevant, and the rising cost of foreign programming, combine to exert increased pressure for high quality Canadian programming" (1989, 7). The first two points of the CAB's seven-point strategy for the new decade were:

1. Strengthen the Canadian character of the broadcasting system and strengthen the capacity of private broadcasting to play its foundation role in the system.
2. Develop an all-industry strategy to produce and exhibit Canadian programming that Canadians want to watch.

"Stations' programming to please governments and regulators, rather than their audiences, will be tuned out," predicted CAB President Michael McCabe. "In today's expanding 100-channel universe if we're not good, we're gone...In the 1990s more hours of Canadian content just won't mean that much" (McCabe, 1989, 19).

Morality Play Ends—Curtain Rises on the Virtual Nation

The 100-channel universe forecast by the CAB's Michael McCabe on the eve of the 1990s was rapidly coming into being by the middle of the decade. The driving force was digital technology, the encoding of all forms of communication—print, audio, and video—in computer language, coupled with advances in telecommunications and reduced prices for computer hardware and software. After several decades of costly trial-and-error experimentation, these factors were converging in the mid-1990s in patterns that threatened to reduce the importance of many forms of print media (books, magazines, and newspapers) and alter traditional radio and television beyond recognition.

The phrase "information highway" was often used in the mass media to attempt to describe these developments. It expressed the notion that radical changes in the means of delivering information to consumers were at the heart of this media revolution. Print, radio, and television media were seen to be converging on this "highway" and assuming new forms in ways that were difficult to predict.

To give a simple example, the impending shift of radio to digital technology will wipe out the distinction between FM and AM radio. The concept of radio frequencies will become meaningless in a digital world that can provide for an unlimited number of radio channels that can be delivered to consumers in a variety of ways—by satellite, by cable, or by telephone line, for example. No one in the radio industry really understands what this will mean even as the technology is being introduced.

Digital technology already is blurring the distinctions between the different players in the old morality play.

The one-time "hero," public broadcasting, is searching for a new role as new competitors emerge. In his annual report for 1992–93, then CBC President Gerard Veilleux forecast that "the existing problem of fragmented audiences for television services is likely to become more acute due to the introduction of new distribution technologies and possible changes in the manner and degree to which the evolving broadcasting industry is regulated."[8] He predicted that direct-to-home satellite services could provide 100 new channels to North American viewers. To prepare for this development, the CBC went into partnership with a Canadian conglomerate, Power Corporation of Montreal, publishers of the daily *La Presse*, and allied itself with a U.S. direct-to-home satellite service owned by General Motors.[9] This CBC-Power collaboration began providing a 24-hour news channel to its American partner from the new CBC headquarters in Toronto in the fall of 1994—a pay television channel received direct from satellite by a growing number of Americans but unavailable to Canadian viewers.

Private broadcasters, the "villains" of the old Canadian morality play, are also adopting new technologies and seeking new alliances. In the fall of 1994, the CTV network went into partnership with GEnie, an on-line information service owned by General Electric in the United States, to provide a print-on-screen news service to computer users in North America.[10]

Private and public broadcasters are also discovering that they no longer have the stage to themselves. Cable television companies want to produce programs and provide computer services to their subscribers. "We no longer just supply the pipe, what we do now defines the product," in the words of Ken Fowler, 1993 Chair of the Canadian Cable Television Association.[11]

Also hovering in the wings are the telephone companies with enormous resources and revenues that outstrip those of cable companies by five-to-one on a per-household basis—$5.9 billion annually compared with $1.1 billion for cable.[12] Bell Canada announced in the fall of 1994 that it would compete with cable companies through a subsidiary, MediaLinx, that would offer telephone subscribers the ability to "exchange video messages...browse through full-motion shopping catalogues, benefit from remote medical diagnosis, take part in distance education sessions and virtual courtrooms, and dial-up a movie for home viewing."[13]

As the stage becomes more crowded, regulation grows increasingly more problematic. CRTC Chair Keith Spicer has identified "consumer sovereignty" as a characteristic of the new era—"Canadians are demanding to see on the screen what they want, when they want, at the price they want"—without clarifying how the national objectives of the current system are going to be implemented in this electronic "marketplace" of the future.

In this explosion of technology, not only is the old morality play ending inconclusively but the theatre itself seems to be disappearing. In an emerging world of virtual corporations and virtual classrooms—businesses and universities that exist only as combinations of information producers and consumers along the information highway—media are becoming elements of a virtual theatre that ignores geographic boundaries. In this theatre of new media, old notions of regulation and cultural protection become absurd, audience and performers become indistinguishable, and perhaps the concept of virtual nation begins to emerge.

NOTES

1. There were 93 private television stations in Canada in 1989, according to the Canadian Association of Broadcasters' strategic plan of July 1989, *Taking the Lead—Private*

Broadcasting Strategies for the 90s. According to the same document, the industry employs more than 8000 people, attracts more than $1 billion annually in advertising, and pays more than $300 million a year in salaries.

2. In the 1990s, the number of stations remained constant but consolidation of ownership left six dominant players in the field, three operating in English, (WIC Western International Communications of Vancouver, CanWest Global Communications of Winnipeg, and Baton Broadcasting of Toronto; one in French, TeleMetropole of Montreal; and two in both languages, the CBC and CFCF Inc. of Montreal. "Canadian TV superpowers," *Marketing*, (November 14, 1994) p. 30. By the mid-1990s, the CBC had more than 9000 employees and spent about $1.4 billion annually operating four TV networks, four radio networks, an international radio service, two international satellite services, and 84 radio and TV stations (Knowlton Nash, *The Microphone Wars*, Toronto: McClelland and Stewart, 1994. p. 10).
3. The author was anchor and Ottawa Bureau Chief for Global TV from 1973 to 1980.
4. Paul Taylor, "Third Service, Third Network: The CanWest Global System," *Canadian Journal of Communication* 18 (1993): 469–77.
5. The most recent example being Nash, *The Microphone Wars*.
6. Professor Nolan's book *Foundation: Alan Plaunt and the Early Days of CBC Radio* was published in 1986 by CBC Enterprises.
7. The CRTC recently approved another proposal designed to lure more viewers from the programming of private television: a service called "Viewer's Choice," which permits cable subscribers to phone in orders to view films that they have selected from a menu provided by the new service.
8. CBC *Annual Report* 1992–93. p. 13.
9. John Ruttle and Ted Davis, "Delivery Dilemma," *Broadcaster* (June 1993): 5.
10. "CTV Steps Onto the Information Highway." *Broadcaster* (September 1994): 22.
11. "1993 CCTA Convention Report—Maximizing the Medium." *Cable Communications Magazine* (July/August 1993): 6.
12. *New Media...New Choices*. (Ottawa: 1992). Department of Communications. Supply and Services, p. 23.
13. "MediaLinx Delivers on the Promise of the Beacon Initiative," MediaLinx Press Release, Toronto, October 5, 1994.

REFERENCES

Task Force on Broadcasting Policy (Caplan-Sauvageau Task Force). (1986). *Report*. Ottawa: Minister of Supply and Services.

Special Senate Committee on Mass Media. (1970). *Report*. Vol. 1. Ottawa.

Canadian Association of Broadcasters. (1989, July). "Taking the Lead—Television Strategic Plan and Analysis." *Internal report*.

Caplan-Sauvageau Task Force. See Canada. Task Force on Broadcast Policy. (1986).

Creery, T. (1989). "Supervised Concentration—Big-Is-Dutiful in Canadian Broadcasting Regulations." A report to the Council of Regulated Industries by the Consumers' Association of Canada. May.

Desbarats, P. (1990). *Guide to Canadian News Media*. Toronto: Harcourt Brace Jovanovich, Canada.

Fulford, R. (1987). "Promises, Promises." *Saturday Night*, July.

Hardin, H. (1985). *Closed Circuits—the Sellout of Canadian Television*. Vancouver: Douglas & McIntyre.

Hosking, C., and S. McFadyen. (1986). "The Economic Factors Relating to Canadian Television Broadcasting Policy: A Non-Technical Synthesis of the Research Literature." *Canadian Journal of Communication* 12, 1.

McCabe, M. (1989). "Challenges and Priorities." *Cable Communications*, December 15.

Mills, M. (1987). "CTV's Troubles Set—If Profitability Is the Accepted God, Are Viewers Not the Ultimate Losers as TV Economics Get Most of the Attention?" *Content*, May/June.

Nolan, M. (1984). "Canadian Broadcasting History: A Time for Revision." *Broadcasting*, January.

Rutherford, P. (1990). *When Television Was Young: Primetime Canada* 1950–1967. Toronto: University of Toronto Press

Starowicz, M. (1989). *Citizens of Video-America—What Happened to Canadian Television in the Satellite Age?* Speech Delivered to a symposium on "Televison, Entertainment and National Culture" sponsored by Duke University and Laval University in Quebec City.

"TV Network News in U.S. Losing Audience, Discovering Budgets." (1988). *The Globe and Mail*, March 2, pp. B1–B4.

Vipond, M. (1989). *The Mass Media in Canada*. Toronto: James Lorimer.

PUTTING THE "PUBLIC" INTO PUBLIC BROADCASTING: A QUESTION OF MEANS

Ross A. Eaman

Ideally, broadcasting should be treated as a two-way medium, with objective, scientifically based audience research providing the feedback by which programmers adjust their output in terms of audience comprehension, interests, desires, and needs.

Sydney W. Head (1985, 337–38).

In the fall of 1994, the Parliamentary Standing Committee on Canadian Heritage began hearings on the future of the Canadian Broadcasting Corporation/Société Radio-Canada in the multichannel universe, with particular reference to the question of whether alternative sources of funding could be found to relieve the pressure on the CBC to sell advertising. In a submission entitled "A New Commitment," the CBC made a number of proposals as to how it might adapt to the changing broadcasting environment, including becoming more innovative, efficient, and diversely funded. It also proposed becoming "more open and accountable to the Canadians who own, fund and enjoy the CBC." What it had in mind was not greater institutional accountability—"the CBC," it noted, "probably has more institutional accountability than any corporation or government department in this country." Rather, what it was proposing was more openness to the public, "a more transparent CBC, a CBC that opens its doors more often." This could be achieved, it suggested, not only by literally opening its physical doors at the Broadcast Centre in Toronto and elsewhere but also by making more use of public response on the airwaves, introducing a broadcast version of its annual report, and creating a citizen's advisory council (Canadian Broadcasting Corporation, 1994, 2, 10, 32–34).

Curiously absent from the CBC's proposed accountability strategy was any direct or substantial mention of audience research. Although emphasis was placed on maintaining the work of its audience relations department, the corporation's audience research unit—now simply called CBC Research—was only alluded to in a brief section on how the CBC measures its programming performance. It is doubtful that this was merely an oversight. But was it the result of a failure to understand or appreciate the role of audience research in terms of public accountability? Or was it perhaps because CBC management is less interested in actually being accountable than in being *perceived* to be accountable? Indeed, is accountability to the public the same thing as, or does it even entail, having meaningful public input into program decision-making? If not, what are the practical requirements for such input, and can audience research realistically fulfil them?

This essay will explore these and related questions. In general, it will be argued that audience research should play a special role within a public broadcasting organization such as the CBC, one that it cannot be expected to have in the private broadcasting sector. That role should be to enable the general public, as distinct from specific audiences, to have a substantial, albeit indirect, say in the determination of the CBC's programming priorities. Provided that it is adequately resourced and intelligently conducted, audience research (admittedly, something of a misnomer) should serve as the voice of the public—of all those Canadians with a stake in what the CBC does—in the corporation's program planning process. In other words, audience research, rather than the personal views of senior executives, advisory councils, members of Parliament, committees of enquiry, or even broadcasting regulators, should be taken as the surest guide to what the public wants from the CBC. Only then can public broadcasting be democratic in the fullest sense of the term.

This is not to say that audience research, especially in the restricted form of program ratings, is the only basis for making major programming decisions. As Neil Morrison, the CBC's first research director pointed out, "it was never intended that Audience Research findings should dictate what should and should not be on the air. No amount of statistical analysis and scientific research can consider *all* factors involved in determining programming policies—especially for a publicly owned broadcasting system" (Morrison, 1957). At the same time, however, the underlying assumption of audience research is that a small group of program planners cannot reliably discern public wants and needs simply by consulting their own personal feelings and desires. As Morrison's successor, Arthur Laird, observed, "it is sometimes possible [for programmers] to uncover the facts of a situation by sheer flashes of insight and personal intuition alone. It is possible—but it is rather rare, and it can be awfully dangerous" (Laird, 1981).

Any discussion of audience research in the context of public broadcasting must, of course, acknowledge and keep in mind that audience research originated to serve the needs of advertisers. It was not until advertisers became seriously interested in radio that any thought was given to knowing more about audiences; to this day, most financial expenditures on audience research are made with advertisers in mind. As a member of the CBC's audience research department stated some years ago, "it is apparent that all commercial audience-measurement data...is designed to serve relatively uniformly the needs of stations, sponsors, time-buyers, agencies and salesmen, and only secondarily the specialized requirements of research practitioners" (quoted in Eaman, 1994, 141). To some extent, public broadcasters like the CBC have been able to use audience data produced primarily for advertisers to answer some of their own questions about public priorities. But they have also found it necessary to conduct their own research using alternative methods such as special surveys, permanent audience panels, and focus groups. One of the problems for public broadcasters today is that, while this supplementary research is essential to giving the public as a whole a meaningful voice with regard to programming, such research is also becoming increasingly expensive at a time when funding for public broadcasting is in a state of crisis. As a result, the nature of public broadcasting itself is threatened by the steady erosion of its financial base.

THE ORIGINS OF AUDIENCE RESEARCH

The first radio broadcast in Canada originated from the Marconi station XWA in Montreal in 1919, about the same time that broadcasting began in the United States. For the next decade, broadcasters had little or no idea how many people were listening to their programs or what they thought of them. As an American radio publication noted in the late 1920s, estimating the size of audiences was "equivalent to determining the number of crickets chirping at any instant in a swamp on a foggy summer evening" (quoted in Barnouw, 1966, 270). Or, as Canadian Merrill Denison observed in 1931, "very little is actually known about the radio audience, either its likes or dislikes, its desires, or even its numbers. And so one may reach knowingly for the salt cellar when he reads forthright statements purporting to tell what the radio audience likes and what it dislikes. No one knows and no one can know for there is no means of finding out" (Denison, 1931, 112–13).

By then, however, a method had in fact been devised for measuring the size of radio audiences. It was the brainchild of Archibald M. Crossley, the head of a small American market research company, and was designed to provide advertisers and their agencies with the information necessary to use radio effectively. The creation of networks in the late 1920s had increased the attractiveness of radio as an advertising medium by making it easier to reach a national market. At the same time, a number of comparative studies of product use in radio and non-radio homes had provided convincing evidence of the selling power of radio. But without reliable data on audiences for particular programs, advertisers still had to make radio-time purchases largely on faith. To alleviate this situation, Crossley developed what became known as the telephone recall method, which basically consisted of selecting numbers from telephone directories and asking respondents to recall what they had listened to the previous day.

One problem with Crossley's method was that it assumed a higher level of memory retention than was probably warranted; another problem was that telephone ownership was much higher at the time among the more well-to-do members of American society. In 1930, nonetheless, Crossley formed a radio audit bureau known as the Cooperative Analysis of Broadcasting to conduct the first continuing survey of American network radio audiences. The bureau was endorsed by the Association of National Advertisers, but in return for its support the ANA required Crossley to work under the direction of a governing committee and consult with an advertising agency advisory committee. It also specifically excluded the networks from its ranks (Beville, 1988, 4–11).

The shortcomings of Crossley's method together with the exclusion of broadcasters from his bureau left the door open for a second audience measurement operation. In 1934, Montgomery Clark and C.E. Hooper set up a competing service using what was called the coincidental telephone method and gave the American networks the opportunity to subscribe. Invented by George Gallup at Drake University, this new method eliminated the problem of memory loss by simply asking people what they were listening to at the time of the telephone interview. In contrast to the Crossley ratings, which consisted of estimated percentages of listening households tuned to particular network programs, the Hooperatings, as they became known after Clark left the company in 1938, measured the percentage of all radio households, whether listening or not. With the support of the networks, Hooper soon began to overtake Crossley. In 1946, after a study which reflected unfavorably on Crossley's methodology, the Cooperative Analysis of Broadcasting folded and sold its subscribers to Hooper (Beville, 1988, 11–13).

By then a new competitor with yet another method for measuring radio audiences had joined the fray. In the mid-1930s, Robert Elder and Louis F. Woodruff of MIT had built and tested an electronic meter for recording listening, but lacked the financial resources to develop it commercially. As a result, they sold their audimeter to Arthur C. Nielsen, the head of a successful market research business. By the late 1940s, the meter-based Nielsen Radio Index (NRI) had achieved 97 percent coverage of U.S. households and plans were laid for expanding into television. In 1950, after CBS decided to cancel the Hooperatings service and rely on Nielsen, Hooper sold his national ratings service to his archrival and withdrew to the local radio and television ratings scene (Beville, 1988, 17–21).

Early Audience Measurement in Canada

None of the early American ratings services made any effort to expand into Canada. But in 1940, Walter Elliott, who had set up a small market-research company in Montreal, travelled to New York to learn about the coincidental telephone method first-hand from Hooper. The same year, together with his partner, Paul Haynes, Elliott established the first comprehensive and continuing radio audience-measurement service in Canada. (Previously, Canadian Facts Limited had conducted occasional coincidental surveys of the audiences for imported soap operas for sponsors like Proctor & Gamble and Lever Brothers.) Beginning with monthly radio reports for Montreal (English and French), Toronto, Vancouver, and Winnipeg, the Elliott-Haynes service included 36 cities by the end of the 1940s, though only the original four were surveyed monthly. In 1952, after two years of experimental research, the company also began issuing monthly reports on television audiences in Canada, encompassing 42 markets by 1960 (Blankenship, Chakrapani, and Poole, 1985, 22–24, 31–32; Elliott-Haynes Limited, n.d.).

The reports of Elliott-Haynes were a mixed blessing for the CBC. They provided the earliest regular data on CBC radio audiences, but their reliability was open to question. Although the coincidental telephone method was a more accurate and valid measurement tool than the recall method, it still suffered from serious weaknesses when applied to Canadian broadcasting in the 1940s. Because it was easier and more economical to conduct telephone surveys in large urban centres, there was a tendency to ignore rural areas. Yet nearly half of Canadian households were located on farms and in small towns of less than 10 000, and the CBC attracted a substantial proportion of its audience in such areas through its regional transmitters and numerous affiliates. As a result, the Elliott-Haynes surveys underestimated the overall audience for CBC radio. It is "easy to see," concluded an independent study, "...how woefully inadequate coincidental telephone surveys in a few urban centres can be in such an area as Saskatchewan, or for that matter in many other parts of Canada" (Canadian Facts Limited, 1949). But this did not prevent the private stations and their lobbying agency, the Canadian Association of Broadcasters, from pointing to the Elliott-Haynes reports as supposed proof that Canadians overwhelmingly preferred their programs to those of the CBC.

Nothing in the Canadian Broadcasting Act of 1936 prohibited the CBC from conducting its own audience research. But initially, at least, the corporation lacked the resources to set up a separate research unit and simply left it up to its commercial department, headed by Austin Weir, to do whatever it could. A study conducted for CBC management by a member of the engineering department in 1948 found "an apparent lack of confidence" in the available ratings services, and acknowledged that "the CBC should be in a position to regularly feel the entertainment pulse of its sponsors, or customers, the Canadian Radio Audience, and should be quick to detect, and act upon, those signals which indicate pleasure, displeasure, or perhaps actual antagonism." But it still concluded that the CBC's "requirements for audience data can be met most economically by an outside agency" (Stewart, 1948). And a few years later, the Massey Commission reiterated that "the limited financial resources of the C.B.C. do not permit systematic listener research on an adequate scale" (Canada, Royal Commission on National Development in the Arts, Letters and Sciences, 1951, 37).

In these circumstances, the CBC welcomed the formation in 1944 of a co-operative, nonprofit audience measurement organization, originally called the Bureau of Broadcast Measurement and later renamed the BBM Bureau of Measurement. However, BBM was initially created mainly to serve the needs of the smaller radio stations in Canada, many of which were not covered in the reports of Elliott-Haynes and often had no need of ratings since they were the only station in town. What such stations required, in order to compete with the print media for advertising, were reliable circulation figures, which BBM undertook to gather by means of a mail ballot survey. As an incentive, participants were given a packet of safety pins.

Although the CBC provided BBM with both financial and technical support, it did not have much need of station coverage statistics. It was more interested, therefore, in the emergence of an alternative method of audience measurement in which representative panels kept diaries of their listening (and later viewing) during a stated period of time. Developed by International Surveys Limited, which Paul Haynes set up in 1946 after parting company with Walter Elliott, the diary technique was able to include all types of households. ISL claimed that this enabled it to produce ratings that could be applied not only to Canada as a whole but to different regions and city sizes. Moreover, by operating its radio panel in conjunction with its consumer panel, ISL was also able to relate listening and viewing habits to purchasing behaviour. However, the use of diaries also had its shortcomings. Participants tended to underreport programs in off-peak periods and to write in what they thought they should be listening to or watching. There was a higher co-operation rate among households whose members had more education and higher socioeconomic status. And keeping diaries became progressively more bothersome as the number of program choices increased and new technologies made it easier to switch from one program to another.

As a result, the CBC tried to interest the A.C. Nielsen Company in extending its meter-based ratings system into Canada. Nielsen had entered Canada in 1944 after pressure from American branch plants to provide general market-research services. But Nielsen considered it too expensive and difficult to set up a meter operation for measuring audiences in Canada. In the late 1950s, Nielsen did begin measuring Canadian television audiences, but it did so using diaries rather than meters. It was not until the development of "people meters" in the 1980s that an electronic ratings service was available in Canada. People meters are small devices wired into television sets and connected to a central computer. They automatically record the age and sex of each person watching, the program being watched, and for how long. Despite lingering problems, people meters are now generally acknowledged to be the most accurate method of measuring television viewing and enable both advertisers and programmers to make detailed analyses of viewing behaviour. In 1987, Nielsen and BBM (which began producing ratings in the 1950s using diaries) reached a tentative agreement whereby Nielsen would extend its people meter service into Canada under the auspices of BBM. However, this agreement broke down, and in 1989 Nielsen introduced a people meter system on its own. BBM tried to develop a rival meter system known as TAM, but this proved unsuccessful, and it was forced to continue its reliance on diary-based measurement.

Creation of the CBC Bureau of Audience Research

For almost a decade after its creation in 1927, the British Broadcasting Corporation (BBC), upon which the CBC was modelled in part, eschewed any form of audience research. John Reith, the BBC's first Director-General, joked to King Edward VIII in 1935 that "water engineers could provide a pretty clear indication of the popularity of broadcast items. When there was anything specially interesting, water consumption fell; immediately afterward there was a sudden, sometimes alarming, peak load" (Reith, 1949, 244). In Reith's view, it was the BBC's duty to determine for itself what was in the public interest. To criticism that listeners did not like BBC programs, his characteristic reply was that "It is occasionally indicated to us that we are apparently setting out to give the public what we think they need—and not what they want, but few know what they want and very few what they need" (1924, 34).

Under pressure from both within and outside the BBC, however, Reith reluctantly agreed in 1936 to the creation of a Listener Research Department on the understanding that it would engage in qualitative as well as quantitative research. The creation of the department was an important turning point in the history of the BBC. As social historians Paddy Scannell and David Cardiff have observed, "it enabled the structural framework of broadcasting—the arrangement of programme output through the days of the week, through the seasons of the year—to be arranged on a rational basis." It also provided "criteria for arbitrating between the competing claims" for time and money of the various production departments. In their view, it was "the clearest acknowledgment of the necessity of basing the activities of broadcasting on real knowledge and understanding of their audiences, not on what the broadcasters thought they might want or need" (Scannell and Cardiff, 1991).

If anything, there was an even greater need for such knowledge and understanding in Canada, with its numerous cultural and regional divisions. But despite the urgings of Weir, the CBC lagged behind the BBC by almost two decades in creating a separate audience research unit. This was not simply the result of inadequate resources, as the Massey Commission suggested, since by that time the budget for the CBC's press and information department was close to $200 000 a year, and an audience research department could have been set up for much less.[2] It was more a question of priorities than of finances. Despite the inadequacy of the existing ratings services from the standpoint of the CBC, it was not until the advent of television that the corporation's management saw the need for an audience research department. At that point, it finally became obvious that program planners would need a great deal more information about audience tastes if they were to meet the challenges of the new medium.

The CBC Bureau of Audience Research came into existence on January 1, 1954. It was given responsibility for "conducting scientific research about the size, composition and characteristics of listening and viewing audiences" and for "investigating the reactions and preferences of the Canadian public about radio and television programs." It was also to make "special opinion and market surveys about broadcasting in Canada" (Morrison, 1954). Its main office was in Ottawa, but it also set up small, regional offices in Montreal and Toronto. It was first run by Neil Morrison, who had previously been the head of CBC talks and public affairs. Morrison saw audience research as a

> way of enabling the CBC to be more responsive to the needs of the public. "Essentially," he told the CBC Board of Governors in 1957, "audience research provides a channel of communication from Canadian audiences back to their national broadcasting system. The findings constitute an evaluation and criticism of the CBC's program service" (Morrison, 1957, iv). The board did not, however, see fit to situate the new bureau, which underwent several subsequent name changes, within the CBC hierarchy so that it could influence programming decisions directly. Instead, it left audience research one step removed administratively from the program planning process, a situation has continued to this day.

The Development of CBC Audience Research

In addition to re-analyzing quantitative audience data purchased from Elliott-Haynes, ISL, BBM, McDonald Research, and later Nielsen, the new department conducted a series of small-scale surveys dealing with reactions to specific programs, scheduling preferences, and so on. Many of these surveys were quite innovative, but most were based on unrepresentative samples and none provided a general view of what the public thought of, or wanted from, the CBC. One result of this was an ill-conceived attempt in 1959 by Kate Aitken, a member of the CBC board of directors, to undertake a study of her own to find out what Canadians thought about CBC programming.

Under Arthur Laird, who succeeded Morrison in 1962 and served as research director until 1983, the department continued to make use of ratings data, principally from BBM for radio and from Nielsen for television. As Laird explained, "given reasonably sound information, and provided you analyse it properly, ratings can be valuable for a variety of purposes—for detecting weak spots in schedules, for examining the effects of lead-in programming, for indicating how programs of different types share audiences when they run against each other, for showing up differences in audience habits in different parts of the country, and so on" (Laird, 1964). This assumed, of course, that the data in question were reliable, which Laird himself would have been the first to admit was not always the case. As a senior member of his staff related, all of the audience measurement services "cut corners and make compromises in their research designs in the interests of both economy and speed" and "the effect of these compromises on the data—the biases introduced and the effect on the sampling error—is just not known" (Purdye, 1962, 123)

Yet even if it were possible to produce accurate ratings, the results would not provide broadcasters with sufficient means to ascertain what the public as a whole wants in terms of programming. By its very nature, audience measurement has a substantial bias toward heavy listeners and viewers. In Canada, 20 percent of listeners account for nearly half of all listening, while 20 percent of viewers account for over 40 percent of all viewing (BBM Bureau of Measurement, 1991, 20; 1990, 42). Although ratings have been described as "democracy in action" (Beville, 1985, 240), their effect is to give some citizens in the world of broadcasting many more "votes" than other citizens. In addition, it has been shown that measurements of audience size or share are not always a reliable guide to audience enjoyment or appreciation (Menneer, 1987). Nor are audience size and share the only way of measuring program popularity. Were it not for the requirements of advertisers, popularity could conceivably be assessed in terms of total population reach or the average number of times that a program is listened to or viewed.

For these reasons, Laird undertook to develop a number of alternative audience-research tools. In the late 1950s, the department had conducted an exploratory study in Toronto on the image of the CBC in the public mind. But it had not sought to determine what a representative sample of all Canadians thought about the CBC. In 1962, therefore, staff member Constance McFarlane organized a national image study involving lengthy personal interviews with nearly 4400 adults from across the country. It was the largest scientific study of the Canadian media up to that time, and its results provided a boost to the CBC's morale (Canadian Broadcasting Corporation, 1963). Similar national image studies were conducted in the mid-1970s and mid-1980s (Canadian Broadcasting Corporation, 1974; 1986). In 1987, CBC Research created a comprehensive Annual Media Survey in order to provide more frequent data on public opinion about the CBC's performance.

Early in its history, the BBC had created audience panels (its so-called listening or viewing thermometer) to assess qualitative reactions to programs. At first, volunteers simply recorded their likes and dislikes on cards over a period of time and the results were presented in the form of an appreciation index. Later, more refined methods were used to measure audience appreciation and the system was extended to television. When the CBC research department was initially set up, the use of panels was ruled out as too expensive and difficult to operate in a country as large as Canada. But in 1965, following pressure from management, the department set up a regular panel for English television network programming; a few years later, a similar panel was instituted for French television. The purpose of the panels, according to Laird, was "to 'go beyond the ratings' and to obtain information on what those who see our programs actually think of them" (quoted in Eaman, 1994, 186). Both panels, which still operate today, were specifically designed to gather qualitative as well as quantitative information.

In addition to recording their program selections, panel members are asked to indicate their level of enjoyment for specified programs. These reactions are then tabulated in the form of an "Enjoyment Index" (EI). This practice has been expanded to include individual characters and specific program elements such as storyline, dialogue, acting, pace, settings, photography, and even humour. Even individual subplots are rated according to enjoyment. In recent years, the panels have also been used to elicit opinions about what *could* be done in terms of programming. For example, the diary for October 4–11, 1987, requested panelists to watch "Degrassi Junior High" and respond to the question, "What are the more serious issues that you would like to see covered on the program?" However, as this example suggests, the panels focus on fairly narrow program matters rather than on the general balance and philosophy of CBC programming.

The same is true of what are known as focus groups, which are the most recent form of a program testing technique first developed by CBS in the 1940s. Focus groups usually consist of eight to twelve people who fit a certain profile, such as being avid watchers of news. Their reactions to specific programs are recorded and displayed on a graph electronically and also elicited through a follow-up discussion and sometimes a questionnaire. This technique yields a substantial amount of concrete information about audience responses to programming. But there are obvious problems in generalizing from such small samples, and the technique can only be used selectively because of cost (about $2500 on a per-unit basis). Ideally, focus groups should be used to flesh out or give additional meaning to general findings from more broadly based surveys or even ratings analysis, not as an independent or self-sufficient guide to the public reception of programming.

The Role of Audience Research for Public Broadcasting

It could be argued that audience research is the most important form of public relations in a public broadcasting organization, but it is clearly not the most visible form. For example, the network television panels are deliberately not identified as a CBC operation in order to obtain more neutral reactions. In fact, most of the work of the CBC's research department is, by its very nature, unknown to Canadians. This is perhaps one reason CBC management might prefer other forms of accountability. But it may also be that there is a lack of faith in the upper echelons of the CBC in the ability of Canadians to determine for themselves what kinds of programming are in their best interests.

CBC audience research provides no basis for any such lack of faith. Over the years, Canadians have consistently supported the idea of using the CBC to foster an indigenous culture, pursue educational goals, and promote understanding between different cultural groups. In its first national survey, for example, the research department found that 94 percent of Canadians agreed that it is important that the CBC "help Canadians in all parts of Canada to understand and learn about each other," while 89 percent felt that it was important for the CBC to "help French Canadian and English Canadians to understand and learn about each other" (Canadian Broadcasting Corporation, 1963) When offered a choice between more entertainment programming and more cultural and information programming, slightly more than two-fifths of the participants in the 1984 national survey chose to leave things as they are, while one-fifth said they would prefer more culture and information and slightly less than one-third favored more entertainment. In the same survey, only about one-quarter of those surveyed indicated that they would like more American and/or European programming, while a slightly larger number preferred more Canadian programming. About two-fifths said they would prefer to leave things as they are. One area in which English-speaking Canadians indicated they would like to see a change was in terms of the relative balance of network and regional programming (Canadian Broadcasting Corporation, 1986).

The problem is not what Canadians say they like and want when they are consulted as a whole, but rather what they appear to say when their views are simply extrapolated from audience ratings. There must, of course, be a balancing act between the value of public input and the practical requirements of running a large broadcasting organization. But if Canadians as a whole had been making key programming decisions over the years, there is every indication that the CBC would have had, among other things, somewhat higher levels of Canadian content; a better balance of local, regional, and national programming; and a greater appreciation of the role of indigenous popular drama in the lives of most citizens. Certainly, as the idea of public broadcasting itself comes under increasing attacks from the ideologues of unrestrained corporate capitalism, it will not be enough simply to have "a CBC that lets Canadians inside the thinking of the Corporation in a more transparent way" (Canadian Broadcasting Corporation, 1994, 10). That "thinking" itself must be a reflection of what Canadians as a whole say they want from the CBC.

It should perhaps be noted in conclusion that the challenge for CBC audience research is somewhat different for radio than for television. Over the last ten years, CBC radio has been able to retain a more or less constant share of the overall radio audience (about 11 percent of anglophone listening and 9–10 percent of francophone listening). In contrast, the overall audience share of CBC television has steadily declined; for example, the CBC's share of prime-time English-language viewing dropped from 20.6 percent in 1989 to 13.9 percent in 1994. In both cases, the CBC faced increased competition from other stations and networks, but the audience erosion that has characterized its television services has generally not occurred in the case of radio. This situation has led some critics to conclude that CBC television is a failure compared to CBC radio, but this conclusion is unwarranted.

To justify its existence, CBC radio necessarily provides services that are not only virtually entirely Canadian but are substantially different on both AM and FM than anything offered by the private stations. The result is that CBC radio has a very strong appeal for a relatively small percentage of Canadians, who tend to be somewhat older, better educated, and better off economically than the norm. According to the BBM Bureau of Measurement, only about 18 percent of anglophones and 15 percent of francophones listen to CBC radio at least once a week. While other measuring agencies give higher estimates than these, it is clear that CBC radio tends to assume either considerable importance in one's life or else hardly any importance; the average CBC listener tunes in for almost twelve hours a week and devotes over half of his or her listening to the CBC. It is for this reason that the growth of other stations has had little if any effect on CBC listenership; those who like CBC radio, whether for its information and current affairs, its arts and culture, or for some combination of the two, are generally not attracted to the additional musical offerings of new private stations. The task for audience research is to discover how CBC radio might expand its reach without alienating the loyal audience which it has successfully cultivated over the years.

CBC television, on the other hand, has always tried to be a full-service Canadian broadcaster. This is reflected in its much higher audience reach; in marked contrast to CBC radio, almost four out of five Canadians watch CBC television at least once a week. Moreover, the demographic composition of CBC viewers is not substantially different from that of other major networks such as CTV. Given that the CBC accounts for over 40 percent of the money spent on Canadian television programming (and attracts over 40 percent of the viewing of Canadian programming in prime time), it is essential that CBC television continue to serve as wide an audience as possible. But this means that, without compensating support for the CBC (such as additional channels), the steady growth of competition inevitably cuts more and more into the corporation's overall television audience. The solution to this problem is not to transform CBC television into a counterpart of CBC radio. Unlike radio, where station loyalty remains a significant factor, the loyalty of viewers in the multichannel television universe is largely to particular programs rather than to networks or channels. To maintain the support of Canadians, therefore, the most important thing for the CBC to do is to produce a sufficient number of high-quality programs in various program categories to retain, even in the face of an overall audience decline, the high level of its audience reach. In this regard, audience research emphasizing qualitative reactions to programming will, if anything, play an increasingly important role in the future.

NOTES

The 1948 internal study had estimated that it would cost $25 000 for salaries to set up a separate research department. At the time, the CBC's overall budget was about $6.5 million.

References

Barnouw, E. (1966). *A Tower in Babel*, Vol. I of *A History of broadcasting in the United States*. New York: Oxford University Press.

BBM Bureau of Measurement. (1990). *1989–1990 Television Data Book*.

————. (1991). *1990-1991 Radio Data Book*.

Beville, H.M., Jr. (1988). *Audience Ratings: Radio, Television, and Cable*, rev. ed. Hillsdale, NJ: Lawrence Erlbaum Associates.

Blankenship, A.B., C. Chakrapani, & W.H. Poole. (1985). *A History of Marketing Research in Canada*. Toronto: Professional Marketing Research Society.

Canada, Royal Commission on National Development in the Arts, Letters and Sciences (Massey Commission). (1951). *Report*. Ottawa.

Canadian Broadcasting Corporation. (1963, June). *What the Canadian Public Thinks of the CBC*. Research Department Report.

————. (1974, February). *What the Canadian Public Thinks of Television and of the TV Services Provided by CBC*. Research Department Report.

————. (1986, January). *How Canadians Feel about the CBC*. Research Department Report.

————. (1990, July). *Street Legal: CBC English Network Panel Results—"Complex Offer"*.

————. (1994, November). *A New Commitment*. Submission to the Parliamentary Standing Committee on Canadian Heritage.

Canadian Facts Limited. (1949). *Saskatchewan Survey*. Report.

Denison, M. (1931). "Thoughts on Radio." In *Open House*, edited by W.A. Deacon and W. Reeves, 107–20. Ottawa: Graphic Publishers,

Eaman, R.A. (1994). *Channels of Influence: CBC Audience Research and the Canadian Public*. Toronto: University of Toronto Press.

Elliott-Haynes Limited. (n.d). Pamphlet, "From Little Acorns Grow ..."

Head, S.W. (1985). *World Broadcasting Systems: A Comparative Analysis*. Belmont, Calif.: Wadsworth Publishing Company.

Laird, A. (1964). *Broadcasting Research in the CBC*. Address to the annual meeting of the Canadian Association of Broadcasters, Quebec City.

————. (1981). "The CBC Research Department: What It Does and Why It Does it." Unpublished talk to CBC head office staff.

Menneer, P. (1987). "Audience Appreciation—A Different Story from Audience Numbers." *Annual Review of BBC Broadcasting Research Findings*. No. 13.

Morrison, N. (1954). "Progress Report." Unpublished report.

————. (1957). "Audience Research Progress Report for Board of Governors. Unpublished report.

Purdye, K. (1962). *A Technical Evaluation of the Radio-TV Audience Measurement Services Available in Canada*. Unpublished research department report.

Reith, J.C.W. (1924). *Broadcast Over Britain*. London: Hodder and Stoughton.

————. (1949). *Into the Wind*. London: Hodder and Stoughton.

Scannell, P., and D. Cardiff (1991). *A Social History of British Broadcasting*, Vol. I: 1922–1939. Oxford: Basil Blackwell.

Stewart, E.C. (1948). *A Report on a Study of Elliott-Haynes Survey Data and its Usefulness to the Canadian Broadcasting Corporation*. Unpublished report, February.

APPENDIX A: BASIC FACTS ON CANADIAN MEDIA

Compiled by Janet Alford, Ellen Eastwood, and Marie Rajic

List of Figures

FIGURE A.1
Basic Canadian Media Statistics

Average television viewing time/week/person	22.8 hours
Average radio listening time/week/person	23.6 hours
Total average circulation of 108 daily newspapers	5 491 150/day
Percentage of households with television sets	99%
Percentage of households with cable	73%
Percentage of households with VCRs	76%
Percentage of households with home computers	39%

Source: Television viewing time: Statistics Canada, *Television Viewing*, Catalogue No. 87–208 (Ottawa: Minister of Supply and Services, 1993) Radio listening time: *Media Digest 94/95*, created by CDMC and member agencies, distributed by *Marketing Magazine*; Newspaper circulation: Canadian Daily Newspaper Association, *1994 Newsletter*; Percentage households cable/VCRs: 1994 Nielsen Marketing Research; Percentage households computers: *Maclean's*/CTV Decima poll, *Maclean's*, January 2, 1995.

FIGURE A.2
Newspaper Circulation by Ownership, Percentage Share

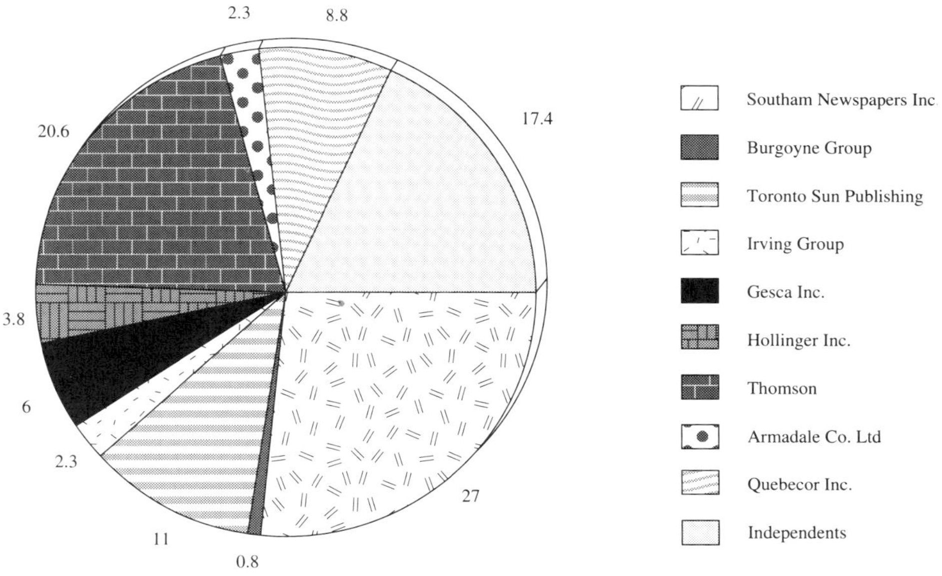

Source: Based on data from the Canadian Daily Newspaper Association, *Research Newsletter* 2, 8 (September 1994).

FIGURE A.3

Top 20 Canadian Newspapers, by Average Daily Circulation

Newspaper	Ownership	Average Daily Circulation
Toronto Star	Independent	536 342
Globe and Mail	Thomson	317 972
Montreal Le Journal	Quebecor	288 096
Toronto Sun	Toronto Sun Publishing	274 521
Montreal La Presse	Gesca	215 369
Vancouver Sun	Southam	214 652
Ottawa Citizen	Southam	172 382
Montreal Gazette	Southam	167 148
Vancouver Province	Southam	165 982
Edmonton Journal	Southam	165 227
Winnipeg Free Press	Thomson	155 701
Hamilton Spectator	Southam	128 841
Calgary Herald	Southam	128 229
London Free Press	Independent	114 817
Quebec Le Journal	Quebecor	104 841
Quebec Le Soleil	Hollinger	102 664
Toronto Financial Post	Toronto Sun Publishing	101 809
Halifax Chronicle-Herald	Independent	96 907
Edmonton Sun	Toronto Sun Publishing	87 145
Windsor Star	Southam	86 236

Source: Canadian Daily Newspaper Association, *Research Newsletter* 2, 8 (September 1994).

FIGURE A.4

Top 10 Canadian Consumer Magazines, by Average Annual Circulation

Rank	Title	Circulation
1	Reader's Digest	1 220 049
2	Chatelaine	899 909
3	TV Guide	810 436
4	National Geographic	684 467
5	Leisure Ways	594 716
6	Canadian Living	577 095
7	Maclean's Canada	542 049
8	Legion	500 028
9	Westworld BC	445 478
10	Touring	445 337

Source: Based on data from the Canadian Circulation Board/Audit Bureau of Circulations (December 1993).

FIGURE A.5

Top-Grossing Canadian Movies
(Winners of the Golden Reel Award)

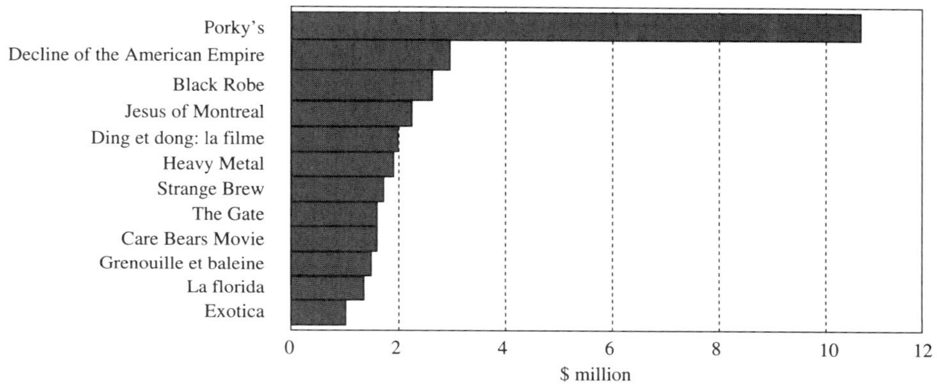

Source: Based on data from the Academy of Canadian Cinema and Television, and Alliance Communications.

FIGURE A.6

Ownership of Home Computer
by Province

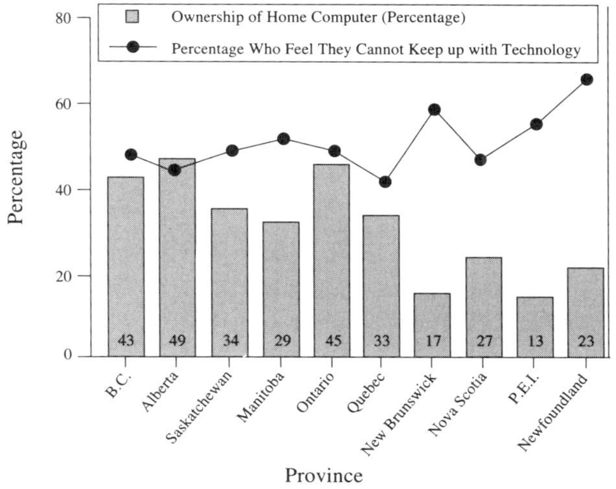

Source: Based on data from *Maclean's*/CTV Decima Poll, *Maclean's*, January 2, 1995.

FIGURE A.7

Ranking Television Against Other Media, Percentage

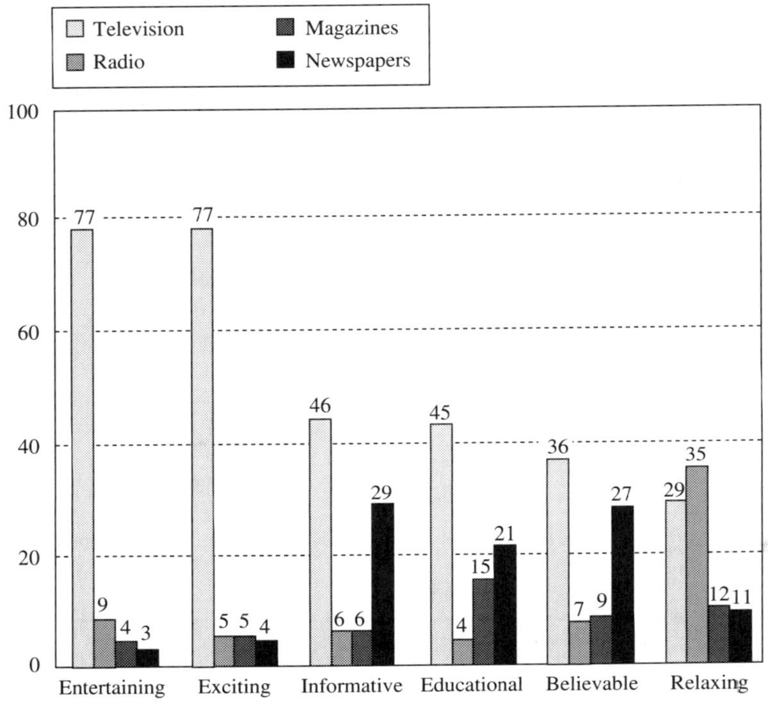

Source: Television Bureau of Canada, *TVB Television Basics* 94/95. Data from Environics.

FIGURE A.8

Average Weekly Viewing Hours per Capita

Demographics	1984	1985	1986	1987	1988	1989	1990	1991	1992	1993	1994
All Canada, 2+	23.3	25.3	26.1	24.8	24.1	23.2	23.9	24.0	23.4	23.3	22.7
Adults, 18+	24.6	26.3	26.9	25.8	25.3	24.3	25.1	25.4	24.7	24.7	24.1
Women, 18+	26.3	28.7	28.9	28.3	27.7	26.7	27.4	27.3	26.7	26.7	26.1
Men, 18+	22.8	23.9	24.7	23.1	22.8	21.9	22.7	23.4	22.7	22.7	21.9
Teens, 12–17	20.9	20.8	22.2	19.7	18.7	18.2	18.3	17.7	17.6	17.6	16.8
Children, 2–11	18.3	22.6	24.7	22.5	20.8	20.3	20.7	19.8	18.5	18.5	18.4

Source: Television Bureau of Canada, *TVB Television Basics* 94/95. Data from BBM Spring Surveys.

FIGURE A.9

Average Weekly Viewing Hours, 1994

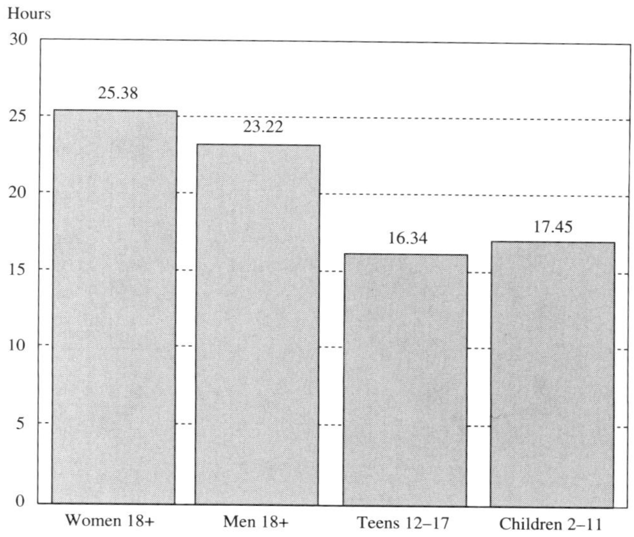

Source: Based on data from Television Bureau of Canada, *TVB Television Basics* 94/95.

FIGURE A.10

Average Hours of Television Viewing by Canadians per Week, and the National Murder Rate

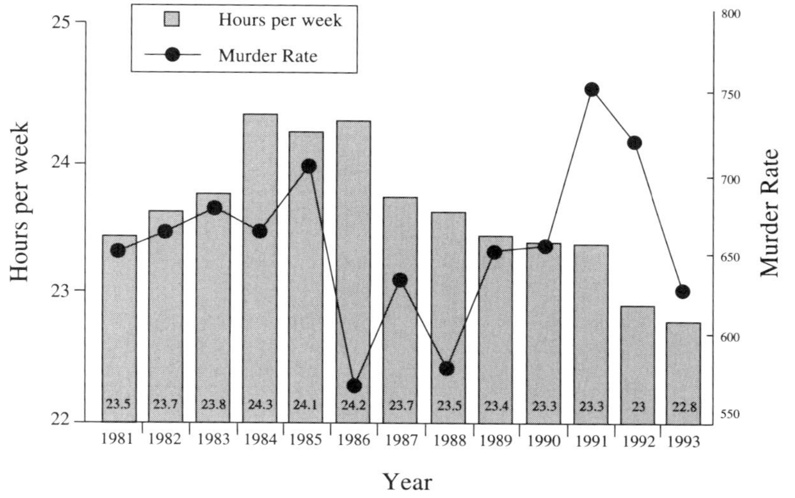

Source: National Murder Rate: Statistics Canada, *National Murder Rate*, Catalogue No. 85-002 (Ottawa: Minister of Supply and Services, 1994) Hours of Television Viewed: Statistics Canada, *Television Viewing*, Catalogue No. 87–208, (Ottawa: Minister of Supply and Services, 1994).

FIGURE A.11

Distribution of Prime-Time Television Viewing by Room of the House, Adults 25–54

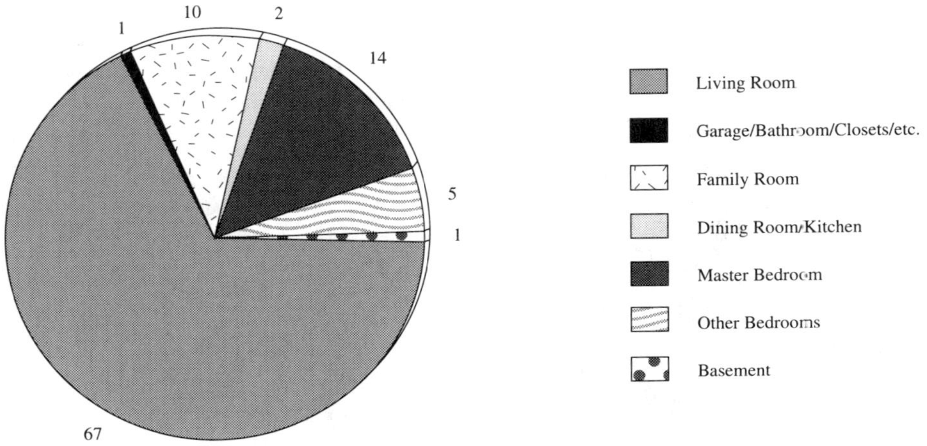

Source: 1993 Nielsen Media Research "TV Audience" U.S. Reproduced from *TVB Television Basics* 94/95.

FIGURE A.12

Percentage of Viewing Time by Network

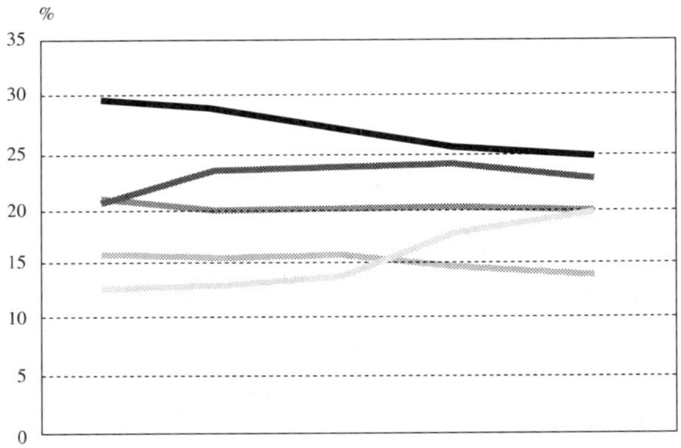

	1989/90	1990/91	1991/92	1992/93	1993/94
CBC	16.1	15.5	15.6	14.2	13.6
CTV	20.9	22.7	23.5	23.1	22.5
Pay/Specialty	12.6	12.8	13.5	17	19.2
Other Cdn.	21.1	20.3	20.4	20.1	19.9
U.S. Stations	29.3	28.6	27	25.5	24.8

Source: Based on data from CBC Research (A.C. Nielsen).

FIGURE A.13

Top 20 Shows in Canada
RATINGS FIGURES
September 5, 1994–April 24, 1995

Ranking	Show	Viewers Age 2+ Rating	Station
1	Seinfeld	11.6	GLOBAL
2	E.R.	9.3	CTV
3	Friends	8.8	GLOBAL
4	Frasier	8.7	GLOBAL
5	America's Funniest Home Videos	8.2	CTV
6	Home Improvement	7.9	BBS
7	Murder She Wrote	7.8	GLOBAL
8	Madman of the People	7.8	GLOBAL
9	X-Files	7.6	GLOBAL
10	Beverly Hills 90210	7.5	GLOBAL
11	Mad About You	7.4	GLOBAL
12	Grace Under Fire	7.4	GLOBAL
13	Melrose Place	7.3	BBS
14	Larroquette	7.3	CTV
15	NYPD Blue	7.2	GLOBAL
16	Roseanne	7.0	CTV
17	CTV Sunday Movie	6.6	CTV
18	60 Minutes	6.6	GLOBAL
19	Sliders	6.5	GLOBAL
20	NHL Hockey	6.4	GLOBAL

RATING—the average percentage of target group population, within a market tuned to a program.
RATING = average target audience / target population x 100 (TVB)

Source: Based on CTV Research (Data by A.C. Neilsen).

FIGURE A.14

Most Watched TV Programs in Canada
September 5, 1994–April 24, 1995
Audience Numbers

Ranking	Show	Viewers Age 2+ (000s)	Station
1	E.R.	2395	CTV
2	America's Funniest Home Videos	2119	CTV
3	Larroquette	1877	CTV
4	Roseanne	1794	CTV
5	Due South	1750	CTV
6	CTV Sunday Movie	1689	CTV
7	On Our Own	1547	CTV
8	Murphy Brown	1497	CTV
9	Law & Order	1434	CTV
10	Cybill	1381	CTV
11	Hockey Night in Canada	1349	CBC
12	CTV Monday Movie	1339	CTV
13	The Mommies	1327	CBC
14	CTV News	1307	CTV
15	Seinfeld	1246	GLOBAL
16	Fresh Prince of Bel Air	1243	CBC
17	Scales of Justice	1208	CBC
18	Royal Canadian Air Farce	1208	CBC
19	Market Place	1206	CBC
20	Fifth Estate	1172	CBC

Audience Numbers = the average number of viewers who tuned into the program weekly.

Source: CTV Research (Data by A.C. Neilsen).

FIGURE A.15

Specialty Services,
Average Weekly Share among Cable Households
(Anglophones Age 2+, Winter 1995)

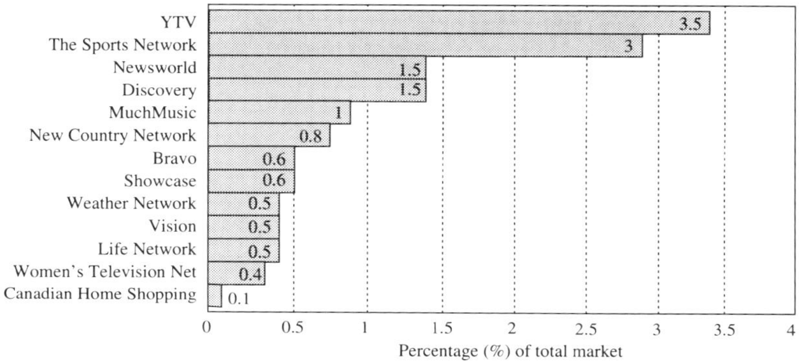

Source: Adapted from Canadian Cable Television Association, Cable TV Facts 1994–95, *Viewing Statistics: Canadian Specialty Services* (Winter 1995). Data from A.C. Nielsen.

FIGURE A.16

Canada's Top 20 Advertisers of 1993

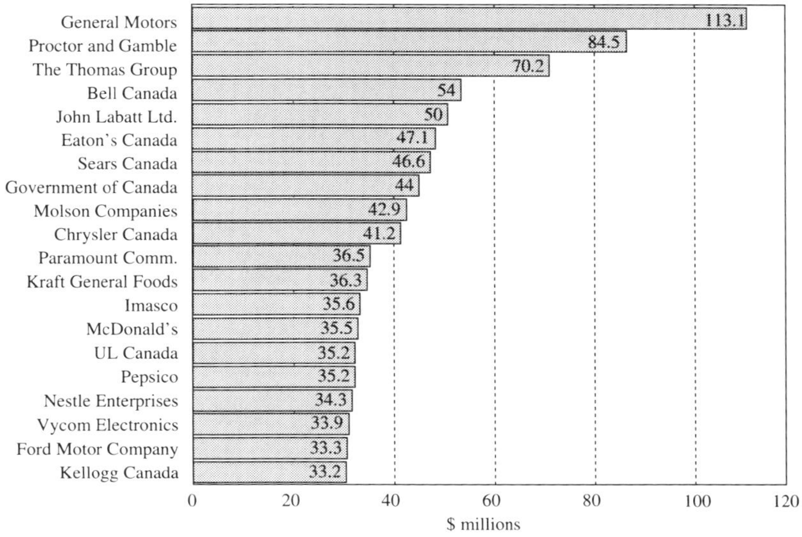

Source: Based on data from Nielsen Marketing Research Data, 1994.

FIGURE A.17

Net Advertising Volume in Canada by Medium (Percentages)

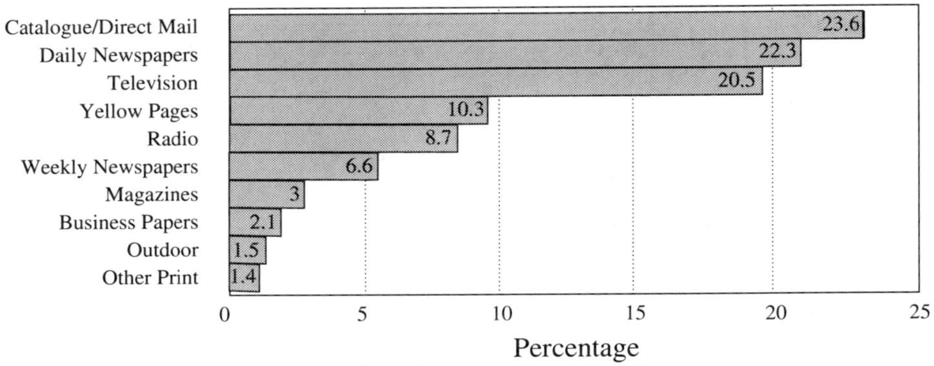

Source: Based on Data from Television Bureau of Canada, *TVB Television Basics* 94/95.

APPENDIX B

The Broadcasting Act of 1991

38-39 Elizabeth II

An Act respecting broadcasting and to amend certain Acts in relation thereto and in relation to radiocommunication.

[*Assented to 1st February, 1991*]

Her Majesty, by and with the advice and consent of the Senate and House of Commons of Canada, enacts as follows:

SHORT TITLE

1. This Act may be cited as the *Broadcasting Act*.

PART I

GENERAL

Interpretation

2. (1) In this Act,

" broadcasting" means any transmission of programs, whether or not encrypted, by radio waves or other means of telecommunication for reception by the public by means of broadcasting receiving apparatus, but does not include any such transmission of programs that is made solely for performance or display in a public place;

"broadcasting receiving apparatus" means a device, or combination of devices, intended for or capable of being used for the reception of broadcasting;

"broadcasting undertaking" includes a distribution undertaking, a programming undertaking and a network;

"Commission" means the Canadian Radio-television and Telecommunications Commission established by the *Canadian Radio-television and Telecommunications Commission Act*;

"Corporation" means the Canadian Broadcasting Corporation continued by section 36;

"distribution undertaking" means an undertaking for the reception of broadcasting and the retransmission thereof by radio waves or other means of telecommunication to more than one permanent or temporary residence or dwelling unit or to another such undertaking;

"encrypted" means treated electronically or otherwise for the purpose of preventing intelligible reception;

"licence" means a licence to carry on a broadcasting undertaking issued by the Commission under this Act;

"Minister" means the Minister of Communications;

"network" includes any operation where control over all or any part of the programs or program schedules of one or more broadcasting undertakings is delegated to another undertaking or person;

"program" means sounds or visual images, or a combination of sounds and visual images, that are intended to inform, enlighten or entertain, but does not include visual images, whether or not combined with sounds, that consist predominantly of alphanumeric text;

"programming undertaking" means an undertaking for the transmission of programs, either directly by radio waves or other means of telecommunication or indirectly through a distribution undertaking, for reception by the public by means of broadcasting receiving apparatus;

"radio waves" means electromagnetic waves of frequencies lower than 3000 GHz that are propagated in space without artificial guide;

"temporary network operation" means a network operation with respect to a particular program or a series of programs that extends over a period not exceeding sixty days.

(2) For the purposes of this Act, "other means of telecommunication" includes wire, visual or other electromagnetic system or any optical or technical system.

(3) This Act shall be construed and applied in a manner that is consistent with the freedom of expression and journalistic, creative and programming independence enjoyed by broadcasting undertakings.

Broadcasting Policy for Canada

3. (1) It is hereby declared as the broadcasting policy for Canada that

(a) the Canadian broadcasting system shall be effectively owned and controlled by Canadians;

(b) the Canadian broadcasting system, operating primarily in the English and French languages and comprising public, private and community elements, makes use of radio frequencies that are public property and provides, through its programming, a public service essential to the maintenance and enhancement of national identity and cultural sovereignty;

(c) English and French language broadcasting, while sharing common aspects, operate under different conditions and may have different requirements;

(d) the Canadian broadcasting system should

(i) serve to safeguard, enrich and strengthen the cultural, political, social and economic fabric of Canada,

(ii) encourage the development of Canadian expression by providing a wide range of programming that reflects Canadian attitudes, opinions, ideas, values and artistic creativity, by displaying Canadian talent in entertainment programming and by offering information and analysis concerning Canada and other countries from a Canadian point of view,

(iii) through its programming and the employment opportunities arising out of its operations, serve the needs and interests, and reflect the circumstances and aspirations, of Canadian men, women and children, including equal rights, the linguistic duality and multicultural and multiracial nature of Canadian society and the special place of aboriginal peoples within that society, and

(iv) be readily adaptable to scientific and technological change;

(e) each element of the Canadian broadcasting system shall contribute in an appropriate manner to the creation and presentation of Canadian programming;

(f) each broadcasting undertaking shall make maximum use, and in no case less than predominant use, of Canadian creative and other resources in the creation and presentation of programming, unless the nature of the service provided by the undertaking, such as specialized content or format or the use of languages other than French and English, renders that use impracticable, in which case the undertaking shall make the greatest practicable use of those resources;

(g) the programming originated by broadcasting undertakings should be of high standard;

(h) all persons who are licensed to carry on broadcasting undertakings have a responsibility for the programs they broadcast;

(i) the programming provided by the Canadian broadcasting system should

(i) be varied and comprehensive, providing a balance of information, enlightenment and entertainment for men, women and children of all ages, interests and tastes,

(ii) be drawn from local, regional, national and international sources,

(iii) include educational and community programs,

(iv) provide a reasonable opportunity for the public to be exposed to the expression of differing views on matters of public concern, and

(v) include a significant contribution from the Canadian independent production sector;

(j) educational programming, particularly where provided through the facilities of an independent educational authority, is an integral part of the Canadian broadcasting system;

(k) a range of broadcasting services in English and French shall be extended to all Canadians as resources become available;

(l) the Canadian Broadcasting Corporation, as the national public broadcaster, should provide radio and television services incorporating a wide range of programming that informs, enlightens and entertains;

(m) the programming provided by the Corporation should

(i) be predominantly and distinctively Canadian,

(ii) reflect Canada and its regions to national and regional audiences, while serving the special needs of those regions,

(iii) actively contribute to the flow and exchange of cultural expression,

(iv) be in English and in French, reflecting the different needs and circumstances of each official language community, including the particular needs and circumstances of English and French linguistic minorities,

(v) strive to be of equivalent quality in English and in French,

(vi) contribute to shared national consciousness and identity,

(vii) be made available throughout Canada by the most appropriate and efficient means and as resources become available for the purpose, and

(viii) reflect the multicultural and multiracial nature of Canada;

(n) where any conflict arises between the objectives of the Corporation set out in paragraphs *(l)* and *(m)* and the interests of any other broadcasting undertaking of the Canadian broadcasting system, it shall be resolved in the public interest, and where the public interest would be equally served by resolving the conflict in favour of either, it shall be resolved in favour of the objectives set out in paragraphs *(l)* and *(m)*;

(o) programming that reflects the aboriginal cultures of Canada should be provided within the Canadian broadcasting system as resources become available for the purpose;

(p) programming accessible by disabled persons should be provided within the Canadian broadcasting system as resources become available for the purpose;

(q) without limiting any obligation of a broadcasting undertaking to provide the programming contemplated by paragraph *(i)*, alternative television programming services in English and in French should be provided where necessary to ensure that the full range of programming contemplated by that paragraph is made available through the Canadian broadcasting system;

(r) the programming provided by alternative television programming services should

(i) be innovative and be complementary to the programming provided for mass audiences,

(ii) cater to tastes and interests not adequately provided for by the programming provided for mass audiences, and include programming devoted to culture and the arts,

(iii) reflect Canada's regions and multicultural nature,

(iv) as far as possible, be acquired rather than produced by those services, and

(v) be made available throughout Canada by the most cost-efficient means;

(s) private networks and programming undertakings should, to an extent consistent with the financial and other resources available to them,

(i) contribute significantly to the creation and presentation of Canadian programming, and

(ii) be responsive to the evolving demands of the public; and

(t) distribution undertakings

(i) should give priority to the carriage of Canadian programming services and, in particular, to the carriage of local Canadian stations,

(ii) should provide efficient delivery of programming at affordable rates, using the most effective technologies available at reasonable cost,

(iii) should, where programming services are supplied to them by broadcasting undertakings pursuant to contractual arrangements, provide reasonable terms for the carriage, packaging and retailing of those programming services, and

(iv) may, where the Commission considers it appropriate, originate programming, including local programming, on such terms as are conducive to the achievement of the objectives of the broadcasting policy set out in this subsection, and in particular provide access for underserved linguistic and cultural minority communities.

(2) It is further declared that the Canadian broadcasting system constitutes a single system and that the objectives of the broadcasting policy set out in subsection (1) can best be achieved by providing for the regulation and supervision of the Canadian broadcasting system by a single independent public authority.

Application

4. (1) This Act is binding on Her Majesty in right of Canada or a province.

(2) This Act applies in respect of broadcasting undertakings carried on in whole or in part within Canada or on board

(a) any ship, vessel or aircraft that is

(i) registered or licensed under an Act of Parliament, or

(ii) owned by, or under the direction or control of, Her Majesty in right of Canada or a province;

(b) any spacecraft that is under the direction or control of,

(i) Her Majesty in right of Canada or a province,

(ii) a citizen or resident of Canada, or

(iii) a corporation incorporated or resident in Canada; or

(c) any platform, rig, structure or formation that is affixed or attached to land situated in those submarine areas adjacent to the coast of Canada and extending throughout the natural prolongation of the land territory of Canada to the outer edge of the continental margin or to a distance of two hundred nautical miles from the baselines from which the breadth of the territorial sea of Canada is measured, whichever is greater.

(3) For greater certainty, this Act applies in respect of broadcasting undertakings whether or not they are carried on for profit or as part of, or in connection with, any other undertaking or activity.

(4) For greater certainty, this Act does not apply to any telecommunications common carrier when acting solely in that capacity.

PART II

OBJECTS AND POWERS OF THE COMMISSION IN RELATION TO BROADCASTING

Objects

5. (1) Subject to this Act and the *Radiocommunication Act* and to any directions to the Commission issued by the Governor in Council under this Act, the

Commission shall regulate and supervise all aspects of the Canadian broadcasting system with a view to implementing the broadcasting policy set out in s0
y from time to time issue guidelines and statements with respect to any matter within its jurisdiction under this Act, but no such guidelines or statements issued by the Commission are binding on the Commission.

7. (1) Subject to subsection (2) and section 8, the Governor in Council may, by order, issue to the Commission directions of general application on broad policy matters with respect to

(a) any of the objectives of the broadcasting policy set out in subsection 3(1); or

(b) any of the objectives of the regulatory policy set out in subsection 5(2).

(2) No order may be made under subsection (1) in respect of the issuance of a licence to a particular person or in respect of the amendment, renewal, suspension or revocation of a particular licence.

(3) An order made under subsection (1) is binding on the Commission beginning on the day on which the order comes into force and, subject to subsection (4), shall, if it so provides, apply with respect to any matter pending before the Commission on that day.

(4) No order made under subsection (1) may apply with respect to a licensing matter pending before the Commission where the period for the filing of interventions in the matter has expired unless that period expired more than one year before the coming into force of the order.

(5) A copy of each order made under subsection (1) shall be laid before each House of Parliament on any of the first fifteen days on which that House is sitting after the making of the order.

(6) The Minister shall consult with the Commission before the Governor in Council makes an order under subsection (1).

8. (1) Where the Governor in Council proposes to make an order under section 7, the Minister shall cause the proposed order to be

(a) published by notice in the *Canada Gazette*, which notice shall invite interested persons to make representations to the Minister with respect to the proposed order; and

(b) laid before each House of Parliament.

(2) Where a proposed order is laid before a House of Parliament pursuant to subsection (1), it shall stand referred to such committee thereof as the House considers appropriate to deal with the subject-matter of the order.

(3) The Governor in Council may, after the expiration of forty sitting days of Parliament after a proposed order is laid before both Houses of Parliament in accordance with subsection (1), implement the proposal by making an order under section 7, either in the form proposed or revised in such manner as the Governor in Council deems advisable.

(4) The Minister shall consult with the Commission before a proposed order is published or is laid before a House of Parliament under subsection (1).

(5) In this section, "sitting day of Parliament" means a day on which either House of Parliament sits.

General Powers

9. (1) Subject to this Part, the Commission may, in furtherance of its objects,

(a) establish classes of licences;

(b) issue licences for such terms not exceeding seven years and subject to such conditions related to the circumstances of the licensee

(i) as the Commission deems appropriate for the implementation of the broadcasting policy set out in subsection 3(1), and

(ii) in the case of licences issued to the Corporation, as the Commission deems consistent with the provision, through the Corporation, of the programming contemplated by paragraphs 3(1)*(l)* and *(m)*;

(c) amend any condition of a licence on application of the licensee or, where five years have expired since the issuance or renewal of the licence, on the Commission's own motion;

(d) issue renewals of licences for such terms not exceeding seven years and subject to such conditions as comply with paragraph *(b)*;

(e) suspend or revoke any licence;

(f) require any licensee to obtain the approval of the Commission before entering into any contract with a telecommunications common carrier for the distribution of programming directly to the public, using the facilities of that common carrier;

(g) require any licensee who is authorized to carry on a distribution undertaking to give priority to the carriage of broadcasting; and

(h) require any licensee who is authorized to carry on a distribution undertaking to carry, on such terms and conditions as the Commission deems appropriate, programming services specified by the Commission.

(2) Notwithstanding subsections (1) and 28(3), no licence of a distribution undertaking may be made subject to a condition that requires the licensee to substitute replacement material for commercial messages carried in a broadcasting signal received by that licensee.

(3) Subsection (2) does not apply in respect of a condition of a licence renewed after October 4, 1987 where before that date the licensee was complying with such a condition.

(4) The Commission shall, by order, on such terms and conditions as it deems appropriate, exempt persons who carry on broadcasting undertakings of any class specified in the order from any or all of the requirements of this Part or of a regulation made under this Part where the Commission is satisfied that compliance with those requirements will not contribute in a material manner to the implementation of the broadcasting policy set out in subsection 3(1).

10. (1) The Commission may, in furtherance of its objects, make regulations

(a) respecting the proportion of time that shall be devoted to the broadcasting of Canadian programs;

(b) prescribing what constitutes a Canadian program for the purposes of this Act;

(c) respecting standards of programs and the allocation of broadcasting time for the purpose of giving effect to the broadcasting policy set out in subsection 3(1);

(d) respecting the character of advertising and the amount of broadcasting time that may be devoted to advertising;

(e) respecting the proportion of time that may be devoted to the broad-casting of programs, including advertisements or announcements, of a partisan political character and the assignment of that time on an equitable basis to political parties and candidates;

(f) prescribing the conditions for the operation of programming undertakings as part of a network and for the broadcasting of network programs, and respecting the broadcasting times to be reserved for network programs by any such undertakings;

(g) respecting the carriage of any foreign or other programming services by distribution undertakings;

(h) for resolving, by way of mediation or otherwise, any disputes arising between programming undertakings and distribution undertakings concerning the carriage of programming originated by the programming undertakings;

(i) requiring licensees to submit to the Commission such information regarding their programs and financial affairs or otherwise relating to the conduct and management of their affairs as the regulations may specify;

(j) respecting the audit or examination of the records and books of account of licensees by the Commission or persons acting on behalf of the Commission; and

(k) respecting such other matters as it deems necessary for the furtherance of its objects.

(2) A regulation made under this section may be made applicable to all persons holding licences or to all persons holding licences of one or more classes.

(3) A copy of each regulation that the Commission proposes to make under this section shall be published in the *Canada Gazette* and a reasonable opportunity shall be given to licensees and other interested persons to make representations to the Commission with respect thereto.

11. (1) The Commission may make regulations

(a) with the approval of the Treasury Board, establishing schedules of fees to be paid by licensees of any class;

(b) providing for the establishment of classes of licensees for the purposes of paragraph *(a)*;

(c) providing for the payment of any fees payable by a licensee, including the time and manner of payment;

(d) respecting the interest payable by a licensee in respect of any overdue fee; and

(e) respecting such other matters as it deems necessary for the purposes of this section.

(2) Regulations made under paragraph (1)*(a)* may provide for fees to be calculated by reference to any criteria that the

Commission deems appropriate, including by reference to

(a) the revenues of the licensees;

(b) the performance of the licensees in relation to objectives established by the Commission, including objectives for the broadcasting of Canadian programs; and

(c) the market served by the licensees.

(3) No regulations made under subsection (1) shall apply to the Corporation or to licensees carrying on programming undertaking on behalf of Her Majesty in right of a province.

(4) Fees payable by a licensee under this section and any interest thereon constitute a debt due to Her Majesty in right of Canada and may be recovered as such in any court of competent jurisdiction.

(5) A copy of each regulation that the Commission proposes to make under this section shall be published in the *Canada Gazette* and a reasonable opportunity shall be given to licensees and other interested persons to make representations to the Commisssion with respect thereto.

12. (1) Where it appears to the Commission that

(a) any person has failed to do any act or thing that the person is required to do pursuant to this Part or to any regulation, licence, decision or order made or issued by the Commission under this Part, or has done or is doing any act or thing in contravention of this Part or of any such regulation, licence, decision or order, or

(b) the circumstances may require the Commission to make any decision or order or to give any approval that it is authorized to make or give under this Part or under any regulation or order made under this Part,

the Commission may inquire into, hear and determine the matter.

(2) The Commission may, by order, require any person to do, forthwith or within or at any time and in any manner specified by the Commission, any act or thing that the person is or may be required to do pursuant to this Part or to any regulation, licence, decision or order made or issued by the Commission under this Part and may, by order, forbid the doing or continuing of any act or thing that is contrary to this Part or to any such regulation, licence, decision or order.

(3) Where an inquiry under subsection (1) is heard by a panel established under subsection 20(1) and the panel issues an order pursuant to subsection (2) of this section, any person who is affected by the order may, within thirty days after the making thereof, apply to the Commission to reconsider any decision or finding made by the panel, and the Commission may rescind or vary any order or decision made by the panel or may rehear any matter before deciding it.

13. (1) Any order made under subsection 12(2) may be made an order of the Federal Court or of any superior court of a province and is enforceable in the same manner as an order of the court.

(2) To make an order under subsection 12(2) an order of a court, the usual practice and procedure of the court in such matters may be followed or, in lieu thereof, the Commission may file with the

registrar of the court a certified copy of the order, and thereupon the order becomes an order of the court.

(3) Where an order that has been made an order of a court is rescinded or varied by a subsequent order of the Commission, the order of the court shall be deemed to have been cancelled and the subsequent order may, in the same manner, be made an order of the court.

14. (1) The Commission may undertake, sponsor, promote or assist in research relating to any matter within its jurisdiction under this Act and in so doing it shall, wherever appropriate, utilize technical, economic and statistical information and advice from the Corporation or departments or agencies of the Government of Canada.

(2) The Commission shall review and consider any technical matter relating to broadcasting referred to the Commission by the Minister and shall make recommendations to the Minister with respect thereto.

15. (1) The Commission shall, on request of the Governor in Coundil, hold hearings or make reports on any matter within the jurisdiction of the Commission under this Act.

(2) The Minister shall consult with the Commission with regard to any request proposed to be made by the Governor in Council under subsection (1).

16. The Commission has, in respect of any hearing under this Part, with regard to the attendance, swearing and examination of witnesses at the hearing, the production and inspection of documents, the enforcement of its orders, the entry and inspection of property and other matters necessary or proper in relation to the hearing, all such powers, rights and privileges as are vested in a superior court of record.

17. The Commission has authority to determine questions of fact or law in relation to any matter within its jurisdiction under this Act.

CONTRIBUTORS

Jeffrey Derevensky is an Associate Professor in the Departments of Educational and Counselling Psychology and Psychiatry at McGill University. He is Director of McGill University's Ready Set Go Parent Education Child Enrichment Project.

Peter Desbarats is Dean of the Graduate School of Journalism at the University of Western Ontario. A former TV news anchor for Global TV, Desbarats has also worked for *The Toronto Star*, the CBC, and the Montreal *Star*. He is the author of *Guide to Canadian News Media* and a biography of Rene Levesque.

Janice Dickin teaches law and Canadian Studies in the Faculty of General Studies at the University of Calgary. She is currently writing a biography of an evangelist, co-editing (with Elspeth Cameron) a collection of biographies of ordinary women, and participating in an NFB film based on her book *Suitable for the Wilds*.

Ross A. Eaman teaches in the School of Journalism and Mass Communication at Carleton University. He is the author of *Media Society: Basic Issues and Controversies*, and *Channels of Influence: CBC Audience Research and the Canadian Public*.

Seth Feldman is Dean of the Faculty of Fine Arts at York University. He is the editor of two anthologies on Canadian cinema: *Canadian Film Reader* and *Take Two*. His commentaries have appeared frequently in the press and on radio and television. He has written and produced for CBC radio's "Ideas" program.

James Gillet is a Ph. D. candidate in the Department of Sociology at McMaster University.

Mary Gerace Gold is an Associate Professor in the Department of Communication Studies at the University of Windsor. Her research and teaching interests include media law, communication policy, and international trade issues related to the media. She has published articles on the use of television cameras in courtrooms and on matters related to personal injury litigation.

Robert Hackett teaches in the School of Communication at Simon Fraser University. He is the author of *News and Dissent: The Press and The Politics of Peace in Canada*, and of a number of important studies on bias in news reporting. He is currently working on Project Censored Canada, a study of why some stories are under-reported by Canadian news organizations.

Helen Holmes teaches in the Faculty of General Studies at the University of Calgary. She is the author (with Michael Markel) of *Technical Writing: Situations and Strategies* and currently serves as President of The University of Calgary Faculty Association.

Colin Hoskins is a Professor in the Department of Marketing and Economic Analysis in the Faculty of Business at the University of Alberta. He is the author (with Stuart McFadyen and D. Gillen) of *Canadian Broadcasting: Market Structure and Economic Performance*, and author or co-author of a number of significant studies on the economics of Canadian and international broadcasting.

Carolyn Klein is a licensed applied development psychologist working for the Baldwin–Cartier School Board in Montreal.

Stephen Kline is Professor in the School of Communication and Director of the Media Analysis Laboratory at Simon Fraser University. He is the author of *Out of the Garden: Toys and Children's Culture in the Age of TV Marketing*.

Martin Laba teaches in the School of Communication at Simon Fraser University. He is the author of numerous articles, book chapters, and reports on issues in communication and popular culture. Professor Laba has written, produced, and edited a number of media productions and is the author of a forthcoming book entitled *Hits and Misses: The Pleasures of Popular Music*.

William Leiss holds the Eco-research Chair in the School of Policy Studies at Queen's University. He is the author of *Under Technology's Thumb*, and *Risk and Responsibility*, and co-author of *Social Communication in Advertising*, among other works.

Stuart McFadyen is a Professor in the Department of Marketing and Economic Analysis in the Faculty of Business at the University of Alberta. He is the author (with Colin Hoskins and D. Gillen) of *Canadian Broadcasting: Market Structure and Economic Performance*, and author or co-author of a number of significant studies on the economics of Canadian and international broadcasting.

John Meisel is President of the Royal Society of Canada. He recently retired from Queen's University where he was the Sir Edward Peacock Professor of Political Science. He served as Chairman of the Canadian Radio-television and Telecommunications Commission and is the author of a number of seminal works on Canadian voting, broadcasting policy, culture and the arts, and on the nature of Canadian society.

Matthew Mendelsohn is an Assistant Professor in the Department of Political Studies at Queen's University. He has published a number of important articles on media coverage of Canadian elections and referendums.

Catherine Murray is the Director of the Centre for Policy Research on Science and Technology and an Associate Professor in the School of Communication at Simon Fraser University. She is interested in evaluating new information services from a consumer perspective.

Richard Pinet teaches and is working on his doctorate at the School of Communication at Simon Fraser University. He has co-produced a number of public forums on interdisciplinary topics and has written articles for *Recovery* magazine, *Our Schools*, Ourselves, and *The Globe* and *Mail.*

Beverly Rasporich is Professor and Associate Dean in the Faculty of General Studies at the University of Calgary. She is the author of *Dance of the Sexes* and co-editor of *Woman As Artist* and *Passion for Identity*, among other works.

Marc Raboy is a Professor in the Department of Communication at the University of Montreal. He is the author of *Movements and Messages: Media and Radical Politics in Quebec*, and *Missed Opportunities: The Story of Canada's Broadcasting Policy*, among other works. He has published widely on Canadian and international policy issues as well as on the political economy of the mass media.

Gertrude J. Robinson is Professor and past director of the Graduate Program in Communications at McGill University. She edited the *Canadian Journal of Communication* from 1987–1993, and her recent publications Include a book (written with Dieta Sixt) entitled *Women and Power: Canadian and* German *Experiences.*

Myles Ruggles is an Assistant Professor in the Department of Communication Studies at the University of Windsor. He is the author of *The Audience Reflected in the Medium of Law.*

Mark Starowicz is Executive Producer of Documentaries for the Canadian Broadcasting Corporation. He was executive producer of CBC radio's "As It Happens", was the producer who launched CBC radio's "Sunday Morning" program, and was the executive producer of CBC television's "The Journal" through its ten-year history.

Gillian Steward has been a journalist and editor for over 20 years. Between 1987 and 1990 she was managing editor of the *Calgary Herald.* Since leaving *The Herald*, she has written a column for Southam News, produced radio documentaries for CBC's "Ideas" program, and has worked with a number of community and volunteer organizations.

Ray Straatsma is a M.A. candidate in the School of Communication at Simon Fraser University. He is completing a thesis on surveillance technologies and the history of market research.

Armande Saint-Jean teaches in the Department of Literature and Communication at the University of Sherbrooke. She was formerly Co-director of the Journalism program at the University of Quebec in Montreal. Her research has focussed on journalistic ethics, feminist theory, and communications research methodology.

David Taras is Professor and Associate Dean in the Faculty of General Studies at the University of Calgary. He is the author of *The Newsmakers: The Media's Influence on Canadian Politics*, and co-editor of *Passion For Identity*; *Prime Ministers and Premier's*; and *The Domestic Battleground*, among other works.

Phil White is an Associate Professor with the Department of Kinesiology at McMaster University. His recent research activity has focussed on how masculinity and femininity are reproduced through sport, the place of bodybuilding and muscles in popular culture, and how the fitness movement reflects class and gender interests.

Kevin Young is an Associate Professor of Sociology at the University of Calgary where he teaches classes on sport, youth crime, and deviance and social control. His most recent research projects involve examinations of sport injury, the political and moral underpinnings of the current health craze, and aspects of sports violence and sports law.

READER REPLY CARD

We are interested in your reaction to *Seeing Ourselves: Media Power and Policy in Canada*, 2/e, by Helen Holmes and David Taras. You can help us to improve this book in future editions by completing this questionnaire.

1. What was your reason for using this book?

   ☐ university course ☐ college course ☐ continuing education course
   ☐ professional development ☐ personal interest ☐ other (please specify) ____________________

2. If you are a student, please identify your school and the course in which you used this book.

3. Which chapters or parts of this book did you use? Which did you omit?

4. What did you like best about this book? What did you like least?

5. Please identify any topics you think should be added to future editions.

6. Please add any comments or suggestions.

7. May we contact you for further information?

   Name: ____________________

   ____

   Address: ____________________

   ____

   ____

   Phone: ____________________

(fold here and tape shut)

MAIL POSTE
Canada Post Corporation / Société canadienne des postes
Postage paid If mailed in Canada
Port payé si posté au Canada
Business Reply
Réponse d'affaires
0116870399 01

0116870399-M8Z4X6-BR01

Heather McWhinney
Publisher, College Division
HARCOURT BRACE & COMPANY, CANADA
55 HORNER AVENUE
TORONTO, ONTARIO
M8Z 9Z9